1 AND 2 THESSALONIANS

THE NIV APPLICATION COMMENTARY

From biblical text . . . to contemporary life

1 AND 2 THESSALONIANS

THE NIV APPLICATION COMMENTARY

From biblical text . . . to contemporary life

MICHAEL W. HOLMES

ZondervanPublishingHouse
Grand Rapids, Michigan

A Division of HarperCollinsPublishers

The NIV Application Commentary: 1 and 2 Thessalonians
Copyright © 1998 by Michael W. Holmes

Requests for information should be addressed to:

 Zondervan Publishing House
Grand Rapids, Michigan 49530

Library of Congress Cataloging-in-Publication Data

Michael Holmes.
    1 & 2 Thessalonians / Michael Holmes.
       p.   cm.—(NIV application commentary)
    Includes bibliographical references and index.
    ISBN: 0–310–49380-3
    1. Bible. N.T. 1 and 2 Thessalonians—Commentaries. I. Title. II. Series.
BS2725.3.H64 1998
227'.81077—dc21
                                                      98–16377
                                                        CIP

Printed in the United States of America

---

98 99 00 01 02 03 04 /❖ DC/ 10 9 8 7 6 5 4 3 2

Contents

The NIV Application Commentary Series

When complete, the NIV Application Commentary
will include the following volumes:

Old Testament Volumes

Genesis, John H. Walton

Exodus, Peter Enns

Leviticus/Numbers, Richard E. Averbeck

Deuteronomy, Daniel I. Block

Joshua, Robert Hubbard

Judges/Ruth, K. Lawson Younger

1-2 Samuel, Bill T. Arnold

1-2 Kings, Michael S. Moore

1-2 Chronicles, Andrew E. Hill

Ezra/Nehemiah, Douglas J. Green

Esther, Karen H. Jobes

Job, Dennis R. Magary

Psalms Volume 1, Gerald H. Wilson

Psalms Volume 2, Gerald H. Wilson

Proverbs, Paul Koptak

Ecclesiastes/Song of Songs, Iain Provan

Isaiah, John N. Oswalt

Jeremiah/Lamentations, J. Andrew Dearman

Ezekiel, Iain Duquid

Daniel, Tremper Longman III

Hosea/Amos/Micah, Gary V. Smith

Jonah/Nahum/Habakkuk/Zephaniah
    David M. Howard Jr.

Joel/Obadiah/Malachi, David W. Baker

Haggai/Zechariah, Mark J. Boda

New Testament Volumes

Matthew, Michael J. Wilkins

Mark, David E. Garland

Luke, Darrell L. Bock

John, Gary M. Burge

Acts, Ajith Fernando

Romans, Douglas J. Moo

1 Corinthians, Craig Blomberg

2 Corinthians, Scott Hafemann

Galatians, Scot McKnight

Ephesians, Klyne Snodgrass

Philippians, Frank Thielman

Colossians/Philemon, David E. Garland

1-2 Thessalonians, Michael W. Holmes

1-2 Timothy/Titus, Walter L. Liefeld

Hebrews, George H. Guthrie

James, David P. Nystrom

To see which titles are available,
visit our web site at http://www.zondervan.com

NIV Application Commentary
Series Introduction

THE NIV APPLICATION COMMENTARY SERIES is unique. Most commentaries help us make the journey from the twentieth century back to the first century. They enable us to cross the barriers of time, culture, language, and geography that separate us from the biblical world. Yet they only offer a one-way ticket to the past and assume that we can somehow make the return journey on our own. Once they have explained the *original meaning* of a book or passage, these commentaries give us little or no help in exploring its *contemporary significance*. The information they offer is valuable, but the job is only half done.

Recently, a few commentaries have included some contemporary application as *one* of their goals. Yet that application is often sketchy or moralistic, and some volumes sound more like printed sermons than commentaries.

The primary goal of The NIV Application Commentary Series is to help you with the difficult but vital task of bringing an ancient message into a modern context. The series not only focuses on application as a finished product but also helps you think through the *process* of moving from the original meaning of a passage to its contemporary significance. These are commentaries, not popular expositions. They are works of reference, not devotional literature.

The format of the series is designed to achieve the goals of the series. Each passage is treated in three sections: *Original Meaning, Bridging Contexts,* and *Contemporary Significance.*

THIS SECTION HELPS you understand the meaning of the biblical text in its first-century context. All of the elements of traditional exegesis—in concise form—are discussed here. These include the historical, literary, and cultural context of the passage. The authors discuss matters related to grammar and syntax, and the meaning of biblical words. They also seek to explore the main ideas of the passage and how the biblical author develops those ideas.[1]

After reading this section, you will understand the problems, questions, and concerns of the *original audience* and how the biblical author addressed those issues. This understanding is foundational to any legitimate application of the text today.

 THIS SECTION BUILDS a bridge between the world of the Bible and the world of today, between the original context and the contemporary context, by focusing on both the timely and timeless aspects of the text.

God's Word is *timely*. The authors of Scripture spoke to specific situations, problems, and questions. Paul warned the Galatians about the consequences of circumcision and the dangers of trying to be justified by law (Gal. 5:2–5). The author of Hebrews tried to convince his readers that Christ is superior to Moses, the Aaronic priests, and the Old Testament sacrifices. John urged his readers to "test the spirits" of those who taught a form of incipient Gnosticism (1 John 4:1–6). In each of these cases, the timely nature of Scripture enables us to hear God's Word in situations that were *concrete* rather than abstract.

Yet the timely nature of Scripture also creates problems. Our situations, difficulties, and questions are not always directly related to those faced by the people in the Bible. Therefore, God's word to them does not always seem relevant to us. For example, when was the last time someone urged you to be circumcised, claiming that it was a necessary part of justification? How many people today care whether Christ is superior to the Aaronic priests? And how can a "test" designed to expose incipient Gnosticism be of any value in a modern culture?

Fortunately, Scripture is not only timely but *timeless*. Just as God spoke to the original audience, so he still speaks to us through the pages of Scripture. Because we share a common humanity with the people of the Bible, we discover a *universal dimension* in the problems they faced and the solutions God gave them. The timeless nature of Scripture enables it to speak with power in every time and in every culture.

---

1. Please note that when the authors discuss words in the original biblical languages, the series uses the general rather than the scholarly method of transliteration.

Those who fail to recognize that Scripture is both timely and timeless run into a host of problems. For example, those who are intimidated by timely books such as Hebrews or Galatians might avoid reading them because they seem meaningless today. At the other extreme, those who are convinced of the timeless nature of Scripture, but who fail to discern its timely element, may "wax eloquent" about the Melchizedekian priesthood to a sleeping congregation.

The purpose of this section, therefore, is to help you discern what is timeless in the timely pages of the New Testament—and what is not. For example, if Paul's primary concern is not circumcision (as he tells us in Gal. 5:6), what *is* he concerned about? If discussions about the Aaronic priesthood or Melchizedek seem irrelevant today, what is of abiding value in these passages? If people try to "test the spirits" today with a test designed for a specific first-century heresy, what other biblical test might be more appropriate?

Yet this section does not merely uncover that which is timeless in a passage but also helps you to see *how* it is uncovered. The author of the commentary seeks to take what is implicit in the text and make it explicit, to take a process that normally is intuitive and explain it in a logical, orderly fashion. How do we know that circumcision is not Paul's primary concern? What clues in the text or its context help us realize that Paul's real concern is at a deeper level?

Of course, those passages in which the historical distance between us and the original readers is greatest require a longer treatment. Conversely, those passages in which the historical distance is smaller or seemingly nonexistent require less attention.

One final clarification. Because this section prepares the way for discussing the contemporary significance of the passage, there is not always a sharp distinction or a clear break between this section and the one that follows. Yet when both sections are read together, you should have a strong sense of moving from the world of the Bible to the world of today.

THIS SECTION ALLOWS the biblical message to speak with as much power today as it did when it was first written. How can you apply what you learned about Jerusalem, Ephesus, or Corinth to our present-day needs in Chicago, Los Angeles, or London?

How can you take a message originally spoken in Greek and Aramaic and communicate it clearly in our own language? How can you take the eternal truths originally spoken in a different time and culture and apply them to the similar-yet-different needs of our culture?

In order to achieve these goals, this section gives you help in several key areas.

First, it helps you identify contemporary situations, problems, or questions that are truly comparable to those faced by the original audience. Because contemporary situations are seldom identical to those faced in the first century, you must seek situations that are analogous if your applications are to be relevant.

Second, this section explores a variety of contexts in which the passage might be applied today. You will look at personal applications, but you will also be encouraged to think beyond private concerns to the society and culture at large.

Third, this section will alert you to any problems or difficulties you might encounter in seeking to apply the passage. And if there are several legitimate ways to apply a passage (areas in which Christians disagree), the author will bring these to your attention and help you think through the issues involved.

In seeking to achieve these goals, the contributors to this series attempt to avoid two extremes. They avoid making such specific applications that the commentary might quickly become dated. They also avoid discussing the significance of the passage in such a general way that it fails to engage contemporary life and culture.

Above all, contributors to this series have made a diligent effort not to sound moralistic or preachy. The NIV Application Commentary Series does not seek to provide ready-made sermon materials but rather tools, ideas, and insights that will help you communicate God's Word with power. If we help you to achieve that goal, then we have fulfilled the purpose for this series.

The Editors

General Editor's Preface

THE TWO LETTERS TO THE THESSALONIANS are often called Paul's eschatological letters—the ones that instruct us in what will happen at the
end of time. We want to know, for example, when Christ will come
again, who will be raised, where we will go, and how all this will happen. Apparently the Thessalonians were curious about these questions
because each chapter of the first letter ends with a reference to the Second Coming. Chapter 4 focuses on these questions.

Paul's answers to such questions, however, seem frustratingly elusive.
He reassures but does not inform. Christ will come again (4:15), but
we don't know when (5:1–3) We will go to be with the Lord (4:17),
but we don't know exactly where. There is security in being believers,
but we cannot know for sure the difference between believers and
unbelievers. Paul communicates hope but does not satisfy our curiosity. Perhaps it is more accurate to say that in order to communicate
hope—true hope—Paul must avoid satisfying our curiosity. Is it possible that too specific answers about questions to which we can only
know partial answers actually discourages hope and instead contributes
to a spiral of despair when we learn about our limitations?

We live in an age where marvelous scientific and technological
achievements condition us to expect more and more precise answers
to all sorts of questions about the lives we lead—including questions
normally reserved for philosophers and religionists. What's wrong
with my life? How should I live? Where is all of this going to end up?
At some levels science and technology have provided interesting
answers to these questions. So our response is to rely more and more
on human wisdom.

We also live in an era that is fast approaching the end of a millennium. In such times people traditionally look heavenward for patterns
of meaning. Expectations of cataclysmic changes increase. The ambi-
guities of everyday living seem to grow in importance and blacken
the light of the sun. The tricksters of day-to-day existence trip us again
and again, and we often retreat to incredible stories, poems, and spir-
itualities that seem to make meaninglessness the norm rather than the

exception. In short, we live in an age where technical precision clashes with a spiritual hunger that only mystery can satisfy.

As Michael Holmes so skillfully reveals in this masterful commentary, our present-day tasks parallel in a remarkable way those facing the apostle Paul as he wrote these two letters. The people of Thessalonica were persecuted Christians, in danger of losing hope in their relatively newfound faith. Paul had left the city abruptly and felt a need to reassure this new believing community. He wanted to give them hope. Indeed, one of the most important lessons we can take away from reading this book is to understand the dos and don'ts of giving hope.

Hope is a common human desire. In order to have meaning in life, we must have confidence that a brighter future lies ahead. We need to know that there is a way out of our human difficulties. Yet it is also apparent that we are severely limited in what we can know about the future (cf. Rom. 8:24). And it is in the interaction between these two truths—our desire for future meaning and the limitations of what we can know—that hope resides. To provide hope we must respect both. If we disregard our desire for future meaning, despair inevitably results. If we disregard our limitations, we begin to predict the future and make mistakes in doing so. The temptation to either of these errors is all the greater because our culture provides a ready market for both. We have a whole industry built around the provision of therapy for despairing people. And we have another whole industry built around predicting the future—prophecy, channeling, and the occult. In either case, true hope is lost.

Paul resists dealing only with the danger of despair, and he resists providing answers that we cannot really know. Instead, he points to Jesus Christ, whose life embodied both human despair and limitation, showing us how faith in God's sovereignty is our only source of hope.

Terry C. Muck

Author's Preface

THE WRITING OF A COMMENTARY is in significant respects a collabora-
tive effort. I am grateful, therefore, for this opportunity to acknowledge
those who have assisted me as I worked on this volume. Because I have
learned far more from others who have studied these two letters than
the format of the series allows me to indicate, I would first like to
express my appreciation for all those whose work has informed and illu-
minated my own, unacknowledged though they must often remain.

I would like to thank Jay Barnes, Provost of Bethel College, for his
steady encouragement and for granting a reduction in course load that
facilitated the completion of the commentary, as well as all the students
in my Greek, Exegesis, and Senior Seminar classes at Bethel who studied 1 Thessalonians with me over the years. I also wish to thank Craig
and Vicki Dahl—Craig for encouraging me throughout the project and
Vicki for reading and commenting on the draft version. Her many
thoughtful observations and questions helped me clarify at a number
of points what I was trying to say. During our walks together my wife,
Molly, helped me talk through thoughts and ideas in various stages of
development. Tom Wagner, my fishing partner, both listened patiently
as I occasionally vented some of my frustrations during the writing
process and helped distract me from them by guiding me to some outstanding crappie and muskie action.

I owe a special debt of gratitude to my friends and fellow believers
at Trinity Baptist Church, which this year celebrates its 125th anniver-
sary. Over the last five years they provided opportunities for and
encouraging support of a series of lessons and sermons on the Thessalonian letters. I wish to mention in particular the Beta, Becomers,
and Sojourners classes for their enthusiastic discussion and feedback,
as well as the congregation for allowing me the privilege of serving as
interim pastor.

Terry Muck offered steady encouragement and helped keep matters in perspective by asking about fishing nearly as often as he asked
about progress on the commentary. My classmate from TEDS days,
Scot McKnight, now an associate editor of this series, read the initial

draft of the commentary and offered valuable suggestions. Verlyn Verbrugge's careful editing of the manuscript made it a better commentary than it would otherwise have been. Beverly Roberts Gaventa graciously provided advance page proofs of her own recent commentary on the Thessalonian letters, and Jeffrey A. D. Weima kept me informed of some of his work on Thessalonians. Jennifer Schmit, my former teaching assistant, helped verify references. Together they have saved me from many slips and errors; the responsibility for those that remain (however much I might wish otherwise) is, of course, mine alone.

The last person I wish to acknowledge is my colleague, John Herzog, chair of the Department of Biblical and Theological Studies at Bethel. Though he had no direct input into the commentary, John nonetheless played a critical role in its completion. We came to Bethel during the 1981–82 school year—he the seasoned teacher and I the rookie fresh out of graduate school. By the way he has led the department—relieving the rest of us of administrative concerns, for example, and consistently arranging schedules and other assignments in a way that permits us both to fulfill our classroom responsibilities and to pursue other interests—John has created an environment that has encouraged, stimulated, and enabled his department to flourish both in and out of the classroom. His is, for example, the only department to win all three of the college's faculty excellence awards (for teaching, service, and scholarship—the last one twice); furthermore, in the last decade his six colleagues in Bible and theology have (to mention only one area of activity) now published seventeen books (and several more are underway). In his own quiet and unassuming, yet clearly effective way he has substantially contributed to my own success as a teacher and a scholar. As a token of my gratitude and appreciation I would like to acknowledge John's contributions by dedicating this volume to him.

Michael W. Holmes
Lent, 1998

Abbreviations

ABD	*Anchor Bible Dictionary*
ACNT	Augsburg Commentary on the New Testament
BAGD	Bauer, Arndt, Gingrich, Danker, *A Greek-English Lexicon of the New Testament*
BDF	Blass, Debrunner, Funk, *A Greek Grammar of the New Testament*
BETL	Bibliotheca ephemeridum theologicarum lovaniensium
BST	The Bible Speaks Today
CBQ	*Catholic Biblical Quarterly*
CEV	Contemporary English Version
CT	*Christianity Today*
DPL	*Dictionary of Paul and His Letters*
EDNT	*Exegetical Dictionary of the New Testament*
EKKNT	Evangelisch-katholischer Kommentar zum Neuen Testament
HNTC	Harper New Testament Commentary
HTR	*Harvard Theological Review*
ICC	International Critical Commentary
JBL	*Journal of Biblical Literature*
JETS	*Journal of the Evangelical Theological Society*
JSNT	*Journal for the Study of the New Testament*
KJV	King James Version
LXX	Septuagint (Greek translation of the Old Testament)
NAC	New American Commentary
NASB	New American Standard Bible
NCB	New Century Bible
NIBC	New International Biblical Commentary
NICNT	New International Commentary on the New Testament
NIDNTT	*New International Dictionary of New Testament Theology*
NIGTC	New International Greek Testament Commentary
NIV	New International Version
NIV[ILE]	New International Version, Inclusive Language Edition
NIVAC	NIV Application Commentary

Abbreviations

NovT	*Novum Testamentum*
NRSV	New Revised Standard Version
NTS	*New Testament Studies*
REB	Revised English Bible
RSV	Revised Standard Version
TCGNT	Bruce M. Metzger, *A Textual Commentary on the Greek New Testament*
TDNT	*Theological Dictionary of the New Testament*
TNTC	Tyndale New Testament Commentary
WBC	Word Biblical Commentary

Introduction

NEAR THE MIDDLE OF THE FIRST CENTURY A.D., Paul wrote a pair of letters to a recently established congregation of Christians in the town of Thessalonica. The people to whom he addressed the two letters we now call 1 and 2 Thessalonians were for the most part new converts to Christianity who had grown up in, and hence were thoroughly socialized in, a Greek cultural environment. One of Paul's major challenges was that of *resocialization*—helping these believers to learn, understand, and live by the very different social and ethical code of early Christianity.

What made this task particularly challenging was that these people were also facing intense persecution from the surrounding culture. As a result of their commitment to Jesus, they were experiencing social ostracism and isolation as well as physical attacks from society around them. As if this were not enough, Paul's task was further complicated by a high degree of apprehension, misunderstanding, and speculation about the return of Jesus. The Thessalonians knew that Jesus was to return, but they were not sure when it might take place or what it meant for them. Not knowing what to think, they had become upset rather than hopeful, unsettled rather than strengthened, by the prospect of Jesus' return.

The parallels between Paul's first-century situation and contemporary times are hard to miss. The approaching millennium has served to heighten an already-intense interest in and speculation about the return of Jesus; at times it seems as though there is no end to a rising flood of books, radio and television shows, and now Web pages devoted to the subject. On a more somber note, even the secular news media has finally noticed that Christians are experiencing severe and sometimes deadly persecution in over eighty countries around the world. Furthermore, anyone involved in pastoring, teaching, or discipling other Christians knows that one of the major challenges facing Christians nearly everywhere today is that of helping believers break free from the shackles of a secular, self-centered, and often hedonistic mindset so that they can begin to think and live on the basis of a genuinely Christian view of reality. Like Paul, we face the challenge of resocialization (or "discipleship," if you prefer): of helping people learn that there is an alternative to contemporary social behavior and ethics, and how to live out that alternative lifestyle consistently.

Granted that there are significant parallels between then and now, just how helpful can letters written over 1900 years ago be to us today? And if they are helpful (as I surely think they are), how and in what ways are they helpful? These are some of the questions I address in the following commentary. As we seek the contemporary significance of these ancient documents, we need to begin by understanding them in their original context and circumstances.

The City of Thessalonica

THESSALONICA (MODERN THESSALONIKI) was the largest and most important city in Macedonia. As the capital of the province it enjoyed numerous civic and commercial privileges, including the right to mint its own coins. In 42 B.C. it became a free city, governed by its own local rulers, a group of five or six men known as "politarchs" (NIV "city officials"; see Acts 17:6, 8). It was situated some ninety miles (150 kilometers) or so west of Philippi on the Via Egnatia, the great Roman highway that connected Rome with its eastern provinces, next to a good natural harbor at the head of the Thermaic Gulf. Major north-south trade routes also passed through Thessalonica, further enhancing its position as a wealthy commercial center.

Religiously Thessalonica offered something for nearly everyone.[1] Not surprisingly for a Greek city, the traditional Greek cults and philosophic traditions were well represented, as were various mystery religions. Known for its early devotion to the cult of the Roman emperor, the city even minted coins declaring Caesar to be divine. It also boasted a sanctuary of the Egyptian gods, among whom Isis and Osiris were prominent. (An inscription recording the spread of the Egyptian cult from Thessalonica to other Greek cities offers an interesting parallel to 1 Thess. 1:8.) In contrast to Philippi (Acts 16:13), there was in Thessalonica a Jewish community large enough to support a syna-

---

1. On the topic of religion in Thessalonica see R. Jewett, *The Thessalonian Correspondence*, 126–33; K. P. Donfried, "The Cults of Thessalonica and the Thessalonian Correspondence," *NTS* 31 (1985): 336–56.

gogue (17:1). There is also archaeological evidence of local devotion to the "highest god" and local cults such as that of Cabirus, which during the first century A.D. was becoming the chief cult of the city. Finally, running through all this is a substantial tendency towards syncretism, a mixing of religious traditions.

Key elements of this religious activity were closely associated with civic and political concerns. In the ancient world religion was always closely linked to politics because dominant social groups realized that religion offered an effective means to legitimize and maintain their power and dominance. In Thessalonica city leaders fostered devotion to the imperial cult in order to solidify good relations with Rome. As a consequence, any perceived attack on the cult of the emperor was viewed as a serious threat to the city's economic and political well-being. The local cult of Cabirus was sponsored by the city's wealthy ruling aristocracy, not only because it reinforced to their advantage the hierarchical nature of Greco-Roman society but also because it gave to all citizens a shared sense of identity and unity. Thus to attack the cult—by proclaiming the exclusive claims of another deity, for example—was virtually to attack the city itself. In such an environment, to preach Christianity was tantamount to treason.

Christianity Comes to Thessalonica

IN A.D. 49, not long after Paul, Silas (Silvanus, cf. NIV note), and Timothy left Philippi, where they had "suffered and been insulted" (1 Thess. 2:2; cf. Acts 16:16–40), they came to Thessalonica. There they stopped, probably because of the presence of a sizable Jewish community and its synagogue. For the next three Sabbaths Paul in particular shared the Christian message in the synagogue, seeking to prove from the Scriptures that Jesus was the predicted Messiah, who had died and risen from the dead on their behalf. The apostle was successful in persuading "some of the Jews" (perhaps only a few), as well as a large number of "God-fearing Greeks" (Gentiles attracted to Judaism who regularly attended the synagogue services but who stopped short of full conversion) and "not a few prominent women" (Acts 17:2–4).

While these converts from the synagogue apparently formed the nucleus of the new congregation, a substantially larger number of converts came to faith directly from paganism as they "turned to God from idols" (1 Thess. 1:9). The workshop that Paul set up in order to support himself, in which he worked, as he put it, "night and day" (2:9), would have been a key place of outreach (and eventually discipleship as well). The private homes of converts, such as Jason, would also have provided a setting for evangelism and instruction. As a result, a new, predominately Gentile congregation came into existence. Paul, Silas, and Timothy devoted themselves to encouraging and instructing the recent converts in the basics of their new faith, becoming deeply attached to them in the process (2:8–12).

Almost from the beginning, however, those who accepted the gospel encountered opposition and hostility from those who were not persuaded by the preaching of Paul and his companions (1 Thess. 1:6; 2:14). This is hardly surprising. On the one hand, the synagogue would have been upset by the loss of members to a new cult. On the other hand, the conversion of leading women of the community inevitably brought the cult to the notice of civic leaders, to whom the proclamation of an alternative emperor (Jesus as the messianic King) would have sounded more than a little seditious.[2] These two groups apparently made common cause against the missionaries and their converts, as civil charges were soon brought against them.

Luke describes the critical episode in Acts 17:5–9.[3] After some disreputable folks from the marketplace (whom the KJV colorfully describes as "certain lewd fellows of the baser sort") had been instigated

---

2. The recent outbreak in A.D. 49 of riots between Jews and Christians in Rome, which led the emperor Claudius to expel the Jews (including, of course, Jewish Christians) from the capital (see Acts 18:2), may well have made the Thessalonian authorities more suspicious of and alert to the possibility of similar troubles in their own city, the more so since in both cases the instigators of the troubles were visitors from the East.

3. How long after Paul's arrival in Thessalonica this event took place is unclear. Paul never indicates in 1 Thessalonians how long he stayed in Thessalonica prior to his expulsion. Luke mentions the incident immediately after describing how Paul preached in the synagogue "on three Sabbath days" (Acts 17:2), which could imply that it took place near the end of Paul's first month in town. Luke, however, often "telescopes" his narrative by skipping over intervening events (compare his relatively brief and episodic account in Acts 18:1–18 of Paul's initial visit to Corinth, which lasted eighteen months). Thus a month or two (or even three or four) may have elapsed between the two episodes narrated in 17:1–4 and 17:5–9. A stay of two to five months would correlate well with the impression given by Paul's description in 1 Thessalonians of his activities during this time, and also with his comment that the Philippians contributed to his support during this time, perhaps (but not necessarily) more than once (Phil. 4:15–16).

to start a riot, they were encouraged to locate the visiting missionaries and haul them before the civil authorities. Failing to find Paul and Silas,[4] they instead seized Jason and some other brothers (clearly members and supporters of the new movement, and perhaps its leaders) and basically charged them with treason for their allegiance to Jesus. The city officials dealt with the resulting turmoil by requiring Jason and the others to post bond, which effectively made them responsible for any further trouble caused by the missionaries.

Given this turn of events, Paul, Silas, and Timothy had little choice but to leave town. That Paul left unwillingly and sooner than he had intended is clear from 1 Thessalonians 2:17, in which he describes himself has having been "torn away" from his new friends and fellow believers. The sudden departure of the missionaries no doubt had a dramatic and shocking impact on the congregation, which unexpectedly found itself alone and facing "persecutions and trials" that severely tested their faith and perseverance (2 Thess. 1:4; cf. 1 Thess. 3:3).

The Setting and Occasion of 1 Thessalonians

FIRST THESSALONIANS 2:17–3:5 offers a glimpse of the emotional turmoil Paul and his companions experienced following their expulsion from Thessalonica. Two concerns seem to have been uppermost on Paul's mind. (1) He was deeply concerned that the young congregation might collapse in the face of hostile external pressures. Even though he had warned them that such pressures would come (3:4), it is one thing to deal with them in theory and quite another to confront them in reality. Paul, apparently not sure that the new congregation was sufficiently instructed to deal with the difficulties and challenges facing them, admits to being afraid (3:5) that these new converts might be persuaded to abandon their commitment to Christianity, thereby wiping out all the time and effort he, Silas, and Timothy had invested.

(2) Paul was also concerned that his behavior and that of his companions might be misunderstood—or more likely, misrepresented—in a

---

4. From 1 Thessalonians it is clear that Timothy was present at this time as well. Luke's mention of only Paul and Silas may indicate that Timothy's responsibilities were more private and less public than those of the other two missionaries, and thus he was less well known to outsiders. If so, this would explain how Timothy was able to return to Thessalonica when Paul was unable to do so (1 Thess. 3:2).

way that would call into question the validity and integrity of the gospel itself. Religious charlatans and frauds were a dime a dozen in the ancient world, and the way Paul and Silas slipped out of town in the middle of the night would have made it only too easy to pigeonhole them as just one more pair of rip-off artists out to scam people. From here it was only a short step to the conclusion that their message was no more truthful than they were, and thus the people might reject it along with them.

The missionaries' first impulse was to return to Thessalonica as soon as possible. This they tried to do—in Paul's case, repeatedly (2:18)—but for unspecified reasons (which he attributed to the working of Satan, 2:18) that proved to be impossible. Frustrated and anxious to learn what was happening in Thessalonica, Paul decided to send Timothy back in his place as his designated representative, in order to strengthen and encourage them (3:1–2). This he did from Athens (where he had arrived by way of Berea, Acts 17:10–15). After a brief time in Athens (17:16–34), Paul moved on to Corinth (probably arriving there in late summer, A.D. 50), where in collaboration with Aquila and Priscilla he began to evangelize that city (18:1–4).

It was while Paul was in Corinth that Timothy returned with the good news from Thessalonica that the congregation was not only standing fast and faithful in the face of persecution, but was even growing in faith and love (3:6–7), to the extent that it was becoming a model for believers throughout Macedonia and Achaia (1:7). The relief, joy, and encouragement Paul felt upon receiving the welcome news is evident throughout 1 Thessalonians, which he apparently wrote and sent to the Christians in Thessalonica immediately after Timothy's arrival.

In the first part of this letter (1:2–3:13) Paul sought to encourage and strengthen the Thessalonians, to defend the integrity and truthfulness of the gospel message, and to affirm and develop his friendship with them as brothers and sisters. In the second part (4:1–5:24) Paul sought to encourage and instruct them regarding some specific matters of Christian living: holiness, sexual ethics, social relationships, the death of believers, the return of Jesus, and congregational behavior. This choice of topics almost certainly reflects something of Timothy's assessment of the situation in Thessalonica; it may also reflect one or more questions raised by the Thessalonians themselves (notice the "now about" in 4:9 and 5:1, and the similar phrase in 4:13) and transmitted to Paul via Timothy (either orally or in writing).

The Setting and Occasion of 2 Thessalonians

IN CONTRAST TO 1 Thessalonians, we know next to nothing about the specific circumstances that led to the writing of 2 Thessalonians. That it was sent by the same three people as 1 Thessalonians and reflects so closely the language and structure of this letter strongly suggests that it was written not long after the first letter, while Paul, Silas, and Timothy were still in Corinth. We do not know how Paul became informed of the new developments in Thessalonica. In view of Thessalonica's location between Philippi and Corinth, one possibility is that someone from the church in Philippi, delegated to deliver a financial gift to Paul in Corinth (see Phil. 4:15–16), shared with Paul information acquired while passing through Thessalonica. This would explain both how Paul learned enough of the situation to write a letter (notice 2 Thess. 3:11, "we hear") and why his information seems rather vague at points (e.g., 2:2).

All we really have to go on are the three main topics Paul addresses in the letter: (1) the intense persecution the church was experiencing (1:3–12); (2) a misunderstanding about the Day of the Lord (2:1–12); and (3) disruptive behavior on the part of some members of the congregation (3:6–15). If these topics offer clues to the circumstances in Thessalonica, it would appear that (1) persecution had either broken out again and/or intensified; (2) a new misunderstanding about the return of Christ had arisen, perhaps under the influence of information allegedly from Paul (see the commentary on 2:2 for details) or based on a misunderstanding of his teaching; and (3) Paul's initial efforts in 1 Thessalonians to deal with the matter of disruptive behavior were unsuccessful, and perhaps even provocative. This second letter represents Paul's effort to deal with these matters while continuing the encouragement and instruction so evident in the first letter (see esp. 2 Thess. 2:13–3:5; also 1:3–12).

Some Technical Matters

Who Wrote the Letters?

BOTH 1 AND 2 Thessalonians were sent out under the name of not one but three people, Paul, Silas, and Timothy. The consistent use of first person plural pronouns ("we," "us") throughout both letters makes it clear that the inclusion of Silas and Timothy in the salutation is no mere formality (contrast Philippians, which includes Timothy in the prescript but uses the first person singular thereafter). All three missionaries stand together in the encouragement, instruction, and commands given to the Thessalonian congregation.[5]

At the same time, the order of the names and the occasional use of "I" (1 Thess. 2:18; 3:5; 5:27; 2 Thess. 2:5; 3:17) reveal that Paul was almost certainly the person who drafted or dictated the letters. Timothy, who had earlier served as the threesome's representative to Thessalonica (1 Thess. 3:2, 5), may have delivered one or both of the letters. It is possible but undeterminable whether Silas was the one who wrote down Paul's dictation.[6]

The Question of 1 Thessalonians 2:13–16

WHILE 1 THESSALONIANS IS widely accepted as genuinely Pauline, not a few scholars have rejected one section of it, 2:13–16, as a later non-Pauline interpolation into the letter.[7] Arguments offered in support of this view include: (1) the condemnation of "the Jews" expressed here is said to contradict Paul's hopeful attitude in Romans 11 regarding the salvation of the Jewish people; (2) the reference in verse 16 to a past judgment of the Jews is said to be a reference to the destruction of the Jerusalem temple in A.D. 70, well after the traditional date for this letter; (3) verses 15–16 contain traditional anti-Semitic language that was current after A.D. 70 and which could not have been written by Paul; (4) in terms of form, verse 13 introduces a second "thanksgiving" section, whereas all other Pauline letters have only a single thanksgiving section; (5) persecution of Christians by Jews (v. 14) is said to be unattested at the time Paul wrote the letter.

None of these arguments is convincing.[8] (1) Paul is not speaking of all Jews, but only those involved in anti-Christian persecution (see

---

5. Similarly E. J. Richard, *Thessalonians*, 40; see BDF §460 (3), and cf. 2 Cor. 1:19, where "by us" means "by me and Silvanus and Timothy" [NASB]). See also J. Murphy-O'Connor, *Paul the Letter-Writer: His World, His Options, His Skills* (Good News Studies 41; Collegeville, Minn.: Liturgical Press, 1995), 19–20.

6. For a discussion of his possible influence, see E. Best, *Thessalonians*, 23–29; E. G. Selwyn, *The First Epistle of St. Peter*, 2d ed. (London: Macmillan, 1947), 9–17.

7. A classic statement of the case against 2:13–16 is given by B. A. Pearson, "1 Thessalonians 2:13–16: A Deutero-Pauline Interpolation," *HTR* 64 (1971): 79–94.

8. For a more detailed discussion of the matter see C. A. Wanamaker, *Thessalonians*, 29–31.

further the commentary below). (2) That Paul has in view here only a small minority of the Jewish people rules out the destruction of the temple as the referent of verse 16. (3) The language is indeed traditional, but its roots are earlier rather than later, as it closely echoes the teachings and language of Jesus. (4) Arguments based on form are inconclusive, as authors occasionally varied their pattern for circumstantial reasons. Galatians, for example, whose authenticity is unquestioned, is the only Pauline letter without an opening thanksgiving. (5) Jewish persecution of Christians goes back to the very beginnings of the church, as the death of Stephen (Acts 7:57–8:1) and Paul's own testimony (Gal. 1:13, "intensely I persecuted the church of God and tried to destroy it"; cf. Phil. 3:6) indicate.

In addition to being based on unconvincing arguments, the case for viewing 2:13–16 as an interpolation faces two major obstacles. (1) No persuasive explanation has been offered to explain why someone at some later time would insert this passage into this letter at this place. (2) Every known copy of 1 Thessalonians contains the passage in question. While this absence of textual disturbance does not prove that the passage is authentic, it does create a significant presumption in its favor.[9] In sum, in the absence of evidence to the contrary, the passage stands as part of the letter.

Is 2 Thessalonians a Fake?

WHILE 1 THESSALONIANS IS almost universally accepted as a genuine Pauline letter, the same cannot be said with regard to 2 Thessalonians. At the present time[10] the balance of scholarly opinion tends toward the view that the letter is a fake (the polite term is *pseudonymous*, i.e., written by one person but falsely published as a letter written by someone else), written by an unknown person sometime between five and fifty

---

9. On this point see M. W. Holmes, "Textual Criticism," *DPL*, 930 (sec. 5).

10. Prior to the early 1970s, 2 Thessalonians, though not unquestioned, was widely accepted as Pauline, and the burden of proof was on anyone who challenged the letter's authenticity. But since the publication of an influential book in 1972 (W. Trilling, *Untersuchungen zum 2. Thessalonicherbrief* [Leipzig, 1972]), the consensus of scholarly opinion has clearly shifted, to the point now that in academic discussions the burden of proof is on those who think the letter is genuine. What is curious about this shift of opinion is that no genuinely new evidence has been offered to justify the now-fashionable rejection of 2 Thessalonians. This suggests that the shift in consensus is more a matter of a climate of opinion than it is of evidence and arguments.

years after Paul's death. The grounds for questioning the authenticity of 2 Thessalonians include the following: (1) the form and structure of 2 Thessalonians is said to be too similar to that of 1 Thessalonians; (2) the vocabulary and style of 2 Thessalonians is said to be too close to that of 1 Thessalonians and too different from that of other Pauline letters; (3) it is claimed that 1 Thessalonians is warm, friendly, and personal, while 2 Thessalonians is cool, distant, and formal; and (4) allegedly there are significant differences in theology between the two letters, especially with regard to eschatology.[11]

None of these arguments is particularly strong or persuasive. With regard to (1) and (2), for example, if 2 Thessalonians is authentic, we are dealing with two documents written by the same author only a short time apart. Under such circumstances, it is difficult to see how or on what basis one might determine that one is "too close" to the other to be authentic. Furthermore, the differences noted under (2) are of questionable value (all Pauline letters differ from one another to some degree; how does one ascertain when that difference is "too different"?). In any case, the claim about differences between 2 Thessalonians and other Pauline letters proves too much, in that it calls into question not only the second letter but also the first.

Item (3) is an opinion, not an argument or reason; the key question is why are the two letters different. Only if one rules out in advance situational reasons for the differences—the same kind of situational differences that are recognized and acknowledged in interpreting other Pauline letters—can one turn these differences into an argument for inauthenticity.[12] As for (4), Robert Jewett rightly observes that a mere "recital of the differences in theological emphasis fails to address the essential weaknesses of such arguments ... many of the arguments concerning differences would eliminate 1 Thessalonians as well as 2 Thessalonians and comparable differences surface when one compares other authentic Pauline letters."[13] In sum, a series of weak argu-

---

11. For more detailed and extensive discussions of the question see I. H. Marshall, *1 and 2 Thessalonians*, 28–45 (who gives particular attention to the arguments of Trilling); C. A. Wanamaker, *Thessalonians*, 17–28; E. Best, *Thessalonians*, 50–58; and R. Jewett, *Thessalonian Correspondence*, 3–18 (all of whom accept the authenticity of the letter). For a brief history of scholarship on the issue and an excellent summary of the arguments against authenticity, see Edgar M. Krentz, "Thessalonians, First and Second Epistles to the," *ABD*, 6:518–23.

12. R. Jewett, *Thessalonian Correspondence*, 12.

13. Ibid., 16.

ments does not add up to a persuasive case against the authenticity of 2 Thessalonians.

Apart from the inconclusiveness of the arguments against 2 Thessalonians, there is the inability of any forgery hypothesis proposed to date to suggest a historically credible situation or circumstance which can explain (1) why a forged letter might have been written, (2) its relationship to 1 Thessalonians, and (3) how it came to be accepted as part of the Pauline corpus.[14] The time frame within which the forgery, if there was one, must have occurred is rather narrow: between the death of Paul in the mid-60s and the formation of the Pauline corpus early in the second century. The closer one places the date of the alleged forgery to Paul's time, the more difficult it is to explain how it went unchallenged by those who knew Paul. The closer one dates it to the formation of the corpus, the more difficult it becomes to explain both why such a letter was written (since the kind of eschatological issues 2 Thessalonians deals with were no longer "hot topics") and how it made it into the collection of Paul's letters. In short, the forgery hypothesis creates as many or more problems as it purports to solve—hardly a characteristic of a convincing theory.

To summarize, three considerations lead me to accept the letter as authentic. (1) It claims to be an authentic Pauline letter. (2) Nothing in the language, style, or theology requires a different conclusion if proper weight is given to the situational character of all the Pauline letters. (3) No one has been able to offer a historically credible explanation of the letter's origin if it is a forgery. I conclude, therefore, that 2 Thessalonians is a genuine Pauline letter.

Was 2 Thessalonians Written First?

IT HAS OCCASIONALLY been suggested that the historical order of the Thessalonian letters is the opposite of the canonical order.[15] Second Thessalonians, it is argued, was in fact the first letter Paul wrote, which Timothy delivered during the visit described in 1 Thessalonians 3:1–6. Since the traditional order of the Pauline letters is based on descending

---

14. On this point see I. H. Marshall, *1 and 2 Thessalonians*, 40–45.

15. Most recently by C. A. Wanamaker (*Thessalonians*, 37–45), who structures his commentary and bases his interpretation on the priority of 2 Thessalonians. For a full listing (with discussion) of the various arguments offered in favor of the suggestion, see E. Best, *Thessalonians*, 42–45; see also R. Jewett, *Thessalonian Correspondence*, 24–30.

length rather than chronology, there is nothing inherently improbable about the suggestion.

But the arguments offered in support of the suggestion are unpersuasive, indecisive, or a matter of assumption. For example, it is claimed that Paul's concern for authenticity in 2 Thessalonians 3:17 ("I, Paul, write this greeting in my own hand, which is the distinguishing mark in all my letters") only makes sense in a first letter. But if so, then it is strange that none of Paul's other letters (most of which are *first* letters) make any such reference. Second, and more significantly, 3:17 implies the possibility of a forged letter. But a forged letter in turn implies the existence of a genuine letter. In short, the verse makes much more sense in a second letter than in a first one. Examples of indecisive arguments include: (1) the observation that in 1:4–5 the Thessalonians are experiencing persecutions, whereas in 1 Thessalonians persecution is referred to as a past experience (persecution could have broken out again after a brief respite); and (2) the claim that the references in 1 Thessalonians to previous instruction (1 Thess. 4:1; 5:1) are to written instruction (they can refer just as well to oral instruction).

In the absence of any persuasive evidence favoring the priority of 2 Thessalonians over 1 Thessalonians, three considerations lead me to accept the traditional order. (1) Second Thessalonians 3:17 makes better sense as part of a second letter rather than a first, especially in light of the references to a purported letter in 2:2 and 2:15. (2) The long description in 1 Thessalonians 1:4–2:12 of Paul's initial visit to Thessalonica seems more appropriate as part of a first letter. (3) The teaching about the return of Christ in 1 Thessalonians 5:1–11 and 2 Thessalonians 2:1–12 makes better sense if 1 Thessalonians is the earlier letter.[16]

---

16. See F. F. Bruce, *1 & 2 Thessalonians*, xlii–xliii, for a full discussion of this last point.

Outline of
1 and 2 Thessalonians

Outline of 1 Thessalonians

I. Prescript (1:1)
II. Remembrance and Encouragement with Respect to the
   Past (1:2–3:13)
   A. Opening Thanksgiving (1:2–10) [focus on the Thessalonians]
      1. Thanksgiving for the Thessalonians (1:2–3)
      2. The Thessalonians and the Gospel (1:4–10)
   B. Apostolic Attitudes Toward the Thessalonians While Present (2:1–12) [focus on the missionaries]
      1. Apostolic Responsibility to God (2:1–4)
      2. Apostolic Ministry, Care, and Nurture (2:5–12)
   C. Second Thanksgiving (2:13–16) [focus on the Thessalonians]
      1. Thanksgiving for the Thessalonians (2:13)
      2. The Thessalonians and Persecution (2:14–16)
   D. Apostolic Attitudes Toward the Thessalonians While Absent (2:17–3:8) [focus on the missionaries]
      1. Apostolic Concern (2:17–20)
      2. Apostolic Action (3:1–5)
      3. Apostolic Relief and Joy (3:6–8)
   E. Third Thanksgiving (3:9–13) [focus on the Thessalonians]
      1. Thanksgiving for the Thessalonians (3:9)
      2. Prayer for the Thessalonians (3:10–13)
III. Exhortation and Encouragement with Respect to the
   Future (4:1–5:22)
   A. General Introduction (4:1–2)
   B. Holiness and Sexual Ethics (4:3–8)
   C. Mutual Love (*philadelphia*) (4:9–12)
   D. Questions Concerning the *Parousia* of Jesus (4:13–5:11)
      1. Questions About the Fate of Deceased Believers
         (4:13–18)

Outline of 2 Thessalonians

Annotated Bibliography

Recent Major Commentaries

Best, Ernest. *A Commentary on the First and Second Epistles to the Thessalonians.* HNTC. New York: Harper & Row, 1972; reprint, Peabody, Mass.: Hendrickson, 1987. An outstanding and thorough treatment that on nearly every issue presents and thoughtfully considers all the interpretive options.

Bruce, F. F. *1 & 2 Thessalonians.* WBC 45. Waco, Tex.: Word, 1982. An excellent, medium-length comprehensive treatment of the Greek text that reflects Bruce's penetrating scholarship, wide knowledge of Paul's other letters, and characteristic thoroughness and attention to detail. Includes a useful excursus on the Antichrist figure.

Elias, Jacob W. *1 and 2 Thessalonians.* Believers Church Bible Commentary. Scottdale, Pa., and Waterloo, Ont.: Herald, 1995. A solid, responsible contribution from a Mennonite perspective, which is deeply concerned about the significance of the text for the church today.

Holtz, Traugott. *Der erste Brief an die Thessalonicher.* EKKNT 13. Zürich: Benziger, 1986. This recent German commentary is part of the influential *Evangelisch-katholischer* commentary series.

Marshall, I. Howard. *1 and 2 Thessalonians.* NCB. Grand Rapids: Eerdmans, and London: Marshall Morgan & Scott, 1983. A solid and reliable medium-length commentary that gives an especially detailed treatment of introductory and critical issues, including extensive attention to (and critique of) the influential work of W. Trilling.

Morris, Leon. *The First and Second Epistles to the Thessalonians.* Rev. ed. NICNT. Grand Rapids: Eerdmans, 1991. A cautious and traditional commentary of moderate length by a careful expositor.

Richard, Earl J. *First and Second Thessalonians.* Sacra Pagina 11. Collegeville, Minn.: Liturgical Press, 1995. A full-length comprehensive critical commentary that takes a fresh and often independent line. Based on the Greek text, but with all Greek transliterated; strong on lexical and grammatical issues.

Rigaux, Béda. *Saint Paul: Les Épîtres aux Thessaloniciens.* Études biblique. Paris: Gabalda, 1956. Still one of the best treatments of the letters.

Trilling, Wolfgang. *Der zweite Brief an die Thessalonicher.* EKKNT 14. Zürich: Benziger, and Neukirchen-Vluyn: Neukirchener Verlag, 1980. A solid commentary based on Trilling's arguments against the authenticity of 2 Thessalonians (W. Trilling, *Untersuchungen zum zweiten Thessalonicherbrief* [Leipzig, 1972]; see the Introduction, fn. 10).

Wanamaker, Charles A. *The Epistles to the Thessalonians: A Commentary on the Greek Text.* NIGTC. Grand Rapids: Eerdmans, and Exeter: Paternoster, 1990. An outstanding full-length commentary on the Greek text that gives particular (and fruitful) attention to the rhetorical aspects of the letters. Written in a South African context, it displays sensitivity to the context of the Thessalonian congregation as a persecuted minority movement and to the challenges Paul faced as he sought to "resocialize" his converts to a genuinely Christian worldview.

Older Major Commentaries

Frame, James Everett. *A Critical and Exegetical Commentary on the Epistles of St. Paul to the Thessalonians.* ICC. Edinburgh: T. & T. Clark, 1912. A full-scale treatment of the Greek text, still useful for its close attention to lexical and especially grammatical questions; draws often on patristic commentators (quoted in the original languages) and provides an often comprehensive survey of earlier scholarship.

Lightfoot, J. B. *Notes on Epistles of St. Paul From Unpublished Commentaries.* London and New York: Macmillan, 1895, pp. 1–136. A relatively brief but penetrating analysis of the Greek text that reflects Lightfoot's encyclopedic knowledge of the ancient world; his lexical observations still warrant close study.

Milligan, George. *St. Paul's Epistles to the Thessalonians: The Greek Text with Introduction and Notes.* London: Macmillan, 1908. Still worth consulting on points of exegesis, though in some respects extremely dated; most of its best points have been taken up by later commentators.

Other Commentaries

Aus, Roger. "II Thessalonians." Pp. 191–221 in *I-II Timothy, Titus, II Thessalonians*, by A. J. Hultgren and R. Aus. ACNT. Minneapolis: Augsburg, 1984.

Calvin, John. *The Epistles of Paul the Apostle to the Romans and to the Thessalonians.* Trans. by R. Mackenzie. Grand Rapids: Eerdmans, 1961 [1540]. A classic example of the Genevan reformer at work, surprisingly exegetical for one better known for his theology. Relatively brief; always worth reading as a supplement to a full treatment.

Gaventa, Beverly Roberts. *First and Second Thessalonians.* Interpretation: A Bible Commentary for Teaching and Preaching. Louisville: John Knox,

1998. A relatively brief (133 pages), nontechnical, always thoughtful treatment of the letter, written in full awareness of the difficulties involved in reading an ancient document through modern eyes. Comments and suggestions for application and preaching are brief but suggestive; particularly notable are the "Reflections" on maternal imagery in Paul and on the persistence of evil.

Hendriksen, William. *I and II Thessalonians*. Grand Rapids: Baker, 1955. Capable exegetical work lies behind his theological discussion; now somewhat dated; uneven in its coverage of issues.

Hiebert, D. Edmond. *The Thessalonian Epistles: A Call to Readiness*. Chicago: Moody, 1971. A lengthy treatment from a pretribulational perspective.

Juel, Donald H. "I Thessalonians." Pp. 211–55 in *Galatians, Philippians, Philemon, I Thessalonians*, by E. Krentz, J. Koenig, and D. H. Juel. ANCT. Minneapolis: Augsburg, 1985. Severely hampered by space constraints imposed by the format of the series, but insightful observations (occasionally expressed with epigrammatic clarity) make it worth consulting.

Martin, D. Michael. *1, 2 Thessalonians*. NAC 33. Nashville: Broadman & Holman, 1995. Competent, but flat and uneven in its treatment.

Morris, Leon. *The Epistles of Paul to the Thessalonians: An Introduction and Commentary*. Revised ed. TNTC. Grand Rapids: Eerdmans, 1984. A short version of his NICNT contribution.

Stott, John R. W. *The Gospel and the End of Time: The Message of 1 and 2 Thessalonians*. BST. Downers Grove, Ill.: InterVarsity, 1991. The best of the nontechnical treatments of the letters by a master evangelical preacher who is also an excellent scholar; it reflects his deep commitment both to Scripture and to the church.

Thomas, Robert L. "1 Thessalonians" and "2 Thessalonians." Pp. 227–337 in *The Expositor's Bible Commentary*, vol. 11. Ed. by F. E. Gaebelein. Grand Rapids: Zondervan, 1978. A brief treatment based on the NIV from a dispensational perspective.

Williams, David J. *1 and 2 Thessalonians*. NIBC. Peabody, Mass.: Hendrickson, 1992. A brief but helpful discussion that nearly always touches on the key interpretive issues.

Special Studies

Collins, Raymond F., ed. *The Thessalonian Correspondence*. BETL 87. Leuven: Leuven Univ. Press and Peeters, 1990. An important and wide-ranging collection of scholarly essays in several languages on nearly all aspects of Thessalonians.

Donfried, Karl P. "The Theology of 1 Thessalonians" and "The Theology of 2 Thessalonians." Pp. 1–113 in *The Theology of the Shorter Pauline Letters*, by K. P. Donfried and I. H. Marshall. New Testament Theology. Cambridge: Cambridge Univ. Press, 1993. A sympathetic treatment of each document separately.

Hock, Ronald F. *The Social Context of Paul's Ministry: Tentmaking and Apostleship.* Philadelphia: Fortress, 1980. An interesting investigation of Paul's use of the workplace as a place for evangelization and discipleship in light of Greco-Roman attitudes toward work and traveling philosophers.

Jewett, Robert. *The Thessalonian Correspondence: Pauline Rhetoric and Millenarian Piety.* Foundations and Facets. Philadelphia: Fortress, 1986. A comprehensive study of critical issues associated with the Thessalonian correspondence and a major contribution to the rhetorical analysis of the letters. Jewett's use of the modern sociological category of "millenarian movements" to interpret the Thessalonian situation has not been persuasive.

Malherbe, Abraham J. *Paul and the Thessalonians: The Philosophical Tradition of Pastoral Care.* Philadelphia: Fortress, 1987. A fine study of Paul and his ministry in light of ancient philosophers and their methods.

Plevnik, Joseph. *Paul and the Parousia: An Exegetical and Theological Investigation.* Peabody, Mass.: Hendrickson, 1997. A recent thorough study that not only analyzes individual issues or passages, but ends with a useful synthesis of Paul's teaching.

Trilling, Wolfgang. *Untersuchungen zum zweiten Thessalonicherbrief.* Leipzig: St. Benno, 1972. A widely influential presentation of the case for understanding 2 Thessalonians as a pseudonymous letter.

Weima, Jeffrey A. D. "'How You Must Walk to Please God': Holiness and Discipleship in 1 Thessalonians." Pp. 98–119 in *Patterns of Discipleship in the New Testament,* ed. Richard N. Longenecker. Grand Rapids: Eerdmans, 1996. An insightful contribution on an important theme in 1 Thessalonians.

1 Thessalonians 1:1

❧

P AUL, SILAS AND Timothy,
To the church of the Thessalonians in God the
Father and the Lord Jesus Christ:
Grace and peace to you.

WITH REGARD TO the letter's structure, 1:1
forms a complete structural unit, the "prescript," and 1:2 begins a new section (the
"thanksgiving"). Like any prescript, it identi-
fies the senders and recipients and conveys an expression of goodwill.
Of all the Pauline letter openings, this is the simplest and most like contemporary Hellenistic letter openings (typically "A to B, greetings";
cf. Acts 15:23, "The apostles and elders, your brothers, To the Gentile
believers in Antioch, Syria and Cilicia: Greetings").[1]

The senders. For reasons we can only guess at, 1 and 2 Thessalonians are the only letters in which Paul does not characterize himself
or his colleagues in some way.[2] The name of the second person is actually "Silvanus" (cf. NIV note), whom Paul mentions elsewhere (2 Cor.
1:19; 2 Thess. 1:1). He is the same person as the "Silas" mentioned in
Acts (see Acts 15:22–40; 16:19–29; 17:4–15; 18:5) and probably the
person mentioned in 1 Peter 5:12.[3] Either he had (like Paul) two names,
one Semitic and one Latin, or "Silvanus" and "Silas" represent Latin
and Greek forms, respectively, of a Semitic name.

Acts presents Silas as a Jerusalem prophet who was delegated (with
Judas Barsabbas) to deliver the results of the Jerusalem Council to the

---

1. See further P. T. O'Brien, "Letters, Letter Forms," *DPL*, 550–53; J. Murphy-O'Connor,
Paul the Letter-Writer: His World, His Options, His Skills (Collegeville, Minn.: Liturgical Press, 1995).

2. Elsewhere Paul describes himself as either a "servant" (Rom. 1:1; Phil. 1:1; Titus 1:1)
and/or an "apostle" (Rom. 1:1; 1 Cor. 1:1; 2 Cor. 1:1; Gal. 1:1; Eph. 1:1; Col. 1:1; 1 Tim.
1:1; 2 Tim. 1:1; Titus 1:1), or a "prisoner" (Philem. 1). When colleagues are named in the
prescript (Timothy in 2 Corinthians, Philippians, Colossians, and Philemon, and Sosthenes
in 1 Corinthians), they are designated as "brother" or "servant."

3. So Peter H. Davids, *The First Epistle of Peter* (Grand Rapids: Eerdmans, 1990), 198; J. Ram-
sey Michaels, *1 Peter* (Waco, Tex.: Word, 1988), xlvi–xlvii, 306–7; but as J. B. Lightfoot
(*Notes on Epistles*, 7) observes, the name is too common to be certain.

---

church at Antioch. After Barnabas and Paul separated (Acts 15:36–39), Paul chose Silas as his coworker, and the two traveled through Galatia, Asia Minor, Macedonia, and Greece (Paul's second missionary trip; cf. Acts 15:40–18:22). Paul apparently viewed him as a fellow apostle (cf. the discussion of 1 Thess. 2:6). He played a substantial role in establishing churches in both Thessalonica and Corinth, as did Timothy, who joined Paul and Silas as a junior member of the team early in their travels (see Acts 16:1–4). Timothy is described in 1 Thessalonians 3:2 as "God's fellow worker," and Paul's own feelings toward him are captured in 1 Corinthians 4:17 ("my son whom I love") and Philippians 2:22 ("as a son with his father he has served with me in the work of the gospel.").

The conjunction of the three names (which also occur in 2 Thess. 1:1) and the frequent use of the first person plural ("we") throughout the letter indicate that all three are cosenders of the letter.[4] The order of the names and Paul's occasional use of "I" (2:18; 3:5; 5:27) indicate that he was the one who actually composed the letter. Timothy, who had earlier served as Paul's emissary to Thessalonica (3:2, 5) may have delivered this letter. It is unclear whether Silas had a hand in its composition or writing.[5]

The recipients. After identifying the senders, Paul identifies the recipients: "the church of the Thessalonians." In the Greek world, *ekklesia* (in the New Testament routinely translated "church") could designate, among other things, a public assembly (Acts 19:32, 39) or a philosophical school, that is, a gathering or a movement. Similarly, in the LXX (Septuagint, i.e., the Greek translation of the Hebrew Bible) *ekklesia* and *synagoge* ("synagogue") each designates Israel both as a gathered assembly and as God's people. As *synagoge* had become the standard term for local Jewish congregations, *ekklesia* was an obvious choice for designating the Christian movement and distinguishing it from Judaism. In Christian usage *ekklesia* could indicate individual house churches (Rom. 16:5), local congregations (Rom. 16:1), or the Christian movement as a whole (1 Cor. 12:28; Col. 1:18, 24). Here it means the local congregation in Thessalonica, as the phrase "of the Thessalonians" clearly indicates. This

---

4. Similarly E. J. Richard, *Thessalonians*, 40; see BDF §460 (3); cf. 2 Cor. 1:19, where "by us" means "by me and Silvanus and Timothy" [NASB]). See also J. Murphy-O'Connor, *Paul the Letter-Writer*, 19–20.

5. For a discussion of his possible influence, see E. Best, *Thessalonians*, 23–29; E. G. Selwyn, *The First Epistle of St. Peter*, 2d ed. (London: Macmillan, 1947), 9–17.

phrase also indicates the relation between the local congregation and God's people elsewhere: the basic concept is the church as a whole, of which the Thessalonians are the local representative.[6]

The local assembly of the Thessalonians is further identified as "in God the Father and the Lord Jesus Christ." The meaning of the phrase is difficult to determine.[7] "In God" is as rare in the Pauline corpus as "in Christ" is common,[8] and interpreters are divided whether to interpret the unusual in light of the common or vice versa. Frequently the phrase "in Christ" "has 'incorporative' force, pointing to believers' participation in Christ's risen life or their membership in his body."[9] If this is what this phrase means here, then the parallel phrase "in God" must be understood similarly. On the other hand, in view of the lack of parallels elsewhere in Paul's letters, some interpreters understand (correctly, in my estimation) the preposition "in" as indicating "means" rather than "position." That is, it designates the community as "brought into being" or "assembled by" God and Jesus.[10]

However one takes the phrase, the close linkage of God and Jesus indicates their unity of purpose and action (cf. 2 Cor. 5:18–21), without which and apart from which the Christian *ekklesia* does not exist. Moreover, the full Christological formula "the Lord Jesus Christ" brings to mind key aspects of God's saving work in Christ that brought the church into existence: The name "Jesus" lays stress on his death, the title "Christ" emphasizes his resurrection, and "Lord" expresses the believer's profession of faith in Jesus the Christ.[11]

---

6. See further J. Roloff, "ἐκκλησία," *EDNT*, 1:410–15; L. Coenen, "Church, Synagogue," *NIDNTT*, 1:291–307; P. T. O'Brien, "Church," *DPL*, 123–31.

7. In addition, the absence of the article before "in God the Father and the Lord Jesus Christ" creates some degree of uncertainty about what word or phrase this statement modifies. The parallel in 2:14 and the pattern of other Pauline prescripts indicate that it modifies the phrase that precedes it. Also, the use of the preposition "in" (*en*) rather than "from" (*apo*) stands against taking it with the following salutation ("grace and peace to you").

8. Outside of 1 Thess. 1:1 and 2 Thess. 1:1, "in God" occurs only five other times, none of which match the usage here (Rom. 2:17 and 5:11, boasting in God; Eph. 3:9 and Col. 3:3, being hidden in God; 1 Thess. 2:2, courage in God), while "in Christ" occurs ca. 170 times.

9. F. F. Bruce, *1 and 2 Thessalonians*, 7; on "in Christ" see further B. Witherington III, "Christ," *DPL*, 98–99; C. F. D. Moule, *The Origin of Christology* (Cambridge: Cambridge Univ. Press, 1977), 54–69.

10. So E. Best, *Thessalonians*, 62; E. J. Richard, *Thessalonians*, 41–42; for the view that it indicates position, see J. E. Frame, *Thessalonians*, 69–70; C. F. D. Moule, *Origin*, 56; J. R. W. Stott, *The Gospel and the End of Time*, 27–28.

11. E. J. Richard, *Thessalonians*, 43.

In addition, it is important to note how this phrase *functions*. By emphasizing the *ekklesia's* theological basis and Christological focus, it serves to differentiate sharply this particular assembly from any others (pagan or Jewish) with which the recently converted Thessalonians were familiar. The monotheistic confession of "God the Father"[12] involves a rejection of the Thessalonians' former gods (cf. 1:9), while the acknowledgment of Jesus as Messiah ("Christ") and Lord distinguishes the Christian movement from Judaism (cf. 1:10).

The greeting. "Grace and peace to you" stands in place of the simple "greetings" (*chairein*) typical of a Greek letter and is similar to greetings found in Jewish letters (e.g., 2 Macc. 1:1 has *chairein* and "peace;" 2 Bar. 78:2 reads "mercy and peace"). But more important than the formal parallels is the theological content of the two evocative terms. For Paul, God is the ultimate source of grace (see 2 Thess. 1:2, "from God the Father and the Lord Jesus Christ"), which is the foundation and basis of all God's actions on behalf of his people. Indeed, grace is not so much an attribute of God as it is his redeeming activity, visible in the ministry, death, and resurrection of Christ. Peace, on the other hand, indicates the outcome of God's saving activity, a restored relationship with God (Rom. 5:1; see also 5:2–11). Here the difference between cultural and biblical definitions of "peace" is clear: not merely the absence of conflict, but the presence (and enjoyment) of whole and harmonious relationships. In short, the phrase "grace and peace" (which functions as both an affirmation and a prayer) calls to mind both the basis and the consequence of God's saving activity, which finds its focus in Jesus Christ.[13]

Bridging Contexts

THIS OPENING VERSE of 1 Thessalonians immediately presents us with at least three interpretive challenges frequently encountered when studying and applying Scripture: (1) the matter of historical precedent; (2) the question of arguments or infer-

---

12. The phrase also occurs at 1 Thess. 1:3; 3:11, 13 (discussed under "Bridging Contexts"); 2 Thess. 1:1–2; 2:16.

13. As J. B. Lightfoot observes, "χάρις [grace] is the source of all real blessings, εἰρήνη [peace] their end and issue" (*Notes on Epistles*, 8). For "peace" see further the discussion of 5:23 below.

ences from silence; and (3) the challenge of evocative language (with the accompanying potential pitfalls of over- or under-interpretation).

The matter of historical precedent. The question of historical precedent arises out of Paul's consistent practice of working as part of a team (exemplified here by his deliberate mention of Silas and Timothy in the address, and the significant role they played in the establishment of the Thessalonian congregation), and of installing teams as the leadership of the churches he established. Unlike itinerant philosophers of his day (with whom Paul will contrast himself in 2:1–12), Paul whenever possible was accompanied by others.[14] Also, he left behind him teams of leaders in the churches he and his colleagues established (Acts 14:23; 20:17, Phil. 1:1; 1 Thess. 5:12; 1 Tim. 4:14; 5:17). Moreover, while the evidence regarding church structure in New Testament times is incomplete, it is nonetheless consistent: Team leadership was the basic pattern. So the question arises: Is this consistent pattern merely a matter of coincidence, or is it an important aspect of Paul's method of ministry that we ought to follow, which may even have normative value for churches today? In other words, is this *description* of how Paul worked also in some way a *prescription* for us?

Gordon Fee and Douglas Stuart, in their excellent discussion of the question of historical precedent, offer helpful guidelines.[15] They correctly note that in general *"unless Scripture explicitly tells us we must do something, what is only narrated or described does not function in a normative way."* They also acknowledge that *"biblical precedents may sometimes be regarded as repeatable patterns—even if they are not understood to be normative."* In this particular instance, I would argue that the *consistency* of Paul's practice with regard to team leadership—a consistency that transcended individual cities, regions, and cultures, and therefore was not a matter of merely local practice—suggests that the pattern exemplified here in 1 (and 2) Thessalonians is indeed worth repeating today, even though it may not be normative.

Inferences from silence. It was noted above that in the prescripts of all Paul's letters except 1 and 2 Thessalonians, he characterizes himself

---

14. On his first journey, he followed his mentor, Barnabas, while Silas and Timothy were with him on his second trip, and Timothy and Erastus (see Acts 19:22; 2 Cor. 1:1) on the third.

15. Gordon D. Fee and Douglas Stuart, *How to Read the Bible for All Its Worth: A Guide to Understanding the Bible*, 2d ed. (Grand Rapids: Zondervan, 1993), 78–112, esp. 105–12. Following quotations are from pp. 106 and 111; italics are in the original.

as either a "servant" and/or "apostle" or "prisoner." In two letters (Romans and Galatians) in which Paul substantially expands his prescript, scholars have found these expansions to be significant for interpreting the meaning and circumstances of those letters. Correspondingly, is there some significance to be found in the *absence* of any characterization here in 1:1? While silence is occasionally significant (e.g., the Sherlock Holmes story in which the clue to solving the mystery was the hound who did *not* bark), as a general rule conclusions or arguments based on silence are at best of only limited value. In this instance in particular (one of his earliest letters, in which he may still have been developing what only later became his characteristic prescript form), it is best not to try to find something significant in what Paul did not say.

The challenge of evocative language. Especially in an opening section like this, phrases such as "church," "grace," "peace," and "the Lord Jesus Christ" often imply more than they explicitly state. These are terms that were for Paul deeply evocative, but which do not necessarily function that way today. Sometimes they evoke little or nothing, or because of changing usage evoke something quite different from what they did for Paul (e.g., "Jesus Christ" as a swear word, or "church" as a designation for a building). Here the twin pitfalls of under- and over-interpretation become apparent: Just how much content or which ideas did Paul intend to communicate?

For example, "grace"—a foundational concept for Paul and a word that occurs one hundred times in the Pauline corpus—is found only twice in 1 Thessalonians (1:1; 5:28). Clearly it is not a significant topic of discussion in this letter. Yet the two places it does occur "frame" the entire document. Moreover, it occurs here in close connection with other phrases (e.g., "in God the Father") that reinforce the basic emphasis of "grace" in Paul's usage.[16] This suggests that grace is in some way foundational for the entire message and therefore ought not to be ignored. Thus, the challenge in this instance is to make clear the foundational nature, the "taken for grantedness," in Paul's thinking of terms such as "grace," without detracting undue attention from the specific topics he does address in the course of the letter.

In the Original Meaning section, I treated, for the sake of clarity, each term or phrase separately. But it is also important to see how the

---

16. For an excellent discussion of grace, see Philip Yancey, *What's So Amazing about Grace?* (Grand Rapids: Zondervan, 1997).

individual pieces fit together as a whole, especially when seeking to bridge from meaning to application. What is the main impression or primary emphasis that Paul, simply by mentioning some foundational terms or phrases, seeks to communicate in his prescript? I suggest that he is emphasizing, from the very beginning of his letter, *the centrality and importance of God for the life of the church.* The phrases Paul links together— "grace," "in God the Father," "the Lord Jesus Christ," "peace"—remind us that the church has no life apart from God's saving work in Christ, work rooted in God's grace and resulting in "peace" (i.e., a restored relationship) with God, of which the gift of the Spirit is evidence. That is, Paul's gospel (see 1:5), in response to which the Thessalonian congregation came into existence, is fundamentally from and about God, and only secondarily for and about humans.

That this *theo*logical emphasis is not some incidental feature of his gospel is clear from the way the apostle will later develop it more fully and explicitly in Romans. There he makes it clear that the gospel is fundamentally the "power of *God* for salvation" (Rom. 1:16); that while humans (who have turned their back on God, worshiping the creature rather than the Creator, 1:25) "were still sinners" (and thus didn't even care if a God existed), "*God* demonstrates his own love for us in [that] . . . Christ died for us" (5:8); that Christ died because "*God* presented him as a sacrifice of atonement" (3:25), in order to demonstrate "that he himself [i.e., *God*] is righteous and that he justifies the one who has faith in Jesus" (3:26 NRSV; cf. 1:17). What Paul spells out in Romans, he implies here in his prescript to the Thessalonians.

THIS OPENING PRESCRIPT offers at least three topics for discussion. One of them, the "church of the Thessalonians," is the primary focus of the following section (1:2–10) and will be dealt with there. The other two are Paul's model of team leadership and the way that important terms and phrases in the prescript emphasize the centrality of God for the life of the church.

Team leadership. If the Pauline pattern of team leadership is indeed worth repeating today (even though it may not be normative), how might one go about applying it? From one perspective, the matter of team leadership can be seen as a question of church structure. This is probably not a fruitful line of approach, however, because most of us already have substantial commitments, both as individuals and as denominations, to one or another of the different forms of church structure that have developed over the centuries for a variety of reasons (historical, theological, and sociological). Moreover, even if we were somehow to slip free of these commitments and agree to start from scratch, there is in the New Testament no definitive model for church structure to guide us. There may be a principle that should guide our thinking about church structure (specifically, the structure should serve the needs of the congregation, rather than the reverse), but there is no definitive model as such. So approaching this matter as a question of church structure is not the most practical way to proceed.

Instead, we might begin by thinking about the Pauline model in terms of how it contrasts with a common feature of many churches today regardless of their particular structure. Whatever their formal structure (congregational, presbyterian, episcopal, or monepiscopal), many individual churches are hierarchically structured in a way that typically concentrates power and authority in the hands of one person. In this respect, they are more like a pyramid-shaped, hierarchically organized corporate structure or military command model than the models of the New Testament, whose dominant images with respect to leadership are those of the family and of servanthood. Consider, for example, the many churches today in which the senior pastor functions essentially as a CEO, with staff and church board subservient to him, or how often (and how quickly!) the latest fads in business organization filter their way down to the church, or the extent to which the jargon of business infiltrates our thinking (e.g., a "business manager" of a church who boasted of turning its day-care ministry into a "profit center").

There are not insubstantial dangers associated with this pattern of church leadership. As Gordon Fee observes, "leadership, especially of the more visible kind, can be heady business.... The great problem with single leadership is its threefold tendency to pride of place, love of authority, and lack of accountability."[17] The last point, accountability, is particularly critical in view of the significant temptation to moral failure (sexual or financial, in particular), temptations to which

---

17. Gordon D. Fee, *Gospel and Spirit: Issues in New Testament Hermeneutics* (Peabody, Mass.: Hendrickson, 1991), 143.

a distressing number of pastors and Christian leaders have succumbed in recent years.

Team leadership, which can be instituted informally within the constraints of any number of different formal structures, offers important advantages in this respect. Accountability to other members of a leadership team works to reduce the chances of a leader falling into sin. Moreover, even in instances where there is significant moral failure of a leader, the presence of a team rather than a single individual in leadership reduces the odds that the failure will devastate the congregation.

The advantages of team leadership, however, are not merely practical. Team leadership reminds us that in the New Testament the critical matter is not office or formal structure but giftedness. In this respect it better models the New Testament idea of what the church is. As Klyne Snodgrass observes, "the body of Christ does not have two classes of members—clergy and laity—or two sets of expectations. Everyone has the same task of building up the body, even though the responsibilities vary."[18] Team leadership is one concrete way of modeling this point for the rest of the congregation.

A contemporary example of team leadership is Willow Creek Community Church, which is often associated with the name of Bill Hybels. From the very beginning, however, this congregation has been led by a *team* of gifted people working together to implement their vision for what a church might be. Nor is this Pauline model limited to congregations. When Billy Graham received his Congressional Medal of Honor, the first thing he is reported to have said upon receiving the award is, "This has been a team effort from the very beginning," and he proceeded to name the people who had ministered with him through the years. In closing he said, "We did this together." Unquestionably, Graham has been blessed with a special gift of evangelism. But he would, I think, be the first to acknowledge that without the support and work of a whole team of differently gifted but equally dedicated people, his ministry would not have been the same. The Willow Creek and Graham teams are potent contemporary examples of something Paul practiced and modeled for the Thessalonians: team leadership in ministry.

The centrality of God for the life of the church. Over the course of the last two decades, a significant shift has occurred in the way

---

18. Klyne Snodgrass, *Ephesians* (NIVAC; Grand Rapids: Zondervan, 1996), 224.

many American Christians view the church. It is no longer uncommon, for example, to encounter a book or speaker describing church members as customers, potential converts or members as prospects, and the gospel, church activities, and programs as products to be marketed. Worship is confused with entertainment, being good with feeling good, and faithfulness with being successful or "blessed." "Meeting the needs of the customers" is said to be the key to church growth. Trends are predicted; for example, increasing numbers of people will select two to five churches "to be their *group* of local churches," and "on any given weekend, they will determine which church to attend according to their own most keenly felt needs."[19] Equally as revealing is the language one hears people using to explain why they changed churches ("my old church wasn't meeting my needs") or to evaluate a Sunday morning service ("that service really blessed me," or "I didn't get anything out of it today"). More and more, in other words, we are viewing "church" in terms of what it can do for *us*.

This shift in how many people view church—no doubt influenced by the narcissism (self-centeredness) and "consumer mentality" of contemporary American culture—is a symptom of a deeper, long-term cultural shift. Over the course of a century or so, substantial segments of American culture have shifted away from a God-centered perspective on reality to a human-centered one. That is, there has been a shift from a theocentric perspective or worldview, in which humans were viewed as the creation of God, to an anthropocentric worldview, in which (under the influence of the ideas of people such as Nietzsche and Freud) "God" is widely viewed as a projection of the human mind. In short, something like the ancient statement of Protagoras, "man is the measure of all things," has become the foundational principle of a contemporary secular worldview. Discussions of right and wrong, law and morality, and good and evil are no longer discussed with reference to God but with reference to human beings and human society as the base line or touchstone.[20]

When viewed from this anthropocentric perspective, the "church" becomes just another human organization, created by human beings to meet human needs. It may differ in style from other groups, but

---

19. George Barna, *The Frog in the Kettle* (Ventura, Calif.: Regal Books, 1990), 142.

20. See further on this point Philip Yancey, "Nietzsche Was Right," *Books and Culture* 4 (January/February 1998): 14–17.

not in substance: it is merely another form of social organization by which human beings seek to bring order and structure to their lives and/or meet personal needs. It is no real surprise, then, that many people view the church primarily in terms of what it can do for them. It is just another instance of the subtle (and therefore insidious) ways contemporary American culture is infiltrating the church today.

Over against this growing tendency stands the opening verse of Paul's letter, with its resounding emphasis on God and Jesus Christ. He reminds us that the church, whether in Thessalonica or elsewhere, is "in God the Father and the Lord Jesus Christ." It does not even exist, and certainly has no life, apart from God and his saving work in Christ. This means that the church is not just another social organization. It is nothing less than the people of God, called together by him for his worship and glory and commissioned to spread the gospel, that is, the good news about God. It is God who calls humans to follow, worship, and serve him, rather than vice versa. God does not exist for the sake of the church; rather, the church exists for the praise and glory of God. Paul emphatically reminds us of that point in the opening of his letter. As John R. W. Stott observes, "What stands out of Paul's vision of the church is its God-centredness."[21]

Grasping this point will fundamentally change the way we think about church. We will think of the worship service, for example, less and less in terms of what it does for us, and more and more as an opportunity for us to glorify, praise, and worship God. We will consider the ministries of the church less and less as a means of meeting our needs, and more and more as opportunities to serve others as disciples and servants of Jesus Christ. We will view gathering together with other believers for worship less and less as an intrusion into our weekend, and more and more as an opportunity to declare (by the way we spend our time) our allegiance to the one true God. In this way, by both understanding and adopting a theocentric rather than an anthropocentric view of the church, we can begin to live out what it means to be a church that truly is "in God the Father and the Lord Jesus Christ."

---

21. J. R. W. Stott, *The Gospel and the End of Time*, 32.

1 Thessalonians 1:2–10

WE ALWAYS THANK God for all of you, mentioning you in our prayers. ³We continually remember before our God and Father your work produced by faith, your labor prompted by love, and your endurance inspired by hope in our Lord Jesus Christ.

⁴For we know, brothers loved by God, that he has chosen you, ⁵because our gospel came to you not simply with words, but also with power, with the Holy Spirit and with deep conviction. You know how we lived among you for your sake. ⁶You became imitators of us and of the Lord; in spite of severe suffering, you welcomed the message with the joy given by the Holy Spirit. ⁷And so you became a model to all the believers in Macedonia and Achaia. ⁸The Lord's message rang out from you not only in Macedonia and Achaia—your faith in God has become known everywhere. Therefore we do not need to say anything about it, ⁹for they themselves report what kind of reception you gave us. They tell how you turned to God from idols to serve the living and true God, ¹⁰and to wait for his Son from heaven, whom he raised from the dead—Jesus, who rescues us from the coming wrath.

WHILE ALL BUT one (Galatians) of Paul's letters addressed to churches have a thanksgiving/blessing section immediately following the prescript, 1 Thessalonians is distinctive in that additional expressions of thanksgiving occur in 2:13 and 3:9. Moreover, there is a clear structural unity to 1:2–3:13. These two points have led some (working from an epistolary perspective) to view the entire section as the "thanksgiving section" of the letter. The difficult-to-explain presence, however, of much nonthanksgiving material in 1:2–3:13 has prompted others to adopt a rhetorical analysis of the letter (e.g., taking 1:1–5 as the *exordium* or introduction, which introduces "thanksgiving" as the principal theme of the letter, and 1:6–3:10 as the *narratio* section, which gives the reasons for thanksgiving).[1] But both approaches emphasize too much the form and not enough the actual content of what Paul says. The shift from "thanksgiving" to speaking directly to the recipients in 2:1 ("You know") clearly marks 1:2–10 as a distinct unit, which functions as the primary "thanksgiving" section of the letter.

Thanksgiving, however, is not the only thing going on here. In the course of his prayer, Paul explains *why* he is thankful; thus on a second level the passage provides us with important details about the founding of the Thessalonian congregation. This thankful remembrance of the church's early history in turn, on yet a third level, serves to praise and confirm the Thessalonians, and thus also to encourage and reinforce the behaviors Paul is praising.[2] Clearly this is a complex and multifunctional (and therefore typically Pauline) prayer report.

In this opening thanksgiving, Paul characteristically touches on several themes that arise later in the letter. For example, in 1:3 "love" anticipates the discussion of *philadelphia* ("love for brother and sister") in 4:9–12, and "hope" anticipates the topic of eschatology in 4:13–5:11; in 1:5, "power" and "Holy Spirit" anticipate the advice about the Spirit and prophecy in 5:19–22; in 1:5–6, the reference to imitation of the founding missionaries prepares for 2:1–12 and 5:12–13; in 1:9–10, the comments on serving God while waiting for the Son anticipate the comments on holiness (4:3–8), vigilance (5:1–10), and mutual exhortation (5:11, 14–22).

This foreshadowing of later topics in the letter, however, should not obscure what is Paul's primary focus in this section: the Thessalonian believers themselves. In particular he focuses on their Spirit-empowered response to the gospel message that Paul and his colleagues shared with them. This focus comes out with clarity when we observe how quickly Paul's thanksgiving for the Thessalonians turns into a description of them.

---

1. R. Jewett, *The Thessalonian Correspondence*, 71–78; cf. C. A. Wanamaker, *Thessalonians*, 72–73, 90.

2. Note, for example, how in verse 5 Paul addresses the Thessalonians directly; this is hardly part of his prayer to God! Clearly what began as a report about his thanksgiving prayer now has a different aim (praise and encouragement).

Thanksgiving, and the Reasons for It (1:2–6)

IN GIVING THANKS and praying for the Thessalonians (1:2), Paul models behavior he will later exhort them to practice (5:17–18). In 1:3 we find the first reason why he is thankful (the "immediate" basis): He "continually remembers" their "work of faith," "labor of love," and "steadfastness of hope" (NRSV). For Paul, there is not a great deal of difference between the "work" produced by faith and the "labor" prompted by love; indeed, in Galatians 5:6 he speaks of "faith working through love." This indicates that his emphasis in each pair of terms is probably on the second word rather than the first; the second word indicates the origin of the first—a point the NIV's interpretative paraphrase ("work produced by faith . . . labor prompted by love . . . endurance inspired by hope") nicely catches. At the same time, the first word indicates something about the character of the second: Paul is giving thanks for an active faith, a hard-working love, and a patient, enduring hope.[3]

This familiar triad of faith, love, and hope (cf. 5:8; Rom. 5:1–5; 1 Cor. 13:13; Gal. 5:5–6; Col. 1:4–5; Heb. 10:22–24; 1 Peter 1:21–22) functions almost as a shorthand summary of the essentials of Christianity: *faith* as the assurance that God has acted in Christ to save his people, *love* ("poured . . . into our hearts by the Holy Spirit," Rom. 5:5) as the present expression and experience of the restored relationship between God and his people, and *hope* as the confidence that "he who began a good work . . . will carry it on to completion" (Phil. 1:6), and that the future, therefore, holds not "wrath but . . . salvation through our Lord Jesus Christ" (1 Thess. 5:9).

In 1:4 (a continuation of the sentence begun in 1:2) Paul gives a second reason (the "ultimate" basis) for thanksgiving: The believers in Thessalonica are "beloved" and have been "chosen" by God. The language here is reminiscent of Deuteronomy 7:7–8 ("The LORD did not . . . choose you because you were more numerous than other peoples. . . . But it was because the LORD loved you"), and Paul is likely thinking of God's people as a whole rather than of individual election.[4]

---

3. For the significance of the full Christological statement, "Lord Jesus Christ," see comment on 1:1.

4. See further I. H. Marshall, *1 and 2 Thessalonians*, 52–53.

When speaking directly to the Thessalonians, as he does in verse 4, Paul frequently addresses them as *adelphoi*, a term traditionally translated as "brothers." The word, however, is in fact inclusive of the whole community, men and women alike. In terms of current English usage it is more accurately translated as "brothers and sisters" (NRSV; NIV^ILE^) or perhaps "siblings." Such a translation reminds us that this is a powerful family metaphor (a point lost in the "dear friends" of the REB and CEV), rooted in the understanding of the one God as "Father,"[5] whose followers are therefore to be viewed as "brothers and sisters," members of a single family. Its use symbolically linked together a community of people, some of whom likely had little if any previous contact, and thus it both functioned to create cohesion within the community and implied a standard of behavior towards one another.[6]

The connecting word (*hoti*) with which verse 5 opens ("because our gospel came to you not simply with words, but also with power, with the Holy Spirit and with deep conviction") can be taken in an explanatory sense ("namely, that . . ."), but is more likely causal ("because," cf. NIV, NRSV). But the primary reasons why Paul "knows" of their election are not given until verse 6. The focus of verse 5 is on how Paul and his colleagues presented the gospel message to the Thessalonians: It was not simply a matter of carefully chosen words, but (1) of a thoughtful message accompanied by[7] both divine confirmation (i.e., "with power" and "with the Holy Spirit") and human corroboration (i.e., "deep conviction" on the part of those preaching the message, not those hearing it), and (2) of a lifestyle consistent with the message being preached (1:5b, which anticipates 2:1–12).

In 1:5a, the phrase "with power and with the Holy Spirit" should probably be understood in light of (and as an instance of) what Paul describes in Romans 15:18–19, where the preposition before both "power" and "Spirit" (Gk. *en*) is exactly the same as the repeated preposition in this verse translated "with": "what Christ has accomplished through me in leading the Gentiles to obey God by what I

---

5. The phrase "God the Father" occurs in 1 Thess. 1:1, 3; 3:11, 13 (discussed there under "Bridging Contexts"); 2 Thess. 1:1, 2; 2:16).

6. Wayne A. Meeks, *The First Urban Christians* (New Haven: Yale Univ. Press, 1983), 87–89; C. A. Wanamaker, *Thessalonians*, 147–48.

7. The "not simply . . . but *also*" here indicates intensification rather than contrast, and the passage should *not* be read in light of 1 Corinthians 2.

have said and done—*by the power of signs and miracles, through the power of the Spirit.*"[8]

In 1:6 Paul finally states two reasons why he "knows" that the Thessalonians have been "chosen by God." (1) They "welcomed the message"—that is, they accepted the gospel preaching and converted to Christianity (cf. 2:13). (2) They then "became imitators" both of the missionaries and, more importantly, of the Lord (cf. 1 Cor. 11:1), in that "in spite of severe suffering," they experienced a supernatural "joy given by the Holy Spirit"[9] (cf. Gal. 5:22).

"Suffering" (Gk. *thlipsis;* NRSV, "persecution"; see also 3:3, 7; 2 Thess. 1:4, 6) indicates the socio-religious dislocation, conflict, persecution, and/or ostracization experienced by the new converts as a result of their turning to a new and socially suspect religion.[10] The refusal of new Christian converts to participate in "normal" social and cultic activities and the exclusivity of their claim to worship the only "living and true God" (1:9) would have left non-Christian friends feeling offended, resentful, or betrayed; similarly, family members would have viewed a refusal to maintain ancestral traditions as evidence of an appalling lack of concern for family responsibilities. Moreover, since civic peace, agricultural success, and freedom from natural catastrophe were thought to lie in the hands of the traditional gods, it was considered extremely dangerous to ignore or offend them.

It is not difficult, therefore, to imagine how conversion to Christianity could result in conflict, persecution, and ostracization. Paul takes it for granted that as a result of this social dislocation believers will "suffer" (a point he develops in 3:2–4; see also 2 Thess. 1:4); he also takes it for granted that the benefits of being a believer, both short-term (the present experience of the Spirit, membership in God's people) and

---

8. For "signs and miracles" in the ministry of Paul, see Acts 14:3; 15:12; 2 Cor. 12:12; elsewhere, Acts 2:19, 22, 43; 4:30; 5:12; 6:8; 7:36, and especially Heb. 2:4. Cf. 2 Thess. 2:9, where Satan's work is characterized by "counterfeit miracles, signs and wonders."

9. In 1:6 the aorist participle *dexamenoi* can indicate either (1) "how" ("by receiving" the message) or (2) "in what circumstances" ("when you received" the message) the Thessalonians "became imitators" of the Lord. Because Jesus presumably cannot have "received the message," the point of comparison must be that of Spirit-inspired joy in difficult circumstances (cf. Heb. 12:2). Option (2), therefore, is to be preferred.

10. J. M. G. Barclay, "Conflict in Thessalonica," *CBQ* 55 (1993): 514–15; C. A. Wanamaker, *Thessalonians,* 81–82; E. J. Richard, *Thessalonians,* 69, 148–49; differently A. J. Malherbe, *Paul and the Thessalonians,* 48, who sees it as only mental "distress and anguish of heart."

long-term (vindication, salvation, the presence of the Lord; cf. 2:19; 4:13–18; 5:9–10; 2 Thess. 1:5–10; 2:13–14), far outweigh any suffering that might be experienced (cf. Rom. 8:18, "our present sufferings are not worth comparing with the glory that will be revealed in us").

Further Description of the Thessalonians (vv. 7–10)

A CONSEQUENCE OF the Thessalonians' becoming imitators of the missionaries and of the Lord was that they in turn became a "model" to believers elsewhere, not just in the two Greek provinces of "Macedonia and Achaia" (1:7), but "everywhere" (1:8). Whether the news "sounded forth"—the image is one of a sound, perhaps that of a trumpet, spreading like stone-caused ripples on a pond—as a result of the efforts of the Thessalonians or of others is not clear. Either way, so well known was the report of the dramatic events in Thessalonica that Paul and his companions did "not need to say anything" (that this is a bit of a rhetorical overstatement is clear from 2 Thess. 1:4).

The two parallel phrases, "the Lord's message" (lit., "the word of the Lord"; cf. 2 Thess. 3:1) and "your faith in God," suggest that the spreading report focused not just on the gospel message, but also its impact on its hearers. Elements of the report are summarized in 1:9–10: It covered (as in 1:5–6) both the activity of the missionaries ("what sort of visit we had with you"[11]) and (more important) how the Thessalonians responded in "turning" (a standard term for conversion, as in Acts 9:35; 11:21; 15:19; 26:18, 20) to God and away from the idols of their pagan heritage (cf. 14:15: the Lycaonians were urged "to turn from these worthless things to the living God").

In language unusual for Paul (perhaps because it borrows from or echoes what is being reported by others), he spells out what this conversion involved. (1) It involved a commitment "to serve[12] the living and true God" (1:9b, a description that echoes Old Testament language; e.g., Jer. 10:10). (2) It included a commitment "to wait for his Son from heaven" (1:10a)—that is, Jesus, here described as the risen

---

11. Pers. trans. The NIV's "reception you gave us" is misleading; the subject of the verb is Paul and his companions, not the Thessalonians, and the noun rendered "reception" is the same one translated as "visit" in 2:1.

12. A common term in the LXX for total commitment to God; cf. K. H. Rengstorff, "δοῦλος," *TDNT*, 2:265–68, followed by E. J. Richard, *Thessalonians*, 55.

and delivering one. (For the linkage of "Son of God" and resurrection, cf. Rom. 1:4; for "deliver" [which in Pauline usage is virtually the equivalent of "save"], cf. Rom. 11:26, citing Isa. 59:20.)

Thus Paul explicates conversion in terms of both present activity (a wholehearted commitment or devotion that expresses itself in active service to God, not merely acknowledgment of him) and future hope (trust in Jesus the Risen One as the agent of God's deliverance at the time of judgment). Both of these elements anticipate later sections of the letter (present behavior, 4:1–12; Jesus as the Risen One, 4:13–18, who delivers, 5:1–11). The reference to the "true and living God" emphasizes the monotheistic nature of Christianity (a characteristic it shared with Judaism) in contrast to the syncretistic polytheism of much of Greco-Roman culture, while the reference to Jesus, "his Son from heaven," once again distinguishes Christianity from Judaism (cf. 1:1).

What Jesus delivers from is "the coming wrath." "Wrath" is not so much a matter of emotion as it is an expression of God's righteous judgment against sin (cf. Rom. 2:5, 8). Though already "being revealed ... against all ungodliness and wickedness" (1:18), it is primarily associated, as here (cf. also 1 Thess. 5:9), with a future time of judgment (cf. Rom. 5:9), which will occur on the Day of the Lord (cf. 1 Thess. 5:2; 2 Thess. 2:2), an event also known as the "coming" (Gk. *parousia*) of Jesus (cf. 1 Thess. 2:19; 3:13; 4:15; 5:23; 2 Thess. 2:1, 8–9). Although the point is not developed here, in Paul's thought the "rescue" or deliverance of believers from the coming wrath is specifically grounded in Jesus' atoning death on their behalf (1 Thess. 5:9–10; cf. Rom. 3:21–26; 5:9–10).[13]

To recapitulate: This section begins as a thanksgiving prayer for the Thessalonians. In the course of his thanksgiving, however, Paul explains why he is thankful, and thus the passage also offers a rich description of the Thessalonians and their response to the gospel message.

Bridging Contexts

THERE ARE A number of ways one might approach the challenge of building a bridge to the twentieth century when confronted by a passage as complex as this one. One way

---

13. See further G. L. Borchert, "Wrath, Destruction," *DPL*, 991–93.

would be to begin with the *form* of this section of the letter. Observing that this section opens with a prayer, one might then seek to identify typical features of Paul's prayer that could serve as a pattern or model for ours (e.g., one writer suggests that Paul's prayer here is "characterized by four qualities: universality, frequency, concreteness, and mutuality"[14]). But since the prayer for the Thessalonians comprises only a small part of this section, a form-based approach leaves much of the section out of account. I would prefer to utilize a form-based approach for a section more completely devoted to prayer (e.g., 3:9–13).

A second way would be to investigate what Paul was trying to accomplish or achieve in this section of his letter. The Original Meaning section is essentially an attempt to answer the question, "What did Paul say?" Here we can ask two additional questions: "Why did he say it?" and, "What was he trying to do or accomplish?" In this section of the letter, for example, Paul could be seen as doing at least three things:

(1) He *praises* the Thessalonians for what they have been doing.
(2) By praising what they have been doing, he implicitly *encourages* them to continue doing it.
(3) He *reinforces* the boundaries that define the Thessalonian congregation as a distinctive group.

These observations might then be utilized as a basis for further reflection about their contemporary application or relevance, or for formulating general principles that might then be applied to the church today.[15]

A third approach to bridging a complex passage like this—and the one I will develop here—takes as its starting point the observation that while this section of the letter begins as a prayer for the Thessalonian congregation, it soon becomes in many respects a narrative account of its origins. One difficulty in bridging contexts when dealing with narrative material is that the order in which material is presented in the narrative is not always the most useful or functional order in which to use or apply it. Thus, we may need to reorganize the material from its narrative order to a more topical or logical order. If we do

---

14. E. J. Richard, *Thessalonians*, 60.

15. For example, "Christian pastoral care builds on the foundation of what God has already done in the life of the individual or congregation" (I. H. Marshall, *1 and 2 Thessalonians*, 60).

this with 1:2–10, we can formulate a number of observations about the Thessalonian congregation (which is, as we noted earlier, the primary focus and topic of this section) that arise out of Paul's description of it.

It was a community rooted in God's grace, love, and election. Paul established this point in 1:1 (by his use of the phrase "in God the Father" and his mention of "grace"). Here he carries forward the point with reference to God's love (cf. Rom. 5:8) and election. Election, as Klyne Snodgrass reminds us, is primarily about God.[16] It is God's grace, love, and mercy in action; it is not so much a matter of some arbitrary atemporal decision (a common caricature), but of a means to an end (cf. Rom. 11:32, "For God has bound everyone over to disobedience so that he may have mercy on them all" [NIV^ILE]). It demonstrates how much God values human beings and reminds us that God is in control. The church exists because God wants it to.

It was a community committed to Jesus Christ. Jesus' death and resurrection (1:10; cf. 4:14; 5:10) is the foundation upon which the church is based (cf. 1 Cor. 3:11); he is the focus of our faith (1 Thess. 1:3); his life is the model by which the church now lives (1:6); and his coming from heaven (1:10) defines the future for which the church waits.

It was a community empowered by the Holy Spirit. It was due to the evident power of the Holy Spirit in the preaching and lives of the missionaries (1:5) that the Thessalonians became convinced that the gospel was not merely a human message, but was in fact what "it actually is, the word of God" (2:13). In turn, the same Spirit (and word, 2:13) is at work in the Thessalonians, giving them (even in the midst of difficult circumstances) joy (1:6) and empowering their own witness to others (cf. 1:7–8).

It was a community that bore witness to the gospel. It is clear that the Thessalonian congregation was actively bearing witness to the gospel they had received (1:8). What is important to notice is both *what* they were bearing witness to and *how* they were doing it. Paul notes that not only the "Lord's message"—that is, the good news about Jesus—had "sounded forth," but also the Thessalonians' "faith in God"—that is, their response to the good news—had "become known." In short, they were sharing both the good news about Jesus and the impact of that good news on their own lives.

---

16. Klyne Snodgrass, *Ephesians* (NIVAC; Grand Rapids: Zondervan, 1996), 58–59, 64, upon whom the following comments draw heavily.

As for the "how," Paul notes (1:9) that others were talking about what the Thessalonians *did*: They turned from idols and served the true God. That is, their behavior was consistent with, and testified to the reality of, their message. Following the example of Jesus (1:6) and the missionaries (1:5–6; cf. 2:3–10), they practiced what they preached.

It was a community characterized by faith, love, and hope. Paul was not the only one impressed by the Thessalonians' active faith (expressing their trust in what God has done), hard-working love (responding to what the Holy Spirit was doing), and patient, endur-ing hope (looking forward to what Jesus would do) (1:3). He specifi-cally mentions that others (1:9) also were talking about their faith in God and their expectation of Jesus' coming (1:8–10), and it seems likely that their love for the brothers and sisters throughout Macedo-nia (4:10) was discussed as well.

It was a community clearly differentiated from other religions. By turning away from idols (1:9), the Thessalonian church differenti-ated itself from paganism; by proclaiming its allegiance to Jesus as res-urrected Messiah, Lord, and Son of God (1:3, 6, 10; cf. 1:1), it distinguished itself from Judaism.

These observations about the Thessalonian congregation arise out of Paul's description of it. None of these characteristics appear to be in any way unique or limited to that particular congregation. This sug-gests that they may offer a yardstick or set of guidelines against which to evaluate our own churches today; indeed, Paul himself observes in 1:7 that the Thessalonians had become a model for others.

ONE WAY TO apply this passage to our con-temporary situation is to take the six obser-vations about the Thessalonian congregation and turn them into a set of questions to ask about our churches (and, for that matter, ourselves).

Are we a community rooted in God's grace, love, and election? This question has implications in two directions. On the one hand, the fact that God loved us so much that while we were yet sinners Christ died for us (Rom. 5:8) reminds us how highly God loves and val-ues his church and the believers who comprise it, despite our sin and failures. This rules out on the congregational level defeatist attitudes, for example, and on an individual level negative self-perceptions. We have worth and value because God loves us. On the other hand, the fact that the church is rooted in God's grace reminds us that the church does not even exist, and certainly has no life, apart from God and his saving work in Christ. This leaves no room for triumphalism or for arrogance or pride, because grace is entirely God's doing. We had nothing to do with it, and have nothing for which to take credit or boast; all we can do is offer praise, glory, and thanksgiving to God for what he has done.

Are we a community committed to Jesus Christ? Have we counted up the cost of following Jesus and decided that it really is worth bearing the cross (i.e., suffering) in order to be his disciple (see Luke 14:25–33)? Do we acknowledge his death and resurrection as the only basis of our salvation? Are his life and teachings the model by which we live, or have we (consciously or unconsciously) imported into our life and thinking some other model or values? Do we seek to minister as his disciples? Do we genuinely believe that the future will be defined by his return in glory? Is he the Lord of all creation (Phil. 2:10–11), or do we view him as merely one more prophet or exalted master or spiritual guide of some sort?

Are we a community empowered by the Holy Spirit? Are the power and gifts of the Spirit evident in our preaching, our evangelism, our ministering? Are the joy and other fruits of the Spirit apparent in our fellowship? Are we open to the leading of the Spirit? It is important to note that the answer to this question is not as simple as charismatic versus noncharismatic, as if the exercise of a few particular spiritual gifts, or their corresponding absence, can indicate whether we are open to the power and leading of the Spirit. It is just as possible for a church that exalts speaking in tongues and prophecy to miss the leading of the Spirit as it is for a church that thinks all the "sign" gifts ceased in the first century. A more reliable indicator is the presence of the fruit of the Spirit and the exercise of those spiritual gifts intended for the building up of the body of Christ.[17]

Are we a community that bears witness to the gospel? Some congregations pride themselves on the way they consistently proclaim the gospel, but they undercut their witness by failing to live it as well.

---

17. On the topic of the Spirit, see comments on 5:19–21.

Others say they evangelize by the way they live the gospel, but they undercut their witness by failing to identify what is it they believe in and live for. Here it is not a matter of either-or, but of both-and. The Thessalonians are our model in this regard: They were sharing both the good news about Jesus and also demonstrating the impact of that good news in their own lives. As John R. W. Stott notes, "No church can spread the gospel with any degree of integrity, let alone credibility, unless it has been visibly changed by the gospel it preaches."[18] At the same time, a congregation that claims that living the gospel excuses them from needing to proclaim it verbally runs the risk of being confused with other non-Christian groups that have similar lifestyles (e.g., the Mormons).

As the Heaven's Gate cult mass suicide at Easter 1997 revealed, our neighbors—for that is what those people, who came from ordinary backgrounds and states across the United States, were—are desperate for hope, so desperate that they are willing to believe virtually anything in order to get it. We who have found a real hope in Jesus must share that hope with our desperately seeking neighbors, both by what we say and by how we live. If that is not happening in our churches, then we need to reflect on why that is the case.

Are we a community characterized by faith, hope, and love? As Paul points out in 1 Corinthians 13:13, these are the things that endure for the long haul. In view of the current political and cultural climate, with its concentration on winning political battles and cultural wars, it may be that love requires the most attention. As John Ortberg observes, the first casualty of the culture wars is not truth but love.[19] Important as it is to promote or contend for biblical values in the so-called culture wars, it is even more important to live them. As Jesus himself said, "everyone will know that you are my disciples, if you have love one for another" (John 13:35, NRSV). There is an obvious and close connection between this point and the previous one: Without love, our proclamation of the gospel will be little more than "a resounding gong or a clanging cymbal" (1 Cor. 13:1).

Are we a community clearly differentiated from other religions? The widespread contemporary interest in New Age religions (in many

---

18. J. R. W. Stott, *The Gospel and the End of Time*, 44.
19. John Ortberg, "Do They Know Us by Our Love?" *CT* 41 (May 19, 1997): 25–26.

respects merely modern forms of ancient Gnosticism) and various other cults and movements is well known. Many of these "religions" are more than happy to incorporate elements of Christianity into their teachings. Often this takes the form of some loosely defined ideas about Jesus as some sort of "exalted master" or a vague concept of some kind of "Christ consciousness." If nothing else, this kind of eclectic syncretism is a matter of "smart marketing" on their part, and it sometimes succeeds in deceiving Christians. But these movements refuse to acknowledge Jesus as the resurrected Messiah, Son of God, and Lord; this is one of the defining differences between them and authentic Christianity.

For the sake of the gospel it is critical that we affirm, maintain, and teach one another what makes Christianity different from any other religion or religious movement. It is equally critical that we identify and repent of the idols of power, ideology, and materialism. To the extent that we worship these in place of Jesus, we are in danger of becoming just another political movement, lobbying organization, or consumer group, scarcely distinguishable from the rest of society.

1 Thessalonians 2:1–12

YOU KNOW, BROTHERS, that our visit to you was not a failure. ²We had previously suffered and been insulted in Philippi, as you know, but with the help of our God we dared to tell you his gospel in spite of strong opposition. ³For the appeal we make does not spring from error or impure motives, nor are we trying to trick you. ⁴On the contrary, we speak as men approved by God to be entrusted with the gospel. We are not trying to please men but God, who tests our hearts. ⁵You know we never used flattery, nor did we put on a mask to cover up greed—God is our witness. ⁶We were not looking for praise from men, not from you or anyone else.

As apostles of Christ we could have been a burden to you, ⁷but we were gentle among you, like a mother caring for her little children. ⁸We loved you so much that we were delighted to share with you not only the gospel of God but our lives as well, because you had become so dear to us. ⁹Surely you remember, brothers, our toil and hardship; we worked night and day in order not to be a burden to anyone while we preached the gospel of God to you.

¹⁰You are witnesses, and so is God, of how holy, righteous and blameless we were among you who believed. ¹¹For you know that we dealt with each of you as a father deals with his own children, ¹²encouraging, comforting and urging you to live lives worthy of God, who calls you into his kingdom and glory.

 **Original Meaning**

IN 2:1, THE word *gar* ("for," omitted in NIV) opens this section; it marks the transition from the primary thanksgiving (1:2–10) to the body or central part of the letter (2:1–5:22). In this section, two points raised in chapter 1—the behavior of the apostles, which the Thessalonians imitated (1:5b–6), and the

character of their visit to Thessalonica (1:9)—are developed in some detail. The repeated appeal to the Thessalonians' own knowledge of these two matters (2:1–2, 5, 9–11) serves both to minimize the distance between Paul and the Thessalonians and to reinforce the relationship between them—points characteristic of ancient "letters of friendship" (see further on 2:17–3:8).[1]

There are several antithetical statements ("not x but y") in this section. These statements have led many to argue that Paul here is defending himself against charges or accusations of some sort.[2] But antithetical statements are also frequently used (a) in nonpolemical situations, and (b) for describing moral examples.[3] The heavy concentration of direct appeals in the last part of the passage (2:9–12), in which Paul reminds the Thessalonians of how he exhorted them to holy living, confirms that the primary function of this section is not defense or apologetics but exhortation. By reminding them of the behavior he and his companions modeled while in Thessalonica (behavior that stands in sharp contrast to that of well-known conventional figures, such as religious charlatans or con-artists), Paul implicitly encourages them to adopt and/or continue such behavior—in the face of hostility and persecution, if necessary (1:6; 2:14; 3:4), as did the missionaries (e.g., 2:1–2).

The repeated use of "for" (*gar*) in the passage (in Greek, at the beginning of verses 1, 3, 5, and 9) notwithstanding, there is no clear or obvious structure to 2:1–12, as the widely varying paragraphing in recent English translations indicates.[4] Where the NIV has three para-

---

1. See further on letters of friendship Stanley K. Stowers, *Letter Writing in Greco-Roman Antiquity* (Philadelphia: Westminster, 1986), 58–70; A. J. Malherbe, *Paul and the Thessalonians*, 68–74.

2. See Jeffrey A. D. Weima, "An Apology for the Apologetic Function of 1 Thessalonians 2.1–12," *JSNT* 68 (1997): 73–99.

3. George Lyons, *Pauline Autobiography: Toward a New Understanding* (Atlanta: Scholars, 1985), 182–84; S. K. Stowers, *Letter Writing*, 25–26; also C. A. Wanamaker, *Thessalonians*, 60–63, 91; E. J. Richard, *Thessalonians*, 87–89; B. R. Gaventa, *Thessalonians*, 5–6, 25–26. For an overview of various proposals regarding (hypothetical) opponents, see C. A. Wanamaker, *Thessalonians*, 53–57.

4. G. Lyons (*Pauline Autobiography*, 192–199), however, takes the repeated use of "for" (*gar*) as an indication that Paul touches on four topics or concerns in this section: (a) a boldness grounded in God (2:1–2); (b) a responsibility to God (2:3–4); (c) a giving of self inspired by God (2:5–8); and (d) a lifestyle worthy of God (2:9–12). This may well catch the missionaries' motivations, but obscures the fact that the primary subject in this section is not God but the missionaries' behavior.

graphs (vv. 1–6a, 6b–9, 10–12), the NRSV has two (vv. 1–8, 9–12), and the NAB only one. With respect to content, in 2:1–4 the focus is on the missionaries' dependence on and responsibility to God; in both 2:5–8 and 2:9–12 the focus is on their behavior toward and care for the Thessalonians.

The Missionaries' Reliance on and Responsibility to God (2:1–4)

VERSE 1 PICKS up the mention of the "visit" in 1:9a: Not only do the Thessalonians[5] indeed know (the "yourselves" [omitted by NIV] after the opening "you" is emphatic) that the visit of Paul and his companions was not a "failure" (*kene*; i.e., "without results"[6]); they themselves are, in view of their conversion, the evidence of success. The rest of the section, however, focuses on the way in which Paul and his coworkers conducted themselves during that visit, rather than on its results.

For the "suffering" and "insults" (2:2) experienced in Philippi, see Acts 16:12–40. Despite the missionaries' experiences in Philippi and despite encountering in Thessalonica "strong opposition" (in light of 1:6, the probable meaning here, rather than "exertion" or "anxiety"), "with God's help" they courageously took the risk ("dared") of speaking out freely and boldly.[7]

In 2:3 Paul reminds the Thessalonians that his "appeal" to them did not involve delusion (i.e., an "error" on Paul's part), "impure motives" (*akatharsia*, used here, as in Rom. 6:19, in a general sense, without any specific implication of sexual misconduct), or trickery (a word that deals with how he preached)—a trio of words that reflect traditional charges against traveling charlatans of various sorts.[8] To the contrary, he says in 2:4, nothing of the sort could have motivated the forthright

---

5. For the significance of *adelphoi*, which includes the entire community, not just the "brothers," see comment on 1:4.

6. Alternatively, some (e.g., E. J. Richard, *Thessalonians*, 89–90) render it "empty," that is, without power or content, and see a reference back to 1:5, "with power." But "without results" reflects the usual sense of this term in Paul's letters (cf. 3:5; also 1 Cor. 15:10, 58; 2 Cor. 6:1; Gal. 2:2; Phil. 2:16) and fits well with 1 Thess. 1:9–10, which emphasize results rather than means (cf. C. A. Wanamaker, *Thessalonians*, 92).

7. Cf. Acts 9:28; 13:46; *parresia*, "boldness" or "frankness," the related noun (cf. 28:31), was a valued characteristic of Greco-Roman orators.

8. Abraham J. Malherbe, "'Gentle as a Nurse': The Cynic Background to 1 Thess ii," *NovT* 12 (1970): 206–7.

behavior of Paul and his companions, especially in the face of such stiff opposition; only a sense of mission and purpose arising out of God's approval and trust could have prompted such boldness. This means further that it is not human approval they seek, but God's, for he is the one who ultimately "tests the heart." That is, God is the one who has examined and approved them, and they are responsible to him, not (in contrast to conventional expectations) to the crowds whom they address (a point emphasized again in 2:6a).

The Missionaries' Behavior Toward and Care for the Thessalonians (2:5–8)

IN 2:5–8 PAUL extends and develops the point made in 2:4. In approaching these verses, it is important to observe that he sets up a fundamental contrast that dominates the entire passage: (2:5) "we never came ... (2:7) *but instead* we became" (NIV, "we never used ... but we were"). That is, the fundamental structure of these verses involves a contrast between the three negative characteristics (flattery, greed, praise) listed in 2:5–6a (which Paul avoided) and the three positive qualities (gentle, caring, loving) described in 2:7–8 (which Paul modeled).

Paul begins 2:5 by once again calling on the Thessalonians to verify the missionaries' claims: They obviously were not seeking human approval, since (1) they avoided the use of flattery (*kolakeia*, a well-known term for a practice despised as much as "boldness" was valued, and which is occasionally connected with financial gain), (2) nor were they seeking to promote their own financial self-interest ("greed," *pleonexia*, which Col. 3:5 labels idolatry), (3) nor were they "looking for"[9] fame or honor ("praise," *doxa*, 2:6a). The context of all three of these terms is popular rhetoric, especially that of hucksters or entertainers seeking their own benefit, in contrast to true philosophers, who sought the moral improvement of their audiences. Behind this concern over means and motives is Paul's obvious concern for the integrity of the message. He deliberately avoided behavior or actions that might lead people to doubt or suspect the integrity of the message or the sincerity of his preaching.

---

9. "Insisting" or "requiring" is the meaning sometimes suggested for *zeteo* in 2:6a (e.g., C. A. Wanamaker, *Thessalonians*, 98), rather than "seeking" (the more common usage). The NIV's "looking for" is nicely ambiguous.

In fact, so concerned was Paul to avoid any hint of financial self-interest that could compromise the gospel that he took an additional precaution. As an apostle he had a right to be supported in his ministry (1 Cor. 9:3–18). But for the sake of the integrity of the message and for the sake of the Thessalonians, he voluntarily gave up that right. This is the point of 2:6b ("As apostles of Christ we could have been a burden to you").[10] The phrase translated "be a burden" (NRSV "make demands") can indicate either financial matters (cf. 2:5, "greed") or a matter involving authority or recognition (cf. 2:6a, "praise"). Since receiving financial support would imply recognition of one's apostolic status, it seems likely that Paul has both nuances in mind. His basic point is clear: Although as apostles[11] they could have made demands or imposed their authority, they chose not to do so.

Having spelled out in 2:5–6 the behaviors he and his companions avoided, Paul goes on to describe in 2:7–8 how they did behave: They were gentle, caring, and loving. As the language of 2:5–6a reflects commonplace rhetorical terminology, so does also 2:7–8. For example, some prominent Cynics of Paul's day stressed the need for those who spoke "boldly" (cf. 2:2) to exercise "gentleness" as well,[12] and philosophers used the nurse metaphor to suggest how one ought to care for those being taught.[13] Paul thus casts not only his negative but

---

10. Among recent translations there is considerable variation in the punctuation (and versification) of 2:6b, "As apostles of Christ we could have been a burden to you," (a concessive participial clause, which is part of a single thought unit running from 2:5 through 2:8). The NIV takes 2:6b (which in some versions is the first part of v. 7) as the beginning of a new paragraph, and by placing a comma after "you," links it with what follows. On the other hand, the NRSV (among others), by placing a period after the phrase, links the phrase with what proceeds it ("⁶ . . . others, ⁷*though we might have made demands as apostles of Christ.* But . . ."). In fact, the phrase has links to both what follows it (with respect to content) and what precedes it (with respect to grammar); thus it serves as a transition in Paul's argument.

11. In view of the strong connection Paul makes between "seeing the Lord" and apostleship (1 Cor. 15:7), it seems likely (but not provable) that the plural "apostles" includes himself and Silas, but not Timothy (cf. I. H. Marshall, *1 and 2 Thessalonians,* 69–70; F. F. Bruce, *1 and 2 Thessalonians,* 31; for an extended discussion, see E. J. Richard, *Thessalonians,* 109–10, who takes it as a designation of all three, as does B. R. Gaventa, *Thessalonians,* 26).

12. See further C. A. Wanamaker, *Thessalonians,* 101; F. F. Bruce, *1 and 2 Thessalonians,* 32.

13. Abraham J. Malherbe, "'Gentle as a Nurse,'" 203–17. Beverly Roberts Gaventa, rejecting Malherbe's proposal, suggests that "instead, Paul draws upon a well-known figure in the ancient world, one identified not only with the nurture of infants but also with continued affection for her charges well into adulthood," and that Paul's reference to himself as a nurse resembles similar references in which Moses (Num. 11:12) and the Teacher of

also his positive points in terms familiar to people well acquainted with the popular rhetoric of the day.

In contrast to whatever way Paul and his companions might otherwise have chosen to act towards the Thessalonians, Paul says they were first of all "gentle."[14] He then indicates what he means by this with the use of a maternal metaphor (cf. Gal. 4:19), that of a nurse. This was a metaphor with strong positive overtones; ancient writers with few exceptions portrayed a nurse as kind and generous. "This suggests that Paul's metaphorical use of the nurse would conjure up in the minds of his audience an important and beloved figure. Whatever the social status of the Thessalonian Christians, they could understand this reference to an important social relationship—one proximate to kinship itself."[15] In this instance, Paul compares himself to a nurse who is also a mother: While competently caring for the offspring of others, she especially nurtures and cherishes her own children.[16]

Verse 8 further develops this image of love and tender concern. So strong was Paul's (and his companions') affection (a rare verb, *homeiromenoi;* cf. Job 3:21 LXX) for the Thessalonians that they freely chose (NIV "were delighted," or "gladly decided") to share with them not only the message they had been commissioned to deliver, but also themselves—because, as things turned out, the Thessalonians had

---

Righteousness at Qumran (1QH 7:19—23, 25) apply to themselves nursing metaphors ("Apostles As Babes and Nurses in 1 Thessalonians 2:7," in *Faith and History: Essays in Honor of Paul W. Meyer,* ed. John T. Carroll et al. [Atlanta: Scholars, 1990], 203). I am not sure that this must be a case of either/or; depending on who heard the phrase, one or the other, or perhaps both, might resonate.

14. There is a much-debated textual variant in 2:7. While a small number of manuscripts read "gentle" (*epioi*), a substantial majority read "infants" (*nepioi*). The single-letter difference between the two readings, however, is so slight in Greek (which was written in all capitals with no spaces between words: HMENHΠIOI vs. HMENNHΠIOI) that either reading could be explained as a scribal slip for the other one. Thus the manuscript evidence is of little help in this instance, and a decision must be reached on other grounds. The most decisive consideration is the basic structure of 2:5—8, specifically the fundamental contrast between the negative behaviors listed in 2:5—6a and the positive behaviors listed in 2:7—8. The three negatives in 2:5—6a (no flattery, no greed, no looking for praise) have to do with means ("how") or motive ("why"), as do the last two of the three positives in 2:7—8 (like a nurse, 2:7; because they loved them, 2:8). This strongly suggests that the first item in 2:7—8 will also deal with either means or motive, a consideration that clearly favors "gentle" (NIV, NRSV) over "infants."

15. B. R. Gaventa, "Apostles As Babes and Nurses in 1 Thessalonians 2:7," 201—2; B. R. Gaventa, *Thessalonians,* 27—28, 31—34.

16. E. J. Richard, *Thessalonians,* 82—83; C. A. Wanamaker, *Thessalonians,* 101.

become "so dear" (i.e., *agapetoi*, "beloved") both to God (cf. 1:4) and to Paul, Silas, and Timothy. The apparent parallelism between 2:7–9 (as a nurse fulfills her duty by caring for others and goes beyond duty in cherishing her own, so the missionaries fulfill their obligations by sharing the gospel and go beyond obligation by sharing themselves[17]) suggests that the development of such deep affection was perhaps unexpected, though certainly welcome. That is, it is not clear that the formation of such *deep* personal friendships was part of the missionaries' original strategy. If so, then we get a glimpse here of how preaching the gospel transformed not only the hearers but also the preachers.

To summarize 2:5–8: In contrast to charlatans and entertainers, who sought in some way either to fill their own pockets or to enhance their public renown, and despite having, as an apostle of Christ, certain "rights" that he could have insisted the Thessalonians recognize (cf. 1 Cor. 9:3–18), Paul deliberately adopted a different strategy of ministry in Thessalonica. For the sake of the gospel, he avoided behaviors that could call into question the integrity of the gospel. On the one hand, their speech was bold and forceful; on the other hand, their actions were characterized by gentleness and care and motivated by love.

Behavior Toward and Care for the Thessalonians: Further Reflections (2:9–12)

THE GAR ("FOR," omitted by NIV) with which 2:9 opens indicates that Paul intends to develop further in 2:9–12 the points made in 2:7b–8, again by appealing (as in 2:1, 5) to the Thessalonians themselves ("you remember," v. 9; "you are witnesses," v. 10; "you know," v. 11). Specifically, his claims that the missionaries were not a financial burden and did give of their very selves were confirmed by their behavior and lifestyle.

In 2:9a Paul uses the proverbial phrase "toil and hardship" (i.e., hard work in difficult circumstances; cf. 2 Cor. 11:27; 2 Thess. 3:8). What this means is indicated by 2:9b: He and his companions not only "preached the gospel" (for the language of this phrase, cf. Mark 1:14, which describes the actions of Jesus), but "night and day" (another proverbial phrase, meaning "both at night and during the day" rather than "continuously") they also "worked"—probably (in light of Acts

---

17. E. J. Richard, *Thessalonians*, 101.

18:3) as tentmakers, or perhaps more generally, leather-workers.[18] Paul and company deliberately gave up any apostolic right of financial support (1 Cor. 9:3–18; Gal. 6:6) specifically "in order *not* to be a burden" (*me epibaresai*, a verb used only here and in 2 Thess. 3:8 in the New Testament) financially to anyone.

This decision to work may parallel the practice of certain Hellenistic philosophers, who viewed it as beneficial to be seen in the midst of society, putting their teachings into practice in the midst of hardships. It probably also offers some clue to one (though not the only) setting in which Paul evangelized and discipled. The artisan's shop that he and his colleagues operated was a recognized setting for discussion and instruction; and in view of the long hours that his low-paying occupation would have demanded, Paul of necessity likely carried out some of his missionary activities while working.[19]

Most important, the decision to work reflects one of Paul's central missionary principles: not to take any financial contributions from those to whom he preached, in order to avoid placing any "obstacle in the way of the gospel of Christ" (1 Cor. 9:12, NRSV). On the one hand, potential converts might think twice about accepting the gospel if it looked as if the missionaries were benefiting financially from their decision. On the other hand, "the Gospel, which turned upon the love and self-sacrifice of Jesus, could not fitly be presented by preachers who insisted on their rights, delighted in the exercise of authority, and made what profit they could out of the work of evangelism."[20]

Verses 10–12 form one long, grammatically awkward (and at points ambiguous) sentence, whose main structure and points are nonetheless clear: verses 10–12a continue the discussion of the missionaries' behavior, while verse 12b indicates its goal. The appeal to both the Thessalonians and God in verse 10 reflects a dual focus already noticed in the letter (cf. 2:5, "you ... God"): a sense of responsibility to and love for both God and the Thessalonians. The use of a trio of unusual adverbs of similar meaning emphasizes, as sort of a generalizing sum-

---

18. See P. W. Barnett, "Tentmaking," *DPL*, 925–26.

19. Ronald F. Hock, *The Social Context of Paul's Ministry: Tentmaking and Apostleship* (Philadelphia: Fortress, 1980), 26–49, 52–59; cf. E. J. Richard, *Thessalonians*, 102–3.

20. C. K. Barrett, *The First Epistle to the Corinthians* (New York: Harper & Row, 1968), 207, to whom the previous point is also indebted. On the topic of financial support, see J. M. Everts, "Financial Support," *DPL*, 295–300.

mary, the character of the missionaries' behavior. The first two (*hosios,* "devoutly" or "purely," only here in the New Testament; *dikaīos,* "justly" or "uprightly," elsewhere in Paul only in 1 Cor. 15:3) were commonly used together in adjectival form, often with reference to the keeping of divine and human statutes,[21] but also of a believer's service to God (Luke 1:75). Because his behavior was proper in the sight of both God and humans, Paul can say he acted "blamelessly" (*amemptos;* also at 1 Thess. 5:23; in adjectival form at 3:13, both in the context of the return of Jesus); that is, no charge can be brought against him when he is examined by God (2:4).

In verses 11–12a Paul then employs a second parental metaphor, this time a paternal one (cf. 1 Cor. 4:14–16, 21; 2 Cor. 6:11–13; Phil. 2:22; Philem. 10). The absence of a verb (suggestions include "deal with," "treat," "counsel," or "bring up") gives the statement something of a timeless cast: Paul is indicating not only how he related to the Thessalonians in the past (during the original missionary visit) but also how he continues to relate to them. Both then in person and now via the letter he sought and seeks to "encourage" (*parakaleo;* also at 3:2, 7; 4:1, 10, 18; 5:11, 14; 2 Thess. 2:17; 3:12) and "comfort" them (*paramytheomai;* in Paul only here and 5:14)—there is no great distinction between these synonyms—and to "urge" them on in the Christian life (*martyromai,* a word with an authoritative tone; cf. Gal. 5:3; Eph. 4:17).

In verse 12b Paul indicates the goal of all this "fatherly" activity: that the Thessalonians might "live a life" (*peripateo,* lit. "walk;" cf. 4:1, 12; 2 Thess. 3:6, 11) that is "worthy of God"—that is, a life that reflects the character of and brings honor to the God to whom they have committed themselves. Paul seeks to inculcate in his converts a "life" (encompassing both attitudes and behavior) in which the characteristics of God himself may be observed.

Two points may be noticed here. (1) Paul directs his converts' attention not to a list of commandments or directory of prescribed behaviors, but to the character of God. This reminds us that for Paul, internal motivation, not simply external actions, is of critical importance. (2) Paul does not view any of this activity as having anything to do with earning or generating God's love or attention. Instead, it is clearly a

---

21. F. Hauck, "ὅσιος, etc." *TDNT,* 5:490.

response to the God who, on his own initiative, "calls"[22] them "into his own kingdom and glory." The life to which Paul urges the Thessalonians is one of thanksgiving (cf. 1:2), a life that by its character and actions is a means of acknowledging and accepting with gratitude what God through Jesus (cf. 1:1, 4) has already done on one's behalf.

Paul's view of the "kingdom" follows closely the teachings of Jesus. The kingdom indicates God's righteous "rule" or "dominion," a dynamic rather than a static concept (in contrast to "realm"). The kingdom has already been inaugurated in the ministry of Jesus, and thus is to some extent present and experienced now (Rom. 14:17; 1 Cor. 4:20), but its full manifestation and experience lies in the future, when God will vindicate his people and fully establish his rule over all creation (2 Thess. 1:5). Thus the kingdom is for Paul a term that is fundamentally eschatological, in that it embodies the "already/not yet" tension that is so central to his theology.[23]

No less eschatological in character is "glory," a word that has in view the radiance or splendor of God's presence, which he confers on people and objects associated with him. Glory is something that humans have lost as a result of sin (Rom. 3:23), but which will be restored when God's children are revealed and creation is released from bondage to sin (8:18–21). In the meantime it is seen most clearly in Jesus (2 Cor. 4:4–6; 3:14–18) and in believers whenever they accept one another as Christ accepted them (Rom. 15:7).[24]

Paul links "glory" closely with "kingdom" (they share a single preposition and article, and a single "his" governs both words). The two terms together indicate a believer's ultimate goal: to live under the dominion and in the presence of God.

To recapitulate, in 2:1–12 Paul focuses on the behavior and attitudes of the missionaries while they were in Thessalonica. Calling on both God and the Thessalonians as witnesses, he first emphasizes their reliance on and responsibility to God (vv. 1–4). He then describes the blameless and gentle, loving way they behaved toward and cared for the Thessalonians as they sought to encourage them to live lives worthy of God (vv. 5–12).

---

22. So most witnesses; a smaller number read "has called," a reading that may reflect the influence of 1:4. See further Metzger, *TCGNT*, 562.

23. See further L. J. Kreitzer, "Kingdom of God/Christ," *DPL*, 524–26.

24. See further R. B. Gaffin, Jr., "Glory, Glorification," *DPL*, 348–50.

MODELING PRINCIPLES. In this and other letters, Paul explicitly calls his converts to imitate him (cf. 1 Cor. 4:16; 11:1; Phil. 3:17; 2 Thess. 3:7) or praises them for having done so (1 Thess. 1:6). In particular, he acknowledges that when he was in Thessalonica, he deliberately chose to act and live in a certain way "in order to make ourselves a model for you to follow" (2 Thess. 3:9). This passage (1 Thess. 2:1–12) is Paul's description of how he chose to act and live in that city. In light of 2 Thessalonians 3:9, it is also, therefore, his own description of specific behaviors and attitudes he wanted his new Thessalonian converts to follow or imitate. Furthermore, there is no hint that his model was intended only for or limited to the Thessalonians, while there is evidence that he modeled essentially the same behaviors and attitudes elsewhere (see, e.g., 1 Cor. 9:3–18). Thus we have a clear indication that what he models in this passage is applicable not only to the Thessalonians, but to other Christians as well, including us.

In terms of the culture of his day, it was important for Paul to offer a model for his converts to follow. As Beverly Gaventa points out,

> a wide variety of teachers in Paul's day employed personal example and urged their students to conform to those examples.... Had Paul avoided the use of example and imitation, he might have appeared to his contemporaries as a person who knew himself unfit as a teacher.[25]

In reflecting on this matter, it is important to notice just what aspects or elements of his lifestyle Paul wanted the Thessalonians to imitate:

> He does not praise the Thessalonians for wearing what Jesus wore or eating what Paul ate. He praises them for embodying in their own setting a response to the gospel that is consistent with Jesus' own faithfulness and with the faith of their teachers.[26]

In other words, what Paul wants the Thessalonians to do is to respond to God and to other people as Jesus did (cf. Phil. 2:5, "Your attitude

---

25. B. R. Gaventa, *Thessalonians*, 16. See Benjamin Fiore, *The Function of Personal Example in the Socratic and Pastoral Epistles* (Rome: Biblical Institute, 1986).

26. B. R. Gaventa, *Thessalonians*, 17.

should be the same as that of Christ Jesus"), and as Paul tried to do as a disciple of Jesus.

So exactly what was it that Paul modeled for the Thessalonians? What attitudes and behaviors did he want them to imitate? I suggest that at least the following four stand out.

(1) *Paul modeled a clear sense of priorities.* Serving God faithfully was clearly Paul's single most important priority. As he says in 2:4, "We are not trying to please men but God." He knew that "no servant can serve two masters" (Luke 16:13). It was God, not someone else, who had called him to proclaim the gospel (Gal. 1:15–16), and it was therefore God to whom he owed his allegiance and who had first place among his priorities.

This sense of calling as an apostle of Christ (1 Thess. 2:6; cf. 1 Cor. 1:1; Gal. 1:1) explains (at least in part) why Paul continued to preach the gospel despite "strong opposition": Proclaiming the gospel was the task that God had entrusted to him (1 Thess. 2:4a), and "it is required that those who have been given a trust must prove faithful" (1 Cor. 4:2). Moreover, it is God "who tests our hearts" (1 Thess. 2:4b; cf. 1 Cor. 4:3–5; 2 Cor. 5:10), not someone else. That is, Paul made it his priority to please God (1 Thess. 2:4; cf. 2 Cor. 5:9) as a servant of Christ (Gal. 1:10).

(2) *Paul modeled a clear sense of concern for the integrity of the gospel.* People in the ancient world were well acquainted with traveling hucksters, alleged miracle workers, and scam artists—smooth and persuasive talkers whose eloquence hid their main goals: to enhance their reputation by winning the adulation of the crowds and/or to line their own pockets. A thin veneer of religious or philosophical terminology was merely a "pretext for greed" (2:5). Public speaking in such a context was often little more than a sideshow characterized by fraud, flattery, impure motives, and trickery (2:3, 5).[27]

Precisely because of the widespread negative perceptions and deep suspicion of traveling preachers, Paul deliberately sought to conduct himself in a manner that (a) would not give an observer any reason whatsoever to stereotype him as just another fly-by-night huckster, and (b) more important, would not call into question in any way the truthfulness of the gospel he preached.

---

27. For two classic examples of such people, see the stories told by Lucian, a second century A.D. Mike Wallace-type person, about Alexander the false prophet and Peregrinus (in the Loeb Classical Library edition of Lucian, 4:173–253; 5:1–51).

Paul did this in two ways. (a) He was careful about how he presented the gospel. His own statement to the Corinthians—"We have renounced secret and shameful ways; we do not use deception, nor do we distort the word of God. On the contrary, by setting forth the truth plainly we commend ourselves to every man's conscience in the sight of God" (2 Cor. 4:2)—summarizes well his goal in this respect. He sought, in short, to proclaim the truth of the gospel truthfully.

(b) Paul was extremely careful with regard to financial matters. For one thing, he refused to take money from those whom he evangelized, lest they think he was somehow benefiting from what he preached. "Unlike so many, we do not peddle the word of God for profit" (2 Cor. 2:17). Instead, as he makes clear in this passage, he worked to support himself "in order not to be a burden to anyone while we preached the gospel of God" (1 Thess. 2:9). For another, when he later was involved in taking up a collection from Macedonia and Achaia for relief of believers in Judea (see 1 Cor. 16:1–4; 2 Cor. 8–9), he made sure that people from the congregations giving the money accompanied it to Jerusalem (1 Cor. 16:3; 2 Cor. 8:19; the delegates included two from Thessalonica, Aristarchus and Secundus, Acts 20:4). Not surprisingly, Paul did this in order "to avoid any criticism of the way we administer this liberal gift. For we are taking pains to do what is right, not only in the eyes of the Lord but also in the eyes of men" (2 Cor. 8:20–21).

As a result of Paul's care for the integrity of the gospel, he was able to call both the Thessalonians and God as witnesses to "how holy, righteous and blameless" he was while in Thessalonica (2:10). More important, the Thessalonians accepted the gospel for what "it actually is, the word of God" (2:13). Paul's behavior and conduct did not compromise or call into question the message he proclaimed.

(3) *Paul modeled a clear sense of love and commitment to those to whom he ministered.* The depth of Paul's love for the Thessalonians is evident not only from his description (in 2:7–12) of the care and gentleness with which he encouraged and comforted them, but also from the sense of loss he felt when he was unexpectedly separated from them (2:17–3:5) and from the way in which his own sense of well-being was bound up with theirs (2:19–20; 3:7–8). That he loved and acted towards them as though they were his own children—which in a sense they were, since he had introduced them to Christ (cf. 1 Cor. 4:15)—is clear from his extensive use of parental images.

In the ancient world typically the mother nurtured the child, while the father was responsible for the child's behavior, moral instruction, and socialization. Paul applies to himself both roles: Like a mother he has given birth (cf. Gal. 4:19, "my dear children, for whom I am again in the pains of childbirth until Christ is formed in you") and nurtures them, and like a father he seeks to instruct and socialize them. (Actually, he seeks to *resocialize* them, so that they would no longer follow the social mores by which they were raised, but to live instead according to the standards of the Christian community into which God called them.)

Paul's sense of commitment to the Thessalonians is evident from his repeated efforts to return to Thessalonica following his forced premature departure (2:17–3:1). Indeed, as he reminds them, he sought repeatedly to return to them. His lack of success in doing so was not due to any lack of effort on his part, but to the opposition of Satan (2:18).

On one level, it is hardly surprising that an evangelist sent by a loving God (1:4) to call people to a life of love (4:9–12) would model a loving and caring attitude toward his converts. In 2:8, however, there is a hint that Paul's feelings for the Thessalonians may have developed more fully than he anticipated: "We loved you so much . . . because you *had become* so dear to us." It appears that the hearts of not only the hearers but also the preachers were transformed. In any case, it is clear that Paul had a deep and genuine love for those to whom he ministered.

(4) Paul modeled a clear sense of the goal toward which he worked. The apostle's goal in ministering to the Thessalonians was not to boost his own reputation or ego by winning their praise and/or approval (2:4, 6) or to flaunt his own authority over them (2:6b). Rather, it was to enable them "to live lives worthy of God, who calls [them] into his kingdom and glory" (2:12; cf. 3:13; 4:1; 4:7). In short, his goal was the well-being of others rather than the enhancement of his own status, reputation, or bank account.

Family imagery. Before leaving this section, we should say a word about Paul's use of family imagery. For some believers, the loss of family relationships was part of the price of accepting the gospel (Matt. 10:34–36; Mark 10:29; 13:12–13; Luke 12:51–53; 1 Cor. 7:12–15). In this light Paul's extensive use of parental and family images is significant. Through the use of such language he essentially portrays the congregation as a new family, whose relationships substitute for those that have been broken or lost.[28]

Not a few of those who come to the church today—as well as a disturbing percentage of those within the church—have lost or never experienced the genuine self-giving love characteristic of healthy family relationships. Thoughtful use of family images today (remembering, of course, that for those who have experienced an abusive situation, paternal or maternal imagery may not carry positive connotation), when coupled with the kind of love and commitment Paul demonstrated toward the Thessalonians, opens up another direction for applying this passage.

 THE FOUR POINTS Paul modeled for the Thessalonians as he ministered to them offer important models and/or reminders for anyone or any group involved in ministry, as well as for individual believers in general.

Goals and Priorities. The need for "goals and priorities" is widely discussed today in Christian and secular books and seminars of all sorts. They are, for example, the second and third items discussed in Stephen Covey's best-selling book, *The Seven Habits of Highly Effective People*.[29] But the fact that the terms have become trendy clichés does not diminish their importance. Most of us learn early on that life is a series of choices, some of which will irrevocably shape the course of the rest of our life. In contrast to the ads that claim that "we can have it all," most of us find life to be more like the 1960s' hit song by the Lovin' Spoonful, "Did You Ever Have to Make Up Your Mind?" The lyrics of the first verse go like this:

Did you ever have to make up your mind?
To pick up on one, and leave the other behind?
It's not often easy, and not often kind,
Did you ever have to make up your mind?

---

28. For an exploration of this idea see Wayne A. Meeks, *The First Urban Christians: The Social World of the Apostle Paul* (New Haven: Yale Univ. Press, 1983), 86–88.

29. Stephen R. Covey, *The Seven Habits of Highly Effective People: Restoring the Character Ethic* (New York: Simon and Schuster, 1989).

Indeed, as the song suggests, a key part of growing up is learning that life requires choices.

For some people making choices seems easy, while others are virtually paralyzed by the prospect of having to choose. The difference often (but not always, of course) is a matter of whether or not a person has a clear sense of goals and priorities. As a college professor, one of my responsibilities is advising students. I find that one of the most frustrating things for many of them, especially the freshmen, is making choices. Apart from simply being overwhelmed by the number of choices they face as they enter college, many of them find it difficult to choose simply because they haven't yet sorted out their goals and priorities in life, and therefore lack criteria by which to make choices. By the time most are juniors, academic decisions have become pretty routine because by then they have focused on a major and so forth, and they have some clear criteria by which to make choices.

Goals and priorities not only help us make choices; they also provide a yardstick by which to evaluate. With respect to many of the programs we are involved in or which our churches offer, we may need to ask: Why are we offering this program, or why are we involved in this activity? What are we trying to accomplish or achieve? Too often programs that once started with a clear goal continue on because of inertia, or "just because that's the way we've always done things." Clear goals can help us assess and perhaps redirect our efforts.

One church I attended while in seminary drew its membership from a large geographic area. Participation levels on Sundays were high, but attendance at the traditional Wednesday night prayer meeting at church was very low. One reason was that the distance people lived from the church made it difficult to gather there in the early evening during the week. When the church leadership began to evaluate the situation, one of the first questions they asked was: What was the goal for Wednesday night activities? The answer: to provide opportunities for mid-week prayer, fellowship, and spiritual refreshment. Clearly the poorly-attended activities scheduled at the church were not achieving these goals. So they took the "radical" step of canceling all Wednesday activities at the church and, instead, offered prayer and Bible study opportunities at four strategically located homes. As a result, involvement in Wednesday night programs nearly tripled.

In short, Paul's example (cf. points 1 and 4 in Bridging Contexts) ought to prompt us to reflect on our own goals and priorities, especially the "big ones." What, for example, do I really want to do with my life? What *am* I doing with my life? What is it that I really value in life? Is serving Jesus and living faithfully in accordance with the gospel really the most important thing for me? Or am I really most committed to accumulating a big enough nest egg so that I can retire by a certain age, or some similar goal? Am I (perhaps without realizing it) trying to serve two masters at the same time? What do my activities say about my priorities? These are the kind of questions that Paul's example prompts us to ask.

Integrity. A Christian talk show host solicits money for a specific purpose but diverts it to others. A nationally known evangelist who preaches often about sexual morality is discovered to have a long-term relationship with a prostitute. A Christian entrepreneur (and former candidate for highest office), who promised investors in his communications empire that everyone would profit equally if part of the business were to be sold, is reported in the secular business press to be negotiating a sale in which he would receive a considerably higher price for his stock than other investors. A Christian fund-raising organization that promises high returns on investments by nonprofit groups turns out to be, when it collapses and leaves them buried in losses, a pyramid scheme. An investigation reveals that an evangelist/healer who claims to receive messages from God about people in his audience is actually being fed information by a colleague in a control room via a radio transmitter. And so on, and so on.

What these examples have in common is a lack of integrity. The people involved in these incidents all said one thing and did something else. In contrast to the familiar saying, "practice what you preach," these people "preached" one thing and "practiced" another. They "talked the talk," but they didn't "walk the walk"; there was a lack of coherence between what they claimed and how they acted. In short, they lacked integrity.

The negative consequences of this kind of "unintegral" behavior hardly need to be spelled out. We've become much too well acquainted with the damage inflicted on the cause of Christ by scandals involving the idols of money, sex, and power. That the topic of TV evangelists is a surefire source of humor and ridicule on late night talk shows is some indication of the dimension of the problem. But we are also familiar with the goodwill earned by those who with faith and discipline have worked hard to live with integrity for the sake of the gospel. We need only contrast the positive impact and image of a Billy Graham, or a Mother Theresa, or former President Jimmy and Rosalynn Carter with any of the well-known causes of scandal whose names are not worthy of mention in the same sentence.

A key point to observe about Graham's reputation for integrity is that it did not happen by accident. The story of how at the beginning of his ministry Graham and his team took deliberate action and established firm guidelines (such as never being alone in a room with a woman other than his wife) to forestall accusations against him is well known. This idea of integrity involving deliberate effort fits in closely with the definition of integrity offered by Stephen L. Carter:

> Integrity, as I will use the term, requires three steps: (1) *discerning* what is right and what is wrong; (2) *acting* on what you have discerned, even at personal cost; and (3) *saying openly* that you are acting on your understanding of right from wrong. The first criterion captures the idea of integrity as requiring a degree of moral reflectiveness. The second brings in the ideal of an integral person as steadfast, which includes the sense of keeping commitments. The third reminds us that a person of integrity is unashamed of doing the right.[30]

In other words, integrity is not something that happens by accident. It involves the hard work of discerning what is right and of learning right from wrong, and then living out—consistently—what has been discerned. It is, to phrase it differently, not just a matter of ethical insight or instruction, but of discipline as well. The subtitle of Richard Foster's famous book on money, sex, and power catches it exactly right: In seeking to live with integrity, we confront "the challenge of the disciplined life."[31] And that may be why, apart from a personal unwillingness to pay the costs sometimes associated with integrity, so many of us find integrity a hard thing to achieve: We lack the discipline to

---

30. Stephen L. Carter, *Integrity* (New York: Basic Books, 1996), 7.

31. Richard J. Foster, *Money, Sex and Power: The Challenge of the Disciplined Life* (San Francisco: Harper & Row, 1985).

do what we say. We find it much easier to talk a good game than to walk one.

The difficulty of living with integrity may explain why we as a society tend to downplay its importance. Stephen Carter goes so far as to assert that in contemporary culture "what matters is not veracity but verisimilitude; it is less important for something to be true than for it to seem to be true."[32] Such an approach may work in the short run, but over the long haul it is an approach destined for failure. In real life it is difficult (as Paul well knew) to separate the message from the messenger. If we do not trust the messenger, we are unlikely to believe the message. Paul's example reminds us of the fundamental importance of integrity on the part of all of us who have been entrusted by God with the gospel of Jesus Christ (cf. 2:4).

Love and commitment. Among the more subtle hazards faced by those engaged in ministry is a temptation (often unconscious) to meet personal needs by ministering to others, or to do things for people in order to win their approval or get them to like us. We are glad to serve or minister to others as long as we somehow benefit from it, or as long as it doesn't place too great a strain on our precious time, energy, and/or money. We greatly admire and honor people like Mother Theresa, but manage somehow to avoid following her example. The human heart being what it is ("deceitful above all things," Jer. 17:9), even when we do something genuinely helpful or loving for someone else, we are not unaware of how we might personally benefit, if only in terms of reputation (Did I go out of my way to help that student in the library because I secretly knew others would observe me being helpful?). Moreover, not only are we experientially familiar with the concept of "fair weather friends," we probably have been one. In short, when it comes to genuine, other-directed love, our "preaching" is often better than our "practice."

There are some broad categories of exceptions, to be sure—family and close friends, for example. The willingness of parents to sacrifice for their offspring, the tenderness and patience with which an adult child will care for an aging parent, or the friend who is there without question or hesitation are familiar to most of us. But even in cases such as these there are no guarantees, and as a culture an increasing number

32. S. L. Carter, *Integrity*, 121.

of us have neither experienced self-giving love nor even observed it in action.

Why is this? Because ours is a self-centered age, and true love is sacrificial. As Bill Hybels observes, "Tell me how to show love without spending time, energy or money, and I will gladly sign up. Tell me that love means sacrifice, however, and I become reluctant to commit myself."[33] Apart from the self-centeredness characteristic of our fallen human nature, so overwhelming are the cultural messages to look out first and foremost for our own interests and to seek first our own happiness that we are reluctant to commit to helping others without fully knowing the cost or limits in advance. The risk to our own interests if we do otherwise, we have been persuaded, is simply too great. We have even convinced ourselves that we can help others be happy only when we are happy. But as Stephen Carter observes, the "trendy contemporary philosophy that we can make others happy only when we are happy ourselves is too often a smokescreen for the pursuit of self interest."[34]

In an age so committed to self-interest, Paul's example of committed, costly love for others is pointedly countercultural. In deciding how to spend his time, he did not think first of his own needs or rights, but those of the Thessalonians. For their sake and because of his love for them, he was willing to endure "toil and hardship" (2:9) and to share with them not only the gospel but his life (2:8). In doing this he was, of course, simply following the model of Jesus, who put a priority on giving rather than getting, on serving rather than being served, on loving rather than being loved.

The irony in this is that in giving of himself for the sake of others, Paul found happiness and satisfaction for himself. Indeed, if 2:8 is any indication, Paul seems a bit overwhelmed by the extent to which the relationship with the Thessalonians developed; in loving others he seems to have received back more than he could have imagined. In so doing, he proved the truth of what Jesus taught when he said, "Whoever wants to save his life will lose it, but whoever loses his life for my sake will save it" (Luke 9:24 NIV [adapted]). Even some therapists have

---

33. Bill Hybels, *Who You Are When No One's Looking* (Downers Grove, Ill.: InterVarsity, 1987), 83.
34. S. L. Carter, *Integrity*, 143.

recognized the principle Paul modeled. Karl Menninger, the well-known psychiatrist, is reported to have said, in answering a question about advice for a person suffering from depression, "Lock up your house, go across the railway tracks, find someone in need and do something to help that person." How different would our churches be if we focused more on meeting the needs of others and less on our own?[35]

---

35. For twelve inspiring profiles of people who exemplify living fully by giving themselves to others, see Jim Langford, *Happy Are They: Living the Beatitudes in America* (Liguori, Mo.: Triumph Books, 1997).

1 Thessalonians 2:13–16

AND WE ALSO thank God continually because, when you received the word of God, which you heard from us, you accepted it not as the word of men, but as it actually is, the word of God, which is at work in you who believe. ¹⁴For you, brothers, became imitators of God's churches in Judea, which are in Christ Jesus: You suffered from your own countrymen the same things those churches suffered from the Jews, ¹⁵who killed the Lord Jesus and the prophets and also drove us out. They displease God and are hostile to all men ¹⁶in their effort to keep us from speaking to the Gentiles so that they may be saved. In this way they always heap up their sins to the limit. The wrath of God has come upon them at last.

THE PRESENCE IN these verses of what appears to be a second "thanksgiving" section (see 1:2–10 for the first) has caused difficulty for attempts to understand the letter in purely epistolary terms (most letters have only one). But if one notices that this is actually the second of three places in the letter where Paul gives thanks, it becomes clear that "thanksgiving" is both a formal epistolary feature and a recurring theme throughout the first major part of the letter. In 1:2 Paul's thanks are ultimately rooted in God's choice of the Thessalonians (1:4); here he gives thanks for their acceptance of the message, and in 3:9 he will give thanks for their continuing steadfastness (3:8).[1]

The passage serves a transitional role in the structure of the letter.[2] In 2:12, Paul's focus shifted from the behavior of the missionaries (the primary subject of 2:1–12) to that of the Thessalonians. Now, still

---

1. Cf. George Lyons, *Pauline Autobiography: Toward a New Understanding* (Atlanta: Scholars, 1985), 189.

2. Cf. C. A. Wanamaker, *Thessalonians*, 109.

focusing on the Thessalonians, he picks up and develops further a point touched on in 1:6: the Thessalonians' acceptance of the gospel in spite of severe suffering (2:13–14). This reference to suffering in turn sets up what he will say in 2:17–20 (where his focus again shifts from the Thessalonians back to the missionaries). Verses 15–16 (whose harsh tone has led some to suggest that they are not part of the letter[3]) have something of the character of a parenthetical editorial comment, prompted by the mention of "the Jews" (at the end of 2:14).

Throughout this section Paul's continuing goal of encouraging his readers is also evident, as he (1) reminds the Thessalonians of their praiseworthy past actions in order to encourage them to maintain that pattern of behavior in the present (v. 13), and (2) seeks to strengthen their sense of group identity and their resolve by showing that "their suffering at the hands of their compatriots was part of a wider apocalyptic pattern of the oppressions of God's people"[4] (vv. 14–16).

Thanksgiving for the Thessalonians (2:13)

AFTER BEGINNING WITH a thanksgiving statement, Paul (as he did in 1:2) quickly reveals why he is thankful (cf. the *hoti*, "because"):[5] The Thessalonians have "received" and "accepted"[6] the message preached by the missionaries not as a merely human message, but in accordance with its true nature, as the "word of God." The clearest evidence of the Thessalonians' acceptance of the gospel as the word of God was their willingness to suffer for it (2:14).[7] The fact that they accepted the gospel despite the "severe suffering" (1:6) that they experienced as a

---

3. For a discussion of the authenticity of 2:13–16, see the Introduction.

4. C. A. Wanamaker, *Thessalonians*, 109.

5. While the "and for this reason" (NIV has only "and") with which 2:13 opens could refer backward or forward, the following "because" shows that it refers forward. A number of interpretations have been offered for the "also" (a second *kai* in the Greek), but in view of the analogous construction in 3:5, it seems best to see it as resuming the theme of thanksgiving from 1:2 (so Peter T. O'Brien, *Introductory Thanksgivings in the Letters of Paul* [Leiden: Brill, 1977], 153–54; for a summary of alternatives see C. A. Wanamaker, *Thessalonians*, 110).

6. "Received" and "accepted" translate respectively *paralambano* and *dechomai*; the former is a technical term used of the reception of authoritative tradition (cf. 1 Cor. 11:23; also 15:1, 3; Gal. 1:9, 12; 1 Thess. 4:1), while the latter (also used in 1 Thess. 1:6) perhaps places more emphasis on the receiver.

7. For the significance of *adelphoi* in 2:14, which includes the entire community and not just the "brothers," see comment on 1:4, above.

result—something they presumably would not have done for a message they considered to be of merely human origin—is for Paul reliable testimony to their commitment. Paul is also confident that God's word is currently "at work" in the Thessalonians, but he does not indicate how he knows this. In light of 1:5 the work of the "word" is probably related to the ministry of the Holy Spirit.

An immediate consequence of the Thessalonians' acceptance of the "word of God" was that they became the focus of hostility from their "own countrymen" (to be understood in a political or local rather than an ethnic sense). Acts 17:5–9 offers a clue as to why this happened: By their acceptance of "Lord Jesus" the Thessalonians implicitly rejected the claims to sovereignty of "Lord Caesar" and the civil religion of the imperial cult, and they thus were perceived as threats to the established social order and government.

The Thessalonians and Persecution: Solidarity in Suffering (2:14–16)

THE SUFFERING THAT the Thessalonians experienced[8] placed them in solidarity not only with the Lord Jesus and the missionaries (1:6), but also with other believers and congregations (2:14). Because the Greek word *ekklesia* ("church") was not yet a technical term, but could indicate a wide range of Hellenistic or Jewish groups, it was necessary for Paul to define more precisely which group he had in mind: It is the "God's churches ... which are in Christ Jesus" (cf. 1:1). This phrase will remind the Thessalonians of the oneness in Christ that they share with other congregations—here, specifically those in "Judea" (i.e., Palestine, including Samaria and Galilee, not simply the restricted area of Roman Judea; cf. Luke 1:5; 23:5; Acts 10:37). We lack the information to know either why Paul chose the Judean churches as an example or what circumstances, past or present, he had in mind.[9]

Paul is clear, however, about the source of the persecution endured by the Judean believers: It was "the Jews" (2:14b). But who did Paul

---

8. The phrase "became imitators of" (cf. 1:6) does not at all suggest that suffering is something the Thessalonians sought; rather, it was something that happened as a consequence of their accepting the gospel.

9. For a list of suggestions as to why he chose Judea, see E. Best, *Thessalonians*, 113; for the possible circumstances to which he refers, see F. F. Bruce, *1 and 2 Thessalonians*, 46, and C. A. Wanamaker, *Thessalonians*, 113.

mean by "the Jews"? In light of the reference to the "churches in Judea," "the Jews" must be Jewish inhabitants of Judea. More specifically, they are "Jewish inhabitants of Judea who killed. ...." That is, the comma that many translations (e.g., NIV, NRSV, NAB, NASB) place after "Jews"—which has the effect of generalizing the reference to include "all Jews"— should be removed.[10] In short, it is not even all Jews in Judea whom Paul designates, but only those who in some way participated or took part in one of the specific activities mentioned in verses 15–16.[11] Those activities include, in addition to persecution of the Judean congregations, (1) having killed the Messiah and the prophets, (2) having driven out "us," (3) not pleasing God, and (4) hindering the missionary effort because of a general hostility towards humanity.[12]

---

10. Frank D. Gilliard, "The Problem of the Antisemitic Comma Between 1 Thessalonians 2.14 and 15," *NTS* 35 (1989): 481–502; cf. C. F. D. Moule, *An Idiom Book of New Testament Greek* (2d ed.; Cambridge: Cambridge Univ. Press, 1959), 106–7. He argues persuasively that the following clause (an articular participial phrase, parallel in form to part of the phrase that defines the churches in 2:14a) is restrictive, not generalizing. Furthermore, from a logical perspective it is unlikely that Paul could have meant literally "all Jews," since a substantial portion of those who acknowledged Jesus as Messiah, including Paul himself, were in fact Jews (cf. Rom. 11:1).

11. W. D. Davies, "Paul and the People of Israel," *NTS* 24 (1977–78): 8, notes that when Paul speaks of the Jewish people as a collective, he calls them "Hebrews" or "Israel/Israelites"); see also W. Marxsen, *Der erste Brief an die Thessalonicher* (Zürich: Theologischer Verlag, 1979), 48–51; L. Morris, *The First and Second Epistles to the Thessalonians*, 83. It must be acknowledged, however, that this is a minority view among commentators.

12. This numeration of charges reflects the four participles in 2:15–16a. The translations vary considerably in their treatment of these participles and the repeated *kai*'s in 2:15–16a: "the ones *kai* having killed the Lord Jesus *kai* the prophets *kai* having driven us out *kai* not pleasing God *kai*, hostile to all people, hindering us. ...." In 2:15a, the NRSV ("who killed both the Lord Jesus and the prophets") treats the first *kai* as if it came after "having killed" rather than before, while the NIV ("who killed the Lord Jesus and the prophets and also drove us out") ignores the first and translates the third as if it were a longer phrase. Preferable is either (1) "who both killed the Lord Jesus and the prophets, and drove us out" (NASB), which links closely the verbs "killed" and "drove out," or (2) "who also killed the Lord Jesus and the prophets, and drove us out" (pers. trans.), which picks up the list-like character of the string of accusations. In 2:15b–16a there are competing structural patterns: While the first three clauses of vv. 15–16 are composed of a noun or pronoun phrase followed by a participle, in the fourth clause the noun phrase is followed by an adjective ("hostile") and then a participle ("hindering"). Both the NIV ("They ... are hostile to all men in their effort to keep us") and the NRSV ("they ... oppose everyone by hindering us") emphasize the adjective, as it immediately follows the noun clause; they treat the adjective as if it were a participle parallel to the first three, and they subordinate the following participle to it. Alternatively, one may emphasize the obvious parallelism of the four participles, as does the NASB ("not pleasing to

The list of charges in 2:15–16 is an odd mix of Christian, Jewish, and pagan complaints. The charge of Jewish responsibility for the death of the Messiah (cf. John 11:45–53; 18:28–31; also Acts 2:23, 36; 3:13–15; 4:10; 7:52; 10:39; 13:28) is accurate to the extent that while the actual execution was carried out by Roman soldiers under the command of Pontius Pilate, he was instigated to do so by a small group of Jewish leaders. The charge of "killing the prophets," found elsewhere in both the New Testament (Matt. 23:29–37//Luke 11:47–51; 13:34; Acts 7:52; cf. Matt. 5:12) and contemporary Jewish literature (Mart. Isa. 5:1–14), is rooted in the Old Testament (1 Kings 19:9–18; 2 Chron. 36:15–16; Jer. 2:30), where it was clearly not intended as a charge against all Jews, but only those not part of the "faithful remnant" (a point Paul himself makes in Rom. 11:2–5, with reference to 1 Kings 19:10, 18; cf. 1QM 13.8–9).

This is clearly an "insider's charge," one typically made by Jews against fellow Jews. In charging some Judean Jews with having "driven out" (the basic, and here quite appropriate, meaning of *ekdioko*) "us," Paul apparently includes himself among the Judean Christians affected (see Acts 8:1, 4; 8:23–25, 29–30). While it is possible that "us" refers only to Paul and his companions, it seems much more likely, in view of the following specific reference to the Pauline missionary effort, that this is a more general reference. In describing the rejection of the prophets (who foretold the Messiah), the Messiah himself, and the Christian missionaries (who proclaim the Messiah), Paul implies "a continuity in the pattern of Jewish rejection of God's agents from OT times to his own."[13]

"They displease God" (2:15; cf. 2:4) is essentially a conclusion based on the other activities mentioned; Paul takes it for granted that those who oppose God's Messiah and his designated missionaries are not pleasing to God.[14] The "hostility toward humanity" (NIV "hostile") echoes a widespread anti-Jewish feeling in the Greco-Roman world, which interpreted Jewish ethnic and religious exclusivism (which to the Jews was a matter of faithfulness to God) as evidence of their lack of concern for or hatred

---

God, but hostile to all men, hindering us"). But it treats the linking conjunction *kai* as though it were a contrasting one ("but," *de* or *alla*); instead, it should be translated, "they are not pleasing to God and, hostile to humanity, are hindering us . . ." (cf. E. J. Richard, *Thessalonians*, 121–22).

13. C. A. Wanamaker, *Thessalonians*, 115.

14. As E. Best, *Thessalonians*, 117, points out, "pleasing to God is one of Paul's favourite expressions for true behavior (Rom. 8.8; 1 Cor. 7.32–4; Gal. 1.10; 1 Thess. 2.4, 15; 4.1; cf. 2 Cor. 5.9); he uses it even of Jesus himself (Rom. 15.3)."

of others.[15] Paul sees this hostility on the part of some Jews as the motivation for the last item on the list of charges, namely, an effort to prevent or hinder (for the verb, cf. Acts 16:6; Rom. 1:13; 1 Cor. 14:39) his mission to the Gentiles, which had as its goal their salvation.[16]

These activities involve "filling up the measure of their sins" (2:16, NRSV). This phrase echoes Gen. 15:16 (cf. Dan. 8:23; 2 Macc. 6:14–15; Matt. 23:32) and expresses an idea not uncommon in Jewish and Christian writings of that era.[17] The grammatical construction used here (*eis to* + infinitive) customarily indicates purpose in Paul.[18] But it can also indicate result (cf. NASB, "with the result that"), which in light of the "always" makes good sense here. In other words, there seem to have nearly always been some people in Israel, whether Judeans of Paul's generation or their ancestors in earlier times, who by their disobedience were "not pleasing to God" and thereby brought judgment on themselves.[19]

Judgment is in fact the subject of Paul's last statement in this section: "But God's wrath has overtaken them at last" (2:16, NRSV).[20] Whereas Jesus will rescue believers from that "wrath" (1:10), those who are opposed to God will be unable to escape it (cf. 5:3)—indeed, Paul says, it "has come upon them" already. I interpret this last phrase along the lines of the idea expressed in John 3:18, "Whoever believes

---

15. For example, the Roman historian Tacitus charges that "among themselves there is unswerving loyalty, ready compassion, but hostility and hatred toward all others" (*Annals* 5.5.2). Cf. further M. Whittaker, *Jews and Christians: Graeco-Roman Views* (Cambridge: Cambridge Univ. Press, 1984), 14–130.

16. This opposition to preaching to Gentiles was not limited to Jews; not a few Christians in the early years of the Christian movement also actively criticized efforts to evangelize Gentiles (cf. Acts 11:2).

17. References in E. J. Richard, *Thessalonians*, 122.

18. Cf. N. Turner, *Syntax*, 143; BDF, §402.2; if so, it is God's purpose Paul has in view (cf. Rom. 11:7–10, 28–32).

19. Cf. 2 Chron. 36:15–17: "The LORD, the God of their fathers, sent word to them through his messengers again and again, because he had compassion on his people and on his dwelling place. But they kept mocking God's messengers, despising his words and scoffing at his prophets, until the wrath of the LORD was aroused against his people, and there was no remedy. Therefore he brought up against them the king of the Babylonians" (NIV, modified).

20. This phrase (which occurs in nearly identical form in Testament of Levi 6:11) bristles with technical interpretive difficulties—the verb is an aorist, where one might have expected either a perfect or a present, and it can be taken at least two different ways; at least four meanings have been suggested for the last two words, *eis telos* (NIV "at last")—which space limitations preclude us from discussing fully here. See E. Best, *Thessalonians*, 119–23; E. J. Richard, *Thessalonians*, 122–23, 125–27; C. A. Wanamaker, *Thessalonians*, 116–18; I. H. Marshall, *1 and 2 Thessalonians*, 80–83.

in [the Son of God] is not condemned, but whoever does not believe stands condemned already because he has not believed in the name of God's one and only Son."[21] That is, rejection of God's Messiah is in and of itself judgment, in that it means the rejection of the one through whom God has made salvation available to all.[22]

OBSERVATIONS. THE PRIMARY topic of concern in this section of 1 Thessalonians is Paul's statement about "the Jews."[23] Is it accurate to say that in this passage Paul holds "an unacceptable anti-Semitic position"?[24] What are we to make of this text, especially in a post-Holocaust era? In the process of understanding this section, several observations may be made.

(1) To restate an earlier conclusion, Paul was not talking about "all Jews" here; his primary focus is those of his day who had not only not acknowledged Jesus as God's Messiah, but were also actively opposing those who did.

(2) Paul wrote as a Jew (cf. Gal. 2:15; Phil. 3:4–6) at a time in history when Christianity was still not clearly differentiated from Judaism. That is, he wrote as an "insider"; his comments are those of one engaged in an intramural debate with other "insiders."

(3) Paul wrote as a member of a minority movement fighting for its identity and survival.[25]

(4) Paul wrote within the context of a rhetorical culture in which hyperbole and exaggeration were recognized and accepted elements

---

21. See on this verse D. A. Carson, *The Gospel According to John* (Grand Rapids: Eerdmans, 1991), 207; R. Bultmann, *The Gospel of John: A Commentary* (Oxford: Blackwell, 1971), 155. For similar interpretations of Paul's phrase see D. A. Hagner, "Paul's Quarrel with Judaism," in *Anti-Semitism and Early Christianity: Issues of Polemic and Faith,* ed. C. A. Evans and D. A. Hagner (Minneapolis: Fortress, 1993), 132–33; C. A. Wanamaker, *Thessalonians,* 117.

22. Implied in this view is the possibility of a reversal of the judgment, if those opposing the gospel cease their hostility to God and his Messiah.

23. Other important topics that arise here turn up elsewhere as well and are treated at those places: giving thanks (3:9), acceptance of the gospel as God's Word (cf. 1:6), and persecution/suffering for the sake of the gospel (3:3–4; cf. also 1:6).

24. E. Best, *Thessalonians,* 122.

25. With respect to points 2 and 3, it is significant that some of the closest parallels to Paul's comments here are found in the writings of another first-century minority Jewish movement, the Jewish community at Qumran; cf. 1QM 3.6–9; 11.10–11; 13.1–12; 1QS 2.4–17; 3.1–6; 4.9–14; CD 1.16–2.1; 5.12–17; 8.1–13.

of public discourse. Moreover, his use of hyperbole must be viewed in the context not just of contemporary Greco-Roman and Jewish rhetorical culture but also of his own practice of using hyperbole, as seen elsewhere in his writings. His comments here about "the Jews" are no more (and possibly less) intense than some of the comments he makes about fellow Christians (see, e.g., 2 Cor. 11). In the same way that his hyperbolic statements about Christian opponents reflected his feelings about them at that point in time and should not be taken as considered or final reflections on their ultimate fate, so too his comments about "the Jews" here in 1 Thessalonians.[26]

(5) Paul's purpose was fundamentally pastoral: He was seeking to encourage and strengthen the Thessalonians by showing them that both their experience of persecution and the activities of their persecutors were part of larger, long-term patterns of behavior. This means that his comments about "the Jews" are not primary, first-level, or fully developed expressions of his views about "the Jews," but a secondary, ad hoc description made in the service of a specific goal, namely, encouraging the Thessalonians.

Implications. Several implications may be drawn from these observations. (1) The observation that Paul was *not* talking about all Jews means, if nothing else, that this passage provides for Christians today absolutely no basis for formulating attitudes or making statements about "the Jews" in general today.

(2) Paul's comments express a theological disagreement with some Jews about the identity of God's Messiah, not a description of or attack on an entire category of people. Paul's comments, therefore, are *not* "anti-Semitic" (i.e., racially based).[27]

---

26. See Carol J. Schlueter, *Filling Up the Measure: Polemical Hyperbole in 1 Thessalonians 2.14–16* (Sheffield: JSOT, 1994); L. T. Johnson, "The New Testament's Anti-Jewish Slander and the Conventions of Ancient Polemic," *JBL* 108 (1989): 419–41. Cf. also C. A. Wanamaker, *Thessalonians*, 118–19.

27. "Anti-Semitism" is a modern concept based on the notion of "race" (itself a problematic modern construction). It differs sharply from a theologically based "anti-Judaism," which is based on an individual's religious commitment, something capable of being changed (e.g., via conversion). That is, an individual who converted from Judaism to Christianity would no longer be seen (from a religious perspective, at any rate) as a "Jew" but as a "Christian." Anti-Semitism, however, is rooted in a characteristic not subject to change (i.e., one's "race"). That is, a Jew who converts from Judaism to Christianity still remains, from an anti-Semitic perspective, a Jew.

(3) The contrast between Paul's circumstances and those of Christians today can hardly be greater. Whereas Paul and the rest of the Christian movement were being opposed by certain members of a widespread, legally and socially recognized religion (Judaism), for many centuries now it is Christianity that has been the dominant and generally recognized religion, and Judaism that has been (and in some cases, still is) the persecuted minority religion. Moreover, when Christians speak about Judaism today, they clearly do so as "outsiders." Consequently, comments that may have been appropriate when made by Paul as an "insider" in the context of persecuted minority movement will *not* be applicable to a context in which Christians are both (a) "outsiders" with respect to Judaism and (b) members of a dominant social group, one that has, moreover, a long and shameful history of persecuting Judaism.[28]

(4) An implication of observations 4 and 5 above is that Paul's comments here must be taken together with, and read in light of, other comments in which he expresses, in more measured and deliberate terms, his views about "the Jews." That is, his comments here, which describe a specific subgroup within Judaism, must be read alongside of passages such as Romans 9–11, in which he discusses in more general terms the future of God's people (*laos*, cf. 11:1a), that is, Israel (cf. 9:4; 11:1b).

(5) This passage is Paul's *description* of certain opponents at a particular point in time; that does not make it a *prescription* for how Christians in other circumstances should view their opponents or enemies.

With these implications in mind, we may turn to consider the contemporary relevance of this passage for believers today.

IN LIGHT OF the preceding observations, it seems to me that responsible application of this text will take advantage of at least three opportunities presented by this difficult passage.[29]

---

28. For a brief overview of Christian anti-Semitism, see Sidney G. Hall III, *Christian Anti-Semitism and Paul's Theology* (Minneapolis: Fortress, 1993), 23–51. On anti-Semitism (and its opponents) among conservative Christians of the twentieth century, see David A. Rausch, *Fundamentalist Evangelicals and Anti-Semitism* (Valley Forge, Pa.: Trinity Press International, 1993).

29. For what implications this passage might have for Christians today who find themselves in a genuinely comparable situation (that is, that of a persecuted minority facing opposition or attack by a socially dominant group), see the discussion of 3:1–5 below.

Confronting the issue of Anti-Semitism. The passage presents us with an opportunity to confront the issue of anti-Semitism. Despite the horrors perpetuated by anti-Semitic ideologies during World War II, the late twentieth-century has witnessed a resurgence of anti-Semitic views and activity, especially in Europe and the United States. While in Europe this resurgence is often associated with neo-Nazi groups, in the United States it is the so-called "militia movements" that have received much of the attention. What is especially troubling is the explicit claims of many of these groups to be both anti-Semitic and Christian (e.g., the Christian Identity movement).[30]

In such circumstances, and particularly because of our long and tragic history of persecuting Jews, Christians need to be aggressively forthright in asserting that anti-Semitism, like any form of racial discrimination, is wrong. Discrimination against, hostility towards, or attacks on any group simply because they allegedly share a common set of social, cultural, religious, or genetic characteristics is not Christian; it is sin. Indeed, any allegedly Christian group that advocates anti-Semitism or other forms of racial discrimination forfeits, in my opinion, any right to be called "Christian."

Because the present passage can so easily be misunderstood and twisted to support anti-Semitic prejudices, it is important to stress that in this passage Paul is *not* anti-Semitic. There is a fundamental theological difference between Christianity and Judaism—the one acknowledges Jesus as Messiah, the other does not—and this *Christologically based* opposition to Judaism as a religion is expressed throughout the New Testament. Scholars have labeled this "anti-Judaism." Regrettably, this theological difference has frequently given rise to racially based discrimination (or worse) against Jews—that is, anti-Semitism. It cannot be stressed too strongly that there is in the New Testament no basis whatsoever for anti-Semitism of any sort.

Not only is Paul *not* anti-Semitic, his comments here apply only to a specific group of Jews of his day and therefore provide absolutely no basis for negative attitudes towards Jews today. It is in Romans 9–11, not in 1 Thessalonians 2:14–16, that we see Paul's thinking about the Jewish people as a whole. There he makes it clear that God has *not*

---

30. See Richard Abanes, *American Militias: Rebellion, Racism, and Religion* (Downers Grove, Ill.: InterVarsity, 1996), esp. 131–88.

rejected his people (Rom. 11:1), and he strongly warns any non-Jews who might be inclined to boast about their allegedly superior status before God that they stand in danger of God's judgment if they do so (11:17–22).

The dangers of using "insider" and/or hyperbolic language. The ease with which Paul has been misunderstood offer us an opportunity to reflect on the inherent dangers of using "insider" and/or hyperbolic language in inappropriate circumstances. What Paul wrote as an "insider" and shared with his close friends made sense and was understandable to them in that context. But as soon as readers lost sight of that original context, Paul's deliberately hyperbolic overstatements sounded different, and over the centuries they have been seriously misinterpreted.[31]

The fate suffered by Paul's words may serve as a warning to Christians today to pay careful attention both to what they say and how they say it, especially if what they say may be repeated or passed on in other contexts. Our goal ought to be (1) to communicate clearly the gospel, our Christian convictions, and our Christian experience, and (2) to do so in a way that does not create unnecessary obstacles or roadblocks to effective communication. Both "insider" language and hyperbole can easily become, as the case of the present passage demonstrates, barriers to clear and effective communication of the gospel. Thus Christians ought to be cautious and careful in using them.

As some of the negative reactions and misperceptions encountered by the Promise Keepers movement in its early years demonstrate, words, ideas, or concepts that mean one thing to "insiders" may sound quite different to those who do not share the same suppositions or insider perspective. What some of the speakers meant by phrases like "taking charge of the home," for example, was not at all what some reporters and outside observers thought they meant. Or, as some Christian political candidates for national office have learned, phrases and

---

31. As W. D. Davies observes, "when [Paul's] letters came to be read by Gentiles who little understood Judaism, the misinterpretation of Paul became almost inevitable. . . . The disputes between Paul and his kinsmen . . . over the true interpretation of their common Jewish tradition . . . once removed from this setting . . . no longer appeared as attempts at the reinterpretation of a shared tradition but as forages in hostility. . . . What was a disruption among Jews came to be spelt out as the denigration and rejection of Judaism and of the people of Israel as a totality"—a tendency against which Paul himself fought (W. D. Davies, "Paul and the People of Israel," *NTS* 24 [1977–78]: 22).

ideas that are easily understood by fellow Christians often either do not communicate at all or (perhaps worse) seriously miscommunicate to non-Christians.

In view of these circumstances—and in view of the current state of communications technology, in which words can circle the globe in literally seconds and thus be heard in contexts that we can scarcely imagine—we would do well to give careful consideration to what we say and to how we say it, especially if it involves any sort of argumentative or polemical language. Christians should never hesitate to engage in forthright discussions of issues or differences, but we ought to seek to do so in ways consistent with the gospel and the values it represents, rather than in ways that unnecessarily polarize or divide, or in ways that raise barriers to genuine understanding. Our goal must be to enlighten, not inflame.[32]

Response to persecutors. This passage offers an opportunity to reaffirm how Christians ought to respond to those who persecute and/or attack them. In 5:15 ("See that none of you repays evil for evil, but always seek to do good to one another and to all" [NRSV]; cf. Rom. 12:17–19), Paul will remind the Thessalonians that doing good, not retaliation, is the proper reaction to persecution (cf. Rom. 12:20–21). As Marshall notes, "Nothing in what Paul writes suggests that the Thessalonians should hate their persecutors or react violently against them. Their task is to live the new life of the Christian in love even to their enemies and to leave vengeance to God himself."[33]

In other words, nothing in the present passage in any way abrogates what Jesus taught in Matthew 5:44 ("Love your enemies and pray for those who persecute you") and Luke 6:27–28 ("Love your enemies, do good to those who hate you, bless those who curse you, pray for those who mistreat you"), and what Paul himself echoed in Romans 12:14 ("Bless those who persecute you; bless and do not curse"), about how believers are to respond to persecution or attacks. Violence against enemies or in response to persecution is not the way of the gospel.

This is an important point to reaffirm in an era when some Christians are becoming increasingly violent in their reaction to social pressures or in the way in which they approach social issues. Examples of

---

32. For an excellent discussion of this matter, see Richard J. Mouw, *Uncommon Decency: Christian Civility in an Uncivil World* (Downers Grove, Ill.: InterVarsity, 1992).

33. I. H. Marshall, *1 and 2 Thessalonians*, 83.

the kind of violence I have in mind include, for example, violent attacks on abortion clinics and even the killing of abortion providers, or the advocacy of robbery, bombings, and killing by allegedly Christian movements (such as the Phineas Priesthood[34]). Moreover, ours is a time when reports of large-scale massacres and atrocities in nominally Christian societies are not uncommon (e.g., "ethnic cleansing" in the former Yugoslavia).

For increasing numbers of Christians, in other words, it appears that the mere perception of someone or some movement as an "enemy" is viewed as sufficient grounds to justify the use of violence against them. Such an attitude overlooks not only the teaching of the gospel (noted above), but also the lessons of history. Attempts to impose, create, or maintain by force a "Christian" society generally have led to unmitigated disaster; and Christian-versus-Christian violence, whether in Europe during the Thirty Years War in the seventeenth century, or in Ireland or Rwanda today (countries in which up to 90 percent of the population are professed Christians), has caused incalculable damage to the cause of the gospel. In Romans 5:8–10, Paul points out how, even when we were all his enemies, God's response was to demonstrate his love for us. Are believers in that God to act any differently towards their enemies?

---

34. As reported by *The CBS Evening News*, October 15, 1996. On the advocacy of violence by militia groups see Richard Abanes, *American Militias: Rebellion, Racism, and Religion* (Downers Grove, Ill.: InterVarsity, 1996), 209–21.

1 Thessalonians 2:17–3:8

B UT, BROTHERS, WHEN we were torn away from you for a short time (in person, not in thought), out of our intense longing we made every effort to see you. ¹⁸For we wanted to come to you—certainly I, Paul, did, again and again—but Satan stopped us. ¹⁹For what is our hope, our joy, or the crown in which we will glory in the presence of our Lord Jesus when he comes? Is it not you? ²⁰Indeed, you are our glory and joy.

³:¹So when we could stand it no longer, we thought it best to be left by ourselves in Athens. ²We sent Timothy, who is our brother and God's fellow worker in spreading the gospel of Christ, to strengthen and encourage you in your faith, ³so that no one would be unsettled by these trials. You know quite well that we were destined for them. ⁴In fact, when we were with you, we kept telling you that we would be persecuted. And it turned out that way, as you well know. ⁵For this reason, when I could stand it no longer, I sent to find out about your faith. I was afraid that in some way the tempter might have tempted you and our efforts might have been useless.

⁶But Timothy has just now come to us from you and has brought good news about your faith and love. He has told us that you always have pleasant memories of us and that you long to see us, just as we also long to see you. ⁷Therefore, brothers, in all our distress and persecution we were encouraged about you because of your faith. ⁸For now we really live, since you are standing firm in the Lord.

IN 2:13, PAUL'S focus shifted from the behavior of the missionaries to that of the Thessalonians, as he picked up and developed further a point raised previously (in 1:6), namely, their acceptance of the gospel in spite of severe suffering (2:13–14). Now Paul's focus shifts back to the missionaries (note the

resumptive "but . . . we") and their attitude towards the Thessalonians. In 2:1−12 Paul stressed the way he and his companions had demonstrated their concern for the Thessalonians while in Thessalonica; here he stresses the ways they have continued to demonstrate their concern for them since being forced to leave the city.

A significant element running throughout the letter, but especially evident in 2:17−3:8, is the theme of friendship. In this passage it carries a double significance. On the one hand, it accurately reflects Paul's deep feelings and concern for the Thessalonians so evident in this section. On the other hand, it also sets up the exhortations that follow in chapters 4−5: A superior could write a letter of friendship to an inferior in order to establish a basis for making a request.[1] Thus what Paul writes here (using traditional themes associated with friendship in the ancient world) not only expresses to the Thessalonians his genuine feelings for them, but also prepares the way for the rest of the letter.[2]

The larger section falls into three clear subsections: Paul's report of his unsuccessful attempts to revisit Thessalonica (2:17−20), his sending of Timothy in his place to encourage the believers in the midst of persecution (3:1−5), and his reaction to the good news when Timothy returns (3:6−8, which spills over into 3:9, the third thanksgiving in the letter).

Apostolic Concern: Attempts to Revisit Thessalonica (2:17−20)

PAUL COMMUNICATES HERE not only his (so far unsuccessful) attempts to return to Thessalonica, but also his deep feelings for them. The primary meaning of the first verb in 2:17 is "to make someone an orphan" (*aporphanizo*), although it can also indicate parents deprived of children, or more generally "deprived of" or "separated from."[3] Paul's earlier use of parental metaphors (2:7, 11) inclines one towards the parental use here. It is not, however, out of the question that Paul has once again

---

1. See Stanley K. Stowers, *Letter Writing in Greco-Roman Antiquity* (Philadelphia: Westminster, 1986), 58−70.

2. C. A. Wanamaker, *Thessalonians*, 119−20, 133; cf. Abraham J. Malherbe, "Exhortation in First Thessalonians," *NovT* 25 (1983): 241.

3. E. J. Richard, *Thessalonians*, 128−29; Johannes P. Louw and Eugene A. Nida, *Greek-English Lexicon of the New Testament Based on Semantic Domains* (2 vols.; New York: United Bible Societies, 1988), 1:726.

switched metaphors (in which case the primary meaning will prevail; cf. NRSV, "were made orphans"). In either case, Paul conveys both the involuntary nature of the separation and the emotional distress it caused him. That the separation was (he hoped) only temporary and that the Thessalonians were never off his mind did little to ease his anguish.

The intensity of his feelings toward them is evident from his description of the repeated attempts he made to return to Thessalonica (vv. 17b–18a). But these attempts failed, he reports, not because of any lack of desire or effort on Paul's part but because "Satan stopped us" (v. 18b). "Satan" (a term used interchangeably with "devil" and other phrases in Paul) designates the one who opposes God (Rom. 16:20), seeks to hinder the progress of the gospel (2 Cor. 2:11; 4:4), and tempts Christ's followers (1 Cor. 7:5; 1 Thess. 3:5). Defeated in the cross (Col. 2:14–15) and doomed to be completely vanquished in the end (1 Cor. 15:24–25), he nonetheless in the meantime continues to attack God's people, as Paul himself knows from personal experience (2 Cor 12:7); against such attacks believers are exhorted to put on "the full armor of God" (Eph. 6:11–17).[4]

How Paul was blocked is not stated.[5] In view of Acts 17:9, it is possible that there were legal barriers to his return. On the other hand, if the "thorn in the flesh" of 2 Corinthians 12:7 was an illness, it may be that poor health prevented Paul from traveling.[6] Timothy no doubt informed the Thessalonians about the circumstances that made it impossible for Paul to visit them, but we must acknowledge that Paul's letter leaves us without a clue.

In 2:19–20 Paul explains why (note the "for" with which 2:19 begins) he was longing so strongly to see them again: To him they represented both the fruit and the evidence of his God-given ministry (cf. 1 Cor.

---

4. See further D. G. Reid, "Satan, Devil," *DPL*, 862–67; J. S. Wright, "Satan," etc., *NID-NTT*, 3:468–77; E. Best, *Thessalonians*, 126–27.

5. The same verb (*enkopto*, cut off, block, hinder) occurs in Rom. 15:22 in a similar phrase, but there the hindrance was the (apparently greater) need first to evangelize other regions (cf. 15:19–21, 23); that is, the hindrance was from God (cf. the "divine passive" in Rom. 1:13), not Satan. We do not know how in the instance involving the Thessalonians Paul "perceived it was Satan who prevented him and not God's Spirit guiding him into other ways. . . . We can only assume that as time went by he saw God's plans being hindered here whereas elsewhere he saw them advanced" (E. Best, *Thessalonians*, 127).

6. I. H. Marshall, *1 and 2 Thessalonians*, 86; on 2 Cor. 12:7, see R. P. Martin, *2 Corinthians* (WBC 40; Waco, Tex.: Word, 1986), 412–17.

9:1).[7] In 2:19 Paul takes for granted a belief he explicitly mentions in 1 Corinthians 3:8, 13–15; 4:5 (cf. Rom. 14:12): At some point in the future, believers will be evaluated with respect to their stewardship of the ministry entrusted to them by God (cf. 1 Thess. 2:4). As Paul understands it, the basis of evaluation is not how hard he may have worked but the fruit he has produced. Thus the health and well-being of the Thessalonian congregation is of no small concern to Paul, for it offers public evidence of his success as God's missionary. "He thus yearns for them in part because, as his converts, their steadfast loyalty to Christ means that his own life has counted for something."[8]

The "crown" in 2:19 is likely the laurel wreath, a symbol of victory (cf. the athletic imagery in 1 Cor. 9:24–27; Phil. 3:12–14). Its equivalent in 2:20 is *doxa*, "glory," which to Hellenistic readers will have indicated "reputation" or "renown."[9] What Paul means by the phrase "in which we will glory" (lit., "of boasting"; the nearly identical phrase occurs in 2 Cor. 1:14 and Phil. 2:16, where the boasting is mutual) is clarified by his statement in Romans 15:17–18, "In Christ Jesus, then, I have reason to boast of my work for God. For I will not venture to speak of anything except what Christ has accomplished through me ..." (NRSV). That is, his boasting is not self-oriented but other-oriented, a taking pride in what others have done or accomplished.

The evaluation and boasting of which Paul speaks are eschatological, in that they will take place "when [Jesus] comes" (2:19). This is the first of four references in 1 Thessalonians to the "coming" (*parousia*) of Jesus (2:19; 3:13; 4:15; 5:23; also 2 Thess. 2:1, 8; the idea is mentioned in 1 Thess. 1:10), a concept discussed at 4:15.

In addition to Paul's evident interest in the Thessalonians as an indicator of his own success or failure, the double mention of "joy" reveals as well (and again, cf. 2:8) his own strong feelings towards the Thessalonians: Even as parents rejoice and take pride in the accomplishments of their children, so it is with Paul and his Thessalonian converts/friends.[10] "Indeed" (which in 2:20 is strongly affirmative), their

---

7. Regarding the grammatical difficulties in the awkwardly placed phrase "Is it not you?" (which in Greek occurs in the middle of 2:19), see C. A. Wanamaker, *Thessalonians*, 123–24; F. F. Bruce, *1 and 2 Thessalonians*, 53; E. J. Richard, *Thessalonians*, 131–32.

8. G. D. Fee, *Philippians* (NICNT; Grand Rapids: Eerdmans, 1995), 249, discussing Phil. 2:16; cf. C. A. Wanamaker, *Thessalonians*, 124; W. Grundmann, "στέφανος," TDNT, 7:630.

9. E. J. Richard, *Thessalonians*, 134.

10. F. F. Bruce, *1 and 2 Thessalonians*, 56.

continuing faithfulness is for Paul a source of deep personal joy. But that joy was not unmixed with anxiety, as the next passage indicates.

Apostolic Action: Timothy Is Sent to Thessalonica (3:1–5)

BECAUSE OF WHAT the Thessalonians represented to Paul, he was more than a little anxious about them, and for good reason: He had been forced to leave those relatively new converts alone and without outside assistance when he and his companions were driven out of town. In a culture in which religion, properly practiced, was supposed to bring positive consequences, the "trials" experienced by the Thessalonians might well have convinced them that they had made a major mistake in abandoning their conventional religions in order to embrace Christianity. Indeed, so concerned was Paul that he, though unable to return himself, was unwilling that the Thessalonians should be left without support, and so a decision was made[11] that Timothy should return as his authorized representative.[12]

Timothy's task was to "strengthen" (or perhaps "firmly establish") and "encourage" (v. 2; the same combination occurs in 2 Thess. 2:17; cf. Acts 14:22; 15:32; Rom. 1:11–12) the Thessalonian converts. The first verb (*sterizo;* also at 1 Thess. 3:13; 2 Thess. 2:17; 3:3) likely focuses more on their spiritual condition, while the second verb (*parakaleo;* also at 1 Thess. 2:12; 3:7; 4:1, 10, 18; 5:11, 14; 2 Thess. 2:17; 3:12) probably focuses more on their attitude. Essentially Timothy is to continue the

---

11. The phrase "we thought it best to be left alone" is awkward: Who does the "we" represent, and if sending Timothy leaves Paul alone, where is Silas (who with Timothy rejoined Paul in Corinth, according to Acts 18:5)? The "we" may be an epistolary plural (cf. the "I sent" in 3:5), but elsewhere in the letter the plurals are genuine (F. F. Bruce, *1 and 2 Thessalonians,* 61). Silas may have remained in Berea while Timothy went to join Paul in Athens, from where he was sent back up to Thessalonica, with Silas then rejoining Timothy on his return trip south. Or he may, after a stay in Berea (Acts 17:14), have traveled with Timothy to Athens and then returned to Macedonia on a different errand (perhaps to Berea) while Timothy went to Thessalonica (J. B. Lightfoot, *Notes on Epistles,* 40). Or the thought here may simply be incomplete, with the intended meaning being something like "we decided that I should be left alone" (I. H. Marshall, *1 and 2 Thessalonians,* 90).

12. In 3:2 "brother" may designate Timothy as an official coworker of Paul (so E. E. Ellis, "Coworkers, Paul and His," *DPL,* 183–85; C. A. Wanamaker, *Thessalonians,* 128; I. H. Marshall, *1 and 2 Thessalonians,* 90, thinks this goes beyond the evidence). More significantly, he is designated, like Paul (cf. 1 Cor. 3:9), as "God's fellow worker" (the textual variants in the NIV footnote reflect scribal efforts to tone down this bold designation).

---

process of socialization that Paul himself had begun (cf. the discussion of 2:11–12 above and Paul's use there of the "father" metaphor)—that is, helping them both to understand and to live out what it means to be members of God's people.

The urgency of Timothy's mission was generated by the "trials" (NIV, which translates the same Greek word in 1:6 as "suffering") or "persecutions" (NRSV) that the Thessalonians were currently experiencing. Whatever the precise nature of these events (see comments on 1:6), they had the potential to "unsettle" or "shake up"[13] the new believers to the point of causing them to abandon their recently adopted faith. Or, as Paul puts it in 3:5, "I was afraid that in some way the tempter [.e., Satan; see comments on 2:18, above] might have tempted you and our efforts might have been useless."

It was apparently the force or extent rather than the fact of the "trials"[14] that generated Paul's concern, for they could hardly have come as surprise to the Thessalonians. They well knew (3:3b), because the missionaries had more than once (notice the imperfect tense) told them ahead of time (3:4), that they would experience such "trials"[15]— that is, socio-religious dislocation, conflict (including persecution), and/or ostracization—if they joined the Christian movement. This is because Christians "are destined" (*keimai* in 3:3b; cf. Luke 2:34; Phil. 1:16) for such things (cf. Acts 14:22). That is, the "trials" that the Thessalonians experienced are not a matter of chance, fate, karma, or bad luck, nor are they unique to the Thessalonians. Rather, they are a consequence of God's election (see comment on 1 Thess. 1:4–6), and part of the common experience of Christians everywhere (note the "we" in 3:4; cf. the believers in Judea in 2:14). Moreover, they are for Paul evidence of God's election (1:6; cf. Rom. 8:33–39) and kingdom (cf. 2 Thess. 1:4–10), a sign that believers really are on God's side.[16] Paul's

---

13. *Sainesthai*, a rare word (only here in the Greek Bible), whose meaning is much debated; in this context it is synonymous with *saleuthenai*, "be shaken," in 2 Thess. 2:2, and here stands as the approximate antonym to "strengthen" or "firmly establish" in 1 Thess. 3:2 (cf. C. A. Wanamaker, *Thessalonians*, 129–30).

14. The Greek word is *thlipsis*, a noun that the NIV variously renders as "trials" (3:3; 2 Thess. 1:4), "persecution" (1 Thess. 3:7), "suffering" (1:6), or "trouble" (2 Thess. 1:6).

15. NIV "would be persecuted," translating *thlibesthai*, a verbal form of the noun *thlipsis*.

16. See further S. J. Hafemann, "Suffering," *DPL*, 919–21; C. G. Kruse, "Afflictions, Trials, Hardships," *DPL*, 18–20; C. A. Wanamaker, *Thessalonians*, 130–31; I. H. Marshall, *1 and 2 Thessalonians*, 92.

point is clear: Properly understood, the experience of "trials" should strengthen, not weaken, one's commitment to Jesus.

But Paul was, apparently, not convinced that the Thessalonians did properly understand how they should view their difficulties, for in 3:5 (which repeats much of the substance of vv. 1–2 and builds on the point made in vv. 3–4), Paul finally indicates the root cause for his concern. It was his fear that the Thessalonian community may have succumbed to the persecution and social pressures they were experiencing—which Paul here characterizes as the means by which Satan ("the tempter") tempted them—and were abandoning their commitment to God, which the missionaries had so recently persuaded them to make. It was the absence of news one way or the other that Paul finally could no longer stand, and which prompted the sending of Timothy to investigate. The charge to Timothy mentioned in 3:2 indicates that Paul hoped for the best, but 3:5 reveals that he feared the worst, which would mean that all the time, love, energy, and money the missionaries had invested in Thessalonica would have been for nothing.[17]

Apostolic Relief and Joy: Timothy Returns with Good News (3:6–8)

ALMOST AUDIBLE IN 3:6 is the sense of relief that Paul felt when Timothy returned with the welcome news that the Thessalonians had indeed successfully resisted Satan's temptations. Whereas Timothy had been sent to inquire about their "faith," he reported back about their "faith and love." This suggests that he not only found them persevering in their confidence in God (which would have been severely tested by the afflictions they experienced), but also maintaining a proper standard of Christian conduct (i.e., love[18]) toward those around them (cf. 1:6–7; 4:9) —no doubt something hard to do under the circumstances. But to Paul, it was evidence of the work of the Spirit (Rom. 5:5; Gal. 5:22) and of the reality of faith (1 Thess. 1:5–6; cf. Gal. 5:6: "For in Christ Jesus . . . the only thing that counts is faith expressing itself through love").

---

17. For the idea of useless efforts (or laboring in vain), cf. Gal. 4:11; Phil. 2:16; and for the Old Testament background see Isa. 49:4; 65:23.

18. See R. Mohrlang, "Love," *DPL*, 575–78; for example, "For Paul, loving others is the single most important characteristic of the Christian life and the heart of Christian living" (576).

Moreover, Timothy also reported the Thessalonians had positive memories of Paul and his fellow missionaries and would welcome a return visit (3:6b). "The apostle gives the impression that he was especially pleased to learn the Thessalonians had a 'kind or affectionate remembrance' . . . of him and his colleagues. This perhaps implies that he was concerned about how the Thessalonians viewed him after his departure."[19] Evidently they understood why Paul left so suddenly under such suspicious circumstances and did not hold it against him.

In 3:7 Paul indicates an immediate consequence of this good news from Thessalonica. In the midst of their own "distress and persecution" (*ananke kai thlepsei*; cf. 2 Cor. 6:4),[20] Paul and his companions were encouraged by[21] the Thessalonians. In short, the encouraged (cf. 3:2) became the encouragers (cf. 2 Cor. 7:4, 13; Philem. 7). For the significance of *adelphoi*, which includes the entire community, not just the (male) "brothers," see comment on 1:4.

Verse 8a, "now we really live," reinforces Paul's sense of relief (v. 6) and encouragement (v. 7). First Thessalonians 2:19–20 provides the context for understanding "live" here: It is not just a matter of a "removal of anxiety,"[22] but of rejoicing in the Thessalonians' continued faithfulness in a way that energizes Paul and his companions.[23]

In verse 8b, the NIV ("since you are standing firm") hides what is really a conditional statement, "if you continue to stand firm" (NRSV). It functions both as an affirmation—it clearly acknowledges that they are currently "standing firm" (for this idiom, see Phil. 4:1; cf. 1 Cor. 16:13; Gal. 5:1; Phil. 1:27)—and as an implicit exhortation ("*if* you con-

---

19. C. A. Wanamaker, *Thessalonians*, 134.

20. The two words form a generic expression encompassing apostolic difficulties and afflictions of all sorts (cf. E. J. Richard, *Thessalonians*, 160; C. A. Wanamaker, *Thessalonians*, 135). Recall that Paul recently had what may have been a disheartening experience in Athens (Acts 17:16–34) and was now working in Corinth in what were, according to what he later wrote (1 Cor. 2:2; cf. Acts 18:6–17), difficult circumstances.

21. As Best notes (*Thessalonians*, 141), the preposition *epi* "after a verb of feeling often has a causal sense;" cf. BDF, §235.2; I. H. Marshall, *1 and 2 Thessalonians*, 95; J. E. Frame, *Thessalonians*, 133; C. A. Wanamaker, *Thessalonians*, 135; differently ("about you") E. J. Richard, *Thessalonians*, 160; F. F. Bruce, *1 and 2 Thessalonians*, 67.

22. E. J. Richard, *Thessalonians*, 155; cf. F. F. Bruce, *1 and 2 Thessalonians*, 67 ("they could now breathe freely").

23. Cf. C. A. Wanamaker, *Thessalonians*, 136; see further (but not always persuasively) E. Best, *Thessalonians*, 142; I. H. Marshall, *1 and 2 Thessalonians*, 95–96.

tinue").[24] If there is any difference between "in Christ (Jesus)" (cf. 2:14) and "in the Lord," it may be that the former "is associated with the *fait accompli* of God's saving *work*," the latter "with its implementation and its working out in human conduct."[25] Finally, it is worth noting how 3:8, like 2:19–20, reveals the extent to which Paul bases his own sense of well-being on the continuing faithfulness of his converts.[26]

IN THE PREVIOUS section, we began by noting that this passage resumes and carries forward Paul's discussion of his attitudes and behavior toward the Thessalonians, both while in Thessalonica (2:1–12) and since being forced to leave town unexpectedly (2:17–3:8). A major theme of this section, Paul's continuing love of and commitment to the Thessalonians, was covered in the treatment of 2:1–12 and need not be discussed again here.

Another major theme, however, that does call for discussion here is the subject of "trials" (3:3) or "persecution" (3:4, 7). Almost from the time Paul arrived in Thessalonica, the believers had experienced "trials" as a result of their conversion to Christianity. Indeed, Paul took it for granted (to the extent that he prophesied ahead of time, 3:4) that they would experience affliction to one degree or another, simply as a result of declaring their allegiance to Christ. The conviction that "trials" are an expected consequence of following Jesus is found not only in Paul (Rom. 8:17; Phil. 1:29–30) but throughout the New Testament, both in the teaching of Jesus (Matt. 5:11–12, 44; 10:17–23; 23:34; 24:9–10) and of the apostles (Acts 9:16; 1 Peter 1:6; 3:13–17; Rev. 2:10).

The "trials" (3:3; 2 Thess. 1:4), "persecution" (1 Thess. 3:7), "suffering" (1:6), or "trouble" (2 Thess. 1:6)—the NIV uses these words to translate the same Greek word, *thlipsis*—that the Thessalonians were experiencing were a consequence of maintaining their allegiance to Christ and to the values he represented in the midst of a pagan culture that held to a different set of values. As we noted in our comments on

---

24. Cf. C. A. Wanamaker, *Thessalonians*, 136, following W. Grundmann, "στήκω," *TDNT* 7:637.

25. C. F. D. Moule, *The Origin of Christology* (Cambridge: Cambridge Univ. Press, 1977), 59; cf. 58–62.

26. Cf. C. A. Wanamaker, *Thessalonians*, 136; I. H. Marshall, *1 and 2 Thessalonians*, 96.

1:6, by "trials" Paul means the social and religious dislocation, conflict, persecution, ostracization, and pressure (informal as well as formal or official) experienced by new converts as a result of their conversion to a new and socially suspect religion.[27]

The refusal of the Thessalonian believers to participate in "normal" social and cultic activities and the exclusivity of their claim to worship the "living and true God" (1:9) would have left non-Christian friends feeling offended, resentful, or betrayed. Family members, meanwhile, would have viewed a refusal to maintain ancestral traditions as evidence of an appalling lack of concern for family responsibilities. Moreover, since civic peace, agricultural success, and freedom from natural catastrophe were thought to lie in the hands of the traditional gods, it was considered dangerous to ignore or offend them.[28] It is not difficult to imagine how conversion to Christianity in such circumstances would routinely result in "trials," that is, conflict, persecution, ostracism, and social pressure.[29]

Paul simply assumed that such "trials" or affliction for the sake of Jesus and the gospel would be part of the common experience of Christians (cf. 2 Tim. 3:12, "In fact, everyone who wants to live a godly life in Christ Jesus will be persecuted."). Can or does this expectation still hold today? In my opinion, the answer is yes, to the extent that the values of the gospel by which one lives run counter to the values of one's surrounding culture. If we find ourselves living for the gospel as a minority in a culture whose controlling values are antithetical to those of the gospel, then our circumstances will closely parallel those of the Thessalonians, and we should expect to experience the same types of

---

27. In other words, I distinguish "trials" or "suffering" that result from opposition and hostility from "suffering" or "trials" that are due to God's discipline of believers. For a thoughtful and sensitive discussion of this latter topic, see D. A. Carson, *How Long, O Lord? Reflections on Suffering and Evil* (Grand Rapids: Baker, 1990), 70–81.

28. Though he wrote over a century later, the comments and observations of Celsus reveal how a conservative, well-educated upper class Roman could view the adherents of this "new superstition" (i.e., Christianity), with its nonsense about an unseen God and a crucified Savior, as a serious threat to the good order and well-being of the Roman empire. See Celsus, *The True Word*, as quoted by Origen, *Contra Celsum*.

29. Did persecution ever result in martyrdom? It has been suggested that the Thessalonians' concern about the fate of those who died before Jesus returned (4:13–18) was a reaction to the death because of persecution of one or more of the members of the congregation. But there is no evidence to indicate that any of the Thessalonians shared the fate of Stephen (Acts 7:54–60), and the suggestion remains an unproven hypothesis.

afflictions as they did. If, however, we find ourselves living as part of a cultural majority in a society whose values match closely those of the gospel, our circumstances will be quite different from those of Paul and the Thessalonians, and there would be little reason to expect the same kind of social ostracism that they experienced.

The application of Paul's words about trials or persecution to Christians living in circumstances quite different from those of the first century—such as the Western democracies (the United States in particular), where Christianity still enjoys a certain measure of freedom, protection, and occasionally even respect—is a complex matter. How one goes about it depends a great deal on how, or on what level, one analyzes or evaluates the contemporary social situation. For example, from a purely statistical standpoint, Christians (broadly defined) comprise a dominant majority in the United States and to some extent need to be at least as concerned about being the persecutor (with respect to their treatment of Jews, Muslims, or other minorities[30]) rather than the persecuted. For another thing, part of what some Christians view as "persecution" is more likely a matter of the "give and take" of politics in a participatory democracy, while yet more is self-inflicted, often as a result of our own shortsightedness or stupidity. Moreover, one can argue that Christians in the United States are in greater danger of being *seduced* by non-Christian cultural values than of being persecuted by them.

Nevertheless, the simple statistic that Christians (broadly defined) comprise a cultural majority is misleading, for several reasons. For one thing, those who call themselves "born again" Christians (a less broad definition that probably gives a truer indication of the actual strength of Christianity in the United States) are reported to be a minority of the population. For another, even though a majority of the population claims to be broadly "Christian," some of our culture's most dominant, influential, and deeply held values are not. Moreover, in certain broadly influential subcultures, such as academia, the news and entertainment industry, or the arts (areas that profoundly affect and shape the culture

---

30. According to an article distributed by the Religion News Service (as reported by the Minneapolis *Star Tribune*, Saturday, June 28, 1997, page B7), for example, a doctor, "a member of the South Carolina state board of education, recently said, 'Screw the Buddhists and kill the Muslims,' in defense of displaying the Ten Commandments in South Carolina's public schools."

as a whole), Christians are clearly in the minority. In addition, there is the matter of regionalism to factor into the equation: In some regions of the country, "born again" Christians are a distinct minority, while in other regions they comprise a majority of the population.

In short, the situation in the United States today is complex, and it is impossible to generalize about how different or similar our circumstances are to those of Paul and the Thessalonians. In some towns and regions, it is entirely possible to go about one's daily or even weekly activities and not have a verbal encounter with anyone who would deny being a Christian (an experience I doubt Paul even dreamed of). At the same time, believers living in a university context or working in certain industries might regularly encounter antagonism or even hostility to Christianity on a regular basis, and would thus find themselves in circumstances roughly similar to those of the first-century believers. The key point to keep in mind when bridging contexts is that Paul has in view "trials" that arise from a conflict of values between the believer(s) and the surrounding culture.

Falling away. For some readers, the language of 3:5 ("I was afraid that in some way the tempter might have tempted you and our efforts might have been useless") and 3:8 ("if you continue to stand firm in the Lord," NRSV) raises a classic theological conundrum: Is it possible for a believer to fall away, that is, lose one's salvation? This is, of course, one of those much-debated points of difference between Calvinists and Arminians. The latter generally argue that it is indeed possible for a believer to fall away or apostatize, while the former argue that a believer who falls away never really believed in the first place.

The answer given to this question is usually shaped as much or more by one's overall theological framework or commitments as it is by the exegesis of any particular passage of Scripture.[31] Nevertheless, to the extent that 3:5, 8 bear on the matter, Paul is genuinely concerned about the fate of his converts: "The danger of their succumb-

---

31. For excellent, exegetically based approaches to this question, see (from the Calvinist perspective) Judith M. Gundry Volf, *Paul and Perseverance: Staying In and Falling Away* (Louisville, Ky.: Westminster/John Knox, 1990), 261–71 (summarized in J. M. Gundry Volf, "Apostasy, Falling Away, Perseverance," *DPL*, 39–45), and the response to Gundry Volf (from an Arminian perspective) by I. Howard Marshall, "Election and Calling to Salvation in 1 and 2 Thessalonians," in *The Thessalonian Correspondence*, ed. Raymond F. Collins (Leuven: Leuven Univ. Press, 1990), 261–62. See also I. H. Marshall, *Kept by the Power of God: A Study of Perseverance and Falling Away* (Minneapolis: Bethany, 1975).

ing to Satan was real, even though they had faith and even though he prayed for them."[32] What Gordon Fee says about the related passage in Philippians 2:16 is relevant here as well:

The question as to whether [Paul's labor] could really be in vain, of course, is much debated. . . . The answer seems to be twofold. On the one hand, such an expression as this only makes sense if such a potential really exists; on the other hand, Paul has such confidence in God regarding his converts that it would be unthinkable to him that the potential would ever be realized.[33]

Satan. In discussing the meaning of 2:18 above, I briefly sketched what Paul says in his letters about *Satan*, a term that designates for him not just personified evil, but an evil personal being. Yet "the critical question facing modern readers of the Bible is whether such a belief is credible and meaningful today. Can we still endorse with integrity belief in the existence of a personal devil and other evil spirits?"[34] To raise this question is to raise the matter of worldviews; indeed, the very form of the question betrays the influence of a particular worldview. A Western worldview shaped by Enlightenment views of science and nature is notoriously unsympathetic to the idea of spiritual beings. But such a naturalistic view of the universe (shaped by a mechanistic cause-and-effect understanding of reality) that disallows any place for spiritual beings also disallows any place for God.

To pursue this matter is beyond the scope of our discussion; my objective here is simply to point out the level at which the discussion must be conducted.[35] In this respect, the observations of N. T. Wright

---

32. I. Howard Marshall, "Election and Calling to Salvation in 1 and 2 Thessalonians," 262; cf. James D. G. Dunn: "*Apostasy* remains a real possibility for the Pauline believer for the duration of the eschatological tension" (*The Theology of Paul the Apostle* [Grand Rapids: Eerdmans, 1998], 497).

33. G. D. Fee, *Philippians* (NICNT; Grand Rapids: Eerdmans, 1995), 250.

34. Sidney H. T. Page, *Powers of Evil: A Biblical Study of Satan and Demons* (Grand Rapids: Baker, 1995), 267.

35. For good introductory discussions of worldview questions, see James W. Sire, *Chris Chrisman Goes to College—and Faces the Challenges of Relativism, Individualism, and Pluralism* (Downers Grove, Ill.: InterVarsity, 1993); Brian J. Walsh and J. Richard Middleton, *The Transforming Vision: Shaping a Christian World View* (Downers Grove, Ill.: InterVarsity, 1984). For a more technical discussion of worldviews with specific reference to biblical studies, see N. T. Wright, *The New Testament and the People of God* (Christian Origins and the Question of God, vol. 1; Minneapolis: Fortress, 1992), 31–144; for a cross-cultural perspective see Charles

regarding Jesus' own understanding of his ministry as involving a struggle against "the accuser" are appropriate. With regard to the accounts of his temptation (Matt. 4:1–11) and the Beelzebub controversy (Luke 11:14–23), he writes:

> How the twentieth century may choose to analyze, psychologize, explain, reduce, or otherwise translate such accounts is no great matter. It may be that, if the mainstream post-Enlightment worldview is correct, all such language must be seen as evidence of religious neurosis. One might equally well, however, wish to suggest that anyone who conceives of themselves as having a vocation—a common enough human experience— might undergo inner struggles which in many cultures would be most readily described in terms of a battle with a hostile power. What we cannot do, in the twentieth or any other century, is to deny that such self-perceptions did, and still do, characterize people of the sort, broadly speaking, that we are discovering Jesus to have been. It should be no surprise to find a description, however stylized and schematized, of such a battle. It might actually be surprising if we did not.[36]

What Wright says about Jesus is no less relevant to Paul, who more than once discerned in the opposition to and hindrance of his ministry the working of Satan.

AS I MENTIONED at the beginning of the Bridging Contexts section, one of the two major themes running through this section of the letter (Paul's continuing love of and commitment to the Thessalonians) is covered in the discussion of 2:1– 12 above. Thus I will concentrate on the other major theme of this section, "trials" or "persecution." As we do so, it will be important to keep in mind that Paul has in view in this passage not suffering as a means

H. Kraft, *Christianity with Power: Your Worldview and Your Experience of the Supernatural* (Ann Arbor, Mich.: Vine, 1989).

36. N. T. Wright, *Jesus and the Victory of God* (Christian Origins and the Question of God, vol. 2; Minneapolis: Fortress, 1996), 457–58.

of godly discipline, but opposition or persecution arising from a conflict of beliefs, values, and conduct between the believer(s) and the surrounding culture.

Persecution. I am a member of the "boomer" generation, who came of age during the turbulent 60s. I have witnessed firsthand the transformation of the United States from a society in which nearly all citizens, Christian or otherwise, embraced values and ethical norms based on the Judeo-Christian moral tradition, into a society in which traditional Christian ethical teachings and values are increasingly not only ignored, but explicitly rejected by a steadily growing (as well as influential and powerful) percentage of society. As American society continues this transition from a Christian to a post-Christian culture, those who seek to live in accordance with the gospel of Jesus Christ can expect to encounter the kind of trials or persecution experienced by Paul and the Thessalonians, if only because the culture at large is less and less Christian. If we are serious about obeying the teachings of Jesus and the words of the apostles, we can expect to find ourselves experiencing opposition, hostility, exclusion, loss, and so forth—what Paul labels "trials"—simply because we are believers.

What form might these "trials" take? The following list is merely suggestive of what a believer might experience:

- an honest employee is fired for disrupting a company's plans to scam consumers or for blowing the whistle on corruption and fraud;
- a law enforcement officer is ostracized and pushed out of line for a promotion by her fellow officers because she refuses to lie in order to cover up misconduct by another officer;
- a college student, the only Christian in her family, is excluded from family activities because after her graduation, she (at least from their perspective) disappoints and embarrasses her family by joining a missions organization working in the inner city rather than taking a "good job";
- high school students experience hostility in taking a stand in an environment where social status and standing is heavily dependent on the extent to which one uses alcohol and/or drugs or is sexually active;

- families who refuse to buy into the consumer mentality of our culture, and thereby implicitly challenge those who do, are rejected by neighbors and friends;
- persons or groups who insist that as a society we do what is right and just, rather than what is merely legal or profitable, experience hostility;
- a teacher who refuses parents who demand that their child be given a grade higher than that earned by the student's work receives harsh criticism;
- a person whose consistent pro-life ethic includes opposition not only to abortion but to the death penalty as well finds himself or herself as a "persecuted minority."

Regardless of what we may experience in countries where Christianity enjoys a certain measure of freedom, protection, and even occasionally respect, the circumstances are vastly different in many other countries. There are substantial numbers of Christians in the world today who find themselves in a situation—that of a persecuted minority facing opposition or attack by a socially dominant group—unambiguously comparable to that of the Thessalonians. These sisters and brothers know all too well the reality of "trials" experienced for the sake of the gospel. In countries such as Laos, Saudi Arabia, Iraq, Sudan, Pakistan, Indonesia, and China (to mention only some), it is dangerous if not illegal to practice Christianity, and afflictions similar to those experienced by Paul and the Thessalonians—including church burnings or closings, harassment, fines, arrest, and/or imprisonment—are a constant and present reality.[37]

Indeed, in more than a few cases it is a matter not only of persecution but also martyrdom. Those who keep track of such matters report that more Christians may have died for their faith in the twentieth century than in the previous nineteen centuries combined.[38] Forced to deny Christ in order to live, they chose to confess Jesus and die,

---

37. See Kim A. Lawton, "The Suffering Church," *CT* 40 (July 15, 1996): 54–64; Paul Marshall with Lela Gilbert, *Their Blood Cries Out: The Untold Story of Persecution Against Christians in the Modern World* (Dallas: Word, 1997).

38. For an account of martyrdom around the globe in the twentieth century, see James and Marti Hefley, *By Their Blood: Christian Martyrs of the Twentieth Century*, 2d ed. (Grand Rapids: Baker, 1996); Nina Shea, *In the Lion's Den: A Shocking Account of Persecution and Martyrdom of Christians Today, and How We Should Respond* (Nashville: Broadman & Holman, 1997).

thereby bearing witness to him as both crucified Messiah and risen Lord and to their hope of the life to come. They bear witness to what Dietrich Bonhoeffer wrote:

> If we refuse to take up our cross and submit to suffering and rejection at the hands of men, we forfeit our fellowship with Christ and have ceased to follow him. But if we lose our lives in his service and carry our cross, we shall find our lives again in the fellowship of the cross with Christ. . . . To bear the cross proves to be the only way of triumphing over suffering. This is true for all who follow Christ, because it was true for him.[39]

For all the persecuted brothers and sisters in Christ wherever they live, we need to emphasize Paul's words of affirmation and encouragement. For Paul, suffering for the sake of Christ and the gospel is evidence of God's love and salvation (1:4–7; 2:13; 2 Thess. 1:5; cf. Rom. 8:17; Phil. 1:28), and is a situation in which God strengthens their faithful endurance and hope (2 Thess. 1:3–4, 11), pouring out his own love and hope:

> We . . . rejoice in our sufferings, because we know that suffering produces perseverance; perseverance, character; and character, hope. And hope does not disappoint us, because God has poured out his love into our hearts by the Holy Spirit, whom he has given us. (Rom. 5:3b–5)

Moreover, it becomes "a witness to others of the truth of Christ, especially as this is seen in their ability to love others even when they are experiencing affliction" (1 Thess. 1:2–7; 2 Thess. 1:3–5).[40] In short, persecution, though not something to be sought,[41] is nonetheless

---

39. Dietrich Bonhoeffer, *The Cost of Discipleship*, rev. ed. (New York: Macmillan, 1963), 101; cf. p. 98: "To endure the cross is not a tragedy; it is the suffering which is the fruit of an exclusive allegiance to Jesus Christ. When it comes, it is not an accident, but a necessity. It is not the sort of suffering which is inseparable from this mortal life, but the suffering which is an essential part of the specifically Christian life. It is not suffering *per se* but suffering-and-rejection, and not rejection for any cause or conviction of our own, but rejection for the sake of Christ."

40. S. J. Hafemann, "Suffering," *DPL*, 920.

41. Persecution is sometimes seen (or even romanticized) as something "good" for the church, in that it is said to purify, unify, strengthen, and grow the church (see, e.g., David H. Adeney, "The Church and Persecution," in *The Church in the Bible and the World*, ed. D. A.

something worth enduring for Christ's sake and the gospel's when it does come.

In 3:2 Paul touches briefly on an important element involved in enduring trials: strengthening and encouraging one another in the midst of them. He touches on this topic only briefly here because in effect the entire letter is intended to strengthen and encourage the Thessalonians. One way he sought to do this was by creating within their community a sense of a counterculture or alternative community that taught, affirmed, and reinforced the values of the gospel. In a sense, he sought to fight "peer pressure" with peer pressure. Rejected by the culture around them, the Thessalonian believers could find in the church support and refreshment from like-minded fellow believers, who were seeking after similar goals. Here is an important ministry today for churches wherever believers find themselves on the receiving end of hostility and opposition because of their faithfulness to Jesus.

Those of us who are by our circumstances insulated from the kind of persecution experienced by our brothers and sisters in Christ "need to be aware of the needs of our suffering brothers and sisters, pray that God will supply them with an unusual abundance of the Spirit of Jesus Christ, and learn from their single-minded devotion to the gospel, in life and in death, how we should live in the service of the gospel in our own time and place."[42] In addition to supporting them in prayer, we should think about other ways, both public and private, that we might use to support and encourage them (for specific suggestions, see the Contemporary Significance section of 2 Thess. 1:1–12)

Finally, we might ask ourselves why we are not experiencing the "trials" that Paul assumes here will be the experience of believers. Three possible reasons spring to mind: (1) We have isolated ourselves in a Christian subculture (dare I say "ghetto"?) of some sort; (2) we are the beneficiaries of fortunate circumstances; or (3) we are not really serious about our commitment to the gospel and its values. Whatever the reason(s), it ought to become a matter of prayer and reflection, so that

---

Carson [Grand Rapids: Baker, 1987], 275–302, who lists only "positive" effects of persecution). But sometimes sustained social and political repression results not in the growth of the church, but rather its disappearance from a geographical area. For a sober assessment and theological analysis of such circumstances, see Mark Galli, "Is Persecution Good for the Church?" *CT* 41 (May 19, 1997): 16–19.

42. Frank Thielman, *Philippians* (NIVAC; Grand Rapids: Zondervan, 1995), 89.

we might be ready when the time comes for the integrity of our own confession of Christ to be put to the test. What will we value more at that time: social acceptance and affirmation, or faithfulness to the gospel, whatever that may cost?

Satan. In thinking about the contemporary relevance of Paul's understanding of Satan, we must avoid two pitfalls. (1) We must avoid ignoring or overlooking the activity of Satan. This applies as much to evil on a societal level as it does a personal level. As the title of Reinhold Niebuhr's famous book *Moral Man and Immoral Society* suggests, it is possible for any human organization, institution, or social structure, even though composed of moral individuals, to become an instrument of sin and oppression.[43] But awareness that Satan may ultimately stand behind manifestations of evil "provides a powerful incentive for combating it"; "the person who discerns a satanic dimension in the evils in the world can hardly rest content with the status quo." Moreover, "the Christian who takes the demonological teaching of the Bible seriously can confront temptation and evil with confidence, knowing that Christ has already defeated the forces of evil and their ultimate doom is assured."[44]

(2) The other pitfall to avoid—and in view of some of the contemporary excesses evident in popular books and magazines, perhaps the greater threat—is that of paying too much attention to the topic of Satan and the demonic. God is the focus of Scripture, and paying too much attention to his defeated opponent runs several risks.[45] "First is the danger of breeding fear and paranoia by exaggerating the power of the devil." "Secondly, there is the danger of appealing to Satan . . . to excuse one's failings."

In this respect it is important to notice what Paul does *not* say about Satan. He discusses, for example, the position of human beings before God, salvation, judgment, and the nature of sin without ever making reference to Satan. "In other words Paul does not offer a systematic understanding of Satan or even a clearly developed doctrine of Satan in which Satan is used to explain either death or sin."[46] That is, nothing

---

43. Reinhold Niebuhr, *Moral Man and Immoral Society: A Study in Ethics and Politics* (New York and London: Scribner's, 1932).
44. S. H. T. Page, *Powers of Evil*, 269.
45. I owe the following points to ibid., 269–70.
46. C. A. Wanamaker, *Thessalonians*, 122.

Paul says about Satan in any way diminishes his understanding of human responsibility for sin and evil. The familiar phrase, "the devil made me do it," is not part of Paul's theology.

The third and fourth points of S. H. T. Page are closely associated: the danger of unthinkingly accepting superstitious or non-Christian practices and beliefs, and

> the danger of unrestrained speculation. The Bible is remarkably free of conjecture regarding the unseen realm. As a consequence, there are many questions it simply does not answer. Unfortunately, many seem to find it difficult to accept the silences of Scripture and speculate about matters concerning which there is no biblical teaching, even when features of the biblical texts discourage such speculation. Speculation about the names and ranks of evil spirits and the realms over which they rule is not only without biblical foundation, it is foreign to the spirit of the Bible.[47]

In short, what is needed when dealing with this topic is balance, neither denying Satan's reality nor paying undue attention to his activities. He is, after all, a defeated power, against whom Paul calls us to "put on the full armor of God so that you can take your stand against the devil's schemes" (Eph. 6:11).[48]

---

47. S. H. T. Page, *Powers of Evil*, 270.

48. See further on the issues raised in the preceding paragraphs the excellent extended discussion by Klyne Snodgrass, *Ephesians* (NIVAC; Grand Rapids: Zondervan, 1996), 347–61, also 109–10.

1 Thessalonians 3:9–13

HOW CAN WE thank God enough for you in return for all the joy we have in the presence of our God because of you? ¹⁰Night and day we pray most earnestly that we may see you again and supply what is lacking in your faith. ¹¹Now may our God and Father himself and our Lord Jesus clear the way for us to come to you. ¹²May the Lord make your love increase and overflow for each other and for everyone else, just as ours does for you. ¹³May he strengthen your hearts so that you will be blameless and holy in the presence of our God and Father when our Lord Jesus comes with all his holy ones.

Original Meaning

THERE IS CLEARLY a substantial connection between these verses and those that precede them. The single sentence comprising 3:9–10 is closely joined with 3:8 by the conjunction *gar* ("for," omitted by NIV, NRSV), and 3:11–13 form a "benediction" that draws to a close the entire first part of the letter (1:2–3:13). Nevertheless, I have chosen to treat these verses separately and as a single paragraph (as does the NAB), largely for pragmatic reasons: (1) because of the important transitional role they play in the overall structure of the letter, and (2) because of the way the theme of prayer draws them together.[1]

Verse 9 draws to a close, in the form of a rhetorical question, the theme of thanksgiving inaugurated in 1:2–10 and continued in 2:13. This thanksgiving has been rooted in events in the recent past and present. In 3:10, however, Paul's prayer looks to the future, signaling a turning point in the letter. Similarly, the benediction in 3:11–13

---

1. While most translations (including the NIV) and commentators take 3:6–10 and 3:11–13 as paragraphs, 3:9–13 are treated as a unit by E. J. Richard, *Thessalonians*, 163–78; Peter T. O'Brien, *Introductory Thanksgivings in the Letters of Paul* (Leiden: Brill, 1977), 156–64; Gordon P. Wiles, *Paul's Intercessory Prayers* (Cambridge: Cambridge Univ. Press, 1974), 52, 59, 64.

both draws together key points in 1:2–3:8 and anticipates the concrete exhortations to follow. Specifically, Paul reiterates (1) his desire to visit Thessalonica (3:11; cf. 2:17–18; 3:6, 10); (2) his hope that their love (which in 3:6 designated a proper standard of Christian conduct; cf. 2:12, "lives worthy of God") will "increase and overflow" (3:12; cf. 1:3; 3:6); and (3) his concern that they persevere until Christ returns (3:13; cf. 1:10; 3:1–5, 8; also 2:19).[2]

But these last two points do not merely summarize what Paul has said to this point in the letter; they also foreshadow the major themes of the following section: proper Christian ethical conduct or holiness (4:1–12; 5:12–22), and the return of Christ (4:13–5:11). Thus 3:11–13 reinforce the transition noted in 3:9–10 and confirm the significance of this section as an important transition in the letter.

Thanksgiving for the Thessalonians (3:9)

THE VERB IN 3:9 (*antapodidomi*), which echoes Psalm 116:12, suggests the translation "what *sufficient* thanks" (Lightfoot; NIV, "thank God *enough*"). The idea is not the inadequacy of Paul's thanks, but the surpassing magnitude of the joy he experiences as a result of God's gracious work in the Thessalonians (cf. 3:7). That this rejoicing is "in the presence of our God" implies that it is happening in the context of prayer.

Prayer for the Thessalonians (3:10–13)

IN 3:10 (IN Greek a direct continuation of 3:9), Paul moves from thanksgiving to a twofold petition: that he might be able (1) to visit the Thessalonians in person (cf. 2:17; 3:7; the request underlines the genuineness and intensity of his desire to see them again), and (2) to "supply what is lacking in [their] faith." In view of Timothy's enthusiastic report (cf. 3:6), "what is lacking" likely designates "things still needed" rather than some kind of spiritual or ethical defect. These "things needed" would include additional instruction on specific points of doctrine and conduct—things they lacked through no fault of their own, but because Paul had been forced to terminate his initial visit prematurely. While Timothy had probably communicated some of the needed instruction, Paul clearly wished to complete the job in per-

---

2. The preceding sentence follows closely C. A. Wanamaker, *Thessalonians*, 140.

son. In the meantime, however, the letter would have to serve as a substitute, and the contents of 4:1–5:22 reveal at least some of the topics he wished to address.

Before turning to those specific issues, however, Paul concludes the first section of the letter with a brief benediction (3:11–13). The form of the prayer reflects a combination of traditional Jewish and specifically Christian elements. For the address ("our God and Father himself and our Lord Jesus," cf. 5:23; 2 Thess. 2:16; 3:16) compare Sirach 23:4, "O, Lord, Father and God of my life" (cf. Sir. 23:1); terms there applied to God (that is, "Lord" and "Father") are here distributed between God and Jesus.[3]

The content of the first petition (3:11) repeats the substance of part of verse 10. The second petition (3:12) both affirms the accomplishments of the Thessalonians (as reported by Timothy, cf. 3:6) and implicitly encourages them to "increase and overflow"[4] in "love," a word that, as was pointed out in the discussion of 3:6 above, encompasses for Paul the full extent of proper Christian behavior. Note that his prayer has in view love not only for those inside the community ("each other"), but those outside as well ("everyone else"). How the Christian community in Thessalonica related to outsiders is to Paul no less important than how they related to each other (cf. Phil. 2:15). With the phrase "as ours does for you," Paul again (cf. 2:1–12) offers himself and his companions as a model for the Thessalonians to follow.

The punctuation of 3:13 as a separate sentence in the NIV and NRSV obscures the fact that this verse, rather than being an additional petition, indicates the goal or purpose of the petition in 3:12 (*eis to* + infinitive, the same phrase as was used in 3:2): "so as to firmly establish your hearts" (cf. NAB, NASB). That is, Paul prays that the Lord will cause the love of the Thessalonians to increase so that "at the coming of our Lord

---

3. With respect to the relationship between God and Jesus in 3:11 (where the plural subject precedes a singular verb), the grammar (the definite article is repeated in Greek, as is the possessive pronoun, "our") distinguishes between the two, who nevertheless act in such concert that it is clear that Paul sees (but here does not discuss or develop) the closest connection between them (see further L. Morris, *The First and Second Epistles to the Thessalonians*, 1078; I. H. Marshall, *1 and 2 Thessalonians*, 100). The claim that "this does not imply Paul held a Trinitarian or Binitarian theology" (E. Best, *Thessalonians*, 147) is a serious understatement.

4. Cf. the observation by John Chrysostom: "Do you see the unrestrained madness of love which is indicated by the words? He says 'increase' and 'overflow' instead of 'grow'" (adapted from J. E. Frame, *Thessalonians*, 138).

Jesus"⁵ (NRSV; cf. on 4:13 below), when they find themselves "in the presence of our God" ("who tests our hearts," 2:4), they may be "blameless in holiness" (lit. trans., cf. 5:23), that is, fully acceptable to God.

The first word (*amemptous*; cf. 2:10) indicates "a condition of blamelessness in which an individual is found to have done nothing deserving condemnation by God." The second word (*hagiosyne*) indicates "moral conformity to the very character of God" (cf. Lev. 19:2; Matt. 5:48).⁶ In short, Paul closely links together both the behavioral and the cognitive aspects of faith. The use of *hagiosyne*, "holiness," which indicates a state or condition—as opposed to *hagiasmos*, "sanctification" (cf. 4:2), which indicates a process leading to the state of holiness— is particularly appropriate here, inasmuch as Paul has in view not a present accomplishment but an eschatological outcome, toward which he will (in 4:1–3; cf. 5:1–11) call the Thessalonians to strive.

Bridging Contexts

IN THIS PASSAGE we find the first of two intercessory prayers in the letter (the other is 5:23; 1:2–3 was a report *about* prayer). Obviously Paul is praying for the specific needs and concerns of a unique congregation dealing with specific problems. Because the prayer is so thoroughly rooted in its particular historical circumstances, it is not possible for us simply to repeat after him the words of his prayer (in contrast to, e.g., the Lord's Prayer, which was given as a model prayer, or the prayer in Eph. 3:16–21).⁷ What we can do is give attention to the pattern of his prayer and its underlying theological assumptions and allow these to shape our own prayers. This does not mean that Paul's prayer is a rigid mold into which ours must be poured, for our prayers must be as situated in and specific to our time

---

5. The "holy ones" who accompany Jesus could be angels (E. Best, *Thessalonians*, 153; I. H. Marshall, *1 and 2 Thessalonians*, 102–3; C. A. Wanamaker, *Thessalonians*, 145; E. J. Richard, *Thessalonians*, 177), "saints" (NRSV, NASB), that is, human beings, or, more likely, both (J. B. Lightfoot, *Notes on Epistles*, 50; L. Morris, *The First and Second Epistles to the Thessalonians*, 112; cf. F. F. Bruce, *1 & 2 Thessalonians*, 74).

6. C. A. Wanamaker, *Thessalonians*, 144; see further S. E. Porter, "Holiness, Sanctification," *DPL*, 397–402; D. Guthrie and R. P. Martin, "God," *DPL*, 363.

7. On the Lord's Prayer see Darrell L. Bock, *Luke* (NIVAC; Grand Rapids: Zondervan, 1996), 307–15; on the prayer in Ephesians see Klyne Snodgrass, *Ephesians* (NIVAC; Grand Rapids: Zondervan, 1996), 183.

just as Paul's were to his. It does mean that his prayer can serve as a guide after which to pattern our prayer life.

Theology. With respect to its underlying theology, Paul's prayer reminds us of the *theo*centric character of his understanding of reality. Every time Paul prayed to God, it was an acknowledgment of God's priority over everything else, a remembering that it is "in him we live and move and have our being" (Acts 17:28). In this respect, prayer becomes a means of bringing our vision and desires into line with God's will (rather than vice versa).

This is so even in the case of intercessory prayer and petitionary prayer, in which we ask God to grant our requests for others and ourselves; the very act of asking "reminds the believer that God is the source of all good, and that human beings are utterly dependent and stand in need of everything."[8] Paul's letters are full of his fervent intercessions and petitions for others and for himself. But even as he makes his requests known to God, he recognizes that it is God who is at work in him "to will and to act according to his good purpose" (Phil. 2:13). Thus, for example, in the case of his "thorn in the flesh" (2 Cor. 12:7–10), Paul prayed fervently that it might be removed, but in the end he accepted God's decision that it would remain, for the sake of Christ and as evidence of his power and grace.

Pattern. With respect to the pattern of Paul's prayer, two points stand out, one related to content and one to chronology. (1) In terms of *content*, note that Paul grounds his petitions in thanksgiving, which amounts to both praise and acknowledgment of God as the one ultimately responsible for the blessings and growth the Thessalonians have experienced. Moreover, there is an interesting contrast in his actual petitions. His requests for the Thessalonians (3:12–13) are that they might experience spiritual growth, while those for himself (3:10–11) are that he might be able to minister to them. That is, his prayer, like his behavior described in 2:1–3:5, is primarily other-directed. That is not to say that Paul never prayed for his own concerns, for we know that he did (e.g., 2 Cor. 12:7–10). It is, however, striking that in this letter, even in his prayers for himself, he models the concern for others that he will encourage the Thessalonians to practice (4:9–12).

---

8. Stanley J. Grenz, *Prayer: The Cry for the Kingdom* (Peabody, Mass.: Hendrickson, 1988), 37.

(2) In terms of *chronology*, we find the same "past-present-future" pattern that turns up elsewhere in the letter (e.g., 1:4–10; 4:13–18; 5:8–11). That is, Paul rejoices and gives thanks for what God has done in the past (3:9); he prays for God to continue to act in the present (3:10–13a); and he prays for the present in light of what God will do in the future (3:13b). Once again he reminds us that the present is profoundly shaped by what God has done and will do.

Two other matters. Before leaving this section, two further matters call for comment. (1) The theocentric emphasis of Paul's prayer reminds us of the proper context in which to consider *the tension between divine activity and human responsibility* that runs throughout this letter. The issue arises here if one compares 3:12 ("May the Lord make your love increase and overflow for each other and for everyone else") and 4:10 ("you do love all the brothers throughout Macedonia. Yet we urge you, brothers, to do so more and more"). On the one hand, Paul consistently emphasizes God's grace and initiative (cf. 3:12). On the other hand, Paul never ceases to exhort and command those to whom he writes (cf. 4:10), even to the point of piling imperative upon imperative (see, e.g., 5:12–22, with its seventeen commands, or for an extreme instance, Rom. 12:9–21).

Texts like 1 Thessalonians 3:12 and 2 Thessalonians 1:11, however, remind us that the "Pauline emphasis lies with God's prior action. . . . For Paul the presupposition behind all such imperatives is the work of the Spirit in the life of the believing community."[9] At the same time, "*moral effort is in no way antithetical to faith;* it is rather the outworking and expression of faith." This means that in response to God's gift and initiative, "believers have a *responsibility* . . . to let the power of grace come to expression in their lives."[10] In short, "dependence on God is fully compatible with human exertions. The Christian is not passive but fully cooperates with God for achieving the divine purpose."[11]

(2) Paul's description of God as Father (3:11, 13; cf. 1:1, 3; 2 Thess. 1:1–2; 2:16) raises a potential difficulty in bringing this concept into

---

9. G. D. Fee, *God's Empowering Presence,* 70; cf. I. H. Marshall, *1 and 2 Thessalonians,* 97. See also D. A. Carson, *Divine Sovereignty and Human Responsibility: Biblical Perspectives in Tension* (Atlanta: John Knox, 1981).

10. James D. G. Dunn, *Romans 1–8* (WBC; Dallas: Word, 1988), 350 (author's emphasis).

11. J. Knox Chamblin, *Paul and the Self: Apostolic Teaching for Personal Wholeness* (Grand Rapids: Baker, 1993), 156.

our day. Overall, "no other description of God is used so frequently in the New Testament";[12] Paul alone refers to God as "Father" forty-two times. For Paul this image is fundamentally and overwhelmingly positive, but for some people it is problematic. In my classes, for example, it is increasingly common to encounter students whose image of God, in part if not in whole, has been shaped by an inadequate or even destructive relationship with their fathers.[13] In such circumstances it becomes important to use the image with sensitivity and care, and when possible to define (rather than take for granted) what the New Testament writers mean by the phrase (the teachings of Jesus offer especially rich resources in this regard). In this way the Pauline view of God as a Father who loved us so much that even when we were still sinners, he sent his Son to die for our benefit as a way of expressing his love (cf. Rom. 5:8), can begin to reshape or replace inadequate images with which we may have grown up.

I SUGGESTED ABOVE that Paul's prayer here in 3:9–13 offers a model to follow rather than words to repeat. What is it that Paul models for us? *A prayer centered around thanksgiving for and intercession on behalf of others.* Nor is this an isolated or unusual phenomenon, as at least forty-two instances of thanksgiving or intercession for others can be found in Paul's letters.[14] To be sure, it is not the only theme or emphasis in Paul's prayers, but it is clearly a significant one that takes up a substantial proportion of the space he devotes to prayer.

One application of this observation is obvious. If we are serious about following Paul's model,

we will never overlook the monumental importance of praying *for others.* Prayer will never descend to the level where it is nothing more than a retreat house in which we find strength for ourselves,

---

12. Klyne Snodgrass, *Ephesians* (NIVAC; Grand Rapids: Zondervan, 1996), 179.

13. For an illuminating example of both the problem and the possibility for healing and change, see Keith Anderson, "What You Get is What You See," *What They Don't Always Teach You at a Christian College* (Downers Grove, Ill.: InterVarsity, 1995), 74–78.

14. For the list of passages see D. A. Carson, *A Call to Spiritual Reformation: Priorities from Paul and His Prayers* (Grand Rapids: Baker, 1992), 67–74.

whether through the celebration of praise or through a mystic communion with God or through the relief of casting our cares upon the Almighty. Prayer may embrace all of these elements, and more; but if we learn to pray with Paul, we will learn to pray for others. We will see it is part of our job to approach God with thanksgiving for others and with intercessions for others. In short, our praying will be shaped by our profound desire to seek what is best for the people of God.[15]

How might we go about praying for others? Paul's prayer suggests at least four ways. Though I have framed them as descriptive statements about Paul ("Paul prays . . ."), each is implicitly a challenge to us ("Pray . . .") to do the same.

Paul prays with thanksgiving (3:9). On one level, this is a matter of basic gratitude, of acknowledging God's graciousness towards us. But in giving thanks to God, we are also sharing (indirectly, at least) with others the reality of God's love and concern for us, and thus thanksgiving to God can become a form of testimony about God.

Moreover, thanksgiving involves remembering what God has done (cf. 1:2–3). Remembering and telling the story of God's faithfulness is important for at least two reasons. (1) When things go well, it reminds us why they are going well: it is due to God's grace and goodness, not our own efforts (cf. Deut. 6:10–13; 8:10–18; 9:4–6). (2) When things are not going well, it gives us hope to remember that the God who has been faithful in the past will be faithful in the future. This is the reason why creating a "community of memory" between the generations is so important (cf. Deut. 6:20–25), and thanksgiving is one way to do this.[16]

Giving thanks to God can also have an important effect on those for whom we give thanks. Paul gives thanks to God for the Thessalonians, but he tells them that he is doing it. "Thus he has simultaneously drawn attention to the Thessalonians' spiritual growth, thereby encouraging them, and insisted that God is the one to be thanked for it, thereby humbling them."[17] In short, Paul encourages and affirms them

---

15. Ibid., 74–75.

16. See further on memory Daniel Taylor, *The Myth of Certainty: The Reflective Christian and the Risk of Commitment* (Waco, Tex.: Word, 1986), 100–107.

17. D. A. Carson, *A Call to Spiritual Reformation*, 87, echoing John Calvin, *The Epistles of Paul the Apostle to the Romans and to the Thessalonians*, 333–34.

in a way that doesn't feed their pride or sense of self-importance. For whom should we be doing the same?

Paul prays that the Thessalonians might be strengthened through loving service to others (3:12–13a). As I noted in the discussion of the Original Meaning above, Paul makes only one petition in this section (3:12, "May the Lord make your love increase"), whose goal or purpose is stated in 3:13 ("so as to strengthen your hearts"). Verse 13 indicates Paul's actual request—that the Thessalonians might be strengthened—while verse 12 indicates the means by which he hopes the strengthening will occur (an increase in their love for others). That is, Paul thinks that the best way for the Thessalonians themselves to be strengthened is through an increase in their love for others, both inside and outside the church.

This love is not merely a matter of emotion or feeling; in 1:3 Paul already gave thanks for the Thessalonians' "labor prompted by love." In short, how might the members of this relatively new church with deep needs of its own gain strength in the face of difficulties and challenges? Through serving others in love, Paul implies—which is advice that flies in the face of the narcissism and self-centeredness of much of contemporary culture. It is not uncommon to hear a statement something like, "I need to get my own act together before I can worry about others," or "I need to take care of my own needs before I can deal with the needs of others." For some of us, who perhaps are suffering the consequences of severe emotional trauma in our life, it may indeed be necessary to deal first with our own needs. But for most of us, one of the surest ways to gain some perspective on our own situation is to serve others. There is more than a little truth in the familiar parable about the man who whined about not having shoes until he met a man with no feet.

Paul prays for the Thessalonians in light of the future (3:13c). The reference to the *parousia* of Jesus reminds us that Paul lived the present in light of the future. He knew that Jesus' coming would be a time not only of salvation but also of judgment (cf. 2 Thess. 1:5–10), and that even believers would at some point come before the God "who tests our hearts" (1 Thess. 2:4) to give an account of their stewardship of life (cf. 1 Cor. 3:10–15). Paul lived his life in light of this reality, and he urged the Thessalonians to do the same (e.g., 1 Thess. 5:4–11). Consequently, he made short-term decisions in light of their long-term consequences, knowing that it was of no value to save one's life in this age if that meant losing it in the next (cf. Luke 9:24–26). Here Paul's prayer is shaped by that same perspective. In a contemporary culture that is as overwhelmingly oriented to immediate gratification and results as ours is, to pray that others might live in light of eternity rather than the present is no small thing—especially since praying in this way on behalf of others inevitably reminds us of our need to do the same.

Paul prays out of his own deep and sincere love for others. For Paul, the Thessalonians' success was the source of his own joy (3:9; cf. 2:19–20). Moreover, his own petition for himself was that he might receive another opportunity to minister to them (3:10–11; cf. 2:17–18). Why was he able to invest so much of himself in them? Simply put, because he deeply and genuinely loved them. As he put it in 2:8, "We loved you so much that we were delighted to share with you not only the gospel of God but our lives as well, because you had become so dear to us."

The first three points above offer guidelines for what to do; this final point forces us to examine who we are. If we do not pray for others out of a genuine love for them, why not? Is it because we secretly despise them, hold something against them, are resentful or bitter, or view them as some kind of a threat? Or are we simply too self-centered to care about them? Whatever the reason, it calls us to personal repentance: "And when you stand praying, if you hold anything against anyone, forgive him, so that your Father in heaven may forgive you your sins" (Mark 11:25). And the standard of forgiveness to which we are called is exemplified by God himself: "Be kind and compassionate to one another, forgiving each other, just as in Christ God forgave you" (Eph. 4:32). Serious prayer for others forces us to get serious with ourselves.

1 Thessalonians 4:1–8

❧

INALLY, BROTHERS, WE instructed you how to live in order to please God, as in fact you are living.

Now we ask you and urge you in the Lord Jesus to do this more and more. ²For you know what instructions we gave you by the authority of the Lord Jesus.

³It is God's will that you should be sanctified: that you should avoid sexual immorality; ⁴that each of you should learn to control his own body in a way that is holy and honorable, ⁵not in passionate lust like the heathen, who do not know God; ⁶and that in this matter no one should wrong his brother or take advantage of him. The Lord will punish men for all such sins, as we have already told you and warned you. ⁷For God did not call us to be impure, but to live a holy life. ⁸Therefore, he who rejects this instruction does not reject man but God, who gives you his Holy Spirit.

IN 4:1–5:22, PAUL communicates in writing what he evidently would have preferred to tell the Thessalonians in person, had he been able to travel there at that time. It is notable that he affirms their present behavior and practices (which he instructs them to pursue with renewed vigor, 4:1, 10) rather than demands changes (contrast 1 Cor. 4:14–5:13). The new information he communicates to them involves a matter not of conduct but of belief, that is, details about the coming of the Lord Jesus (4:13–18). Thus Wanamaker (and others) are right to see here an example of *epideictic* or *demonstrative* rhetoric, intended to affirm and praise (in contrast to *deliberative* rhetoric, which was intended to persuade).[1]

From 4:1–2, which serve as a general introduction to what follows, Paul moves immediately into the first topic, holiness (4:3–8), with a specific focus on sexual morality. The next three sections are each

---

1. C. A. Wanamaker, *Thessalonians*, 146, 46–48.

introduced by the phrase *peri (de)*, "now concerning" or "now about"; 4:9–12 (love for others), 4:13–18 ("those who fall asleep"), and 5:1–11 ("times and dates"). A request formula ("Now we ask you") introduces the final section, 5:12–22 (on congregational matters).

A general introduction (4:1–2)

IN 4:1 THE adverb *loipon*, routinely (and somewhat mechanically) translated as "finally," functions as a transitional particle; "and now" (REB) catches its point nicely. The strong conjunction *oun*, "therefore" (omitted in NIV), closely links the two major portions of the letter (1:2–3:13; 4:1–5:22). For the significance of *adelphoi* ("brothers"), which includes the entire community and not just the male members, see comments on 1:4.

In verse 1 Paul does three things.[2] (1) He reminds the Thessalonians of the instructions (*to pos dei*; perhaps "precepts" or "guidelines") they had received[3] from him during his time in Thessalonica (a point he repeats in 4:2, where their authoritative source is emphasized). (2) He affirms and commends them for following those instructions. (3) He exhorts (*parakaleo*; cf. 2:12; 3:2, 7; 4:10, 18; 5:11, 14; 2 Thess. 2:17; 3:12) them "to do this more and more" (cf. 1 Thess. 4:10). In other words, it appears that he is affirming that they have done well, while making it clear that there is much more to do. For both "how to live" (*peripateo*, lit., to walk) and "to please God," see comments on 2:12.

Holiness (4:3–8)

PAUL VIEWS THE instructions he passed on to the Thessalonians (4:2) not merely as precepts to be followed but rather as nothing less than an expression of "God's will" for them (4:3), which can be summarized in a single word: *hagiasmos*, "sanctification" or "holiness." Whereas in

---

2. The NIV substantially obscures the awkwardness of Paul's sentence. Here is a more literal translation: "We ask and urge you in the Lord Jesus that—just as you learned from us how you ought to live so as to please God, just as you are indeed currently living—that you do so more and more" (cf. NASB).

3. Literally, "you received from us"; the NIV's "we instructed you" reverses (and thus obscures) Paul's emphasis on the Thessalonians' own willing acceptance of what Paul and his companions handed on (the verb is *paralambano*, often used as a technical term indicating the reception of authoritative tradition; cf. 1 Cor. 15:3).

3:13 *hagiosyne* indicated a state or condition of holiness, here *hagiasmos* indicates a process leading to a state of holiness (i.e., conformity to God's character); thus the NIV's transformation of this noun into a verbal phrase ("should be sanctified") accurately catches Paul's nuance.[4]

While the term *holiness* itself is broad enough to encompass the full range of Christian behavior, Paul focuses on a single aspect of what it entails, namely, sexual morality. This topic would have been of particular significance for anyone recently converted from pagan culture, in view of the wide range of sexual mores and practices that existed in Greco-Roman society. Sexual fidelity was demanded of wives (in order to guarantee the parentage of legitimate offspring), and in some circles upheld as a virtue in husbands as well. At the same time, however, a wide range of pre- and extramarital activity was tolerated and occasionally even encouraged. Thus it could not be assumed that converts brought with them into the church any common understanding or expectation regarding sexual behavior. This was an area where socialization into the norms of the new community was definitely a necessity.

Against such a backdrop Paul counsels the Thessalonians to "avoid sexual immorality" (4:3b; cf. 1 Cor. 6:18), that is, *porneia*, a general term for nearly any type of sexual sin, including prostitution, adultery, or fornication. In 4:4 he spells out an important means of avoiding immorality: "each of you," he advises, "should learn to control your own body" (NIV^ILE).

This last phrase presents a major interpretive problem: Does Paul mean that each of the Thessalonians should learn (1) "how to acquire a wife for himself" (NAB, NRSV margin), or (2) "to control your own body" (NIV^ILE; cf. NIV, NRSV, REB)? The phrase in question is, apparently, an idiomatic euphemism whose interpretation is made difficult by the circumstance that the meaning of both the verb (*ktaomai*, frequently "acquire," but also "possess" or "control") and its object (*skeuos*, "vessel," "tool," "body," "wife") is a matter of debate.[5]

---

4. Cf. J. E. Frame, *Thessalonians*, 147.

5. In support of (1), cf. J. E. Frame, *Thessalonians*, 149–50; C. Maurer, "σκεῦος," *TDNT*, 7:365–67; E. Best, *Thessalonians*, 160–63; O. Larry Yarbrough, *Not Like The Gentiles: Marriage Rules in the Letters of Paul* (Atlanta: Scholars, 1985). In support of (2), cf. I. H. Marshall, *1 and 2 Thessalonians*, 107–9; C. A. Wanamaker, *Thessalonians*, 152–53; E. J. Richard, *Thessalonians*, 198; L. Morris, *The First and Second Epistles to the Thessalonians*, 119–21; G. D. Fee, *God's Empowering Presence*, 51–52.

The considerations offered in support of (1), "acquire a wife," are either ambiguous (the alleged similarity in form between 4:4 and 1 Cor. 7:2 amounts in Greek to only two words, and in 1 Peter 3:7 both husbands and wives are "vessels") or of uncertain relevance (late rabbinic usage, which might illustrate but cannot establish Pauline usage). Moreover, had Paul meant "wife," 1 Corinthians 7:2 (cf. 7:27) demonstrates that he could have said so clearly.

Option (2) fits well with the use of *skeuos* elsewhere in Paul (cf. 2 Cor. 4:7, where he refers to the human body as an earthen *skeuos;* cf. Rom. 9:21–23), in the Old Testament (cf. 1 Sam. 21:5; in the LXX, *skeuos* is specifically a euphemism for the genitals, a usage also attested in secular Greek with respect to both sexes), and in early Christian writings (Barnabas 21:8). In addition, it correlates closely with what Paul says in 1 Corinthians 6–7. Finally, it better accords with both the immediate context (the verses before and after are aimed at the entire community, which makes it unlikely that Paul would abruptly interject a command aimed at only a small subset within it, namely, men eligible for marriage) and the cultural environment (many marriages were arranged). In sum, the translation "to control your own body" accurately communicates Paul's meaning.

The self-control Paul commends is to be exercised "in a way that is *holy* and *honorable*" (4:4b), two terms that stand as the antithesis of the "passionate lust" and ignorance mentioned in 4:5. The very definition of "holiness" (conformity to God's character) implies a knowledge of God, and thus it stands as the antithesis of ignorance of God in 4:5b. Similarly "honor," a matter both of respect for the opinion and concern for the well-being of others, is primarily *other*-centered (cf. Rom. 12:10, "honor one another above yourselves"), and thus stands in contrast to "covetous passion" (1 Thess. 4:5a; NIV "passionate lust"), which involves a *self*-centered concern for one's own needs or drives.

For Paul, sexual activity is not just an inconsequential private activity involving one or more consenting adults; on the contrary, it has an impact on both one's relationship with God (cf. 1 Cor. 6:12–20) and with other people (cf. 1 Thess. 4:6); therefore, it ought to be exercised in a way that is respectful of both. In short, sexual behavior ought to be altruistic (a matter of giving to) rather than self-serving (a matter of taking from).

Some commentators think that Paul starts a new topic in 4:6, that of business dealings among believers.[6] But it seems more likely that he is developing an idea implicit in his use of "honorable" in 4:4. Whereas moral sexual relationships seek the honor of others, dishonorable sexual activity amounts to a "sinning against" (NIV "wrong") or "exploitation" (NIV "take advantage of") of one's Christian brother or sister (e.g., an adulterous spouse robs his or her marriage partner of the trust, security, and intimacy the couple shared before the adultery took place). Paul's concern here is probably pragmatic as well as moral: Sexual misconduct involves both a breakdown of the ethical standards that distinguish the Christian community from outsiders and a significant threat to the sense of kinship and unity within the community.

In 4:6b–8, the seriousness with which Paul approaches this matter of sexual behavior is evident. Verse 6b ends the long sentence started in 4:3 by indicating *why* believers should not wrong or exploit one another: The Lord (i.e., Jesus) "is an avenger in all these things" (NRSV; cf. Ps. 94:1; Rom. 12:19; 2 Cor. 5:10; 2 Thess. 1:5–10); that is, sooner or later such sinners will be brought to judgment.[7] Verse 7 gives an additional reason why believers should behave in a morally responsible manner: God's "call," upon which their standing as believers is based (1:4; cf. 2:12; 5:24), is essentially a call to "holiness" (cf. 4:3; also Rom 1:7, 1 Cor 1:2: "called to be holy")—that is, a call to become like God. In short, these ethical standards are rooted in God's own character (his holiness). This means, therefore (4:8), that whoever "rejects this instruction" is in fact rejecting no mere human precept or standard, but God himself.

God does not merely define by his character the standard according to which his followers are to live; he provides as well the power by which one can live. He is the one who *gives* to believers[8] "his *Holy*

---

6. See, for example, E. J. Richard, *Thessalonians*, 200–202. The transitional particle that allegedly signals a new topic is in fact ambiguous in its implications, and while the vocabulary in the verse could be used of business, none of it is in any way limited to business (indeed, *pragma*, "matter," in the singular hardly ever refers to business, for which the plural is customary); the vocabulary, in fact, occurs most often in more general ways. Finally, in 4:7 Paul returns to the theme of 4:3–5; it seems unlikely that he changed topics for a single verse (4:6).

7. See further S. H. Travis, "Judgment," *DPL*, 516–17.

8. Literally, "into you" (*eis hymas*); see Ezek. 37:6, 14, for the Old Testament background; cf. 1 Cor. 6:19 (where the literal word order is, "the temple of the in-you Holy Spirit"); 2 Cor. 1:22; Gal. 4:6.

[this word is emphasized by the word order] Spirit." The present tense "almost certainly stresses the ongoing work of the Spirit in their lives," especially with respect to the struggle against sin:

> For Paul the presence of the Spirit was not simply God's gift as an option against sin; nor would he have understood the Spirit as present but ineffectively so. To the contrary, the dynamic that makes Paul's argument against sexual impurity possible is the experienced reality of the Spirit.[9]

 **SIMILAR CONTEXTS.** IN some respects, bringing this passage into our generation is relatively straightforward, for two reasons. (1) The sexual ethic Paul sets forth here has a theological rather than a cultural basis. That is, Paul offers in this passage what may be termed a "theological ethic." As Beverly Roberts Gaventa observes, in contemporary discussions of ethics, behavior is often analyzed in terms of a psychological model (i.e., whether a certain behavior is psychologically "healthy" or "unhealthy"), or in terms of its social impact or consequences.[10] Paul, however, works from a different starting point: He bases his ethical instructions on his understanding of God. This theological basis gives a high level of authority to his instructions, because, as he points out in 4:8, anyone who rejects them is not rejecting Paul, but God. It also means that his instructions are transcultural, since they are not rooted or grounded in any particular culture or historical circumstances.

In regard to Paul's understanding of God, an important assumption underlying his discussion needs to be highlighted. "Paul assumes that our bodies—our persons—belong to the God of creation.... If we believe that God created us, then we remain obligated to do what pleases God. We do not belong to ourselves, and no amount of protest will make it so"—a perspective that stands in sharpest contrast to the "ethic of the autonomous self" so popular in contemporary culture.[11] In other words, what Paul states explicitly in 1 Corinthians 6:19–20

---

9. G. D. Fee, *God's Empowering Presence,* 52–53.
10. B. R. Gaventa, *Thessalonians,* 55–56.
11. Ibid., 60–61.

("you are not your own; you were bought at a price. Therefore honor God with your body") is a working assumption behind his discussion here in 1 Thessalonians.

(2) The circumstances of the church in the first century and today are relatively similar. Many have noted, of course, the extensive parallels between the sexual license of first-century Mediterranean culture and contemporary Western cultures. But I have an additional parallel in mind: The church, now as then, faces the challenge of socializing or acculturating to a biblical sexual ethic people who bring with them, when they come into the church, no common standard or set of expectations regarding sexual behavior. Even those raised within the church cannot be assumed to be of one mind regarding sexual ethics and behavior, due in part to the church's wavering and uncertain voice on the subject (when it speaks at all) and in part to the widespread but widely varying impact of contemporary culture on believers through movies, television, music, books, and the arts.

In view of these similar circumstances, Paul's strategy for developing a common sexual ethic is worth noting. What Paul offers to people coming from widely differing backgrounds is an ethic based on the one thing he knows they all share, a relationship with the one true God. In other words, what they already have in common becomes the starting point for building towards a common understanding of sexual conduct in a Christian context.

Holiness. One potential difficulty in bridging contexts, however, involves a central concept in the passage, *holiness*. This has become something of a lost word in the vocabulary of the contemporary church. When it is used, it is often seen as a negative concept, usually "separation from" (when I ask, "From what?" my students often answer, "Anything that's fun"). For this reason it is important to note that for Paul holiness is fundamentally a positive concept, rooted in the very character of God: "For I am the LORD your God; sanctify yourselves therefore, and be holy, for I am holy" (Lev. 11:44 NRSV). In other words, holiness for Paul is a matter of becoming more and more like the God who has chosen, called, and saved us. To be sure, modeling ourselves after his character may well involve separating ourselves from anything not pleasing to him or incongruent with his character, but to over- (or only) emphasize the idea of separation obscures the primary aspect of the term.

It is also important to observe that God made the statement about holiness in Leviticus 11 to a people with whom he had already established a personal relationship. This means that the call to holiness is a call to discipleship, not a requirement for salvation. Viewing holiness in this way helps us understand how Paul can view it as a future goal (*hagiosyne*, a state or condition of holiness, as in 3:13), a past gift (see comment on 5:23), and a journey (*hagiasmos*, a process leading to a state of holiness, as in 4:3) to which God calls us (4:7). This view of holiness also helps us understand how Paul can use the term as an overarching one-word summary of God's will for his people (4:3). Finally, we should notice that God does not simply call us to holiness, he provides the power to make progress towards that goal in the person of the *Holy* Spirit (4:8).

Human sexuality and behavior. While Paul sees holiness as encompassing the full range of Christian behavior, in this passage he quickly focuses on a specific area of concern, sexual behavior. In approaching his discussion, it is important to note that Paul takes for granted the Bible's fundamentally positive view of the essential goodness of human sexuality, both as created and when exercised in its intended context of heterosexual marriage.[12] His concern is not to disparage sex, deny it, or pretend it doesn't exist, but to see that it is exercised in a manner that builds up the community rather than tears it down.

With respect to sexual behavior, Paul gives two guidelines in this passage, one negative and one positive: negatively, "avoid sexual immorality" (4:3), and positively, "control your own body in holiness and honor" (4:4 NRSV). Because these guidelines are relatively abstract, it is necessary to unpack them and spell out more concretely what he means.

Porneia, "sexual immorality," is (as noted above) a broad term that includes both adultery (sexual intercourse involving a married person and someone other than his or her spouse) and fornication (sexual intercourse involving individuals who are not married). In other words, Paul states here in a concise negative form what the Scriptures teach positively about sexual activity: The biblical context for sexual intercourse is heterosexual marriage. Holy living, with respect to sexuality,

---

12. To paraphrase my colleague Keith Anderson, God values people, relationships, and sex, and the reason why sex outside of marriage is sin is because it does not value these things highly enough (Keith Anderson, *What They Don't Always Teach You at a Christian College* (Downers Grove, Ill.: InterVarsity, 1995), 103–5.

involves disciplined fidelity to one's spouse for those who are married and disciplined abstinence for those who are not.

Whereas Paul's words about avoiding sexual immorality deal with the *context* of sexual intercourse, his words about "holiness" and "honor" deal more broadly with the *conduct* of sexual behavior in general (including, but not limited to, intercourse). Sexual behavior is to be *holy*, that is, congruent with our relationship with God. Moreover, it is to be *honorable*, that is, respectful of the other person, as well as of any other people who might be affected by the relationship (e.g., one's spouse and children, in the case of marriage, or potential future spouses, in the case of those who are unmarried, or the congregation of which one is a part).

In short, Paul is calling for behavior that is altruistic rather than selfish, other-centered rather than self-centered. He also reminds us that sexual behavior has both spiritual and social consequences. However much contemporary secular culture tries to insist that sex is a private matter between consenting adults and therefore of no concern to anyone else, private sexual behavior can (and often does) have social consequences.

IN THIS SECTION we will apply the principles discussed in the previous section in terms of concrete personal behavior. While the following comments barely scratch the surface of the matter, they will indicate what a contemporary application of Paul's teaching might involve.[13]

On a personal level. For those who are married, it means first of all faithfulness to one's spouse. It also means treating each other with respect and love and rules out, as John R. W. Stott writes, "the selfish sexual demands which are sometimes made by one married partner on the other, in terms of aggression, violence, cruelty and even rape." "There is," as Stott observes, "a world of difference between lust and love, between dishonorable sexual practices which use the partner and true love-making which honours the partner, between the selfish desire to possess and the unselfish desire to love, cherish and respect."[14]

---

13. See further Lewis B. Smedes, *Sex for Christians: The Limits and Liberties of Sexual Living*, rev. ed. (Grand Rapids: Eerdmans, 1994); Tim Stafford, *Sexual Chaos: Charting a Course Through Turbulent Times* (Downers Grove, Ill.: InterVarsity, 1993).

14. J. R. W. Stott, *The Gospel and the End of Time*, 85.

For those who are not married, it means obedience to the spirit, not just the letter, of the biblical teaching about the proper context for sex. There are those who interpret the injunction against intercourse outside of marriage as implying permission for just about anything else (including, e.g., oral sex and manual stimulation to orgasm). This results in the odd circumstance of people who in a technical sense are virgins, yet who are in some respects more sexually experienced than some married couples. Such behavior hardly seems to square with Paul's call for disciplined holiness. Moreover, to the extent that various sexual behaviors function or are viewed by a couple as preparation for intercourse (foreplay), they would be inappropriate in a relationship in which intercourse is inappropriate.

It also means taking into account what is best for the long-term well-being of one's friend/date/partner, rather than what feels good or seems right at the moment. Feelings and memories stay long after the relationship that gave rise to them comes to an end. People engaged in a nonmarital sexual relationship (particularly if the relationship involves exploitation of any form) accumulate emotional and physical "baggage," which is often carried forward into subsequent relationships (marriage in particular). This amounts to a form of doing wrong (cf. 4:6) to a future spouse.[15]

For some people (married people in particular), following Paul's guidelines may require lowering the level of (or even breaking off, if necessary) an intimate friendship with someone to whom one is improperly attracted. In a dating situation it means avoiding behavior or contact that arouses a level of sexual desire inappropriate for the level of the relationship. For anyone it means avoiding visual or verbal stimulation or input that arouses inappropriate or wrongly focused sexual desires.[16]

On the positive side, following Paul's guidelines means thinking about one's sexual life not as a separate segment of one's life, but within the larger framework of one's personal walk with God. It may mean

---

15. One member of a group of male Christian college students captured well the positive side of this point: "The facts of life are that the woman I date today may be the wife of one of these other guys in another year or two. My relationship with them is important to me, and I want a strong and positive relationship with both of them if that happens" (Keith Anderson, *What They Don't Always Teach You at a Christian College*, 108).

16. Much of this last paragraph follows Craig Blomberg, *1 Corinthians* (NIVAC; Grand Rapids: Zondervan, 1994), 129.

developing healthy relationships that supply those personal psychological and social needs for which sexual involvement is sometimes a substitute. It may require a willingness to exercise short-term discipline for long-term gain.[17]

On a congregational level. So far we have been talking about what Paul's teaching means on a personal level. But it also has implications for the congregation as a whole. To begin with, Paul's starting point—holiness (or "sanctification," NIV) as God's will for *all* of life (4:3)—suggests that the church might do well to integrate its teaching on the subject of sexual ethics and conduct into a larger framework of discipleship in general. The principles of holiness and honor that Paul applies to the matter of sexual behavior are applicable to other areas of behavior or conduct (e.g., personal relationships, how we behave towards strangers, how we handle our money) as well.

Furthermore, when the church sets forth holiness and honor as its standard for sexual behavior, it must also make a serious attempt to facilitate and enable the challenging process of character formation necessary if people are to make progress in that direction. It is unfair and unrealistic to establish a standard without also providing the means and assistance to achieve it.

Similarly, in proclaiming abstinence as a genuine option (and, from a biblical perspective, the only option) for its singles, the church must not minimize the challenge or difficulty of living up to that ethic. It must also be willing to discuss the "why" of waiting (one of the strengths of the "True Love Waits" program utilized by some churches is that it offers a clear goal and reason for waiting). It also needs to acknowledge that sometimes people get involved in a sexual relationship in hopes of finding the acceptance, love, and friendship they feel is missing from their life, and then seek to provide an environment in which important relational needs can be met in more healthy ways.

---

17. For some singles, it means the exercise of more than a short-term discipline. John R. W. Stott (himself single) writes, "We too must accept this apostolic teaching, however hard it may seem, as God's good purpose both for us and for society.... It is possible for human sexual energy to be redirected ... both into affectionate relationships with friends of both sexes and into the loving service of others.... Alongside a natural loneliness, accompanied sometimes by acute pain, we can find joyful self-fulfillment in the self-giving service of God and other people." (J. R. W. Stott, *The Gospel and the End of Time*, 84–85). See further Rhena Taylor, *Single and Whole* (Downers Grove, Ill.: InterVarsity, 1984).

The church must also reconsider some of the distinctions it makes between various categories of sexual misbehavior. For Paul, whether sexual immorality occurred in an opposite-sex or same-sex context was essentially insignificant (cf. 1 Cor. 6:9–10, "neither the sexually immoral ... nor adulterers nor male prostitutes nor homosexual offenders ... will inherit the kingdom of God"). That can hardly be said of most evangelical congregations today, and to the extent that we treat or categorize one form of sexual immorality differently from another, we fall short of the New Testament's understanding of sexual ethics. Moreover, in fixating on one category of sexual immorality, such as homosexual activity,[18] while more or less ignoring others, such as adultery, we run the risk of noticing the speck in someone else's eye but not seeing the log in our own (Matt. 7:3–5; Luke 6:41–42).[19]

In the last few years, more than a few cultural observers have noticed that secular culture is, for various pragmatic reasons, seriously reconsidering the value of the kind of sexual ethic traditionally proclaimed by the church. It is both ironic and tragic that at such a moment many denominations or segments of the church have lost their ability and authority to speak clearly on sexual matters. The reasons (e.g., confusion, hypocrisy and scandal, cultural accommodation) are less important than the consequences: the loss of ability to speak not only prophetically but also pastorally to people seeking an alternative to the sexual confusion and emptiness of contemporary culture. Paul's instructions to the Thessalonians offer a biblical antidote to our current confusion.

---

18. For a superb discussion of the Bible's teaching about homosexuality and its ethical and practical implications for how the church should respond to people who have a homosexual orientation, see Richard B. Hays, *The Moral Vision of the New Testament: Community, Cross, New Creation* (San Francisco: HarperSanFrancisco, 1996), 379–406.

19. My adaptation of a point made by David P. Gushee, "The Speck in Mickey's Eye," *CT* 41 (August 11, 1997): 13; in a similar vein William Bennett, in remarks to the Christian Coalition in 1994, observed that divorce, not homosexuality, was the greater threat to the survival of the family (Richard L. Berke, "From the Right, Some Words of Restraint," *New York Times*, September 17, 1994, sec. 1, p. 9, as reported by Stephen L. Carter, *Integrity* [New York: BasicBooks, 1996], 143).

1 Thessalonians 4:9–12

❦

NOW ABOUT BROTHERLY love we do not need to write to you, for you yourselves have been taught by God to love each other. ¹⁰And in fact, you do love all the brothers throughout Macedonia. Yet we urge you, brothers, to do so more and more.

¹¹Make it your ambition to lead a quiet life, to mind your own business and to work with your hands, just as we told you, ¹²so that your daily life may win the respect of outsiders and so that you will not be dependent on anybody.

CONTRARY TO THE impression given by the NIV, these verses comprise a single segment of the letter composed of just two sentences, verses 9–10a and 10b–12. After signaling the beginning of this section with the phrase "now concerning" and announcing the topic (*philadelphia*, "love for brothers and sisters"), Paul employs a figure of speech (*paralipsis;* cf. BDF §495) in which a speaker pretends to skip over a subject ("we do not need to write to you") that he does in fact discuss. It offers Paul a diplomatic way simultaneously both to affirm the Thessalonians for what they are doing well (4:9–10a) and to encourage them to develop in areas that need further attention (4:10b–12).

In pre-Christian usage, *philadelphia* refers to love for one's siblings. Its use in Christian circles (cf. Rom. 12:10; Heb. 13:1; 1 Peter 1:22; 2 Peter 1:7 [twice]) to designate love for fellow believers probably arose out of the practice of Christians addressing each other as "brother" or "sister."[1] In 4:11–12, however, Paul will make it clear that love for those within the community has implications for how Christians ought to relate to those outside the community as well.

The Thessalonians' exemplary mutual love (*philadelphia*), not just for one another but towards believers throughout Macedonia (4:10a;

---

1. For the significance of *adelphoi* (4:10), which includes the entire community, not just the male members of the church, see comments on 1:4.

cf. 1:7–8), leads Paul, using a strongly affirmative present tense (lit., "are"; NIV "have been"), to characterize them as *theodidaktoi*, "taught by God" (4:9). This word was almost certainly coined by Paul, though the concept itself was not new (cf. John 6:45, quoting Isa. 54:13, which describes the messianic age of salvation). This Greek word assumes the existence of a relationship with God; this in turn implies that the Spirit (4:8) is the means by which God teaches them, an idea Paul develops in 1 Corinthians 2:9–16 (cf. also John 14:25–26; Rom. 5:5; Gal. 5:22, 25–26).

Even as Paul affirms the Thessalonians for doing well with respect to *philadelphia* (4:10a), he urges (*parakaleo*) them, as he did in 4:1, "to do so more and more" (4:10b, a phrase that both looks back to 4:9–10a and forward to what follows; cf. also 3:12). Verses 11–12 (which with 4:10b comprise a single sentence) spell out (indeed, remind them, "just as we told you") what Paul has in mind. Specifically, he wants them (1) "to make it your ambition [a] to lead a quiet life and [b] to mind your own business," and (2) "to work with your hands."[2]

The meaning of these three phrases, both individually and as a group in the context of 4:9–12, is a matter of debate.[3] They are often interpreted, in light of 2 Thessalonians 2:1–3 and 3:6–15, as Paul's response to a situation generated by excessive interest in and excitement about the imminent return of Jesus, which led some members of the church to abandon their jobs and behave in ways that disrupted the fellowship and irritated their pagan neighbors.

But this scenario is at best only a possible hypothesis. Against it stand three considerations. (1) There is the awkwardness of inter-

---

2. In terms of grammar and syntax, the infinitive "to make it your ambition" could govern the first (so F. F. Bruce, *1 & 2 Thessalonians*, 90), the first and second (so C. A. Wanamaker, *Thessalonians*, 162; E. J. Richard, *Thessalonians*, 211), or all three of the following infinitives (i.e.,, "to lead . . . and to mind . . . and to work"). Similarly, it is unclear whether the following "just as we told you" refers to just the last infinitive or to all of 4:11. Decisions on these points reflect judgments about content and context, rather than grammatical or syntactical considerations. I have linked the first two together in view of (a) their similar meaning and (b) the correlation this creates with the two reasons given in 4:12.

3. See further E. J. Richard, *Thessalonians*, 211–23; C. A. Wanamaker, *Thessalonians*, 162–64; I. H. Marshall, *1 and 2 Thessalonians*, 116–17; E. Best, *Thessalonians*, 174–78; A. J. Malherbe, *Paul and the Thessalonians*, 95–106; Bruce W. Winter, *Seek the Welfare of the City: Christians as Benefactors and Citizens* (Grand Rapids: Eerdmans, and Carlisle: Paternoster, 1994), 41–60; Ronald F. Hock, *The Social Context of Paul's Mission: Tentmaking and Apostleship* (Philadelphia: Fortress, 1980), 42–49.

---

preting the earlier letter (1 Thessalonians) in light of the later one (2 Thessalonians). (2) Paul himself does not connect the refusal to work with the expectation of Jesus' return. (3) Paul repeatedly stresses that he is bringing to their attention things he had already taught them (4:11; cf. v. 2). Almost certainly this would have to have happened at the time the community was established—before, in other words, any specific problems or misunderstandings arose.

Taken in their own right (i.e., not in light of 2 Thess. 2–3), the phrases in 1 Thessalonians 4:11 are richly evocative of social and political concerns (indeed, the first two have unmistakable political connotations). Moreover, from its inception the Christian community, willingly or unwillingly, had been visible in the public arena, with sometimes painful consequences for the new believers (cf. Acts 17:5–9; also the discussion of persecution in 1 Thess. 1:6; 3:1–5). Any member of the congregation who remained active in the public arena, either in his or her own right or as someone's client (whose obligations included looking after the public interests of one's patron, upon whom a client was financially dependent), ran the risk of attracting continued negative public attention—that is, *thlipsis,* "persecution" (1:6; 3:3–4, 7)—to the congregation as a whole. In such a setting, Paul argues that *philadelphia* (i.e., love and concern for the well-being of one's Christian sisters and brothers) requires that the members of the congregation fulfill their "ambition" (4:11; cf. Rom. 15:20; 2 Cor. 5:9) in private rather than public ways.

As a result, Paul urges the believers in Thessalonica "to lead a quiet life" and "to attend to their own concerns" (NIV "mind your own business"), two idioms with similar meaning. In secular usage both phrases can describe a principled withdrawal from the public arena. The first one evokes the image of a withdrawal from the noise, antagonism, and strife of public matters in favor of a quiet, more contemplative setting; in the Old Testament (Job 3:26; 11:19; Ezek. 38:11) and elsewhere it is associated with images of virtue, peace, tranquillity, and security.[4] The second phrase suggests a withdrawal from public matters to devote

---

4. Cf. the following description (Philo, *Abraham,* 20) of the antithesis of the "quiet life": the "vulgar man, who spends his days meddling, running around in public, in theaters, tribunals, councils, and assemblies, meetings and consultations of all sorts; he lets loose his tongue for unmeasured, endless, indiscriminate talk, bringing chaos and confusion into everything, mingling truth with falsehood . . . the private with the public, the sacred with the profane, the serious with the ridiculous, not having learned to remain quiet [*hesychian*] . . . and he pricks up his ears in an excess of bustling busyness."

time to one's own private interests, or to give attention to that for which one is best suited (in Pauline terms, that to which one has been called). In the context of Paul's concern for *philadelphia* (4:9), he is advising the Thessalonians to avoid as much as possible the strife, social pressures, and tumult of the public arena (and the attendant potential for violence against the congregation), and to focus instead on the needs and the building up of the congregation.

The proper context for understanding the command "to work with your hands" (v. 11; cf. 1 Cor. 4:12; Eph. 4:28) is not that of Greco-Roman culture (in which philosophers and moralists debated the propriety and fitness of various types and kinds of work, including manual labor), but the Old Testament. There this expression occurs as an idiomatic phrase (Deut. 2:7–8; Job 1:10; Ps. 89:17 [LXX]; Jer. 1:16), in which the emphasis falls not on "hands" but on "work" (cf. Isa. 5:12, with its parallelism between "the deeds of the LORD" and "the work of his hands"). Thus, Paul is not discussing manual labor as opposed to other kinds of work, but simply "work" in general, as a means of providing for the needs of individuals and the community.[5]

This understanding of 4:11 fits nicely both with the two commands that precede it, where Paul is basically telling the Thessalonians to keep a low profile, to give attention to their own affairs, and to stay busy, and with the reasons that follow in 4:12. This understanding also means that it is not necessary to drag back (anachronistically, in my opinion) 2 Thessalonians 2:1–3 and 3:6–13 in order to understand this verse.

In 4:12 Paul spells out the specific goals of the behavior he encourages in 4:10b–11. The first goal (which ties in most closely with the first two commands in 4:11, but can encompass all three) is that the believers in Thessalonica will live (lit., "walk," *peripateo;* cf. 2:12; 4:1; 2 Thess. 3:6, 11) in a manner that will "win the respect of outsiders" (cf. 1 Cor. 10:32–33; Col. 4:5; 1 Peter 2:12). Not only will this make it easier for the young community to thrive in the midst of a hostile pagan environment, it will also significantly and positively affect opportunities for further outreach and evangelism in the community.

The meaning of the second goal (linked closely to the command to work in 4:11) is doubly ambiguous. In terms of the grammar, the

---

5. See further E. J. Richard, *Thessalonians*, 220.

phrase can be translated either as "have need of no one" (cf. NIV's "not be dependent on anybody" [similarly NRSV]) or as "have need of nothing" (cf. NASB, "not be in any need"). Of more importance is the contextual ambiguity. On the one hand, Paul's concern may be that believers should work in order to be self-sufficient and free from entanglements with *outsiders* (in particular, free from financial dependence on patrons). On the other hand, Paul's concern may be that believers should work in order not to be a burden on *insiders*, that is, fellow believers who would feel compelled to provide the necessities of life for any brothers or sisters in the congregation who lacked them.

The "outsider" option makes good sense in light of 4:12a; on this view, all three commands in 4:11 have to do with how the congregation relates to outsiders. But I favor slightly the "insider" option, since (1) it is not without its implications for how outsiders view the congregation, and (2) it makes good sense in light of the overall topic of 4:9–12: The proper exercise of *philadelphia* includes working to support one's needs and not taking financial advantage of one's brother or sister in Christ.

Throughout 4:1–12 Paul has sought to establish clear standards of community conduct (holiness and honor) and to foster a particular community ethos (private rather than public, active rather than idle); in doing so, he has consistently used insider/outsider language (the community vs. those "who do not know God," 4:5; "outsiders," 4:12). In these ways he has continued the process of (re-)socializing the new Thessalonian converts by fostering a unique sense of congregational identity within the larger community and by establishing a clear boundary between it and the larger culture.[6]

PHILADELPHIA WITH RESPECT to outsiders. Determining the historical context of a text is a critical aspect of bringing this section into our day and age. In the case of 4:11, one's understanding of the historical context is determined by the exegetical decisions one makes regarding the meaning of "lead a quiet life," "mind your own business," and "work with your hands." If one concludes that

---

6. Cf. the similar analysis of B. R. Gaventa, *Thessalonians*, 59.

the passage is Paul's response to a situation generated by excessive interest in and excitement about the imminent return of Jesus, which led some members of the church to abandon their jobs or behave in ways that disrupted the fellowship and irritated their pagan neighbors, then one will reconstruct the situation with which Paul is dealing as a matter of *internal church discipline*. On this view, some members of the congregation have let their eschatological excitement get out of hand and have quit their jobs, and Paul is telling them to calm down a bit and get back to work.

If, however, one concludes (as I have done) that Paul is dealing with a situation in which some members of the congregation are active in the public arena and are bringing unwanted attention to the congregation, then one will interpret the situation with which Paul is dealing as a matter of *external church/community relations*. On this view, Paul is instructing members of the congregation about the (in)advisability of being involved in the public affairs of the community.

Regardless of how one decides this matter, it is important not to lose sight of Paul's starting point, which is also the basis for his instructions. The topic of this section of the letter is *philadelphia*, love for brother and sister (4:9), and the instructions given in 4:11 (however we interpret them) indicate a specific way in which the Thessalonians can practice *philadelphia* "more and more" (4:10b). Here it is crucial to observe not simply what Paul is saying, but also what he is doing: In advising individuals who have made (or are making) decisions about the extent to which they can or should be involved in the larger community, Paul indicates that such decisions ought to be significantly influenced by *philadelphia*.

In other words, Paul takes it for granted that genuine love and concern for others will influence (if not determine) an individual's decisions (here, about mundane matters such as whether to become involved in public affairs). Moreover, it is clear, given the way this topic appears throughout his letters, that this is not an isolated element in Paul's theology (see, e.g., Rom. 14:19; 15:1–3; 1 Cor. 12:7; 14:12; Gal. 5:13). As Paul says in Philippians 2:4, "Each of you should look not only to your own interests, but also to the interests of others."

Discerning this underlying principle—that *philadelphia* should influence an individual's decisions—is a key to applying this passage today. In some countries today Christianity is, like the church in Thessalonica, a persecuted minority movement. Public attention to one member of the group can and often does result in a spotlight being cast on others as well. The wrong kind of public activity on the part of one believer can have devastating consequences for the entire congregation. Where the circumstances of the church today mirror closely those of the Thessalonian congregation, the applicability of the specific advice in 4:11 is apparent.

In many countries and regions, however, Christians form a substantial part of cultural majorities. In these circumstances the consequences of public involvement are substantially different, and it may be that engagement with rather than withdrawal from the public arena is called for. Regardless, however, of how similar or different our circumstances are, Paul's fundamental point in this passage (the need for *philadelphia*) will be applicable, even if his specific instructions may not be.

In addition to this primary concern for *philadelphia*, Paul spells out in 4:12a another (clearly secondary) factor that should shape decisions: concern for the respect of outsiders.[7] In the larger context of the letter, it is clear that there are substantial limits to this factor. For example, Paul certainly would not want the Thessalonians to give up their faith in Jesus simply to win the respect of the larger community! Paul himself was always far more concerned about being faithful to God than he was to impress unbelievers. At the same time, and quite pragmatically, he appears to have sought to avoid behavior that needlessly brought disrespect or shame to the gospel or the church. This suggests that Paul's concern here is that the Thessalonians not give unnecessary or needless offense to those outside, for the well-being of the congregation as well as for the sake of the gospel.

Philadelphia with respect to insiders. The matter of work (4:11) reappears in 2 Thessalonians 3:6–13, where it is the major focus of attention. Nevertheless, a few comments may be in order here. Elsewhere Paul makes it clear, in close conjunction with instructions about *philadelphia* (Rom. 12:10), that he expected believers to "share with

---

7. At first glance, 4:12b ("not be dependent on anybody") appears to give yet a third reason. But if 4:12b has "insiders" in view (as I suggest above in the discussion of Original Meaning), then it reinforces the need to take *philadelphia* into account when making decisions. On the other hand, if 4:12b has "outsiders" in view, then it basically reinforces the reason given in 4:12a ("win the respect of outsiders"). In neither instance does it add a substantive third reason, so I have subsumed it under the other two (*philadelphia* and respect for outsiders).

God's people who are in need" and to "practice hospitality" (Rom. 12:13; cf. 2 Cor. 8:7–14; 9:12; also Heb. 13:1–3; 1 Peter 4:8–9). Here he is dealing with the flip side of the matter: the implications of *philadelphia* for those who might be recipients of such sharing. Those who are able to work (a point assumed by his instructions here) ought to do so; they should not take advantage of the willingness of fellow believers, motivated by mutual love, to help out.

Philadelphia, in other words, is bi-directional: It entails both a willingness to assist those who are in need and a responsibility not to exploit or take advantage of the willingness of fellow believers to help. As John R. W. Stott observes, "It is an expression of love to support others who are in need; but it is also an expression of love to support ourselves, so as not to need to be supported by others."[8]

 TO THIS POINT in chapter 4, Paul has emphasized two fundamental points, holiness and *philadelphia*. The first focuses primarily on our relationship with God, while the second focuses, by the very nature of the term, on our love for others. In this respect, Paul's discussion parallels what Jesus identified as the most important commandment: "Love the Lord your God with all your heart and with all your soul and with all your mind and with all your strength"; and, "Love your neighbor as yourself" (Mark 12:30–31; cf. Matt. 22:37–40)—which Paul himself cites elsewhere (Rom. 13:9).

Paul's broad understanding of *philadelphia* challenges us to reconsider what it means to love our neighbor. In light of his own application of the principle in 4:9–12 to the matter of work, two closely related topics suggest themselves: choice of occupation and choice of how we spend out money.

Occupational choice. Ours is a culture that increasingly measures an individual's worth not by the quality of one's character but by the quantity of one's wealth and possessions ("The one who dies with the most toys wins"). Thus it is hardly surprising that high-paying jobs are more highly valued than low-paying ones. What is surprising is the extent to which this attitude has infiltrated the church. In a recent

---

8. J. R. W. Stott, *The Gospel and the End of Time*, 90.

study of religion and attitudes towards money, Robert Wuthnow reports that "weekly churchgoers" were more likely to admire "people who make a lot of money by working hard" than "people who take a lower-paying job in order to help others."[9]

This is a troublesome finding, especially since it involves weekly churchgoers, who are more likely to be serious about their faith than occasional attenders. It suggests that the long-standing tradition of Christians valuing most highly career choices that focused on helping others—choices like teaching, missions, medicine, and social services—is declining. One reason such service-oriented careers have been highly respected among Christians is precisely because they represented various ways to practice *philadelphia* by serving others.

The shift observed by Wuthnow away from valuing jobs for what they accomplish toward valuing them for what they pay represents a shift towards a more self-centered perspective. Since self-centeredness is a central characteristic of contemporary American culture, it is difficult not to view this shift as evidence of the church's accommodation to the values of the surrounding culture, a trading of biblical values for secular ones. Precisely at this point Paul's instructions to the Thessalonians about making occupational choices in light of their impact on others, believers and unbelievers alike, challenge us to reconsider the value of this trade. As believers, what really is more important to us: accumulating wealth or serving others? An honest answer to this question can function as an important diagnostic tool as we reflect on this issue. While the answer we give in real life is often a compromise, Paul reminds us where the emphasis clearly ought to fall.

As I worked on this section, a local newspaper ran a feature about an African-American man in his late twenties who left a respected job in private industry to take a position with the city Park District as a supervisor of a community recreation center. In the space of two years he turned the building and grounds from a hot spot for drug dealing and gang activities into a safe place for the neighborhood kids to hang out after school, and he instituted several successful mentoring and self-improvement programs. When asked why he had left the better-paying position for his current one, he indicated that he did so in order to serve his community better and more directly. This is the

---

9. Robert Wuthnow, *God and Mammon in America* (New York: Free Press, 1994), 131.

kind of choice that Paul's emphasis on *philadelphia* calls us to affirm and model.

It is not enough, however, to affirm and model career choices in isolation, for they are frequently related to lifestyle choices. Our culture defines success increasingly in material terms and places great emphasis on affluence as evidence of success. Thus lifestyle choices about the size and location of one's house, the vehicle one drives, the clothes one wears, the organizations one joins, or the places one visits all become ways of demonstrating one's affluence—concrete evidence of one's success (or lack thereof). Magazines like *The Robb Report* ("for the affluent lifestyle"), prominently displayed at the checkout counter of the upscale grocery store, offer advice on the proper ways of demonstrating one's affluence. Wealth is to be displayed ("If you've got it, flaunt it"), and excess and extravagance are widely celebrated. In view of this contemporary emphasis on material affluence, it is no surprise that people feel pressure to choose a job primarily for what it pays rather than for its social usefulness or value.

How we spend our money. If the church is to affirm and model choosing jobs in terms of service rather than salary, it will also have to affirm and model lifestyle choices that encourage people to live on lower levels of income. But here too, as was the case with career choices, the trends are disturbing. In an analysis of the "anatomy of a giver," Tim Stafford, drawing on several recent authoritative surveys and analyses, compared the giving habits of Christians with those of non-Christians. One of his key findings about Christians as a whole: "Their affluence is indistinguishable from their neighbor's." Moreover, the key variable predicting giving levels was not age (the younger were no less generous than their elders) but income. The weakest givers were those making from $40,000 to $100,000 per year, who gave *less* as a percentage of their income than those making under $20,000 a year. Even among conservative and evangelical believers, who rank among the most generous givers, the per-member contributions between 1985 and 1993 actually shrank, in constant dollars, from $651 to $621.[10]

It is difficult not to draw a connection between the culture's emphasis on affluence and the finding that Christians who as their income rises could afford to give more in fact give less (as a percentage of income).

---

10. Tim Stafford, "Anatomy of a Giver," CT 41:6 (May 19, 1997): 22, 24

It appears that many Christians, like their unbelieving neighbors, are making lifestyle choices based on affluence rather than *philadelphia*.

What might it mean to make spending decisions on the basis of *philadelphia* rather than affluence? (1) It might mean making lifestyle choices on the basis of need or utility rather than label or status (e.g., is a car being chosen primarily for its transportation value, or for the nameplate it bears?).

(2) It might mean making lifestyle choices in light of their impact on one's ability to contribute to the needs of others. For example, not a few people cite "a large mortgage" as a reason why they cannot contribute more. But why did they end up with such a large mortgage? Perhaps because they followed a common bit of real estate advice to buy as much as they could "afford," a choice that then set limits on how much they could give. Why not turn the process around: Decide first on a giving level and then settle on a mortgage consistent with that decision. This is not always easy to do; one couple was ridiculed by various real estate professionals for adopting such a "stupid" strategy.

(3) When considering a discretionary purchase (perhaps a new hi-tech golf club in order to gain a yard or two from the tee?), it might mean asking whether there is some other use to which the money might be put, from which others might benefit.

(4) It might mean taking seriously what Jesus said about those to whom much has been given: "From everyone who has been given much, much will be demanded; and from the one who has been entrusted with much, much more will be asked" (Luke 12:48). Note too what Paul says in 2 Corinthians 8:13–15:

> Our desire is not that others might be relieved while you are hard pressed, but that there might be equality. At the present time your plenty will supply what they need, so that in turn their plenty will supply what you need. Then there will be equality, as it is written: "He who gathered much did not have too much, and he who gathered little did not have too little."

True, individuals may find it difficult to withstand on their own the cultural onslaught regarding wealth and spending. Consequently, the church needs to create an environment, a countercultural community, in which believers can mutually encourage and support one another in going against the cultural tide.

1 Thessalonians 4:13–18

BROTHERS, WE DO not want you to be ignorant about those who fall asleep, or to grieve like the rest of men, who have no hope. [14]We believe that Jesus died and rose again and so we believe that God will bring with Jesus those who have fallen asleep in him. [15]According to the Lord's own word, we tell you that we who are still alive, who are left till the coming of the Lord, will certainly not precede those who have fallen asleep. [16]For the Lord himself will come down from heaven, with a loud command, with the voice of the archangel and with the trumpet call of God, and the dead in Christ will rise first. [17]After that, we who are still alive and are left will be caught up together with them in the clouds to meet the Lord in the air. And so we will be with the Lord forever. [18]Therefore encourage each other with these words.

Original Meaning

THE PHRASE "WE do not want you to be ignorant" (i.e., "we want you to know") is a common formula often used to introduce information (cf. Rom. 1:13; 11:25; 1 Cor. 10:1; 12:1; 2 Cor. 1:8). Together with "about" (*peri*; cf. 1 Thess. 4:9; 5:1), this expression clearly signals a new topic: "those who have died" (NRSV; NIV "those who fall asleep"). Paul appears to be responding to a question asked by the Thessalonians (whether it was asked in a letter or orally via Timothy is a matter of speculation). Paul's reply consists of a statement of the topic (v. 13), a theological affirmation (v. 14), information (vv. 15–17), and application (v. 18).

Even though Paul here turns to a new topic, there is a point of contact with the preceding section, 4:9–12. There he was concerned that the Thessalonians live in a way that would "win the respect of outsiders" (4:12). Here he does not want them to grieve like "outsiders," that is, like those "who have no hope." In both instances he wants them to conduct themselves in a way that is genuinely Christian, that is, in a manner consistent with the gospel message to which they have committed themselves.[1]

Preliminary observations. What Paul writes here appears to draw on early Christian teaching about what is often called the *parousia* ("coming") of Jesus;[2] it has close parallels to the Olivet Discourse in the Synoptic Gospels.[3] This tradition about Jesus' *parousia* represents it as taking place from or in heaven (4:16; cf. 1:10; Matt. 24:30; 2 Thess. 1:7), with clouds (1 Thess. 4:17; cf. Matt. 24:30//Mark 13:26//Luke 21:27; Rev. 1:7), accompanied by angels (cf. 1 Thess. 3:13; 2 Thess. 1:7; Matt. 24:31//Mark 13:27; Matt. 16:27//Mark 8:38//Luke 9:26; Matt. 25:31) and manifestations of power and glory (cf. 2 Thess. 1:9; Matt. 24:30//Mark 13:26//Luke21:27; Matt. 16:27//Mark 8:38//Luke 9:26; Matt. 25:31), announced by a trumpet blast (1 Thess. 4:16; cf. Matt. 24:31; 1 Cor. 15:52; Rev. 11:15), and associated with judgment (cf. 1 Thess. 1:10; 5:3; also Matt. 25:31—46; 2 Thess. 1:7—10; 2:8).

Presumably Paul had introduced the Thessalonians to much of this tradition. The frequency with which he mentions the topic in 1 Thessalonians (in addition to 4:13—5:11, see 1:10; 2:19; 3:13; 5:23) suggests that it was part of his basic missionary preaching. But it is also clear that a question arose that these believers were unable to answer satisfactorily on the basis of what they learned or remembered. Despite a great deal of speculation about the matter, we simply do not know why or how the question arose,[4] why it apparently caused confusion and turmoil, or even exactly what the question was (were they worried that those who died before the Parousia might miss the event, or that they would in some way be disadvantaged with respect to it?).

It has been noted that Paul's use of "sleep" as a euphemism for death probably reflects the way in which the Thessalonians themselves formulated their question. This observation may offer a basis for a

---

1. Compare the analysis of Abraham Smith, who suggests that in 4:13—18 and 5:1—11 Paul discusses specific examples of "good behavior" towards outsiders in circumstances beyond one's control (*Comfort One Another: Reconstructing the Rhetoric and Audience of 1 Thessalonians* [Louisville, Ky.: Westminster/John Knox, 1995], 88, 90).

2. For the specific Greek word see 2:19; 3:13; 5:23; 2 Thess. 2:1, 8; also Matt. 24:3, 27, 37, 39; 1 Cor. 15:23; James 5:7—8; 2 Peter 1:16; 3:4, 12; 1 John 2:28. A wide range of other terms and expressions are also employed in the New Testament to refer to the return of Jesus; for the Pauline vocabulary, see L. J. Kreitzer, "Eschatology," *DPL*, 259—60 (section 3.4.1).

3. F. F. Bruce, *1 and 2 Thessalonians*, 95, from whom much of this paragraph is taken.

4. For an overview of five major hypotheses, see I. H. Marshall, *1 and 2 Thessalonians*, 120—22 (cf. E. J. Richard, *Thessalonians*, 231—32); for a sixth, see C. A. Wanamaker, *Thessalonians*, 166.

working hypothesis. At least some of the Thessalonians had only recently been converted from a pagan culture in which death ("sleep") was widely associated with an utter lack of hope (see comments on v. 13). If some of these relatively new believers still understood death in a largely pagan sense, it is understandable how distressed they might have been by the death of fellow believers prior to the Parousia; it would have meant the end of any hope of being "with the Lord" (v. 17) in the future, that the "wait for his Son from heaven" (1:10) would have been in vain. In response Paul offers a profoundly different understanding of death, the future, and the fate of believers, one grounded in what was for him the most fundamental event in history: God's resurrection of Jesus.

The Topic (4:13)

IN VERSE 13, Paul introduces the topic. It concerns "those who fall asleep," that is, Christian brothers or sisters who have died before the Parousia of Jesus. He writes to inform ("we do not want you to be ignorant") the Thessalonians,[5] "so that" (*hina*, an expression of purpose, which the NIV's "or" misses completely) they will not "grieve like the rest" (i.e., those "who have no hope"). Paul does not say that the Thessalonians should not grieve, but that they should not grieve in the same way or to the same extent as those without hope grieve. The hope that is characteristic of a believer (cf. 1:3; 2:19; 5:8; 2 Thess. 2:16; also Rom. 5:2; 8:24) must, Paul believes, affect the way one deals with death: "Grief at a friend's death (Phil. 2:27) is normal, but a grief of despair, one that sees only helplessness, is a denial of hope itself."[6]

"Sleep" was widely and frequently used as a euphemism for death both by pagans and by Jews and Christians. There were, however, significant differences in how the reality (death) behind the euphemism was understood. "In contemporary paganism it was too often viewed as a sleep from which there would be no awaking; cf. Catullus (5.4–6): The sun can set and rise again / But once our brief light sets / There is one unending night to be slept through.'"[7] People who viewed death

---

5. The Greek word Paul uses here, *adelphoi* (NIV "brothers"), includes the entire community, not just the male members; see comments on 1:4 .

6. E. J. Richard, *Thessalonians*, 225.

7. F. F. Bruce, *1 and 2 Thessalonians*, 96.

in this perspective were accurately characterized by Paul as those "who have no hope" (4:13);[8] see, for example, Theocritus (*Idyll*, 4.42): "Hopes are for the living; the dead are without hope." For Jews and Christians, death was no less real, but the hope of resurrection meant that death was viewed not as a permanent state but as a temporary condition, one that might interrupt but could not terminate life as part of God's people.

A Theological Affirmation (4:14)

INDEED, IT IS precisely the resurrection of Jesus that provides—as the *gar*, "for" (omitted by NIV), with which 4:14 begins indicates—the foundation on which Paul bases his encouragement (4:13; cf. 4:18) and the rest of this section. "Since[9] we believe," Paul writes, "that Jesus died and rose again," then we must also believe (a phrase not in the Greek, but clearly implied by the sentence construction) "that God"— whom Paul elsewhere consistently describes as the God who raised Jesus from the dead (e.g., 1:10; Rom. 4:24; 6:9; 8:11; 10:9; 1 Cor. 15:4, 15, 20; Gal. 1:1)—"will bring with Jesus those who have fallen asleep in him" (cf. 2 Cor. 4:14; also Rom. 6:4; 8:11; 1 Cor. 15:22). That is, for Paul so close is the connection between Jesus and those who believe in him that belief in his resurrection carries with it, as a necessary corollary, belief in the resurrection of his followers (cf. 1 Cor. 15:20, "Christ has indeed been raised from the dead, the *firstfruits* of those who have fallen asleep").

In other words, there is a fundamental and decisive difference between a typical pagan and a Christian attitude toward death. Whereas for the former it meant a permanent end to life, for the latter it was a transition to an even better mode of existence, life in the presence of Jesus (cf. Phil. 1:21–23). Thus Paul took it for granted that Christians should face death not with despair but with hope—a hope in what God will do, grounded in what he has already done.

---

8. Regarding the NIV's "rest of men, who have no hope," (1) the comma is misleading; Paul does not mean "all other humans, who have no hope" but "all other humans who have no hope" (in contrast to some who do have hope, false though it may be). (2) The added phrase "of men" is needlessly sexist (the Greek phrase is simply an inclusive "the rest").

9. This sentence in the Greek begins with the word *ei*, "if" (omitted by NIV). But inasmuch as Paul takes it for granted that the conditional statement (*ei* + indicative) is factual, the NRSV's "since" accurately reflects his logic (cf. BDF, § 372.1).

Additional Information (4:15–17)

IN VERSES 15–17 Paul spells out the implications of all this for those who have already died. "According to the Lord's own word,"[10] the apostle writes in verse 15, "we[11] who are alive" when the Parousia takes place "will certainly *not* precede" or have some kind of advantage over those who have already died.[12] They will not miss the event, nor will they be disadvantaged in any way; if anything, they will have a slight *ad*vantage. For when the "Lord himself" descends from heaven (4:16), announced by archangel and trumpet, "the dead in Christ [cf. 1 Cor. 15:18; Rev. 14:13] will rise first"; only then, Paul goes on to say (cf. 1 Cor. 15:23), will those still alive when the event occurs "be caught up together with them."

The details Paul associates with the Lord's descent are a collection of richly evocative images. The "command" or order, a military term, evokes the Lord's authority and power (cf. Philo, *Rewards and Punishments*, 117: God is able to gather together the scattered exiles with a single command) and may be associated with the calling forth of the dead (cf. John 5:24–25). For the "trumpet call" see (in addition to the parallels noted above, esp. 1 Cor. 15:52), Isaiah 27:13 (the trumpet summons the exiles to return to Jerusalem); Joel 2:1; Zechariah 9:14.[13] Finally,

---

10. Paul is probably referring to an otherwise unrecorded teaching of Jesus, similar to or perhaps associated with the Synoptic Apocalypse (cf. the parallels noted at the beginning of this Original Meaning section), which apparently circulated as part of early Christian tradition. While the content of the teaching apparently predates Paul, the wording of the following verses likely reflects his own paraphrase and application of the tradition. For a discussion of various hypotheses and possibilities, see E. Best, *Thessalonians*, 189–94; F. F. Bruce, *1 and 2 Thessalonians*, 98–99; C. A. Wanamaker, *Thessalonians*, 170–71; Richard. *Thessalonians*, 239–41; I. H. Marshall, *1 and 2 Thessalonians*, 125–27.

11. Paul's use of "we" (4:15, 17) implies (but does not prove) that he expected to be alive when the Parousia occurred. As time went on, he appears to have recognized that he might not survive until that event (cf. 2 Cor. 1:8–9; 4:14; Phil. 1:20–24). For discussion see B. Witherington III, *Jesus, Paul and the End of the World* (Downers Grove, Ill.: InterVarsity, 1992), 24–25; F. F. Bruce, *1 and 2 Thessalonians*, 99; E. Best, *Thessalonians*, 194–96; C. A. Wanamaker, *Thessalonians*, 171–72; I. H. Marshall, *1 and 2 Thessalonians*, 127.

12. Secular ideas about the disadvantages of an "untimely death" may be part of the background here. Cf. Plutarch, *Ad Apollonium*, 113C: "Some may assert that there need not be mourning for every death, but only for untimely death, because of the failure of the dead to gain what are commonly held to be the advantages of life, such as marriage, education, manhood, citizenship, or public office." There were also some Jewish traditions that suggested that when the End arrived, the living might have some advantage over the dead (cf. 4 Ezra 13:16–20).

13. The "voice" and the trumpet may be a single sound; cf. Ps. 47:5 (LXX 46:6), "God has ascended with a shout, / the Lord with the sound of a trumpet," and Rev. 1:10; 4:1.

throughout the Bible clouds have symbolized God's presence, whether during the Exodus (Ex. 16:10), at Mount Sinai (24:16), in the desert (Num. 11:25), at Solomon's temple (1 Kings 8:10), or at the Transfiguration (Mark 9:7) and Ascension (Acts 1:9).[14]

Those alive at the Parousia are said to be "caught up" together with the risen dead "to meet the Lord" (lit., "to a meeting with the Lord"). "Caught up" translates *harpazo*, "to seize, snatch" (in Latin *rapere*, from which comes the English word "rapture"). In using this particular word Paul may be making a play on words; Plutarch, a near contemporary of Paul, used the word (or compounds of it) for those who die an untimely death and thus are "disadvantaged" in that they are "snatched away" from the opportunity for education, marriage, citizenship, and so on.[15]

The word for "meeting," *apantesis*, is used in the LXX for God's meetings with Abraham (Gen. 14:17), with David (2 Sam. 19:16), and with the Israelites at Sinai (Ex. 19:17). It was frequently used in secular Greek as a technical term for the formal reception of a visiting dignitary, in which a delegation of citizens or city officials would go out to meet a guest on his way to the city and escort him back into town with appropriate pomp and circumstance.[16] In the New Testament (Matt. 25:6; Acts 28:15) *apantesis* describes exactly this same kind of movement of a welcoming party going out to meet someone and escorting him back to the destination. The implication of Paul's use of this word here is that the resurrected dead and raptured living together will meet the descending Lord "in the air"[17] and accompany him in glory and honor the rest of his way to earth.[18]

Paul's emphasis in these verses, however, is not on the sequence, details, or direction, but on the outcome and result. (1) He assures the

---

14. See also Dan. 7:13; Rev. 14:14.

15. Plutarch, *Ad Apollonium*, 111D, 117B–C (for the word); 113C (for the discussion; see footnote 12); cf. Abraham J. Malherbe, "Exhortation in First Thessalonians," *NovT* 25 (1983): 255–56.

16. In this sense it is closely associated with the Greek word *parousia*, which in Hellenistic usage often indicated a visit by a dignitary or official.

17. The "air" (Gk. *aer*) was often viewed as the dwelling place of demons; that the triumphant meeting between Jesus and his followers takes place there may indicate just how complete is the victory over death and sin.

18. Cf. F. F. Bruce, *1 and 2 Thessalonians*, 103; I. H. Marshall, *1 and 2 Thessalonians*, 131. But nothing in the word itself or the context demands such an interpretation, and an ascent to heaven (rather than descent to earth) remains a possibility (cf. C. A. Wanamaker, *Thessalonians*, 175–76; E. J. Richard, *Thessalonians*, 247–48).

Thessalonians that contrary to what some of them may have thought, both groups, the dead and the living, will end up together. (2) The most important point to note in all this is the result: *All* believers in Jesus, whether alive or dead at the time of his Parousia, "will be with the Lord forever." That is, death—the one thing that some Thessalonians (apparently still influenced by pagan perspectives) thought would stand as an insurmountable barrier, preventing those followers of Jesus who died before the Parousia from experiencing the presence of Jesus—is in reality no barrier at all. Here is the real antidote to the grief some Thessalonians were experiencing: The final destiny of Christians who died before the Parousia is not death, but rather resurrection leading to life with the Lord forever.

Application (4:18)

THIS CHRISTOLOGICALLY BASED conviction is the source of the hope Paul mentioned in 4:13, in light of which he urges the Thessalonians (4:18) to "encourage [*parakaleo* again, as in 4:1, but here more in the sense of "comfort," as in 3:7] each other with these words" (cf. 5:11). This is, in fact, the goal of the whole paragraph: Paul's discussion of what will happen in the future was not an end, but only a means to an end. Knowledge of the future ought to shape and influence how we live in the present, even in the presence of death, and it is on this basis that the apostle exhorts and encourages the Thessalonians.

To recapitulate: After stating the topic ("those who have died") in verse 13, Paul shares a fundamental theological affirmation: God will bring with Jesus those who have died (v. 14). He then shares some additional information (vv. 15–17) and indicates how the Thessalonians should use this information: to encourage one another (v. 18).

Bridging Contexts

THIS PASSAGE IS the first of several in the Thessalonian letters that deal with what are often termed "things to come"—that is, experiences or events in the future such as death, resurrection, the return of Jesus, and judgment. Because these passages deal with events that have not yet happened (on both the individual and the global level), they have, for obvious reasons, long fascinated people, particularly in times of distress or great turmoil. Unfortunately, these texts also have a long history of being misunderstood, misused, and fiercely debated.

For this reason, it is important to keep several things clearly in mind regarding this section as we attempt to bring it to our day and age. (1) In this passage Paul is dealing with a fairly narrow question: the fate of believers who die before Christ returns. To this question he gives a clear and unambiguous answer: The ultimate fate of all believers, regardless of when or if they die, is to "be with the Lord forever" (4:17). This is the final word of his answer and the central point of the passage.

(2) Paul's expectations of what God and Jesus will do in the future are grounded in his convictions about what God and Jesus have already done in the past. What Paul says here is not a matter of optimistic speculation but of a confident hope: The future resurrection of those who are "dead in Christ" (4:16) is an unavoidable corollary of God's past resurrection of Christ himself.[19]

(3) Paul writes about the dead for the sake of the living. That is, while his main topic is the future fate of the believing dead, his primary focus is the present conduct of the living. If 2:1—12 offered a portrait of Paul the missionary, here we catch a glimpse of Paul the pastor as he clarifies how the affirmation about what the Thessalonians *believe* (4:14) ought to shape and influence how they *live*, even in the face of what he terms elsewhere "the last enemy," death itself (1 Cor. 15:26). He expects that what he says about deceased brothers and sisters will shape the attitudes and behavior of the brothers and sisters still living in Thessalonica.

(4) This means that Paul's fundamental purpose in this section is not to answer any and all questions that his readers (then or now) may have about their future, but to equip the Thessalonian believers to encourage one another (4:18). Whatever he says by way of instruction is in the service of his exhortation.

(5) Finally, it is important to note the differing assumptions underlying the question and its answer. Those asking the question apparently assumed that death was the ultimate end of human existence, whereas for Paul the ultimate end for believers is life.

---

19. Throughout this passage Paul takes the historicity of the resurrection of Jesus for granted. For a full discussion from both theological and apologetic perspectives, see Murray J. Harris, *From Grave to Glory: Resurrection in the New Testament* (Grand Rapids: Zondervan, 1990); also Craig Blomberg, *1 Corinthians* (NIVAC; Grand Rapids: Zondervan, 1994), 293—322.

The pitfall of a literal interpretation of metaphoric language. If we keep these points in mind, it may be possible to navigate successfully around two major pitfalls that one encounters in this passage (and others like it), pitfalls that have the potential to bog down or sidetrack application of the passage. The first potential pitfall has to do with the nature of the events the passage describes. Resurrection and the return of Jesus, for example, are events that are beyond the range of present human experience and which strain the ability of language to describe them. In order to communicate the truth about these future events that transcend the boundaries of human experience and the limits of language, Paul follows the example (and often borrows from the language) of the Old Testament prophets.

The prophets sometimes used figurative language or metaphors to alert their audience to the significance of predicted events in human history. For instance, in Isaiah 13 the prophet utilized images of cosmic disaster (e.g., the stars, sun, and moon not giving light, and the heavens trembling; see vv. 10, 13) to describe the historical event of God's judgment of Babylon. The prophet Joel associated similar language ("I will show wonders in the heavens and on the earth, blood and fire and billows of smoke. The sun will be turned to darkness and the moon to blood," Joel 2:30–31) with his prophecy of the coming of the Holy Spirit in the last days (2:28–32). According to Peter, who quotes Joel 2:28–32, this prophecy was fulfilled on the day of Pentecost (see Acts 2:16–21). Examples like this indicate that the biblical writers made use of at least some degree of metaphor or figurative language in speaking of future events.

Like the prophets, Paul also occasionally used figurative or metaphorical language, as his use of "sleep" as a metaphor for death in 4:13 demonstrates. But this has not always been recognized, and metaphorical language in Paul's letters has sometimes been (mis-)interpreted too literally.[20] Two quite different outcomes have resulted from this literalistic misreading of Paul's teachings about future events. (1) Some have rejected Paul's message. Shaped by an Enlightenment perspective that draws a sharp distinction between the supernatural and the natural and understands that the world as a closed continuum of natural cause and effect, these interpreters have either rejected Paul's

---

20. For example, some readers, encountering a passage such as 2 Thess. 1:7 that speaks of Jesus coming from heaven "in blazing fire," have taken it as a literal description.

statements as "mythical" and/or irrelevant to a modern scientific world-view, or they have decided that they must be radically reinterpreted or "demythologized" in order to make sense today.[21] Such approaches, which essentially see Paul as only a "child of his times" and ignore the divine inspiration of Scripture, have been unanimously rejected by evangelical scholars.[22]

(2) Other interpreters, taking Paul's metaphorical language too literally, read into his letters meanings or ideas he never intended to communicate. For example, the idea of "soul sleep" (the erroneous idea that believers are unconscious between the time of death and the coming of Christ), taught by Jehovah's Witnesses and Seventh-Day Adventists, is based on a misunderstanding of Paul's use of sleep as a metaphor for death.[23]

Those who reject the Pauline message basically deny any reality behind Paul's figurative language or metaphors, while those who read extraneous ideas into Paul's message confuse the metaphor with the reality it represents. How can we avoid these two outcomes? While both approaches misunderstand too literally the symbolic language that Paul uses to speak of future events, at least the second approach recognizes that Paul is speaking of historical realities. This is an important point to emphasize: The New Testament in general, and Paul in particular, places the future events of resurrection, judgment, and the return of Christ on the same historical level as his ministry, death, and resurrection. In fact, Paul's belief in what God will yet do is grounded in his convictions about what God has already done. The future is shaped by the past. While this perspective may be viewed with skepticism by an Enlightenment worldview, in reality it calls into question the Enlightenment's radical separation between natural and supernatural, a distinction that seems odd to much of the non-Western world.

---

21. The well-known New Testament scholar and theologian Rudolph Bultmann is most often associated with this latter approach. He understood Paul's idea of Christ's return at the end of history as judge of the living and the dead to mean that every person must have an existential encounter with Christ, which will be determinative for her or his destiny.

22. On this question of figurative or metaphorical language, see further I. H. Marshall, *1 and 2 Thessalonians*, 128–29; Douglas J. Moo, *2 Peter, Jude* (NIVAC; Grand Rapids: Zondervan, 1996), 173–78; and especially G. B. Caird, *The Language and Imagery of the Bible* (with a Foreword by N. T. Wright; Grand Rapids: Eerdmans, 1997).

23. See further Frank Thielman, *Philippians* (NIVAC; Grand Rapids: Zondervan, 1995), 84.

But at the same time that we affirm the historical realities of which Paul speaks, we must acknowledge that he sometimes utilizes symbolic or metaphoric language to express them. This means that in interpreting passages in which Paul speaks about the future, there may well be some degree of uncertainty or disagreement about some of what he says, especially with regard to details. As a consequence, we do well to follow John R. W. Stott's guideline:

> We will be wise to combine affirmation (we are eagerly expecting a cosmic event which will include the personal, visible appearing of Jesus Christ and the gathering to him of all his people, whether dead or alive at the time) with agnosticism about the full reality behind the imagery.[24]

That is, we must affirm the central elements of what Paul teaches (Jesus is coming again) while acknowledging the possibility of uncertainty about some of the details (will Jesus and his followers descend to earth or return to heaven after the "meeting in the air"?).

The pitfall of unanswered questions. A second pitfall arises out of the circumstance that in answering one specific question, Paul raises (but does not answer) several other questions. These include the nature of the resurrection body, whether any change takes place to the bodies of those who are caught up, the state of the Christian dead between death and resurrection, the resurrection of unbelievers, judgment and the Judgment Day, and so forth.[25]

Some of these questions can be answered on the basis of other Pauline passages. The apostle, for example, discusses the nature of the resurrection body in 1 Corinthians 15:35—49 and indicates in 15:50—53 that while not all believers will die (and consequently be resurrected), "we all will be changed" or transformed. Similarly, 2 Corinthians 5:1—10 and Philippians 1:23 indicate that between death and resurrection, deceased believers are aware of "being with Christ." In many instances when one is preaching or teaching on 1 Thessalonians 4:13—18, it will be advisable and legitimate to answer these other questions by looking at other passages of Scripture. The

---

24. J. R. W. Stott, *The Gospel and the End of Time,* 105—6.
25. For an excellent discussion of these and other related issues, see Harris's *From Grave to Glory* (see note 19).

challenge is to deal with them in a way that meets the needs or interests of the audience without distracting attention from the main points Paul makes here.

But some of the questions cannot even be answered, simply because the New Testament does not address them. In such instances, the challenge is to avoid becoming distracted by or dogmatic about points concerning which there are grounds for legitimate differences of opinion. One example of a question like this is the matter of the timing and direction of the "rapture" mentioned in 4:17. Some interpreters insist that this "catching up" of believers to be with the Lord is a separate event from the Parousia (the second coming) of Jesus, and that after being "caught up," the gathered assembly returns to heaven. But in view of the close correlation between 1 Thessalonians 4:13−18 and 1 Corinthians 15:51−52, and the way in which the events of 1 Corinthians are associated with Christ's return, many scholars (myself included) conclude that the events described in the present passage take place at the same time as the Parousia and that the gathered assembly of believers accompanies the Lord Jesus in a triumphal procession to earth.[26] In view of such differences, it seems unwise to become dogmatic about a particular interpretation of this passage or to make it a test of faith or fellowship.

ONE OF MY all-time favorite *Peanuts* cartoons involves a conversation between Lucy and Linus. Looking out a window, Lucy wonders: "Boy, look at it rain ... what if it floods the whole world?" "It will never do that," says Linus. "In the ninth chapter of Genesis, God promised Noah that would never happen again, and the sign of the promise is the rainbow." "You've taken a great load off my mind," replies Lucy, to which Linus responds: "Sound theology has a way of doing that!" The cartoon captures the essence of what Paul was doing in this passage in 1 Thessalonians: Offering "sound theology" as

---

26. See also the discussion of 2 Thess. 2:1−12 below. See further regarding this debate Gleason L. Archer, Paul D. Feinberg, Douglas. J. Moo, and Richard R. Reiter, *Three Views on the Rapture: Pre-, Mid-, or Post-Tribulational?* (Grand Rapids: Zondervan, 1984). A clear (and to my mind, decisive) presentation of the post-tribulation position is Bob Gundry, *First the Antichrist* (Grand Rapids: Baker, 1997).

a comfort and encouragement to friends trying to make sense of that universal human experience, death.

Death is a "hot" topic in contemporary American culture. Since the publication of Kübler-Ross's accounts of near-death experiences,[27] a steadily increasing number of books have appeared that deal with dying, death, and the afterlife, and mainstream media (both print and visual) now regularly deal with the topic. But if the more popular-level media offer any indication, the real point of interest is not simply death itself as much as what happens *after* death. Books that claim to offer a glimpse of what happens after death or that describe "walking towards a light" fill the shelves of retail outlets; major movies visualize fictitious stories of people who die, yet are still able to interact with the living; supermarket tabloids scream for attention with headlines like "What Really Happens After You Die."

Personal concerns regarding death. Behind all this intense general *interest* in death and its aftermath lies, I suspect, an even more intense personal *concern*: What will happen to *me* at death? It should come as no surprise that our culture's general interest in death turns out to be intensely personal, for as I noted above, death is one of the few things universal to human experience. Even the Thessalonians' question to Paul fits this pattern. Their general concern—"What about those who have died before Jesus comes?"—hides a more personal question: What will happen to me if I die before Jesus comes? In short, the underlying question back then is essentially the same as the one being asked today.

This means, in turn, that Paul's answer to their question is also an answer to ours. Keeping in mind that he is speaking specifically about believers (not humans in general), there are at least three specific aspects of his answer that probably need to be emphasized today.

(1) The future of believers is not so much a place as a relationship. To believers who, like people around us, wonder about what happens or "where we go" when we die, Paul says: "We will be with the Lord forever" (4:17). Compared to the detailed answers available from other sources (e.g., the Muslim portrayal of Paradise or those propounded by the New Age movement), this seems almost too basic, hardly sufficient to satisfy our intense curiosity. Yet this answer seems "basic" only if we fail

---

27. Elisabeth Kübler-Ross, *On Death and Dying* (New York: Macmillan, 1969).

to sense the substance of what Paul's affirmation implies. As Paul develops the point elsewhere,[28] resurrection (or rapture, as the case may be) to "be with the Lord forever" includes (a) the acquisition of a transformed resurrection body that is glorious and imperishable, and (b) the enjoyment of a relationship with Christ that is closer, richer, and fuller than the relationship we currently experience—in sum, a state of existence that Paul himself considers to be "better by far" (Phil. 1:23). Our present experience of Christ, in other words, is only a foretaste of what lies before us.

If Paul's answer about the future seems somewhat basic in comparison to other answers, it nonetheless has something they do not: a solid historical foundation. What Paul says about our future as believers is not a matter of baseless speculation, but is grounded in God's resurrection and exaltation of Jesus the Messiah. Our confident outlook towards the future is grounded in our knowledge of the past. What God has already done—rather than human speculation, unfounded optimism, or sheer wishful thinking—is the foundation on which our genuine hope for the future rests.

(2) *For believers, death is not an end but a transition.* The questions the Thessalonians raised reflect at least in part an assumption on their part that death was the final reality of human existence, an end point or barrier that even the return of Jesus could not cross or affect. Similar views of death are not uncommon today; even some Christian theologians argue that on an individual level there is nothing beyond death.[29] Against any materialistic philosophy or viewpoint that asserts such a view of death, Paul clearly declares that *there is a reality beyond even death.*

In contrast to the cynicism expressed in much of Ecclesiastes, whose author, after surveying everything that happened "under the sun," found only meaninglessness, frustration, and despair, Paul affirms that there is more to life than can be known only on the basis of human experience. In view of God's resurrection of Jesus, the death of a believer must be viewed not as an end to life, but as a transition to an even better experience of life: life in the presence of Jesus the Lord. Martin Luther King Jr. expressed this with characteristic eloquence in

---

28. Primarily in 1 Corinthians 15 and 2 Corinthians 5; for a full discussion see Murray J. Harris, *From Grave to Glory*, 185–231.

29. For examples, see Stephen H. Travis, *Christian Hope and The Future* (Downers Grove, Ill.: InterVarsity, 1980), 93–95.

a sermon at the funeral of the four young girls killed by a racist's bomb in Birmingham, Alabama, in 1963:

> I hope you can find some consolation from Christianity's affirmation that death is not the end. Death is not a period that ends the great sentence of life, but a comma that punctuates it to more lofty significance. Death is not a blind alley that leads the human race into a state of nothingness, but an open door which leads man into life eternal. Let this daring faith, *this great invincible surmise,* be your sustaining power during these trying days.[30]

To affirm with Paul that death is not an end but a transition is not at all to deny or minimize the destructive effects of death, which include the disruption of valued and significant human relationships. As John R. W. Stott observes, "However firm our Christian faith may be, the loss of a close relative or friend causes a profound emotional shock. To lose a loved one is to lose a part of oneself. It calls for radical and painful adjustments, which can take many months" or even years.[31] In such circumstances, mourning is a natural, even necessary, response; as D. A. Carson observes, "The Bible everywhere assumes that those who are bereaved will grieve, and their grief is never belittled."[32]

But even in the midst of our mourning and sorrow, Paul reminds us not to lose sight of God's resurrection of Jesus, that decisive victory over death in which all departed believers will participate eventually when God also raises them (4:14). For this reason the way in which we mourn ought to be qualitatively different from those "who have no hope" (4:13). "What Paul prohibits is not grief but hopeless grief."[33] In seasons of loss, testifying to the hope we have in Christ may not be easy. "The struggle," as Leighton Ford, the noted evangelist and mission leader, whose oldest son died at age twenty-one, notes, "is to bring our faith and our emotions together."[34] That is precisely the chal-

---

30. Quoted by Susan Bergman, "In The Shadow of the Martyrs," *CT* 40:9 (August 12, 1996): 25.

31. J. R. W. Stott, *The Gospel and the End of Time,* 92–93.

32. D. A. Carson, *How Long, O Lord? Reflections on Suffering and Evil* (Grand Rapids: Baker, 1990), 112.

33. J. R. W. Stott, *The Gospel and the End of Time,* 94.

34. Leighton Ford, *Sandy: A Heart for God* (Downers Grove, Ill.: InterVarsity, 1985), as quoted by J. R. W. Stott, *The Gospel and the End of Time,* 93.

lenge that death presents to Christians: to live out their beliefs when it is most difficult to do so.

(3) *What we know and believe about the future ought to shape how we live in the present.* While Paul's subject was the fate of believers who had died, his audience was believers who were alive, and his last word is to them: "Therefore encourage each other with these words" (4:18). Paul clearly expects the information he has imparted to the Thessalonians to affect their attitudes and behavior. If the assumption of some of them (namely, that death is the end) were true, then an Epicurean approach to life—"Let us eat and drink, for tomorrow we die"—would be appropriate, as Paul himself recognizes (1 Cor. 15:32). But precisely because that view of life is not true, because we do look forward to the resurrection of the dead, we live not for the moment but with an eye to the future. More important, how we live now ought to be shaped in fundamental ways by that future.

Suicide bombers, tragically convinced that they will enter Paradise when they die, willingly give their lives for political or religious causes. Jehovah's Witnesses labor in hope that they might be found among the 144,000 who qualify for heaven, and Mormons strive toward extraterrestrial rewards. If mistaken beliefs such as these can have such an impact on those who hold them, should the beliefs of Christians, grounded as they are in the resurrection of Jesus, have any less impact? Yet it often appears that many Christians are indistinguishable from their neighbors in critical respects. Risk-averse and security-conscious, we seem unwilling to risk much of anything, let alone our lives, for the sake of the gospel. Yet it is in fact risk-taking living in this world to which the gospel calls us ("For whoever wants to save his life will lose it, but whoever loses his life for me and for the gospel will save it," Mark 8:35).

The early church understood this. For example, when an epidemic broke out in a city and the inhabitants fled to the countryside in fear, many Christians stayed to minister to the sick (Christian and non-Christian alike) in the spirit of Matthew 25:35–40, secure in the knowledge that dying in the service of the gospel meant life with Christ forever. Moreover, their ministry became a powerful means of evangelism that contributed significantly to the long-term expansion of Christianity.[35] If an Ebola-like epidemic were to break out in our city

---

35. See Rodney Stark, *The Rise of Christianity* (Princeton: Princeton Univ. Press, 1996), 73–94.

today and a call for volunteers to serve and minister went out, how would we respond? This is the kind of question with which this passage confronts us.

Confronting our own mortality. More generally (and less hypothetically), the passage challenges us to confront our own mortality. It invites us to ask about the extent to which our thinking about and behavior regarding death is motivated by either fear or denial of it. It offers an opportunity to decide if we really believe, with Paul, that for believers "to die is gain" (Phil. 1:21, 23). None of these questions is easy to deal with, since they force us to confront death. The good news is that we do not need to confront death only on the basis of our own resources, but on the basis of faith in the God who has already conquered death in the resurrection of his Son, our Lord. The refrain to a familiar hymn captures well Paul's basic point in this passage:

> Because He lives I can face tomorrow,
> Because He lives all fear is gone;
> Because I know He holds the future.
> And life is worth the living just because He lives.[36]

I read recently about a woman who described how, when her mother's death had become inevitable, she nonetheless wanted the doctors to do everything they could to keep her mother alive because, as she only later realized, she did not want to be the "next in line." This kind of denial is not uncommon; as Martin Marty points out, "a strong majority of Americans share that belief [in eternal life], yet they live in terror of death."[37] How different, however, was the attitude exemplified by the late Archbishop of Chicago, John Cardinal Bernardin. The faith, grace, and courage with which he faced, very publicly, his death from cancer won him wide and genuine respect from people across the nation, indeed around the world. In the manner in which he lived his life in the face of his own imminent death, he modeled a genuinely Christian attitude toward death. For the archbishop, death

---

36. "Because He Lives," text by Gloria Gaither and William J. Gaither, music by William J. Gaither. Copyright 1971 by William J. Gaither.

37. Quoted in Kenneth L. Woodward and John McCormick, "The Art of Dying Well," *Newsweek*, November 25, 1996, 63 (a news report about Archbishop Bernardin).

may have been, in Paul's words, the "last enemy" (1 Cor. 15:26); but it was not the final victor, for the ultimate victory belongs to God, who "gives us the victory through our Lord Jesus Christ" (15:57). And therein lies our hope.

1 Thessalonians 5:1–11

NOW, BROTHERS, ABOUT times and dates we do not need to write to you, ²for you know very well that the day of the Lord will come like a thief in the night. ³While people are saying, "Peace and safety," destruction will come on them suddenly, as labor pains on a pregnant woman, and they will not escape.

⁴But you, brothers, are not in darkness so that this day should surprise you like a thief. ⁵You are all sons of the light and sons of the day. We do not belong to the night or to the darkness. ⁶So then, let us not be like others, who are asleep, but let us be alert and self-controlled. ⁷For those who sleep, sleep at night, and those who get drunk, get drunk at night. ⁸But since we belong to the day, let us be self-controlled, putting on faith and love as a breastplate, and the hope of salvation as a helmet. ⁹For God did not appoint us to suffer wrath but to receive salvation through our Lord Jesus Christ. ¹⁰He died for us so that, whether we are awake or asleep, we may live together with him. ¹¹Therefore encourage one another and build each other up, just as in fact you are doing.

Original Meaning

THE TOPIC OF this unit, "times and dates" (introduced by the "now ... about," as in 4:9), is closely connected with the previous one. Whereas 4:13–18 dealt with the fate of the Christian dead at the Parousia of Jesus, 5:1–11 deals with the attitude of the living towards the same event. There he reassured the community about the fate of the deceased believers at the time of the Parousia; here he reassures them regarding the fate of living believers at the time of the Parousia (as children of the day, they will not be subject to wrath) and reminds them of the need to "be alert and self-controlled" (5:6) in the meantime.

After describing how the Parousia will seem to non-Christians (5:2–3), Paul addresses the Thessalonian brothers and sisters[1] in 5:4–11. Within this section verses 4–5, 7, and 9–10a state "indicatives," which are followed by "imperatives" in verses 6, 8, and 10b–11. The reference to "awake or asleep" in 5:10 demonstrates the close connection in Paul's mind between this section and the preceding one, as does the concluding exhortation in 5:11 (cf. 4:18), which functions as a general conclusion for 4:13–5:10.

"Times and Dates" (5:1–2)

THE STARTING POINT in this passage is the issue of when the Lord will return. As in 4:13, Paul appears to be responding to a Thessalonian question. It cannot be determined, however, what prompted it. It is often suggested that the question about the timing of the Day of the Lord arose out of an intense (perhaps even overheated) interest in or curiosity about when that Day would come, and that Paul was trying to moderate or control this "eschatological fervor."

But in view of (1) the way in which Paul goes out of his way to assure the Thessalonians of what they *are* (children "of the light" and "of the day," 5:4, 8), (2) his reminder that "God did not appoint us to suffer wrath" (5:9; cf. 1:10), and (3) the way he encourages them to encourage one another (5:11), it is possible that the Thessalonians' question was prompted not by curiosity but rather fear and concern about the fate of the living believers at the time of the Parousia. That is, the question here may closely parallel the question behind 4:13–18. There the concern was for the fate of deceased believers at the Parousia (would they miss it?), while here the concern is for the fate of living believers at the Parousia (who apparently did not want to be caught unprepared for the coming wrath that would accompany it; cf. 1:10).[2]

The words translated as "times" and "dates" (*chronōn* and *kairōn*, "times and seasons," KJV, NRSV; cf. Dan. 2:21; 7:12) are in the New Testament

---

1. For the significance of *adelphoi* (NIV "brothers") in 5:1 (which includes the entire community, not just the male members), see comments on 1:4.

2. Similarly I. H. Marshall: "The members were worried not only about the fate of those who had already died at the imminent parousia but also about their own position; the character of the parousia as sudden, unexpected judgment upon unbelievers filled them with anxiety regarding themselves also" ("Election and Calling to Salvation in 1 and 2 Thessalonians," in *The Thessalonian Correspondence*, ed. Raymond F. Collins [Leuven: Leuven Univ. Press, 1990], 260).

period basically synonymous (cf. Acts 3:19–21). Together they form an idiomatic phrase whose meaning here is essentially "when" (cf. Acts 1:7). The event about whose timing the Thessalonians are curious is identified in 5:2 as the "day of the Lord" (cf. 2 Thess. 2:2; also 1 Cor. 5:5). In the Old Testament this was described as a day of judgment for the opponents of God, but a day of deliverance for the faithful (e.g., Isa. 2:1–4:6; Joel 1:15; 2:1, 11, 31–32; Amos 5:18–20; Zeph. 1:14; Zech. 14). Paul consistently carries over this double aspect of the "day of the Lord," which he also terms the "day of our Lord Jesus [Christ]" (1 Cor. 1:8; cf. 2 Cor. 1:14), or simply as the "day of [Jesus] Christ" (Phil. 1:6, 10; 2:16), or even just "the day" (1 Thess. 5:4; 2 Thess. 1:10; cf. 1 Cor. 3:13). The phrase designates the same event as the Parousia (1 Thess. 4:15) of Jesus. Paul likely switches terms here because his emphasis falls more on the aspect of judgment than deliverance.

As to when the Day will occur, Paul writes that there is nothing more he can say on the point ("we do not need to write you"), since the Thessalonians already "know very well" the only thing one needs to know about "when" it will occur: It "will come like a thief in the night" (5:2; cf. 2 Peter 3:10; Rev. 3:3; 16:15). The most likely source of this metaphor is the teaching of Jesus (cf. Matt. 24:43//Luke 12:39), where this expression occurs in a context stressing the necessity of readiness or watchfulness (Matt. 24:44//Luke 12:40)—a theme Paul picks up in 5:4–6. Its use here throws emphasis on the unexpectedness of the Day's arrival and on its threatening character as a time of judgment for those who are unprepared.

"Peace and Safety" (5:3)?

BOTH OF THESE aspects are developed in 5:3 (which, like 5:2, draws heavily on Gospel tradition; cf. Luke 21:34–36). At a time when all *appears* well, "destruction" will arrive with the suddenness of labor pains (a common biblical image for pain and agony, though here the emphasis is more on the suddenness with which they begin). Anyone who is not "with the Lord" (cf. 4:17) will certainly *not* (the negative is emphatic) escape (any more than a pregnant woman can avoid the inevitable labor pains).

While the phrase "peace and safety" (or "security") has partial Old Testament antecedents (Jer. 6:14; 8:11; Ezek. 13:10–16; Mic. 3:5), its more likely context is a political one, inasmuch as *pax et securitas* was a popular slogan of the imperial Roman propaganda machine. The promise of peace and security was what Rome offered to those peoples who submitted (willingly or unwillingly) to Roman rule and military power; it was seen as Rome's gift to those it conquered, virtually equivalent to an offer of deliverance or "salvation" from turmoil and danger.[3] But from Paul's perspective, any such claims are illusory and deceptive and therefore dangerous. Only trust in God will deliver one from the "destruction" accompanying the coming Day of the Lord.

"Destruction" (or perhaps "disaster") can indicate loss of property, death, or eternal punishment. In 2 Thessalonians 1:9, the phrase "eternal destruction" stands as the opposite of "eternal life." Here, however, where the adjective is "sudden" rather than "eternal," the idea seems to be one of some sort of historical catastrophe or disaster, perhaps as a foreshadowing or anticipation of an eternal loss or judgment to follow.[4]

Alertness and Self-Control (5:4–8)

IN 5:4–8 PAUL extends the metaphor and imagery of 5:2–3 ("day," "thief," "night"). The imagery of light and darkness (often in phrases like "offspring of light" and "offspring of darkness") was commonly utilized to designate "insiders" and "outsiders" (cf., e.g., Luke 16:8; John 12:36; Eph. 5:8; 1 John 1:6–7; 2:9–11; 1QS 1:9–10; 3:13; 3:24–25; 1QM 1:1, 3). "Night" and "darkness" are associated with alienation from God and ignorance about the imminence of the Day of the Lord; correspondingly, "day" and "light" are associated with salvation and knowledge about the Day of the Lord. In 5:7 Paul picks up yet another aspect of "night"; its association with undisciplined behavior (drunkenness).

Verse 6, like much of this passage, has parallels in the Gospels (cf. Matt. 24:42–44; Mark 13:33, 36: "Be on your guard! Be alert!" "Do not let him find you sleeping"). Paul spells out two implications of the Thessalonians' status as children of light (1 Thess. 5:5). Unlike the "others" (i.e., unbelievers; cf. 4:5, 13), who sleep in ignorance (and will thus be caught off guard), the Thessalonians are to be "alert [cf. 5:10; also 1 Cor.

---

3. E. Bammel, "Romans 13," in *Jesus and the Politics of His Day*, ed. E. Bammel and C. F. D. Moule (Cambridge: Cambridge Univ. Press, 1984), 375–80. E. J. Richard (*Thessalonians*, 260) develops from a different direction a similar point.

4. See further on this term G. L. Borchert, "Wrath, Destruction," *DPL*, 992–93.

16:13; Col. 4:2; 1 Peter 5:8] and self-controlled" (NRSV "sober"; cf. 2 Tim. 4:5; 1 Peter 1:13; 4:7; 5:8). The first word (lit., "stay awake") emphasizes the need for vigilance; the second (lit., the opposite of drunkenness, cf. 5:7) conveys the idea of balance or discipline.

In 5:8a, where the phrase "since we belong to the day" essentially summarizes the point (and draws on the imagery) of 5:2–7, Paul repeats (and thus emphasizes) the call for self-control. He then drops the metaphors and images and associates[5] self-control with the familiar triad of faith, love, and hope (see comments on 1:3), which Paul describes using military images (chest protector, helmet; cf. Eph. 6:11–18; also Rom. 13:12) likely drawn from the Old Testament (cf. Isa. 59:17; also Wis. 5:17–20). In this triad the emphasis falls on "the hope of salvation," a phrase that reveals how for Paul salvation is in its fullness a future gift (cf. Rom. 5:10; 8:24; 13:11), which believers currently experience (cf. 1 Cor. 1:18; 2 Cor. 2:15) only in part and thus look forward to in hope.[6]

Salvation, Not Wrath (5:9–11)

ALTHOUGH IN 5:4–5, 8a Paul has already stated a basis for his exhortations about vigilance and in 5:6, 8 about discipline, in 5:9 (note the "for") he gives what amounts to an additional reason, one that not only supplements what he gave in 5:4–5 but also states its theological basis. The Thessalonians' status as "children of the light" (NIV[ILE]), who on the "Day of the Lord" are "appointed . . . to receive salvation," is grounded in God's activity on their behalf. That is, the Thessalonians can stay alert and be self-controlled in genuine hope because God himself has destined (cf. 1:4; 2:12; 3:3; 4:7; 5:24) them not "to suffer wrath" (see comments on 1:10), but rather "to receive salvation" (cf. 2 Thess. 2:13).[7]

---

5. It is an interesting question whether the verb "putting on" (NIV; cf. NRSV) signifies (1) an action simultaneous with the action of exercising self-control (in which case it indicates perhaps the means of exercising self-control), or (2) an action that precedes (already "having put on," NASB) the exercise of self-control (in which case it indicates a reason for exercising self-control). The word order (the aorist participle follows the main verb) slightly favors (1), but on the basis of the Old Testament background of the terms used here, B. R. Gaventa (*Thessalonians*, 72) makes a strong case for (2).

6. See further L. Morris, "Salvation," *DPL*, 858–62.

7. It is worth noting that "Paul does not suggest that the appointing of certain people to salvation means that others are appointed to wrath" (I. H. Marshall, *1 and 2 Thessalonians*, 140). It would be unwise to make any inferences about predestination to wrath on the basis of this text, since Paul himself does not address the topic here.

Paul spells out what this involves both negatively (the avoidance of wrath, 5:9) and positively (to "live together with" Jesus, 5:10b). This salvation comes "through our Lord Jesus Christ" (cf. Rom. 5:1, 11; 1 Cor. 15:57), who "died for us" (1 Thess. 5:10a; cf. Rom. 5:6, 8; 8:3; 14:15; 1 Cor. 15:3; 2 Cor. 5:14–15). Though Paul does not develop the idea here, "the implication is inescapable that through the death of Jesus something happened which transformed the destiny of believers. Had Jesus not died," they too would be subject to wrath, just like "the others" (5:6).[8] Paul no doubt intends this point to reassure the Thessalonians that their salvation is rooted in God through Jesus and is thus a genuine source of hope.

In 5:10–11 it becomes clear that Paul is linking 5:1–11 with 4:13–18 as well as 4:9–12. (1) Given that Paul viewed Jesus' death and resurrection as two sides of a single coin (cf. Rom. 14:9; 1 Cor. 15:3–4), his mention of the former here cannot but bring to mind his mention of the latter (cf. 1 Thess. 4:14). (2) Paul's description in 5:10b of the purpose of Christ's death—"that, whether we are awake or asleep, we may live together with him"—is phrased in words that obviously echo 4:15–17. (3) In 5:11a ("Therefore encourage one another") Paul essentially repeats 4:18 (though here he stresses encouragement more than comfort), while the rest of the verse ("build each other up, just as in fact you are doing") recalls what he said in 4:9–10 about *philadelphia*. Concerns about the fate of those who die before the Parousia and questions about its timing do not, for Paul, override the need to practice *philadelphia*; to the contrary, they provide concrete occasions for its exercise, as believers comfort and encourage one another in the midst of difficult circumstances, confident in the hope of a salvation grounded in the death and resurrection of the Lord Jesus.

CENTRAL POINTS. A common (and often effective) first move when bridging contexts in the Pauline letters is to identify the problem or question that generated Paul's comments. But since we do not really know what prompted Paul to address the topic of the Day of the Lord, a good alternative first move is to

---

8. I. H. Marshall, *1 and 2 Thessalonians*, 140.

identify the central points Paul makes in response. These include at least the following:

(1) No human being knows when the Day of the Lord will come (5:2).

(2) To unbelievers (who are asleep, "clueless," and "in the dark"), the coming of the Day will be a sudden and unexpected surprise (5:3, 5).

(3) To believers (who are "with it" and "in the know," because "the lights are on" for them), the coming of the Day will *not* be a surprise (5:4).

(4) In contrast to unbelievers, who have a false sense of security (5:3), believers have genuine security in the salvation grounded in the death (and, by implication, resurrection) of the Lord Jesus Christ (5:9—10).

(5) For believers (regardless whether they are dead or alive at the time), the coming of the Day of the Lord will mean life together with him (5:10).

(6) In the meantime, we should stay alert (5:6) and disciplined (5:6, 8) as we encourage and build up one another (5:11; cf. 4:18) in faith, love, and hope (5:8; cf. 1:3).

After identifying these central points, an important second move is to highlight Paul's central focus in this passage. In 5:4, it becomes clear that Paul's primary concern is not to develop the implications of the Day of the Lord for unbelievers but rather to spell out clearly its implications for believers. As in 4:13—18, his focus is not on passing along information for its own sake, but on developing the implications of that information about the future for how the Thessalonians should both think and live in the present. Thus, having said in 5:2 all he can about "when" the Day of the Lord will occur, in 5:4 he directs his readers' attention away from the question of "when" to the matter of *how* they should conduct themselves in light of the unexpectedness of its coming. This strongly suggests the direction that any application of this passage ought to take.

Two secondary points. Beyond this, there are in this passage at least two substantial points that Paul touches on but does not discuss. Clearly, they are of no more than secondary interest with respect to this particular passage. But in some circumstances (such as working with new believers), it may be appropriate (or even necessary) to give them more attention than they receive here. (1) A significant aspect of Paul's theology underlies 5:9–10, where he alludes to but does not develop his theology of the cross. To grasp more fully his understanding of the death of Jesus and its significance, it will be necessary to bring in passages such as Romans 3:24–26 (cf. 5:6–10) and 2 Corinthians 5:19–21.[9] (2) A difficult question that arises out of 1 Thessalonians 5:2–3 is that of the fate of *unbelievers* on the Day of the Lord. Paul is so focused on the significance of the Day for believers that he simply does not develop this other issue. (He does, however, take up this point in 2 Thess. 1:5–10.)

A potential pitfall. Finally, we must avoid a major temptation when dealing with this passage: the temptation to speculate about—or even claim to know!—when the Day of the Lord will occur. No time in church history appears to have been free from people who have attempted to discern the time of Jesus' return. Certain periods or eras, however, have been plagued by it far more than others, generally because of calendrical or social conditions. The approach of the year 1000, for example, generated turmoil in parts of Europe, where the expectation that the world would end is said to have been widespread. In the fourteenth century widespread plagues and famines led many to think that the end was near, as did also the religious and political turmoil of the Reformation era.

The origins of groups such as the Jehovah's Witnesses and Seventh-Day Adventists can be traced back to nineteenth-century date setters. And now the late twentieth century—because of the combined effect of the approach of a new millennium and the founding of the modern state of Israel in 1948—is overrun with its own plague of date setters. The early 1970s saw Hal Lindsey's *The Late Great Planet Earth* (which, while scrupulously avoiding setting a date, nonetheless left the clear impression that 1988 was the year). More recently Edgar Whisenant gave eighty-eight alleged reasons why the Rapture would happen between September 11 and 13, 1988; when it did not, he then announced with even more conviction that 1989 was the year.[10]

---

9. See further A. E. McGrath, "Cross, Theology of the," *DPL*, 192–97; J. B. Green, "Death of Christ," *DPL*, 201–9.

10. "Edgar Whisenant: His New Predictions" (interview by Steven Lawson), *Charisma* 14 (February 1989), 58–61, 89.

Now, as the twentieth century draws to a close (I am writing this in 1997), the hypnotic, almost magnetic, effect of the coming millennium (combined, no doubt, with the lure of quick profits) is drawing date setters out of the woodwork. Representative advertisements that have crossed my desk recently include ones for *The Return of Jupiter* (the ad copy for this book, on the back page of the February 1997 issue of a magazine I have, reads: "A terrible earthquake is going to break the oceanic Earth crust under the Pacific Ocean by the year 1996 A.D."), *Earth's Two-Minute Warning: Today's Bible Predicted Signs of the End Times*, and *The End: Why Jesus Could Return by A.D. 2000* (ad copy: "50 Events Pointing to the Return of Christ by A.D. 2000! . . . *Get your copy while there is still time!*).

Not surprisingly, the tabloids are getting into the act, with headlines like "Judgement Day's exact date, time, and place" (January 31, 2001, in the Sinai region), or "The Date Jesus Will Return to Earth" (answer: "Unknown to the world, Jesus Christ will return to Earth on Dec. 25, 1997, ushering in an era of perfect peace and harmony, after a massive comet strikes our planet and eradicates most of mankind on Dec. 31, 1999"), appearing frequently on their covers. Nor is it a surprise, given today's cyber culture, to find Websites devoted to prophecy and the future.

In view of what both Jesus and Paul have to say about when Jesus will return (cf. Mark 13:32: "No one knows about that day or hour, not even the angels in heaven, nor the Son, but only the Father"), there is one thing we may confidently conclude about all attempts to identify in advance the date when Jesus will return: They are all wrong.[11] The temptation to try and figure out the date should be recognized for what it is, a temptation. Like most temptations, it distracts us from what we ought to be doing instead: encouraging and building up one another.

MUCH OF WHAT Paul says in this passage sounds as if it were his application of the teachings of Jesus, specifically Matthew 25:1–13 (the parable of the ten virgins) and

---

11. See further C. Marvin Pate and Calvin B. Haines, Jr., *Doomsday Delusions: What's Wrong with Predictions About the End of the World* (Downers Grove, Ill.: InterVarsity, 1995).

Luke 12:35–46 (exhortations to watch and be ready). Especially strik-ing is Luke 12:42–46:

> The Lord answered, "Who then is the faithful and wise man-ager, whom the master puts in charge of his servants to give them their food allowance at the proper time? It will be good for that servant whom the master finds doing so when he returns. I tell you the truth, he will put him in charge of all his possessions. But suppose the servant says to himself, 'My master is taking a long time in coming,' and he then begins to beat the menservants and maidservants and to eat and drink and get drunk. The mas-ter of that servant will come on a day when he does not expect him and at an hour he is not aware of. He will cut him to pieces and assign him a place with the unbelievers.

Key points emphasized in those two Gospel texts, alertness and discipline, are exactly the ones that Paul emphasizes (cf. 5:6, 8). Tak-ing this into consideration along with the summary of Paul's key points and primary focus given above suggests the following theses as a start-ing point for the contemporary significance of this passage.

The proper preparation for the coming Day of the Lord is service rather than speculation. Human beings are naturally curious, especially about the future. Add God to the mix, and it is easy to understand why speculation about the return of Jesus is so attractive and fasci-nating to so many people. But while it might seem like a harmless activity, there are several potential negative aspects associated with it. (1) Since no one knows when Jesus will return, speculation about when he will return is largely a waste of time, time that could be bet-ter invested in more productive activities.

(2) It often produces a waste of resources. When the Gulf War against Iraq broke out in 1991, publishers rushed to market updated editions of previously published books on Bible prophecy, seeking to cash in on the heightened interest in the Near East in Bible prophecy that the war generated. Not long afterward, one could hardy give these books away (one widely advertised book by a "name" author was later available by the case for forty cents a copy). This does not strike me as good stewardship of our time, energy, or money.

(3) Speculation about dates can lead to behavior that brings need-less ridicule to the gospel. Numerous Korean Christians in the early

1990s were not the first, nor will they likely be the last, to sell or give away property (or, conversely, run up big credit card debts), quit jobs, and generally withdraw from society to wait for an end that did not come when predicted (much to the amusement of secular society).[12]

(4) Finally, speculation feeds the development of a crisis mentality with regard to the return of Jesus. It generally feeds on fresh information—for example, a war, a major earthquake or natural disaster, some change in Europe that might possibly be construed as having something to do with the rise of a reconstituted Roman empire—that prompts people to ask if this could be a sign of the end. As Douglas Moo points out, "by doing so, they imply that Christ's return can be imminent only if the signs—as they interpret them, of course—are in place." The danger "is that Christians will adopt the appropriate eschatological mindset only in times of crisis" and pay less attention (if any) at other times.[13] In light of 5:3 ("while people are saying, 'Peace and safety'"), there is irony in this "crisis approach," since Paul's words at least allow for the possibility that Jesus will return at a moment when people think a crisis may have just passed.

This "crisis approach" is the opposite of what Paul recommends. In contrast to this binge-like approach, he advises self-control and discipline; in contrast to paying attention only in times of crisis, he urges alertness at all times. And in contrast to idle speculation, he recommends encouraging and building up one another—things we should be doing anyway. His mention of faith, love, and hope in 5:8 provides a clear pointer to what he has in mind: The "work produced by faith," the "labor prompted by love," and the "endurance inspired by hope in our Lord Jesus Christ" (1:3). In short, Paul is calling us to stay alert and to keep busy: to conduct ourselves as though Jesus may return soon (which he might), and to minister as though his coming may be delayed indefinitely (which it might).

Practically speaking, this is a matter of combining a short-term attitude with long-term planning. A short-term attitude is one that does not take the future for granted; it is an attitude that remembers that the future is in God's hands, not ours. Jesus told a parable about a "certain rich man" who said to himself, "You have plenty of good things laid up

---

12. See C. Marvin Pate and Calvin B. Haines, Jr., *Doomsday Delusions*, 10–14.
13. Douglas J. Moo, *2 Peter, Jude* (NIVAC; Grand Rapids: Zondervan, 1996), 195.

for many years. Take life easy; eat, drink and be merry." Yet that very night he was called to meet God (Luke 12:16–21). This man had an attitude the opposite of the one that Paul encourages us to adopt, in that he forgot that the future was in God's hands, not his own. To summarize, Paul wants us to plan and minister for the long haul, but to do so with the attitude he shared with James: *"If it is the Lord's will,* we will live and do this or that" (James 4:15, italics added).

For believers, the Day of the Lord is a cause of anticipation, not apprehension. At least some of the Thessalonians appear to have felt a degree of apprehension about the return of Jesus. There may be those today who share this sense of apprehension regarding the Parousia, perhaps because they associate it primarily with wrath, destruction, and judgment. Paul goes out of his way, however, to emphasize that it really ought to be a cause of anticipation.

He gives at least three reasons for this anticipation. (1) It means that as believers we will be with the Lord forever (a point Paul makes twice; cf. 4:17; 5:10). That is, the coming of Jesus will mean a transition to an even higher level of fellowship and life together with our risen Lord. (2) Even though wrath will be one aspect of the return of Jesus, God has destined us for salvation rather than wrath (5:9), which is the very thing from which Jesus will deliver us (1:10). (3) As Paul will say in a later letter, nothing—not even death or God's wrath—can "separate us from the love of God that is in Christ Jesus our Lord" (Rom. 8:39).

The only source of genuine security is God, not human institutions. As I noted above, *pax et securitas,* "peace and security," was what Rome offered to the peoples under its power and domination, and to many it was an appealing slogan. The same slogan is no less appealing today in the tumultuous world of the late twentieth century, where political, economic, and social turmoil leave many, many people with a deep longing for some degree of stability and safety. Even in the United States, which in comparison with much of the rest of the world enjoys unprecedented levels of peace and security, there is a deep sense of unease and insecurity. Its massive military power cannot guarantee domestic security, as the terrorist bombings of the World Trade Center and the federal office building in Oklahoma City have demonstrated. Its massive economic power does not guarantee personal economic security, as waves of corporate "down-sizing" and layoffs have shown.

Marketers have not been slow to exploit the resulting anxiety. Investment firms promise financial security. Ads for dead bolt locks, personal protection devices, and gated communities promise personal security (a promise now even making its way into automobile advertising). Ads for various other products promise to secure our health or future in other ways.

But from Paul's perspective, any and all such claims are illusory and deceptive. No social institution can guarantee our future. No economic organization or enterprise can guarantee our economic security. No form of government, whether it be a liberal welfare state or fascist regime, a "Committee for National Salvation" or an anti-government militia, can deliver on the promise of peace and safety. In an age when we are bombarded with promises of peace and security, it is important to remember that the only genuine source of eternal peace and security is trust in God and his Messiah, Jesus Christ the Lord. That, and that alone, not promises of peace and security, will deliver us from the wrath and destruction that will accompany the coming Day of the Lord.

To summarize: As believers today we should not become so fascinated by (or apprehensive about) the future return of Jesus that we fail to be his ministers in the present. Thessalonian concerns about the fate of those who died before the Parousia and questions about its timing did not, for Paul, override the need to practice *philadelphia*, "love for brother and sister"; on the contrary, they provided concrete occasions for its exercise. So too it is today: A proper understanding and awareness of the return of Jesus will energize us in the present, as we comfort and encourage one another in the midst of difficult circumstances, confident in the hope of a salvation grounded in the death and resurrection of the Lord Jesus.

1 Thessalonians 5:12–22

NOW WE ASK you, brothers, to respect those who work hard among you, who are over you in the Lord and who admonish you. [13]Hold them in the highest regard in love because of their work. Live in peace with each other. [14]And we urge you, brothers, warn those who are idle, encourage the timid, help the weak, be patient with everyone. [15]Make sure that nobody pays back wrong for wrong, but always try to be kind to each other and to everyone else.

[16]Be joyful always; [17]pray continually; [18]give thanks in all circumstances, for this is God's will for you in Christ Jesus.

[19]Do not put out the Spirit's fire; [20]do not treat prophecies with contempt. [21]Test everything. Hold on to the good. [22]Avoid every kind of evil.

THIS SECTION AT first sight appears to be something of a grab bag of miscellaneous exhortations and instructions. Scholars have long debated whether such sections in Paul's letters reflect specific issues in a particular church or are merely generic admonitions that have no intrinsic connection with the circumstances of the recipients. The observation that 5:12–22 have numerous parallels and similarities with Romans 12:3–18 has led some to conclude that here Paul shares with the Thessalonians traditional material applicable in a general way to any church. The differences between the two passages, however, are as significant as the similarities and suggest that while Paul does incorporate some general pastoral admonitions, he has shaped them to some extent in light of his knowledge of the situation in Thessalonica.[1]

---

1. See further I. H. Marshall, *1 and 2 Thessalonians*, 145–46 (who offers the most extensive list of possible parallels with Rom. 12); C. A. Wanamaker, *Thessalonians*, 190–91; E. J. Richard, *Thessalonians*, 272–74.

In terms of structure the section appears to fall into four segments: (1) verses 12–13; (2) verses 14–15; (3) verses 16–18; and (4) verses 19–22. The first and last of these segments likely deal with issues specific to Thessalonica. The middle two are more general in character and probably should not be pressed for clues about the state or problems of the congregation.

Congregational Responsibilities Toward Leaders (5:12–13)

VERSES 12–13A COMPRISE a single sentence in which Paul asks the congregation[2] to "respect" and to "hold ... in highest regard in love because of their work" a specific group within the church. The second verb elsewhere means "to think, consider," but the context here requires something like "to esteem, regard, respect," especially in view of the following adverb, "most highly, beyond all measure" (hence the NIV's "hold ... in highest regard"). But this means that "respect" is not the best translation of the first verb, since "respect" and "esteem/regard" are closer in meaning than the two words Paul has used. Either "acknowledge" or "recognize" (cf. 1 Cor. 16:18, "deserve recognition") better catches Paul's nuance here.[3]

In short, Paul is calling for proper recognition and appreciation of "those who work hard among you, who are over you in the Lord and who admonish you." The grammar makes it clear that he is describing a single group with three characteristics. Paul often uses the verb "to work" (*kopiao*, which sometimes indicates manual labor) to characterize his own activities on behalf of the gospel (1 Cor. 15:10; Gal. 4:11; Phil. 2:16; Col. 1:29) or those of members ministering within a congregation (1 Cor. 16:16; cf. Rom. 16:6, 12). This is its meaning here (the corresponding noun, *kopos*, occurs in 1:3 in the expression "labor prompted by love").

The second verb (*proïstemi*; NIV "are over"; NRSV "have charge of") can mean "to lead, protect, care for." Its meaning in Romans 12:8, where it occurs as one of a series of spiritual gifts, is subject to the

---

2. For the significance of *adelphoi* (NIV "brothers"), which includes the entire community, not just the "brothers," see discussion on 1:4 above.

3. Cf. C. A. Wanamaker, *Thessalonians*, 191–93; E. J. Richard, *Thessalonians*, 267–69; "respect" is supported by E. Best, *Thessalonians*, 224; I. H. Marshall, *1 and 2 Thessalonians*, 146–47.

same uncertainty we find here (although its position there between "contributing" and "showing mercy" suggests "care for" rather than "lead"). In 1 Timothy 3:4, 5, 12 it describes a father's relation to his household and children (which involves all three aspects), and in 1 Timothy 5:17 that of elders to the church. In Titus 3:8, 14 it involves "caring for" (i.e., "promoting") good works. The corresponding noun is used in Romans 16:2 of Phoebe, the benefactor who cared for (in a financial sense) Paul and others. The most consistent nuance running through these occurrences is that of "care for," a meaning that makes good sense in relation to the third term, "admonish" (*noutheteo*; cf. 5:14).[4]

Our difficulties in determining exactly what kinds of "work" these people are performing should not obscure the point that it is precisely "because of their work" (5:13) within and for the congregation that Paul directs the other brothers and sisters to acknowledge and appreciate them. Had Paul himself appointed them (as he did in some situations; cf. Acts 14:23), presumably such a request would not have been necessary, since the people in question would have had clear apostolic backing and support. The implication is that these people have surfaced within the congregation as "servants" or "ministers" (i.e., *diakonoi*; cf. Rom. 16:1 NRSV; 1 Cor. 16:15), and Paul is calling on the rest of the community to recognize that fact.

It is possible that 5:13b hints at a bit of tension between leaders and the rest of the congregation. But the call to "live in peace with each other" is common in Paul and elsewhere (see Rom. 12:18; 14:19; 2 Cor. 13:11; Eph. 4:3; Col. 3:15; 2 Tim. 2:22, Heb. 12:14; cf. Mark 9:50). In other words, Paul's purpose here may be preventative rather than curative. (For the meaning of "peace" see comments on 1 Thess. 1:1.)

Congregational Responsibilities Toward Individuals (5:14–15)

HAVING "SPOKEN OF the need of the community to respect its leaders," Paul "moves on to advise the community on how it ought to treat

---

4. See further E. Best, *Thessalonians*, 224–25 ("care for"); F. F. Bruce, *1 and 2 Thessalonians*, 118–19; I. H. Marshall, *1 and 2 Thessalonians*, 147–48 (who combines the ideas of "lead" and "care for"). C. A. Wanamaker (*Thessalonians*, 191–94) argues for the idea of "benefactor" or "patron"; similarly but more cautiously E. J. Richard, *Thessalonians*, 268, 275.

those with special spiritual problems and needs."[5] (1) He instructs them to "warn those who are idle." While the verb (which in 5:12 the NIV renders as "admonish") can carry a positive sense (e.g., Rom. 15:14), here it clearly includes a note of disapproval (cf. 1 Cor. 4:14). While "idle" is attested as a meaning for Paul's word here (*ataktos*), in fact it represents only a narrow part of the term's broader semantic range, which touches on ethical and social/political conduct. In light of 1 Thessalonians 4:11–12 above, which deal with responsible conduct or behavior, and how the related adverb and verb are utilized in 2 Thessalonians 3:6–15 (see esp. v. 11), it should probably be given here its more fundamental sense of "undisciplined, irresponsible, disorderly" (cf. NASB).

(2) They are to "encourage [*paramytheomai*; see 2:12] the timid." The range of meaning of the uncommon word translated "timid" (*oligopsychous*; NRSV "faint hearted") includes worried, discouraged, fearful, inadequate, lacking in confidence, despondent, sad, and weak. Nothing in the immediate context offers a clue to its precise nuance here or about its cause.

(3) "Help the weak" (cf. Rom. 15:1) is similarly imprecise.[6] The verb can be rendered "support, supply, help," or even "defend," while the "weakness" can involve moral temptation, spiritual shortcomings, physical weakness, or economic need.[7]

(4) The command to "be patient with everyone" in the congregation (echoed in Eph. 4:2; Col. 3:12) should be compared with Gala-

---

5. I. H. Marshall, *1 and 2 Thessalonians*, 150. Some have argued that 5:14–15 are directed to the leaders referred to in 5:12–13, but this is unlikely. The entire community is addressed in 5:12–13 and 16–18, and the introductory phrase in 5:14 is nearly identical to that of 5:12 (note esp. the repetition of *adelphoi*, "brothers and sisters"). Had Paul intended a change of subject in 5:14, he surely would have signaled it more clearly. Cf. E. Best, *Thessalonians*, 229.

6. Fee (*God's Empowering Presence*, 57; cf. J. E. Frame, *Thessalonians*, 196) suggests that the first three imperatives in 5:14 relate to earlier sections of the letter: The reference to the "idle" reprises 4:9–12, the "faint hearted" (NRSV; NIV "timid") would be those concerned about believers who have died (4:13–18), and the "weak" would be those at whom 4:3–8 were directed. But David Black, while agreeing with Fee regarding the first two points, argues that the "weak" are those addressed in 5:1–11 ("The Weak in Thessalonica: A Study in Pauline Lexicography," *JETS* 25 [1982]: 307–21). That the "weak" can plausibly be identified with passages as different as 4:3–8 and 5:1–11 demonstrates how vague the term is (similarly E. Best, *Thessalonians*, 231).

7. I. H. Marshall (*1 and 2 Thessalonians*, 151) thinks Paul means people susceptible to temptation or sin (cf. Rom. 4:19; 5:6; 8:3, 26) or overcome by difficult circumstances (1 Cor. 2:3; 2 Cor. 11:30; 12:5); Best (*Thessalonians*, 231) suggests those who are hesitant about or lacking insight into matters of faith and practice, such as idol food (cf. Rom. 14:1–15:6; 1 Cor. 8; 10). Richard (*Thessalonians*, 277) sees it as the most general of the commands in 5:14–15.

tians 5:22 (patience as a fruit of the Spirit), 1 Corinthians 13:4 (a characteristic of love), as well as Exodus 34:6 (a quality of God). The relevance of this injunction to a community under pressure or stress (e.g., persecution or concern about deceased believers) is evident.

(5) In 5:15, "Make sure that nobody pays back wrong for wrong, but always try to be kind to each other and to everyone else," Paul appears to be quoting a saying that formed a part of his basic instructions to new converts. It is closely paralleled by Romans 12:17–21 and echoes the Golden Rule in both its negative form (Don't do to others what you do not want done to you) and its positive form ("Do to others what you would have them do to you," Matt. 7:12//Luke 6:31). It is probably grounded in the teachings of Jesus regarding vengeance (Matt. 5:38–42; cf. Luke 6:29–30; also Prov. 20:22; 25:21–22; Sir. 28:1–7) and love for enemies (cf. Matt. 5:43–48; Luke 6:27–28, 32–36).

Verse 15a is a categorical prohibition against repaying evil for evil; verse 15b is an equally absolute command to *"always"* (the word order is emphatic) actively pursue or strive for "what is good" (lit. trans.).[8] Note that pursuing what is good is not limited to other members of the congregation ("each other"). Even in a context in which believers have been ostracized and persecuted by outsiders, Paul includes within the scope of his command all people (*"everyone* else," in the climactic position in the sentence), thereby repeating and reinforcing a point he made earlier in 3:12.

Congregational Responsibilities Toward God (5:16–18)

IN 5:16–18 PAUL turns from instructions covering attitudes and actions toward fellow believers and other human beings to instructions dealing with attitudes toward God. Whereas 4:3 established "holiness" as God's will with respect to individual behavior, here three closely connected imperatives (5:18b goes with all three commands, not just the last one in the series) spell out "God's will in Christ Jesus" for the Thessalonians as a community.[9]

---

8. The NIV's "try to be kind" misses by a considerable margin the forcefulness of Paul's statement. For the verb, cf. Rom. 12:13; 14:19; 1 Cor. 14:1; 1 Tim. 6:11; 2 Tim. 2:22.

9. 5:12–15 are clearly aimed at the community as a whole, and 5:16–18 continue without a break the pattern of plural imperatives found in the preceding verses. Moreover, the

With regard to the command to "rejoice always" (NRSV; cf. Phil. 4:4), "the emphasis on joy is not so much on the experience of joy, but the active expression of it."[10] Thus the translation "rejoice" (NRSV, NASB), which makes it clear that an action or attitude is involved, is preferable to "be joyful" (NIV), which misleadingly suggests more an emotional state. Though the basis for joy is not indicated here, the earlier references in the letter to joy (1:6; 2:19–20; 3:9) make it clear that the basis is God's activity and work among his people.

In urging the Thessalonians to "pray" and to "give thanks" (5:17–18a), Paul is giving advice he himself modeled (cf. 1:2; also 2:13; 3:9–10, 11–13; 5:23; 2 Thess. 1:3, 11; 2:13, 16–17). Similar encouragement to pray occurs in several letters (cf. Eph. 6:18; Phil. 4:6; Col. 4:2; 2 Thess. 3:1). For "continually" (cf. 1 Thess. 1:3; 2:13), "persevere in prayer" (Rom. 12:12, NRSV) gives the sense.[11]

Giving thanks (5:18) is another common command or theme (cf. Rom. 14:6; 1 Cor. 14:16; 2 Cor. 1:11; 4:15; 9:11; Eph. 5:4, 20; Phil. 4:6; Col. 2:7; 3:17). Like the command to rejoice, it is deeply rooted in Paul's *theology*, that is, his understanding about God. Because he was convinced that in any and all circumstances God was at work on behalf of his people (Rom. 8:28), he could therefore urge the Thessalonians to "give thanks in all circumstances" (1 Thess. 5:18). This was so even if the circumstances involved the death of a believer because, even though death was an awful reality, it was not the last word or act (cf. Rom. 8:31–39). The last word or act belongs to God, and it is resurrection and life. Thus for Paul, both rejoicing and giving thanks become forms of worship or praise of God.

Congregational Responsibilities Toward the Spirit (5:19–22)

IN 5:19–22, PAUL moves from the Spirit-connected activities of rejoicing (cf. 1:6; Gal. 5:22), praying (cf. Rom. 8:26–27; Eph. 6:18), and giving thanks to matters concerning the Spirit and prophecy. The five imperatives in these verses fall into two sets (vv. 19–20;

---

obvious context for the reading of the letter (cf. 5:27) would have been the community gathered together. Cf. J. R. W. Stott, *The Gospel and the End of Time*, 124.

10. G. D. Fee, *God's Empowering Presence*, 54.

11. F. F. Bruce, *1 and 2 Thessalonians*, 124.

vv. 21–22), structured as follows (using NIV wording but different punctuation):

> ¹⁹Do not put out the Spirit's fire;
> ²⁰do not treat prophecies with contempt;
> [instead,]
> ²¹test everything:
> hold on to the good;
> ²²avoid every kind of evil.

In isolation, 5:19 can be taken rather generally. But in the context of 5:20 and 5:21a it is clear that Paul is focusing on charismatic manifestations of the Spirit, specifically prophecy.[12] Thus one can paraphrase 5:19–20 as, "Don't quench the Spirit,[13] that is [or perhaps, 'for example'], don't treat prophecies with contempt."

The closest Paul comes to defining "prophecy" is in 1 Corinthians 14. Apparently "it consisted of spontaneous, Spirit-inspired, intelligible messages, orally delivered in the gathered assembly, intended for the edification or encouragement of the people," by men or women (1 Cor. 11:4–5) who remained "in control" of the activity.[14] Although there seem to have been some who spoke this way more often than others, who were thus called "prophets," it appears to have been an activity potentially open to everyone (cf. Joel 2:28–30; Acts 2:17–18). There is no evidence that such utterances were ever given the same authority as inspired texts (i.e., Scripture) or that they involved what is sometimes referred to as "personal prophecy." Rather, its focus was on the corporate life of the community; and in view of the present passage, Romans 12:6, and 1 Corinthians 12–14, it seems to have been a familiar aspect of the Spirit's activity in early Christian congregations.

It is unclear (because of a lack of information) whether these commands are meant to be curative or preventative. The grammar of the imperatives suggests (but certainly does not require) translating them as "stop quenching . . . stop despising." Converts from a pagan

---

12. G. D. Fee, *God's Empowering Presence*, 58–59; I. H. Marshall, *1 and 2 Thessalonians*, 157.

13. That is, "put out the fire." The vivid and picturesque image of fire picks up the frequent association of the Holy Spirit and fire (e.g., Acts 2:3–4). The NIV ("do not put out the Spirit's fire") attempts to catch this imagery, but obscures the fact that "Spirit" is the direct object of the verb.

14. G. D. Fee, *God's Empowering Presence*, 170.

background would have been familiar with various sorts of "ecstatic" activities associated with different pagan shrines and cults, and they may have been leery or suspicious of what appeared to be similar activities within the church. If so, then Paul writes both to affirm and to regulate what he viewed as legitimate and normal.

Alternatively, one can link the problem here with the issue of leadership in 5:12–13. Because genuine prophecy is subject to the control of the Spirit, it is outside the control of human leadership within the congregation and thus enables those not part of any formal leadership structure to exercise an informal leadership. Perhaps "those working hard," whom Paul called the congregation to acknowledge (5:12), may have felt threatened by any behavior that appeared to undermine or compete with their role in the congregation.[15]

At the same time, it is important to recognize that it was possible to "fake" or imitate genuine Spirit-produced activity. Because it is hard to challenge something said or done in the name of the Spirit without appearing to be unspiritual, gifts such as prophecy are subject to potential abuse and manipulation. In short, charismatic prophetic activity was potentially threatening and divisive, and it is easy to see how some people within a congregation might have wished or sought to minimize it.

In any case, speculation about the reason for the command ought not to obscure Paul's instructions regarding what was from his perspective a valued aspect (cf. 1 Cor. 14:1, "eagerly desire spiritual gifts, especially the gift of prophecy") of Christian corporate experience. Do not, he says, quench the Spirit by treating prophetic utterances with contempt. The proper solution to the problem of potential abuse is not to throw out the baby with the bath water; it is instead to "test everything" (5:21a). Paul strikes a careful balance here: "Because such utterances are from the Holy Spirit, they must not be 'despised'; but also because such utterances come through merely human vessels," they are not to be accepted blindly just because someone claims to have the Spirit.[16] The proper course is to "test" them, in the sense of examining or investigating something with regard to its trustworthiness or genuineness (cf. Luke 14:19; also 1 Thess. 2:4 above). In

---

15. Cf. C. A. Wanamaker, *Thessalonians*, 202–3.
16. G. D. Fee, *God's Empowering Presence*, 60.

1 Corinthians, Paul apparently refers to this activity as discerning (1 Cor. 12:10) or weighing (14:29) the content of a prophecy.

Once a prophecy has been "tested," the next step is clear: Hold on firmly to those that are good, and have nothing to do with those that are not (5:21b–22). Prophecies that pass the test are from the Holy Spirit and therefore ought not to be rejected or treated with contempt. On the other hand, any prophecy that fails the testing process is not from the Spirit and should therefore be rejected and avoided (the verb here, *apecho*, is the same as in 4:3, "avoid sexual immorality").

The structure of the passage clearly links 5:21b–22 closely with 5:21a. But the wording of these last two commands goes beyond the needs of the immediate context: verse 21b ("Hold on to the good") echoes 5:15b ("always seek to do good," NRSV), and verse 22 is probably best taken as "every kind of evil" (rather than "every kind [of prophecy that is] evil"). This may be a clue that Paul intended verses 21b–22 not only as an explication of verse 21a but also as a statement of broader application.

IN BRINGING THIS section of the text to us today, it is important to keep in mind that verses 15–22, no less than verses 12–14, are in the first place directed to the community, not individuals (a point missed, for example, by the commentator who assigned to verses 16–18 the heading "Responsibilities to Oneself," thinking that they deal with "the believer's inner life"). Stott's analysis of this section—under the heading of "Christian Community, or How to be a Gospel Church," he discusses leadership (vv. 12–13), fellowship (vv. 14–15), and worship (vv. 16–22)—points us in the right direction. This is not to suggest that these verses have nothing to say to individuals, but rather that we must keep in mind that they are addressed first to the congregation, and only indirectly to individuals. This will help us, for example, to avoid misapplying a verse like 5:16 or 5:21.

Leadership issues. In the civic or social clubs and associations that were common in first-century Greco-Roman culture, there was a noticeable relationship between wealth, status, and leadership. Often wealthy members were given leadership positions because they were patrons of the group (or in hopes that they would become patrons).

Indeed, in many cases wealthy members of an association or group who functioned as patrons or benefactors took it for granted that they would exercise leadership. Within the Christian congregation, however, the key qualification for leadership (in theory, if not always in practice) was not wealth or status but giftedness for ministry. As F. F. Bruce has observed, in general "leaders did not do the appropriate work because they had been appointed as leaders; they were recognized as leaders because they were seen to be doing the work."[17]

In this respect, Paul's instructions in 5:12 are countercultural. He wanted the congregation both to acknowledge and to respect as its leaders those people who were actually doing the work of ministry, rather than accepting (perhaps by default) those who had, from the perspective of secular culture, the "proper" social or financial qualifications. In such circumstances, the possibilities for misunderstandings, hurt feelings, or even divisions within the congregation (e.g., consider Corinth!) are obvious, and that may have prompted Paul to include at this point the command to "live in peace with each other" (5:13).

Congregational pastoral ministry. Every church, no matter how strong, has what J. R. W. Stott terms "the 'problem children' of the church family," that is, those who are struggling with "problems of understanding, faith, and conduct."[18] Moreover, most individuals, no matter how strong or mature spiritually, are likely to encounter in the course of life times of grief, doubt, or even despair (as Paul himself acknowledges, see 2 Cor. 1:8). In this section, Paul sketches some of the responsibilities of a congregation as a whole to individuals within it who happen to find themselves in need of some kind of encouragement, help, or even warning.

With respect to 5:14, it is important to notice that Paul calls on the entire congregation, not just the leaders, to take responsibility for mutual care and encouragement (cf. 5:11 above). As Ernest Best observes,

> Paul lays the responsibility for the whole community on the community itself; each member, and not the leaders alone, must be aware of his or her responsibility for others and seek to help them. At no stage can the ordinary member lean back and say, "This is the task of the ministry alone." Paul knows

---

17. F. F. Bruce, *1 and 2 Thessalonians*, 120.
18. J. R. W. Stott, *The Gospel and the End of Time*, 122.

nothing of an inert mass, the congregation, on which the ministry operates.[19]

In short, Paul is trying to develop in the entire congregation a sense of pastoral responsibility.

With respect to 5:15, we should not water down or ameliorate the force of Paul's absolute statements about not repaying "wrong for wrong" and seeking instead to do good. Paul's statements "can only mean that even when somebody does wrong to a Christian the latter must respond by doing good in return."[20] That is, Paul does not merely forbid retaliation, he commands, in the spirit of the Golden Rule, that we seek to do good. Moreover, we are to do good not just for the congregation, but for everyone, including those who may be attacking the church. As some of the disciples said in another context, "This is a hard teaching" (John 6:60).

Joy in all circumstances. In thinking about the application of verses 16–18, it is important to keep clearly in mind just what Paul meant by them. In 5:18, for example, Paul does not say to give thanks *for* all circumstances, but *in* all circumstances. Similarly, 5:16 is *not* a command to individual believers to "be joyful always"; as Stott observes, joy is not something that can be turned on and off like a faucet.[21] Moreover, such a command contradicts what Paul urges in Romans 12:15 ("mourn with those who mourn"). Rather "to rejoice always is to see the hand of God in whatever is happening and to remain certain of God's future salvation."[22] Paul has in mind "a stable and deep-rooted joy which enables him"—but even more so a congregation—"to cope with disappointments and see them in their true perspective."[23] And that true perspective is rooted in the conviction that in any and all circumstances, God is at work on behalf of his people—reason enough to give thanks and rejoice and thereby fulfill God's will for us (v. 18).

On prophecy. It is clear that in 5:19–22 Paul is focusing on a particular manifestation of the Spirit, namely, "prophecies" (5:20). It is sometimes claimed that prophecy ceased at the close of the apostolic

---

19. E. Best, *Thessalonians*, 233.
20. I. H. Marshall, *1 and 2 Thessalonians*, 152–53.
21. J. R. W. Stott, *The Gospel and the End of Time*, 124.
22. C. A. Wanamaker, *Thessalonians*, 200.
23. I. H. Marshall, *1 and 2 Thessalonians*, 155.

age,[24] a conclusion that would render these verses largely irrelevant today. There is, however, in my opinion no biblical basis for such a cessationist view of prophecy (or any other spiritual gift, for that matter), despite efforts to find one in 1 Corinthians 13:8–12 or Ephesians 2:20.[25] Paul took it for granted that prophecy was part of the common and normal experience of the Spirit's activity in the congregations he established, and there is no biblical basis to think that the situation is or should be any different today.

In this respect, Paul would never bother to "regulate" (as he does here) anything that ought not to be happening in the first place—he would simply forbid it! As Gordon Fee rightly notes, "despite the fact that the ministries of the Spirit can be abused in the Christian community, Paul's own deep appreciation for the central role of the Spirit in individual and corporate life will not allow for correcting abuse by commanding disuse. Rather, the antidote for abuse is proper use,"[26] which he defines in 5:21 as a matter of "testing" prophecies.

To affirm the present-day validity of prophecy is not to say that "not quenching the Spirit" (5:19) is merely a matter of being open to the possibility of prophecy or other specific manifestations of the Spirit. On an individual or a congregational level, obedience to 5:19 cannot be reduced to a matter of Pentecostal versus non-Pentecostal experience, as if being Pentecostal or charismatic automatically means that one is open to the Spirit and that a non-Pentecostal is automatically guilty of quenching the Spirit. As Keener observes, "Contrary to their own claims . . . some charismatic churches plainly follow a charismatic tradition by rote; by contrast, in some noncharismatic churches . . . only the most spiritually insensitive person could fail to sense the overwhelming presence of God's Spirit."[27]

---

24. See, for example, John F. MacArthur, Jr., *Charismatic Chaos* (Grand Rapids: Zondervan, 1992); Richard B. Gaffin, Jr., *Perspectives on Pentecost: Studies in New Testament Teaching on the Gifts of the Holy Spirit* (Phillipsburg, N.J.: Presbyterian and Reformed, 1979). See also Gaffin's essay in Wayne A. Grudem, *Are Miraculous Gifts for Today? Four Views* (Grand Rapids: Zondervan, 1996), 25–64.

25. See Gordon D. Fee, *Gospel and Spirit: Issues in New Testament Hermeneutics* (Peabody, Mass.: Hendrickson, 1991), 76–77; Craig S. Keener, *Three Crucial Questions about the Holy Spirit* (Grand Rapids: Baker, 1996), 95–107. On 1 Cor. 13:8–12 see Craig Blomberg, *1 Corinthians* (NIVAC; Grand Rapids: Zondervan, 1994), 260, 262–63; on Eph. 2:20, see Klyne Snodgrass, *Ephesians* (NIVAC; Grand Rapids: Zondervan, 1996), 144.

26. G. D. Fee, *God's Empowering Presence*, 59.

27. C. S. Keener, *Three Crucial Questions about the Holy Spirit*, 171–72.

To put the matter a bit differently, it is accurate to observe that some traditions, denominations, or movements do seem to be more open to certain expressions of the Spirit's working than others. But it is impossible on the basis of this generalization to make predictions or judgments about the openness of any particular congregation or individual to the leading of the Holy Spirit. All congregations and all individuals need to take seriously Paul's command against "quenching the Spirit."

One difficulty in applying 5:21a ("Test everything") is that Paul nowhere provides a list of criteria by which to test prophecy. Nonetheless Gordon Fee suggests that two principles may be inferred from his letters.[28] (1) In 2 Thessalonians 2:15, in a context in which some Thessalonians had been badly shaken by misrepresentations of Paul's teaching (misrepresentations that may have had their origins in a prophecy, cf. 2 Thess. 2:2), Paul urges the believers to "stand firm" and "hold to the teachings we passed on to you." This suggests that one test of any prophecy is its agreement with the apostolic preaching and teaching about Jesus; any prophecy that does not agree with the apostolic proclamation is immediately suspect (cf. 1 John 4:1–3). Since today the apostolic preaching and teaching is preserved in Scripture, in practical terms this means that Scripture is the standard or norm by which prophecy is to be tested, not the other way around. This is the test of content.

(2) In 1 Corinthians 14:3, Paul says that genuine prophetic activity serves to strengthen, encourage, and comfort—that is, it works "for the common good" (12:7). This is the test of purpose and effect.

With regard to 5:21–22, in context these commands clearly have in view the matter of prophecy. But the way in which Paul states them hints at a wider application. Paul himself appears to make a broader application of 5:21b ("hold on to the good") in Philippians 4:8 ("whatever is true, whatever is noble, . . . if anything is excellent . . . think about such things"). In applying 5:22 more broadly, however, it is important to keep clearly in mind precisely what Paul meant by it. It is still not uncommon to hear people, influenced by but misunderstanding the King James Version of 5:22 ("Abstain from all appearance of evil"), paraphrase the verse as, "Avoid even the appearance of evil." This in turn is taken to mean that we should "avoid anything—

---

28. G. D. Fee, *God's Empowering Presence*, 61.

even if it is good—that might somehow under some circumstances possibly seem to be evil." But Paul does not say to avoid something that might (mistakenly) somehow appear to be evil; he commands us to avoid evil whenever and however it appears (as the NIV makes clear).

AS JACOB W. Elias observes, this passage "prescribes both spontaneity and freedom as well as structure and accountability for worship and church life generally."[29] Maintaining this tension between openness and control while seeking to apply faithfully the many imperatives presents a major challenge to responsible application.

Congregational responsibilities toward leaders (5:12–13a). Paul's instructions in 5:12–13a call on congregations today to do two things. (1) They should recognize or acknowledge those who are actually doing the work of ministry. Those with the titles, positions, visibility, or recognition are not always the ones doing the hard work that keeps a congregation going. Factors other than spiritual giftedness (e.g., ambition, connections, personality, education, natural talent, or good looks) often influence which people are placed in positions of leadership or visibility in a congregation. In and of themselves, however, these considerations neither qualify nor disqualify one for ministry. The key consideration is giftedness by the Spirit, something that usually becomes evident in the exercise of the gift. Thus Paul calls us to recognize as our congregational leaders those who are actually leading the congregation.

(2) The congregation should respect or "hold . . . in highest regard" its leaders. This may be the greater failure of congregations today. We usually know who our leaders are, but far too often we do not respect or follow them. To be sure, to some extent respect is something that must be earned, as we like to remind ourselves, but far too often even when it has been earned, it is not given. A leader does something less than perfectly, and we think to ourselves, "I could have done better than that." A solid message is preached, but it lacks the flair and drama of the big-name personality we watched earlier on TV, and we say to

---

29. J. W. Elias, *1 and 2 Thessalonians*, 235.

ourselves, "Why can't he preach like so-and-so?" A song is well sung from the heart, but it lacks the production values of the latest video from our favorite Christian recording artist, and we are disappointed. In these and other subtle (and sometimes not so subtle) ways we fail to give those who minister to us the respect they deserve.

Ben Franklin, who was both printer for and friend of George White-field, the famous colonial era evangelist, claimed that when he was listening to Whitefield preach, he could easily tell the difference between a new sermon and one previously delivered. The latter were highly polished in both content and delivery and had a tremendous impact on the audience, including the somewhat skeptical Franklin himself. (He reports that prior to a particular sermon appealing for funds, he had resolutely determined to give nothing; he was so moved, however, by Whitefield's eloquence that by the time the offering plate came by, he emptied his pockets!)[30]

In view of Whitefield's impact and reputation, it is hardly surprising, as Franklin reports, that not a few of the local preachers were less than happy to have Whitefield preaching in their area. It is easy to understand how they might have felt threatened by his presence and the inevitable comparisons drawn between his preaching and theirs. But any such comparison was hardly fair; they were responsible for two or three new sermons per week, while Whitefield had the opportunity to polish and refine his sermons through repeated delivery. But the unfairness of such comparisons did not prevent them from being made.

The problem of unfair negative comparisons is still around; if anything, the advent of mass-media communication has exacerbated the problem. No longer do we know of nationally renowned preachers, teachers, or speakers only by reputation; we have usually seen and heard them, either via television or videos. What we tend to forget when watching them, however, is that much of what we see on these TV shows or videos is produced with the benefit of substantial production support and post-production editing. So we see them on-screen in all their edited perfection, speaking powerfully and moving deeply large, enthusiastic studio audiences. Compared to such well-presented personalities, it is hardly a surprise that our own pastor, Sunday

---

30. L. Jesse Lemisch, ed., *Benjamin Franklin: The Autobiography and Other Writings* (New York: New American Library, 1961), 116–20.

School teacher, or seminar leader somehow seems a bit "lacking" in some respect.

Though such comparisons are inherently unfair, we make them anyway, sometimes without even realizing it. When we do so, we fail to give our local leaders the respect they deserve for doing the work to which God has called them. Paul's command here reminds us of the need to grant our respect to those who have earned it by their work and care for the congregation.

Living in peace (5:13b). Paul's command to live in peace with one another is a hard saying for many people and congregations. The peace that the apostle has in mind is not merely the absence of conflict (hard enough to achieve for many of us!), but the presence of positive, healthy relationships. Too often, however, we place a higher value on a superficial harmony than on genuine peace. We are "nice" to one another and coexist without open warfare (at least most of the time). Because we value so highly "niceness" and not upsetting or disturbing someone, we avoid the hard work it takes to maintain a relationship.

When a problem occurs, we do not follow the guidelines of Matthew 18:15 and go to the other person to clear up the matter (after all, it's not "nice" to be confrontational). Instead we pretend that there's nothing wrong (meanwhile gossiping about it with others). But this leaves wounds untreated and hurts unhealed, allows misunderstandings to linger, and eventually gives rise to suspicion and mistrust. We have superficial harmony, but no peace, because we have avoided the hard work of reconciliation necessary for genuine peace to flourish. Only as we "care enough to confront," to paraphrase the title of Milton Mayerhoff's little classic, will we be able to fulfill Paul's command to live in peace with one another.

Congregational responsibilities toward individuals (5:14–15). In reviewing Luci Shaw's poignant book *God in the Dark: Through Grief and Beyond*, Margaret D. Smith writes:

> Through the book, she calls to God, asking like the Psalmist, "Where are you? I call but you don't answer. You have left me here, alone. . . ." If she hasn't abandoned God in this crisis, and if God has promised to be with her always, then where is he? Why doesn't he make himself known? This is her aching prayer, and she never knowingly receives a satisfactory answer.

Through the book, friends flit in and out like fireflies, giving off brief sparks in the darkness, telling Luci in a thousand thoughtful ways that they love her. But while she appreciates these friends, Luci never seems to connect the two wires: Where is God? and, Here are God's people.[31]

Smith's insight—that God often makes his presence known through his people—underscores the importance of Paul's command to the Thessalonian congregation in 5:14. In nurturing those who are weak, in caring for those in distress, by encouraging those who are fearful, and, if necessary, disciplining those who require it, we can become ministers of the grace of the gospel, servants of God through whom he reaches out to those looking for him or in need of his presence.

The congregational activities of rejoicing, praying, and giving thanks mentioned in 5:16–18 tie in closely here as well. There are times when a group of believers can do what an individual believer may find herself or himself unable to do and in this way minister to that individual. I remember vividly a faculty worship service when, overwhelmed with grief, I found myself completely unable to rejoice or give thanks and hardly able to pray. But as I listened to my colleagues pray, give thanks, and rejoice in God's grace and goodness, their words broke through my sorrow. Unable to give thanks or rejoice at the moment, I nevertheless felt carried along by their praise, thanksgiving, and prayers. As they did what I was unable to do alone, my colleagues became for me tangible evidence of God's presence.

Ministering to those in the body who have deep needs or hurts, as Paul here urges us to do, is often difficult, sometimes simply because people do not always respond, heal, or grow as fast as we think they should. This may be why Paul adds a word about patience at this point. Our society not only encourages us to want things our way, but to want them our way when we want them. But if we are to be genuinely patient with others,

> we must renounce the tyranny of our own agendas. . . . The idea that we should not have to wait on anything or anyone is merely another form of self-centeredness. Patience . . . values other people

---

31. Margaret D. Smith, "Waiting for an Answer," *The Reformed Journal* 39 (October, 1989): 29.

enough to give them room and time to fail, learn, and develop
... to mature at their own rate rather than expect them to do
everything right and to do it now.[32]

If impatience is one form of self-centeredness, retaliation (5:15) is
another. Perhaps that is why judgment and vengeance are tasks God
has *not* entrusted to his people to carry out. As humans we are too
prone to identify our enemies as God's enemies; we too easily confuse
our desires for revenge with God's justice. Perhaps it is precisely
"because of our strong natural tendency to seek revenge," as Calvin puts
it, that *any* form of retaliation or "vengeance is forbidden to us without exception."[33] This may be the only way to break the otherwise
unending spiral of violence that retaliation generates.

In place of retaliation, we are commanded instead to "always seek
to do good" (NRSV), not only to those within the congregation but to
everyone else as well. This kind of nonretaliatory behavior has a much
different motivation: "Such treatment of opponents has as its goal reconciliation and peace, not another's defeat and suffering. That is the
way God dealt with us when we were his enemies. That is the way God
deals through us with those who continue to oppose him."[34]

It is important to notice a significant consequence of Paul's command to do good to everyone (friend and foe alike): It hinders the
development of a dualistic perspective—the tendency to view everyone outside our group or aligned against us as evil (or at least on the
side of evil). Instead, it reminds us of God's love, care, and concern for
everyone. It forces us to expand our perspective toward that of God's,
rather than reduce his to the limitations of ours.

Congregational responsibilities toward God (5:16–18). I have
labeled this section "responsibilities toward God" primarily in order to
maintain the parallelism with the other headings in this section. Moreover, to do so recognizes that in these verses, as throughout the passage, Paul speaks in the imperative mood, that is, in the language of
command. In many respects, however, it might well be as accurate to
label this section "opportunities to acknowledge and affirm our faith
in God." For just as reciting a formal written creed (such as the Nicene

---

32. Klyne Snodgrass, *Ephesians* (NIVAC; Grand Rapids: Zondervan, 1996), 219.
33. J. Calvin, *The Epistles of Paul the Apostle to the Romans and to the Thessalonians*, 374.
34. Paul Achtemeier, *Romans* (Interpretation; Atlanta: John Knox, 1985), 202.

Creed or Apostles' Creed) is an intellectual statement of faith, so the actions of rejoicing, giving thanks, and praying are an experiential statement of faith. They are ways of expressing by our behavior what we believe with the mind.

Charles Wesley's famous hymn "Rejoice, the Lord is King" catches well this coordination between belief and expression:

1. Rejoice, the Lord is King! Your Lord and King adore!
    Rejoice, give thanks, and sing, And triumph evermore:

    Refrain   Lift up your heart, lift up your voice!
    Rejoice, again I say, rejoice!

4. Rejoice in glorious hope! Our Lord the Judge shall come
    And take His servants up To their eternal home: (Refrain)

In these verses, the rejoicing and giving thanks are both based on and give concrete expression to our convictions that our Lord is indeed King, and that he will come to take us to be with him for eternity. Viewed in this light, rejoicing, praying, and giving thanks are less things we "have to do" and more expressions of what we truly believe. In this sense, then, Paul's commands in verses 16–18 become more opportunities than responsibilities—opportunities, moreover, that constitute nothing less than God's will for us.

The real challenge in verses 16–18 comes out, however, not when times or circumstances are good and it is easy to rejoice and give thanks, but when (as in Thessalonica) our material circumstances may not seem so good. Do we truly believe that God's salvation is of more value than the cost of persecution that comes as a result of accepting the gospel? Then let us demonstrate that conviction by rejoicing in the midst of it. Are we really persuaded that God will indeed deliver his people and bring justice on their behalf? Then let us pray with persistence and patience, waiting and watching expectantly for God to act (cf. Luke 18:1–8, the parable of the persistent widow).[35] Are we genuinely convinced that "in all things God works for the good of those who love him" (Rom. 8:28)? Then let us demonstrate that conviction by giving thanks in all circumstances.

---

35. See on this passage Darrell L. Bock, *Luke* (NIVAC; Grand Rapids: Zondervan, 1996), 453–59.

Congregational responsibilities toward the Spirit (5:19–22).
There is a double responsibility in these verses: not to quench anything
that is genuinely of the Spirit, and not to attribute anything false to the
Spirit. As J. W. Elias succinctly puts it, "During worship the Spirit
needs to have freedom to move prophets to speak, yet what is said also
needs to be tested."[36]

The worship services of a great many churches in America today
are so tightly structured, choreographed, and controlled that there is
virtually no opportunity for "spontaneous, Spirit-inspired, intelligible
messages, orally delivered in the gathered assembly, intended for the
edification or encouragement of the people" (the definition of
prophecy given above). The key word here, I think, is "control": Some
services are so much under human control that there is virtually no
room for the Spirit to move.

In considering this last statement, it is important to emphasize that
this is in no way a matter of "liturgical" versus "nonliturgical" traditions. It is not difficult for a skilled worship leader, even one working
from a well-defined liturgy or service book in which everything is
printed out in advance, to provide room and opportunities for the
Spirit to move in and through the congregation during worship. On
the other hand, nonliturgical congregations, including some that would
faint at the sight of a printed order of service, can be observed following, week after week, an "order of service" as rigid and predictable—
as "controlled," in other words—as any printed liturgy.

In other words, it is not so much a matter of liturgical style as it is
a matter of attitude and approach. Some of us are simply more com-
fortable when things are "under control"; we dislike the unexpected and
prefer the comfort of the predictable. But the hidden cost of pre-
dictability is a loss of spontaneity, and a consequence of too much
control is a quenching of the Spirit. In such cases, part of the solution
may be building into the congregation's worship activities "space" or
room for the Spirit, perhaps during one of the less formal gatherings
(such as a Saturday or Sunday evening service).[37]

---

36. J. W. Elias, *1 and 2 Thessalonians*, 235.

37. See further Wayne A. Grudem, *The Gift of Prophecy in the New Testament and Today*
(Westchester, Ill.: Crossway, 1988), 253–62, who offers several useful suggestions to
"churches which do not use the gift of prophecy but would like to."

It is also possible to quench the Spirit by valuing cultural expectations or norms more than the Spirit. This may be a matter of labeling only certain styles of music or forms of worship as fitting, proper, or "Christian," of placing a high value on having the service end by a certain time so as not to interfere with other scheduled activities, or of insisting on gender distinctions or social roles that are cultural rather than biblical. In these and other ways some congregations run the risk of quenching the Spirit in their midst.

If the problem for some churches is too much control, the problem for others is too little discernment. Some churches or movements are so in awe of prophets and prophecy that they neglect to test anything at all that happens in the name of the Holy Spirit. This is a blatant contradiction of Paul's command to "test *everything*," and then to hold on to what is good and stay away from everything else. The results of this failure have been widely documented; they include not only questionable behavior, but worse, the propagation of false teaching and heresy.[38] This failure to take seriously Paul's command to test all prophecies is a major shortcoming of the contemporary charismatic movement.

As was indicated in the Bridging Contexts section, there are two means by which to test prophecy. (1) One test is that of purpose and effect: Genuine prophetic activity serves to strengthen, encourage, and comfort. In short, it works to edify and to build up God's people. If the effects of an alleged prophecy are otherwise, then there is good reason to suspect it. The same goes for prophecies that exalt or serve the interests of an individual.

(2) The primary means of testing prophecies, however, is Scripture. It is axiomatic that nothing that is truly of the Holy Spirit will contradict anything that God has said in his Word. Any alleged prophecy or revelation must be tested against the one reliable, Spirit-given source of revelation that has already been received, namely, Scripture. Moreover, as was pointed out in the Original Meaning section, there is no evidence that prophetic utterances in the early church were ever given the same authority as Scripture. Though I disagree in general with the cessationist view of prophecy, I share their concern for the centrality of Scripture in the life of the church. Nothing

---

38. For examples see C. S. Keener, *Three Crucial Questions about the Holy Spirit*, 171–75, and (from the opposite end of the spectrum on this issue) John F. MacArthur Jr., *Charismatic Chaos* (Grand Rapids: Zondervan, 1992).

must be allowed to supplant God's written Word as the final guide for faith and life.

Wayne Grudem offers three important guidelines for churches that use the gift of prophecy, which incorporate the key points discussed thus far.[39] (1) "Remember that what is spoken in any prophecy today is not the word of God, but is simply a human being reporting in merely human words something which God has brought to mind." (2) "Be sure to test prophecies, to *evaluate* them by Scripture and by what else you know to be true." (3) "Be sure you emphasize *Scripture* as the place where people can always go to hear the voice of the living God." If these guidelines are followed, it would eliminate much of the unbiblical, sub-biblical, and even heretical activity that is falsely attributed to the Spirit today.

---

39. Grudem, *The Gift of Prophecy*, 262–63.

1 Thessalonians 5:23–28

M AY GOD HIMSELF, the God of peace, sanctify you through and through. May your whole spirit, soul and body be kept blameless at the coming of our Lord Jesus Christ. ²⁴The one who calls you is faithful and he will do it.

²⁵Brothers, pray for us. ²⁶Greet all the brothers with a holy kiss. ²⁷I charge you before the Lord to have this letter read to all the brothers.

²⁸The grace of our Lord Jesus Christ be with you.

Original Meaning

THIS PART OF the letter is a combination of rhetorical and epistolary forms. Just as an intercessory prayer (3:11–13) draws the first section of the letter (1:2–3:10) to a close, so too a similar prayer (5:23–24) draws to a close the second section (4:1–5:22). Both share a similar form, reflect liturgical echoes, and end on an eschatological note. Moreover, as the first prayer summarized major themes of the first section of the letter, so this one touches on the major themes of the second section: Note the emphasis on holiness ("sanctify," 5:23) and on the coming of Jesus. Thus the prayer fulfills the function of a *peroratio*, the concluding part of a speech or document that summarizes major themes of a discourse and seeks to secure the goodwill of the recipients.[1]

Verses 23–24 also form part of the epistolary framework of the letter, specifically the letter closing (vv. 23–28). Secular letters usually ended with greetings and a farewell statement (e.g., "Many salutations to your wife and to Serenus and to all who love you, each by name. Goodbye."[2]). Paul's letters typically close with a prayer, an exhortation, greetings, and/or a command to greet one another (often accompanied

---

1. See further P. T. O'Brien, "Letters, Letter Forms," *DPL*, 553; G. W. Hansen, "Rhetorical Criticism," *DPL*, 822–26.

2. Cited by Calvin J. Roetzel, *The Letters of Paul: Conversations in Context*, 3d ed. (Louisville, Ky.: Westminster/John Knox, 1991), 60.

by a request for prayer), and a closing benediction. While 1 Thessalonians lacks any greetings, the other elements are clearly present.[3]

A Closing Prayer (5:23-24).

THE PRAYER IN 5:23 essentially echoes the thought (and even some of the words) of the prayer in 3:13. The phrase "God of peace" (cf. Rom. 15:33; 16:20; Phil. 4:9; cf. also 2 Thess. 3:16) identifies God as the source of peace, which for Paul is not merely the absence of conflict but, more positively, a state of wholeness and well-being characterized by reconciled relationships (cf. Rom. 5:1-11); as such, it is virtually a synonym for "salvation." The verb "sanctify" (*hagiazo*) is the verbal form of the noun translated as "holiness" (*hagiasmos*) in 4:3. The expression "sanctify you through and through" restates in different words the idea of "blameless in holiness" from 3:13 (see the discussion there). Like the noun "holiness," the verb "sanctify" indicates a process rather than a state, whose goal is associated (as in 3:13) with "the coming of our Lord Jesus Christ."

The second part of 5:23 stands (in the Greek word order) in a chiastic parallel relationship with the first part:
(May God himself, the God of peace)

> sanctify
>> you
>>> through and through (*holoteleis*);
>>> may your whole (*holokleron*)
>> spirit, soul and body
> (blameless at the coming of our Lord Jesus Christ)
> be kept.

The structure of the verse makes it clear that the phrase "spirit, soul and body" is essentially a synonym for "you," in much the same way that "heart" (*kardia*) was in 3:13. Coming as it does after the emphatic "whole," the phrase is Paul's way of stressing the comprehensive nature of salvation, which encompasses a person in her or his entirety, including in particular the body, which significant elements of Greek culture tended to deprecate. In Greek thought the body was a tomb or prison from which the soul sought escape, while for Paul there is no existence apart from the body.

---

3. See further Jeffrey A. D. Weima, *Neglected Endings: The Significance of the Pauline Letter Closings* (Sheffield: Sheffield Univ. Press, 1994), 174–86.

Verse 24 takes the form of a solemn affirmation, in which Paul grounds his prayer and with which he probably hoped to reassure any who might still be concerned about their fate at the Parousia of Jesus. Two points come through strongly. (1) In the phrase "the one who calls" (which picks up a theme running throughout the letter; cf. 1:4; 2:12; 4:7), "the present tense . . . stresses that God does not merely call Christians once and then leave them on their own. Instead God continues to call the followers of Christ to salvation."[4]

(2) The "one who calls" is also "faithful," that is, will not reject them or go back on his word to them. This is a point Paul will share with the Corinthians (cf. 1 Cor. 1:8–9) and develop more fully in Romans (cf. Rom. 8:30, 38–39; esp. 11:29). Thus with respect to their salvation, Paul confidently affirms that God "will [indeed] do it," that is (as he says in Phil. 1:6), "he who began a good work in you *will carry it on to completion* until the day of Christ Jesus" (italics added).

Closing Requests and Benediction (5:25–28)

EVEN AS PAUL on more than one occasion in the letter prayed for the Thessalonians (cf. 1:2–3; 3:10; 5:23), so he in turn requests (in 5:25) their prayers for him and his companions (cf. 2 Thess. 3:1–2; also Rom. 15:30–32; 2 Cor. 1:11; Col. 4:3–4). Despite the difference in spiritual maturity between Paul, Silas, and Timothy, on the one hand, and the Thessalonians on the other, Paul implicitly acknowledges, by his request for prayer, their fundamental equality before God.

The instruction to greet one another "with a holy kiss" occurs in four of Paul's letters (here; Rom. 16:16; 1 Cor. 16:20; 2 Cor. 13:12; cf. 1 Peter 5:14). A customary greeting in the ancient world in both Greco-Roman and Jewish cultures, the kiss was a sign of affection between family and friends and of honor towards superiors. There is some evidence (cf. 1 Cor. 16:20; Justin Martyr, *First Apology*, 65.2) that the "kiss of peace" may have been part of the ritual that preceded the celebration of the Lord's Supper.[5] Its use likely picked up on the "family" metaphors so common in early Christianity (including the repeated use of *adelphoi*, "brothers and sisters," throughout the letter) and served as a sign of unity and of mutual affection.

---

4. C. A. Wanamaker, *Thessalonians*, 207.
5. I. H. Marshall, *Last Supper and Lord's Supper* (Grand Rapids: Eerdmans, 1980), 145.

The probable explanation of the abrupt switch in verse 27 from the plural to the singular pronoun ("I") is that Paul took the pen from the scribe (Silas?) and wrote the last two sentences himself (cf. 2 Thess. 3:17; also Gal. 6:11; 1 Cor. 16:21).[6] In a culture in which only a small percentage of the population was literate, Paul took it for granted that the letter would be read aloud (cf. Rev. 1:3) during a gathering of the community (cf. Col. 4:16). The force and solemnity of his order is surprising and unusual, as is the triple occurrence of *adelphoi*, "brothers and sisters" (see comments on 1 Thess. 1:4), and the repeated "all" in 5:25–27. The reason is probably related to his purpose in writing: there is in the letter

> something for everyone, something which troubled, doubtful, working, and attentive members need to hear and to repeat to one another as exhortation (4:18). . . . Public reading of the letter in the presence of every brother and sister assures that each member of the community is either admonished, encouraged, or assisted with patience, love, and concord (5:12–14).[7]

Just as in the prescript (1:1) Paul replaced the usual brief word of greeting with a phrase, so here in 5:28 for the customary "farewell" (see Acts 15:29) Paul substitutes, "The grace of our Lord Jesus Christ be with you" (cf. 2 Thess. 3:18; also 1 Cor. 16:23; Gal. 6:18; Phil. 4:23; Col. 4:18). The content of Paul's opening greeting ("grace and peace") finds its echo in 5:23 ("God of peace") and here ("grace"), forming an *inclusio* that unifies the letter. For the significance of this last term and of the phrase "Lord Jesus Christ," see the comments on 1:1 above.

Bridging Contexts

IN THIS SECTION verses 23–24, with respect to both form and content, duplicate or summarize earlier portions of the letter (for details see the discussion in the Original Meaning section). Appropriately for a letter closing, Paul does not introduce new

---

6. For a photograph of a papyrus letter in which the switch from the neat, precise writing of the scribe to the irregular (and nearly illegible) scrawl of the author is strikingly obvious, see Everett Ferguson, *Backgrounds of Early Christianity*, 2d ed. (Grand Rapids: Eerdmans, 1993), 121.

7. E. J. Richard, *Thessalonians*, 292; for a survey of alternative hypotheses, cf. F. F. Bruce, *1 and 2 Thessalonians*, 135.

material but rather alludes once more to the topics and themes he has already discussed. In addition, in 5:23 Paul does for the Thessalonians what he asks them to do for him and his companions in 5:25.

Paul's prayer. Paul's prayer in 5:23 that we might "be kept" blameless, which stands parallel to the phrase "may God ... sanctify you," reminds us that sanctification is a gift as well as a goal. It is a gift given in grace, in that at conversion believers have already passed from death to life (Col. 2:13), so that we are new creations in Christ (2 Cor. 5:17), in whom we stand before God blamelessly. Yet it is also a goal (cf. 1 Thess. 3:13), in that we are called to live it out in our lives. This means that "discipleship is life between the times, for God has not yet finished what he began." But it is important to note that "the life of faith is not a striving for more; it is living more fully in what has already been given, knowing that even efforts to live more appropriately as 'saints' (4:1–3) depend upon God who sanctifies."[8]

The holy kiss. The "holy kiss" (5:26) apparently at first was a social custom. But early on it became (and continues to be in some traditions) part of the church's celebration of the Lord's Supper. It signified mutual reconciliation between believers before they took communion together as fellow Christians. In its Pauline context the key aspect is not the greeting's form but its function as a sign of unity and mutual affection within the congregation. Any culturally acceptable form of greeting, whether a kiss on each cheek, a hug, a hearty handshake, or whatever, that conveys warmth and symbolizes unity would likely be acceptable to Paul.

On instruction. At first glance the command in 5:27 about reading the letter to everyone seems so tied to its first-century setting that it may appear to be of no relevance today in a culture where literacy is more widespread. But the *result* of Paul's command—that the entire church *be instructed* in what he had to say—is no less relevant now. Christian discipleship is not a matter of developing our own individual spiritual intuitions, but of following after Jesus, in accordance with what he modeled and taught, both in person and through the writings of the New Testament. Thus *instruction*—learning (and remembering) the good news about what God through Jesus has done on our behalf, and about its implications for how we live—is a central element of discipleship for everyone.

The definition of instruction given in the previous sentence is shaped in light of what Paul has done in this letter. In the first three

---

8. Donald H. Juel, *1 Thessalonians* (Minneapolis: Augsburg, 1985), 250.

chapters, Paul basically tells the story of (i.e., he "remembers") not only how God brought the gospel to the Thessalonians, but also all that God has done in their midst since then. Moreover, he does not present this as "new" material, but basically asks them to remember and think about what they already know (cf. "you know," 1:5; 2:1, 2, 5, 11; 3:3, 4; 4:2; 5:2; "you remember," 2:9; "you are witnesses," 2:10; see also 4:9). Then in the last two chapters, when he finally deals with their specific issues and questions about the present and future, he consistently does so in light of what God has already done in the past (see 4:1, 7, 9, 14; 5:9, 10, 24; also 4:2; 5:2).

Thus, by insisting that the letter be read to everyone in the congregation, Paul ensures not only that they will hear the answers he gives to their questions and problems, but also that they will hear and recall the narrative of what God has done among them that provides the basis for those answers. Whatever their current difficulties, he does not want them to forget what God has already done in their midst.

A caution. Some interpreters find in 5:23 (with its reference to "spirit, soul and body") a basis for developing a "tripartite" view of human nature (the view that we consist of body, soul, and spirit). But the fact that only here in the entire New Testament does this phrase occur ought to make us cautious in building any major conclusions about the human personality on this verse. Moreover, as we noted above, Paul's emphasis is on the wholeness of human beings rather than on constituent elements. In addition, Paul tends to use terms like these rather broadly and somewhat interchangeably; as a consequence it is difficult to find any consistent distinctions between them in his letters.[9]

> We can no more take his words here to mean that our nature is threefold than we can take some of his words elsewhere to indicate that we are twofold (body and spirit, 1 Cor. 7:34), or those of Jesus in Mark 12:30 to show that we are fourfold (heart, soul, mind, and strength).[10]

---

9. As Gordon Fee observes, "it is very likely, given the way Paul here expresses himself, that he might think of the human spirit and soul as distinct entities in some way. But how he might think of them as different is not at all clear from the rest of his letters. . . . Moreover, the emphasis on entirety suggests that he could easily have included 'mind' without for a moment deviating from his concern. That is, whatever distinctions he may have understood are quite secondary to the greater concern of completeness" (*God's Empowering Presence*, 66).

10. L. Morris, *The First and Second Epistles to the Thessalonians*, 182.

In short, it does not appear that Paul is here offering any kind of anthropological definition.

 THESE CLOSING VERSES of the letter offer an opportunity to reflect on a theme that has been running beneath the surface throughout the letter and to reprise a theme that has been explicit since the opening verse. The theme for reflection is the importance of *remembering what God has done*, and the theme to reprise is *the centrality of God for the life of the church*.

The importance of remembering what God has done. This theme was touched on briefly in discussing Paul's thanksgiving prayer in 3:9–13, where I suggested in passing that remembering and telling the story of God's faithfulness is important for at least two reasons. (1) When things go well, it reminds us why they are going well (it is due to God's grace and goodness, not our own efforts; cf. Deut. 6:10–13; 8:10–18; 9:4–6). (2) When things are not going well, it gives us hope to remember that the God who has been faithful in the past will be faithful in the future. This second point is the one I will focus on at the moment because of the way that Paul throughout his letter so consistently models it for the Thessalonians.

As we noticed in the Bridging Contexts section, Paul repeatedly deals with the present and future in light of the past. Why, for example, is Paul not worried about the fate of those who have died before Jesus returns? Because God raised Jesus from the dead and will therefore raise those who are in Jesus (4:13, 16). Why is he unconcerned about the coming judgment? Because Jesus, who "died for us so that . . . we may live together with him" (5:10), will deliver us from the coming wrath (1:10). How can Paul (and we) be so utterly confident that "the one who calls [us] is faithful and he will do it" (5:24)? *We are confident that in the future God will do for us what he has promised because of the faithfulness to his promises that he has already demonstrated in the past.*

It is on the basis of these foundational facts about God that we are able, no matter how difficult our circumstances, to encourage and comfort one another in the present as we look forward to the future with confident hope. Remembering what God has done in the past—not as dead history but as the living and ongoing narrative of a faithful and powerful God in his relationship with his people—provides the basis for life in the present and hope for the future.

Psalm 13 exemplifies vividly this kind of approach to life. The first four verses are David's lament, an angry accusation that God has forgotten and abandoned him to his enemies. But then in verses 5–6 he says: "But I trust in your unfailing love; my heart rejoices in your salvation. I will sing to the LORD, for he has been good to me." In the midst of his despair and sorrow, he remembers what God *has* done and that God *is* faithful, and this gives him hope regarding the future. Indeed, the only reason he bothers crying out to a God who apparently has abandoned him (an ironic waste of time, if it were true) is because he remembers God's faithfulness in the past. Psalm 77 strikes a similar theme. The answer to the hard questions (v. 8, "Has his unfailing love vanished forever? Has his promise failed for all time?") involves remembering what God has done (vv. 11–12):

I will remember the deeds of the LORD;
    yes, I will remember your miracles of long ago.
I will meditate on all your works
    and consider all your mighty deeds.

For us today, remembering what God has done includes not only remembering the scriptural narrative of God's faithfulness, love, and power, but also what God through Jesus has accomplished during all the time since the close of the book of Acts, as well as what he continues to accomplish today. This has always been one of the strengths of "testimony time" at church, when believers share their testimonies about what God has done in their lives. Not only does it forcefully remind us that God is still active and powerful, but listening to the testimony of others often prompts us to recall our own memories of what God has done in our lives. Remembering and sharing God's faithfulness in the past can become a powerful means of encouraging and strengthening one another in the present.[11]

It is also important, I think, to observe that remembering who God is and what God has done provides not only the basis for confidence in the future, but also a basis for discerning how we should live in the

---

11. For more on memory, see Daniel Taylor, *The Myth of Certainty: The Reflective Christian and the Risk of Commitment* (Waco, Tes.: Word, 1986), 100–107.

present. The God who has called us, for example, has demonstrated in Christ Jesus his love for us and has given us the Holy Spirit; in light of this, we should not be surprised that God's will for us (4:3) includes living a holy life (4:7) and loving others (4:9).

In this respect the current popularity of WWJD bracelets is an encouraging development. The letters WWJD represent the question, "What Would Jesus Do?" When confronted by a problematic situation, the bracelet is supposed to remind the wearer to ask the question, "What would Jesus do?" in these circumstances. The bracelet thus becomes a means of encouraging believers to live their lives in light of the teaching and deeds of Jesus.

It is just here, however, that we encounter a significant weakness of contemporary Christianity: its lack of knowledge of the Bible. In order to answer the WWJD question, obviously knowledge of the Gospel narratives about Jesus is necessary. But as various polls by Gallup and Barna have revealed, the level of Bible literacy in America is abysmal. Details of the polls' findings have been widely reported: Only half of the Christians polled identified correctly Jesus as the person who delivered the Sermon on the Mount; barely three of five could recall the names of the first four books of the New Testament. When asked to quote a Bible verse, the most frequent response was "God helps those who help themselves"—a line written by Benjamin Franklin.

It seems rather pointless to wear a WWJD bracelet if one has never read a Gospel, nor does it do much good to ask "What would Jesus do?" if we have no idea of what Jesus did. Nor can we discern how to live in the present or look forward in hope if we do not learn and remember what God has done in the past.

The centrality of God for the life of the church. In echoing in these closing verses the key ideas of his opening verse, Paul closes the letter as it began: with the spotlight, focus, and emphasis squarely on God and Jesus Christ. In the course of his letter Paul has talked a fair amount about both himself and the Thessalonians, but at the end the last word is not about themselves but about God. The final thing he wants on our minds is God, the one who has called and saved us through Jesus Christ, who gives us the Holy Spirit in power and holiness, and who will bring us into his kingdom and glory when Jesus returns. In this respect the two *theological* affirmations in 5:24—virtually a one-sentence summary of the last half of Romans 8—deserve emphasis: "The one who calls you *is faithful* and he *will do* it." That is, not only is God able to do all that he has promised, but because he is trustworthy and reliable, he will in fact do it.

Our future, in other words, rests entirely in the power and faithfulness of God. Paul implied as much by the way he linked together in 1:1 phrases like "grace," "peace," "in God the Father," and "the Lord Jesus Christ." Here he makes it explicit: Our future as believers rests entirely on the power and faithfulness of God as revealed through Jesus the Messiah. If that is a good place to begin, it is an even better place to end, as we anticipate "the coming of our Lord Jesus Christ" (5:23).

2 Thessalonians 1:1–12

PAUL, SILAS AND Timothy,
To the church of the Thessalonians in God our
Father and the Lord Jesus Christ:

²Grace and peace to you from God the Father and the Lord Jesus Christ.

³We ought always to thank God for you, brothers, and rightly so, because your faith is growing more and more, and the love every one of you has for each other is increasing. ⁴Therefore, among God's churches we boast about your perseverance and faith in all the persecutions and trials you are enduring.

⁵All this is evidence that God's judgment is right, and as a result you will be counted worthy of the kingdom of God, for which you are suffering. ⁶God is just: He will pay back trouble to those who trouble you ⁷and give relief to you who are troubled, and to us as well. This will happen when the Lord Jesus is revealed from heaven in blazing fire with his powerful angels. ⁸He will punish those who do not know God and do not obey the gospel of our Lord Jesus. ⁹They will be punished with everlasting destruction and shut out from the presence of the Lord and from the majesty of his power ¹⁰on the day he comes to be glorified in his holy people and to be marveled at among all those who have believed. This includes you, because you believed our testimony to you.

¹¹With this in mind, we constantly pray for you, that our God may count you worthy of his calling, and that by his power he may fulfill every good purpose of yours and every act prompted by your faith. ¹²We pray this so that the name of our Lord Jesus may be glorified in you, and you in him, according to the grace of our God and the Lord Jesus Christ.

VERSES 1–2 COMPRISE the prescript of the letter. It follows closely the prescript of 1 Thessalonians. The only differences are all in the direction of patterns found in Paul's other (later) letters.

From an epistolary perspective, 1:3–12 comprises the "thanksgiving" section of the letter. The complex character of Pauline thanksgivings (present in every letter except Galatians) was noted in the discussion of 1 Thessalonians 1:2–10. The same holds true here, as Paul not only prays but also praises and instructs in this thanksgiving section.

From a rhetorical perspective, 1:3–12 functions as the *exordium*, or introduction, which has two primary purposes: (1) to win the goodwill of the audience while setting a mood or tone for the letter, and (2) to announce its main themes. The former goal is accomplished by the praise and affirmation in 1:3–4, while 1:5–10 raise the central topic of the letter, the "Day of the Lord."

Grammatically, the entire section contains just three sentences in Greek: verses 1–2 (the prescript), 3–10, and 11–12. In terms of content, the NIV (cf. NRSV, NAB) is right to break the long second sentence into two paragraphs. The first section (vv. 3–4) comprises the thanksgiving proper, while the second (vv. 5–10) is largely instructional and encouraging in character. The last paragraph (vv. 11–12) is what is termed a "prayer report"—that is, a report about a prayer rather than an actual prayer itself.

The Prescript (1:1–2)

EXCEPT FOR TWO minor differences, 1:1–2 is identical to what Paul wrote in 1 Thessalonians 1:1. (1) The first difference is the addition of "our" to "Father," an instance of what Paul commonly does in the rest of his letters. The designation of God as "our" Father "reflects Paul's conception of Christians as forming the family of God in a metaphorical sense and is to be seen alongside those texts where believers are called the children of God (cf. Rom. 8:14–23; Gal. 3:26; 4:4–7)."[1] (2) The other difference is in verse 2, where the source of the "grace and peace" (which is assumed by Paul in 1 Thess. 1:1) is explicitly

---

1. C. A. Wanamaker, *Thessalonians*, 213.

identified as "God the Father and the Lord Jesus Christ." The same (or similar) phrase is found in all of Paul's letters except 1 Thessalonians and Colossians (which has only "God our Father"). For the meaning of these verses, see the discussion of 1 Thessalonians 1:1.

The Thanksgiving (1:3–4)

THE STATEMENT IN 1:3a about giving thanks (repeated in 2:13 below) echoes closely what Paul wrote in 1 Thessalonians 1:2. The phrase "we ought" is otherwise unparalleled in Paul's writings, as is the phrase "and rightly so." Some argue that here thanksgiving is viewed as a duty rather than a joy, and they take it as an indication of non-Pauline authorship. But this consideration overlooks the reasons for thanksgiving, two of which are given in 1:3b: The Thessalonians' "faith is growing more and more," and the love they have "for each other is increasing"—the very thing for which Paul said he was praying in 1 Thessalonians 3:10, 12.[2] Any sense of "obligation" in 2 Thessalonians 1:3a is driven not by duty but by gratitude to God for the divinely inspired growth experienced by the Thessalonians, a gratitude so overwhelming that one has little choice but to give thanks for it.

The Thessalonians' growth in faith and love (cf. 1 Thess. 1:3) was taking place under the most adverse conditions: the continuing experience of "persecutions" (*diogmois*; cf. Acts 8:1; Rom. 8:35; 2 Cor. 12:10) and "afflictions" (*thlipsesin*, NIV "trials"; cf. 2 Thess. 1:6; also 1 Thess. 1:6; 3:3, 7). The church's circumstances do not appear to have changed much since the time of Paul's writing the first letter (cf. 1 Thess. 3:1–5). But adverse external circumstances have not hindered the fellowship's growth in the critical areas of faith and love; if anything, they may have promoted it.

Consequently (NIV "therefore") Paul reports two more reasons why he gives thanks and "boasts" (cf. 1 Thess. 2:19) to other congregations about the Thessalonians. These are the "perseverance" (cf. 3:5; also 1 Thess. 1:3, "endurance inspired by hope") and "faith" (primarily in the sense of "trust," but perhaps also a bit of the sense of "faithfulness") that they have demonstrated. In short, the Thessalonian brothers and

---

2. Lightfoot notes that the two verbs "are carefully chosen; the former implying an internal, organic growth, as of a tree; the other a diffusive, or expansive character, as of a flood irrigating the land" (*Notes on Epistles*, 98).

sisters[3] have become for Paul an exemplary model of enduring Christian commitment under difficult conditions.

Instruction and Encouragement (1:5–10)

IN 1:5, PAUL goes on to say that "all this"—that is, the four reasons he has just mentioned for giving thanks—is at the same time "evidence" (in the sense of a clear indication) of "God's righteous judgment" (NIV "that God's judgment is right").[4] The significance of affliction and persecution is potentially ambiguous; such experiences can be interpreted either as attacks on God's people by forces hostile to God, or as punishment suffered by God's people for their sins. Paul interprets the fact that the Thessalonians are not only persevering and trusting in the midst of persecution, but actually growing and increasing, as a sign of God's blessing, not judgment. The Thessalonians, Paul implies, having placed their faith in God, are being attacked by forces hostile to God.[5] God in turn has judged the situation correctly, as his blessing of them in the midst of their suffering indicates.

In other words, the growth, increase, perseverance, and faith demonstrated by the Thessalonians together give evidence that they are indeed part of God's people. "As a result," they "will be counted worthy" (for this verb, see comment on 1:11) of God's kingdom. In 1 Thessalonians 2:12 Paul had urged them "to live lives worthy of God, who calls you into his kingdom and glory." Here he offers them assurance that they are, by God's power, in fact living such lives, and he helps them understand that the continuing persecution and afflictions they are experiencing are not evidence to the contrary, but in fact confirmatory evidence.

---

3. The Greek word *adelphoi*, "brothers"(1:3) includes the entire community, not just the male members; for the significance of the term, see comments on 1 Thess. 1:4.

4. The antecedent of "all this" (NIV; "this is," NRSV; the phrase is not in the Greek, but is implied by the construction) is ambiguous. I take it to be all the reasons mentioned after the "because" (*hoti*) in 1:3 (similarly J. R. W. Stott, *The Gospel and the End of Time*, 146). For the view that it is the Thessalonians' perseverance and faith, see I. H. Marshall, *1 and 2 Thessalonians*, 172–73; F. F. Bruce, *1 and 2 Thessalonians*, 149; E. Best, *Thessalonians*, 254–56; E. J. Richard, *Thessalonians*, 304, 316–18; for the view that the antecedent is the persecution and affliction (NIV "trials"), see C. A. Wanamaker, *Thessalonians*, 220–23.

5. For the idea of affliction as a consequence of following Jesus, see comments on 1 Thess. 3:4.

In terms of the Greek word order, there is some ambiguity regarding the phrase "as a result you will be counted worthy of the kingdom of God" (1:5b). (1) It can be taken with either "God's judgment" or "persecutions and afflictions." (2) The phrase can indicate either purpose ("in order that") or result ("with the result that"). In view of the last clause in 1:5 ("for which you are suffering") and 1 Thessalonians 2:12 (where the actions of the Thessalonians are linked by Paul with the idea of being "worthy of God"), it seems most likely that the phrase should be linked with "persecutions and afflictions." This decision in turn strongly suggests that the phrase indicates result rather than purpose—exactly as the NIV renders it.

> It was not necessary for the readers to suffer in order to be considered worthy of God's dominion, but the writer certainly wished to comfort them with the fact that as a result of their experience of affliction they were considered worthy of it by God.[6]

In 1:6 Paul picks up (from 1:5a) and develops the idea of God's righteous judgment. There are, he says, two sides to this judgment, one negative (v. 6, retribution "to those who trouble" God's people) and one positive (v. 7a, "relief to [those] who are troubled"). The negative side is discussed further in 1:8–9. The troublers of God's people are part of a larger group identified as "those who do not know God," that is, who "do not obey the gospel of our Lord Jesus"[7] (v. 8). The second clause makes it clear that the first clause is not talking about simple ignorance but willful rejection (cf. 2:10 below; also Rom. 1:18–23, 25, 28; contrast John 17:3).

The punishment (exdikesis, 1:8; a noun, the same one usually translated "vengeance" in Rom. 12:19, cf. NRSV) that this group will experience is

---

6. C. A. Wanamaker, Thessalonians, 223; cf. F. F. Bruce, 1 and 2 Thessalonians, 149. For the idea of God's dominion or "kingdom," see comments on 1 Thess. 2:12.

7. In light of Old Testament usage, some argue that "those who do not know God" (cf. Ps. 79:6; Jer. 10:25) refers to Gentiles, and "those who do not obey the gospel" (cf. Isa. 66:4 LXX; Rom. 10:16) refers to Jews (see, e.g., I. H. Marshall, 1 and 2 Thessalonians, 177–78; cf. NRSV). But this distinction cannot be maintained consistently in either the Old Testament (cf. Jer. 4:22; 9:3, 6; Hos. 5:4) or Pauline usage (cf. Rom. 11:30–32). Moreover, the passage is cast in the poetic style of Old Testament prophecy, and the two clauses are an example of synonymous parallelism. Together they identify a single group that includes both Jews and Gentiles (cf. F. F. Bruce, 1 and 2 Thessalonians, 151–52; C. A. Wanamaker, Thessalonians, 227).

identified in verse 9. The words "and shut out" are not in the Greek, which reads "everlasting destruction from the presence of the Lord and from the glory of his power." This suggests that Paul is not talking about two things (destruction and separation) but only one thing. The second part of the sentence defines what he means by the first part: "everlasting destruction," that is, separation from the Lord's presence (for this phrase cf. Isa. 2:10, 19, 21, a judgment passage) and glory.[8] In other words, Paul's definition of "destruction" (cf. 1 Thess. 5:3) here is precisely the opposite of his definition elsewhere of salvation as being with the Lord always (1 Thess. 4:17) and sharing in God's glory (Rom. 8:17–18, 30; 2 Cor. 4:17; Phil. 3:21).[9]

The positive side of God's judgment, first mentioned in verse 7a ("relief"), is explicated (if only briefly) in verse 10. In sharpest contrast to those who "disobey the gospel" (1:8), "those who have believed" will experience both the presence and the glory of the Lord himself (the very things the other group will not experience). This is because the Lord "will be glorified in the presence of his holy people."[10] They will also "marvel," either in the sense of "admire" or (in view of the parallelism with the preceding phrase) perhaps "worship."

In the last part of verse 10 Paul applies his point directly to the Thessalonians: The group that will experience the Lord's presence, he assures them, "includes you." In the context of their present experience of affliction, the statement is both reassuring and comforting (and thus rein-

---

8. Similarly F. F. Bruce, *1 and 2 Thessalonians,* 152; I. H. Marshall, *1 and 2 Thessalonians,* 179; C. A. Wanamaker, *Thessalonians,* 229; L. Morris, *The First and Second Epistles to the Thessalonians,* 204–5. The term *destruction* here in 1:9 is sometimes taken in the sense of annihilation. This is linguistically possible, but "as there is no evidence in Paul (or the rest of the NT for that matter) for a concept of final annihilation of the godless, the expression 'eternal destruction' should probably be taken in a metaphorical manner as indicating the severity of the punishment awaiting the enemies of God" (C. A. Wanamaker, *Thessalonians,* 229).

9. Cf. also Matt. 25:46, where the similar phrase "eternal punishment" (a different Greek word for "punishment" is used) is defined in contrast to "eternal life"; everything that eternal life is, eternal punishment is not.

10. The preposition *en* ("in") can indicate (1) location (e.g., NIV "in his holy people;" cf. L. Morris, *The First and Second Epistles to the Thessalonians,* 206), (2) cause (e.g., "because of his holy people;" so J. E. Frame, *Thessalonians,* 237), (3) means (e.g., NRSV "by his holy people"), or (4) presence ("in the presence of his holy people"; so C. A. Wanamaker, *Thessalonians,* 231). Option 3 includes the idea of option 4 (at least implicitly) and makes good sense in the following phrase as well; it is thus the preferable choice (cf. I. H. Marshall, *1 and 2 Thessalonians,* 180). For the Old Testament background of the phrase cf. Ps. 88:8, and for the following phrase cf. 67:36, or possibly 88:6.

forces the point of 1:3–4). At the same time, it is a veiled exhortation to keep on persevering, lest they find themselves in the other category.

All that Paul has been talking about "will happen when the Lord Jesus is revealed from heaven" (1:7b), that is, "when he comes ... on that day" (1:10, NRSV).[11] This is the same event that Paul in his first letter referred to as Jesus' "coming" (*parousia*, 1 Thess. 4:15) or "the day of the Lord" (5:2). The phrase "is revealed" actually renders a noun, *apokalypsis* ("revelation;" cf. Rom. 2:5; 1 Cor. 1:7; for the corresponding verb, see Rom. 8:18; 2 Thess. 2:3, 6, 8). Paul likely uses this word (rather than *parousia*) because of its nuance of present hiddenness or veiledness: Even though Jesus currently is indeed Lord, not all of creation yet recognizes or acknowledges that fact—indeed, some actively persecute the Lord's people. But the day is surely coming when the Lordship of Jesus will be revealed for all to see clearly, and with consequences that Paul outlines in verses 6–10 (i.e., either judgment or salvation).

A Prayer Report (1:11–12)

IN THESE VERSES Paul reprises some of the key themes of verses 5–10 in a prayer report (rather than an actual prayer, as in 1 Thess. 3:11–13). In it he informs the Thessalonians of the contents (2 Thess. 1:11) and purpose (1:12) of his "constant" (cf. 1 Thess. 1:2) prayers for them. (1) His first petition (which resumes the idea of v. 5) is that "God may count you worthy of his calling." The verb here (*axioo*) is a simple form of the verb in verse 5 (*kataxioo*). There is considerable debate whether these two verbs mean "make worthy" or "consider worthy." The first option better fits the context, but the second option better fits with usage elsewhere.[12] God's "calling" (*klesis*; for the related verb cf. 1 Thess. 2:12; 4:7; 5:24) is essentially equivalent to God's "election" or "choice" (*ekloge*, 1 Thess. 1:4; see also 2 Thess. 2:13–14).

---

11. With respect to the phenomena accompanying the Lord's return, see comments on 1 Thess. 4:13–18. The fire imagery emphasizes the judgmental aspects of the event; cf., for example, the words of John the Baptist (Matt. 3:10, 12), and for the Old Testament background, Isa. 66:15–16. Indeed, Isa. 66, with its themes of vindication and vengeance (e.g., 66:14, "the hand of the LORD will be made known to his servants, but his fury will be shown to his enemies") is illuminating for the present passage.

12. For "make worthy" see I. H. Marshall, *1 and 2 Thessalonians*, 182; E. J. Richard, *Thessalonians*, 310; E. Best, *Thessalonians*, 268–69; for "consider worthy" see C. A. Wanamaker, *Thessalonians*, 233; L. Morris, *The First and Second Epistles to the Thessalonians*, 197–98, 209.

(2) The other petition is that God might "fulfill" or "bring to completion"—the verb has the idea of finishing something already begun—"every good purpose of yours [cf. Rom. 10:1; Phil. 1:15; 2:13] and every act prompted by your faith" (the same phrase as in 1 Thess. 1:3). These two phrases are likely an instance of hendiadys, in which the second phrase explains the first. The emphasis on God's power reinforces the thought that God through the Holy Spirit (cf. 1 Thess. 1:5) is at work in the Thessalonians' midst[13] (cf. 2 Thess. 1:3–5), and thus they do not stand alone in their afflictions.

Whereas verse 11 echoed verse 5, the statement of purpose in verse 12 echoes verse 10 (cf. also Isa. 66:5; indeed, images from Isa. 66 occur throughout the passage). Here, however, there is an element of reciprocity not mentioned earlier ("you in him"). Also, the time frame in view is different: In verse 10 it is future (eschatological), while in verse 12 the emphasis is on the present. That is, when God's people do in fact live in a manner worthy of their calling (cf. 1 Thess. 2:12; also Phil. 1:27; Col. 1:10), one consequence is that the "name of our Lord Jesus" is presently glorified, foreshadowing the future glorification that will occur at the Parousia (2 Thess. 2:10).[14]

The glorification of the Lord and his name in turn results in the glorification of his followers ("and you in him"), a process that begins with the work of the Spirit in the lives of believers now (2 Cor. 3:18) and culminates with the revealing of the "glorious freedom of the children of God" at the Parousia (Rom. 8:18–21; cf. Phil. 3:20–21).

All of this is due solely to "the grace of our God and the Lord Jesus Christ" (v. 12).[15] The fact that grace is most often associated with the initial experience of salvation in the past should not cause us to overlook the fact that the present (cf. Rom. 5:2, "this grace in which we now stand") and the future of salvation are no less a matter of grace. With respect to the phrase "our God and the Lord Jesus Christ" (lit., "the God of ours and Lord Jesus Christ"), it is possible that "God" and "Lord" both refer to Jesus (a single article controls the whole phrase). But in view of both the immediate context (in v. 11 "our God" is clearly the Father,

---

13. Similarly G. D. Fee, *God's Empowering Presence*, 70.

14. Cf. Rom. 15:7: When believers accept one another as Christ accepted them, it is possible to catch a glimpse now of the glory that was lost as a result of sin (3:23) but which will be restored fully at the Parousia (5:2; 8:18–24).

15. For "grace" see comments on 1 Thess. 1:1; see also 5:28; 2 Thess. 1:2; 2:16; 3:18.

distinct from "the Lord Jesus" in v. 12a) and usage elsewhere in the Thessalonians letters (1 Thess. 1:3; 3:11; 3:13; 2 Thess. 1:1—2; cf. 2:16), this seems unlikely, and the NIV accurately catches the sense.[16]

A NUMBER OF themes, topics, and elements in this complex section have already appeared or have close parallels in 1 Thessalonians. For how one might approach the prescript (with respect to both Bridging Contexts and Contemporary Significance), see the discussion of the prescript of the first letter (1 Thess. 1:1), from which 2 Thessalonians 1:1—2 scarcely differ. With regard to love, faith, and perseverance, see comments on 1 Thessalonians 1:2—3. The question of the relation between divine initiative and human responsibility arises in 2 Thessalonians 1:11 (cf. also 2:13—15; 3:3—4); see comments on 1 Thessalonians 3:9—13 (Contemporary Significance).

With respect to the thanksgiving (1:3—4) at the beginning of the passage and the petitionary prayer report (1:11—12) at the end, see the discussion of 1 Thessalonians 3:9—13 (Bridging Contexts and Contemporary Significance).[17] In giving thanks for what the Thessalonians have done and by praying for what God might accomplish through them in the future, Paul implicitly encourages them as well.

The matter of persecution is clearly a major concern in this passage. As in 1 Thessalonians, Paul has in view "persecutions and trials" (v. 4) that are specifically the result of living for Christ and the gospel in an openly hostile world, which rejects God and his love.[18] Thus what I said about this subject in 1 Thessalonians 3:1—5 (cf. also 1:6; 2:13—16) is also relevant to this passage and should be consulted (including the Bridging Contexts section). In particular, the discussion there of how and in what ways various contemporary situations or circumstances do or do not parallel those of the Thessalonians is important here.

---

16. Cf. Murray J. Harris, *Jesus as God: The New Testament Use of Theos in Reference to Jesus* (Grand Rapids: Baker, 1992), 265—66.

17. See further D. A. Carson, *A Call to Spiritual Reformation: Priorities from Paul and His Prayers* (Grand Rapids: Baker, 1992), 39—62. Carson devotes two chapters to 2 Thess. 1:1—12, discussing what the passage reveals about "the framework of prayer" and about "worthy petitions."

18. Paul discusses suffering in general in Rom. 8:17—30.

In addition to what Paul said earlier about persecution, 2 Thessalonians 1 has a particular angle on this topic that has not come up before and that is central to the discussion. That is the matter of persecution *as it relates to the question of God's justice.*

Persecution and God's justice. Although we do not know for sure why or how the question about God's justice arose, it seems likely that it is closely connected with the confusion about whether the Day of the Lord has already arrived (the topic of ch. 2). In 1 Thessalonians, Paul had informed the believers in Thessalonica (1) that the trials or afflictions they were experiencing were not due to God's judgment of them, but were instead the result or consequence of their allegiance to God's word, the gospel (1 Thess. 1:6; 2:14; 3:4), and (2) that when the Day of the Lord, with its accompanying judgment, did occur, they would experience not wrath but salvation (5:9). In short, the coming of the Day of the Lord would bring an end to their afflictions—the "relief" Paul mentions in 2 Thessalonians 1:7.

But since the first letter, there has been a new development. In light of 2 Thessalonians 2:2, it seems as if at least some in the congregation were persuaded that the Day of the Lord had already arrived. But if that is true, then why were they still being persecuted? The righteous were supposed to be vindicated, and only the wicked were supposed to experience suffering and judgment after the return of Jesus. Yet as chapter 1 makes clear, they were still being persecuted, perhaps more heavily than before. What did this mean? One can easily imagine how under such circumstances questions could easily arise about God's justice and judgment.

Paul responds to this problem in two ways. In chapter 2 he corrects the misunderstanding regarding the coming of the Day of the Lord that generated the question about whether God is just. Before that, however, he addresses the question itself. His answer is relatively straightforward. (1) Almost as an axiom not requiring proof, he insists that "God is just" (1:6) and "[his] judgment is right" (1:5). (2) He affirms that the justness and rightness of God's judgment will become evident to all "when the Lord Jesus is revealed from heaven" (1:7).

By placing the public vindication of God's justice and judgment in the future, Paul implicitly acknowledges that at the present time and in light of their circumstances, it might indeed appear that God is not just. In this respect his answer has much in common with the perspective of the writer of Ecclesiastes. This author acknowledges that if one views things from a purely human perspective—that is, "under the sun"—it does not appear as if God is just, for the righteous die young and poor while the wicked die old and wealthy (Eccl. 7:15). Moreover (4:1),

> I saw the tears of the oppressed—
>> and they have no comforter;
> power was on the side of their oppressors—
>> and they have no comforter.

But, the writer goes on to assert, there is more to reality and life than what can be learned or observed from the merely human perspective. This observable life is not all there is to reality; a time is coming when "God will bring every deed into judgment, including every hidden thing, whether it is good or evil" (12:14). This is essentially the point Paul makes in 2 Thessalonians 1:7–10, where he describes God's coming judgment, which will set right the scales of justice.

Paul differs from Ecclesiastes in one important respect, however, in that he does not place the vindication of God's justice entirely in the future. The faith and endurance of the Thessalonians in the face of continuing persecution *already* offer a clear indication (1:4–5) of God's justice. This idea is similar to what he says in Philippians 1:28: Opposition to the gospel "is an omen to them that they will be destroyed, but that you will be saved—and that by God" (NIV, modified).[19] In short, the faithfulness of God's people is, from Paul's perspective, evidence now of God's justice, which will be fully vindicated in the future.

A question which well might arise at this point, but which Paul does not address here, is this: Why does God delay his judgment? Why doesn't he vindicate his people now? Is he unable to, or does he not care? Some have seized on the "delay" in the appearance of God's judgment as an excuse to ignore or reject the idea of God's justice. In Romans Paul suggests an answer: It is a matter of God's gracious patience towards sinners. As he says in Romans 2:4, "Do you show contempt for the riches of his kindness, tolerance and patience, not realizing that God's kindness leads you toward repentance?" (see also 3:25).

---

19. On this passage see Gordon D. Fee, *Paul's Letter to the Philippians* (NICNT; Grand Rapids: Eerdmans, 1995), 169–72; Frank Thielman, *Philippians* (NIVAC; Grand Rapids: Zondervan, 1995), 93–94, 100–101.

In passing we may note that there is in 2 Thessalonians 1:6−8 an implicit explanation of why the Thessalonians are suffering. God's coming judgment on "those who trouble you" (1:6), Paul says, will fall on those who "do not know God and do not obey the gospel of our Lord Jesus" (1:8). In other words, those who are persecuting the Thessalonians are persecuting them not so much because they hate them, but because they are hostile to the God in whom the Thessalonians believe and trust.

Finally, it is important to observe that when Paul asserts that God will vindicate his people, he is repeating a theme at least as old as the Exodus. In the "Song of Moses" in Deuteronomy 32:40−41, for example, the Lord himself declares:

> I lift my hand to heaven and declare:
>> As surely as I live forever,
> when I sharpen my flashing sword
>> and my hand grasps it in judgment,
> I will take vengeance on my adversaries
>> and repay those who hate me.

And in 32:36, 43, this declaration by the Lord becomes on the lips of Moses virtually a confession of faith:

> The LORD will judge his people
>> and have compassion on his servants
> when he sees their strength is gone
>> and no one is left, slave or free. . . .
> Rejoice, O nations, with his people,
>> for he will avenge the blood of his servants;
> he will take vengeance on his enemies
>> and make atonement for his land and people.

Isaiah takes up the same theme and finds in it a word of encouragement (Isa. 35:4):

> Say to those with fearful hearts,
>> "Be strong, do not fear;
> your God will come,
>> he will come with vengeance;
> with divine retribution
>> he will come to save you."

In Jeremiah 11:20 (cf. 20:12), it becomes a prayer from the mouth of the prophet:

> But, O LORD Almighty, you who judge righteously
>   and test the heart and mind,
> let me see your vengeance upon them,
>   for to you I have committed my cause.

This confident hope on the part of Moses, Isaiah, and Jeremiah that God will indeed vindicate his people and take vengeance on his enemies is the background for Paul's confident assertion that "God is just," and it offers us a clue to the significance of his statement: To declare that God is just and will vindicate his people is virtually equivalent to a confession of faith in God. In this respect, Paul views the Thessalonians' perseverance in the face of persecution as nothing less than a declaration of their trust and hope in God. This observation offers a point of departure for thinking about how we might apply this passage today.

A growing faith. Before leaving this section, a short phrase—Paul's observation in 1:3 that the Thessalonians' "faith is growing"—may need a word or two of explanation. To people accustomed to thinking in somewhat static terms of "faith" as something one either has or does not have (e.g., "So-and-so has lost his faith"), this phrase may sound a bit odd. But as John R. W. Stott, observes, "Faith is a relationship of trust in God, and like all relationships is a living, dynamic, growing thing."[20]

Perhaps an appropriate analogy is the various ways we speak of "love." True, we say that someone is "in love" or "not in love." But we also speak of a couple "in love" as growing in their love for each other. Similarly, it is not inappropriate to speak of "faith" as something one does or does not have, as long as we realize that faith is, as Stott points out, a living and (one hopes) growing relationship with God.

 IF ONE COMES to this chapter after first working through 1 Thessalonians, many of the topics and themes in this passage sound familiar, and it may not be necessary to treat all of them again. On the other hand, if one begins with 2 Thessalonians

---

20. J. R. W. Stott, *The Gospel and the End of Time*, 144.

rather than 1 Thessalonians, then much more in this chapter calls for treatment or discussion. In this instance, the references given under "Bridging Contexts" (above) to the discussion of the various topics in the commentary on 1 Thessalonians offer guidance in dealing with them here and should be consulted.

In either case, however, there are some themes or perspectives that are distinctive to this chapter and which therefore call for reflection here. These include the importance and consequence of our response to the gospel and the matter of God's justice.

A choice that makes all the difference. A hard-to-miss characteristic of a modern consumer culture is choice. To walk into a supermarket or department store is to find oneself immediately surrounded by a mind-dazzling (or is it numbing?) array of choices. Two dozen varieties and sizes of soap, fifteen different brands of snack chips, a dozen kinds of toilet paper, nine shoe stores in the same mall, and so on and so on. The range and variety of products—and thus choices—seem endless.

But even as the range of choices has multiplied, the significance of those choices has decreased. Much of the difference between similar products is superficial rather that real, involving distinctions without a real difference. All the brands of soap clean effectively; my car runs the same regardless of which brand of gas I put in it. More and more of our choices mean less and less, despite the efforts of advertisers to convince us otherwise. In the long run, most of the decisions one makes in the course of the day are inconsequential. A year from now, it is unlikely that my life will have been affected by which brand of paper towels or variety of soup I purchased yesterday. Ironically, it seems that a second characteristic of a modern consumer culture is its tendency to trivialize choices even as it multiplies them.

Another aspect of contemporary culture, this one tragic rather than ironic, is the tendency to try to avoid responsibility for our choices. The tendency to "pass the buck" or shift responsibility is everywhere observable. Rather than take responsibility for the consequences of our actions, we seek to blame someone or something else: the way we were raised, the environment in which we were raised, the absent parent who wasn't there, or the dysfunctional one who was there. Antisocial or personally destructive behaviors have been medicalized and are now treated as diseases rather than viewed as character faults or shortcomings. Our heavy reliance on no-fault divorce, easily accessible abortions, lawsuits as a means of settling minor social problems, or deficit spending as a means to avoid paying for present consumption offers further evidence, I suggest, of a culture fundamentally unwilling to bear responsibility for the consequences of our actions.

But not all choices are trivial, and not all consequences of our choices can be avoided. Despite the ads that try to persuade us that "we can have it all," there are still times when we are confronted by mutually exclusive choices, whose consequences are more or less irrevocable. Examples include choices about education, which person to marry, what career to pursue, whether to use drugs, whether to terminate a pregnancy, or whether to be faithful to a commitment. They are choices, in other words, that "make all the difference" in the fabric and shape of our lives, to borrow a phrase from one of Robert Frost's most famous poems, "The Road Not Taken." This poem reads, in part:

> Two roads diverged in a yellow wood,
> And sorry I could not travel both
> and be one traveler, long I stood. . . .
> Then took the other. . . .
> Oh, I kept the first for another day!
> Yet knowing how way leads on to way,
> I doubted if I should ever come back. . . .
> Two roads diverged in a wood, and I—
> I took the one less traveled by,
> And that has made all the difference.[21]

Here the choice is unavoidable ("sorry I could not travel both"), and the consequences are both irrevocable ("knowing how way leads on to way, I doubted if I should ever come back") and significant ("I took the one. . . . And that has made all the difference").

Paul's description in 1:5–10 of God's future judgment—in particular, the basis of it—focuses a spotlight on a particularly consequential and unavoidable choice: the decision whether to accept or reject "the gospel of our Lord Jesus" (1:8). When the time of judgment comes, as it inevitably will, those who, in response to the gospel, believed the

---

21. Robert Frost, "The Road Not Taken," *Collected Poems of Robert Frost* (Garden City, N.Y.: Garden City Publishing, 1942), 131.

message and placed their trust ("faith") in God will "be with the Lord forever" (1 Thess. 4:17) in his presence. Those, however, who have rejected the gospel will find themselves "shut out" (2 Thess. 1:9) from the Lord's presence and majesty.

Here we have what J. R. W. Stott describes as "the solemn alternative": the opportunity to find and fulfill our true identity as human beings ("to glorify God and enjoy him forever," in the words of the Westminster Shorter Catechism) by believing in the gospel, or by rejecting it to place ourselves among those who "will be alienated from their own true identity as human beings. Instead of being fulfilled or 'glorified,' their humanity will shrink and shrivel.... Instead of shining with the glory of Christ, their light will be extinguished in outer darkness."[22]

By sharing with the Thessalonians this vision of the future consequences of a choice they have already made, Paul seeks to encourage them to remain faithful to the God who has called them (1:11), in spite of whatever persecution they may experience in the meantime. To those of us who have made the same choice as the Thessalonians, it likewise offers encouragement to us. But for those of us who may not yet have made that decision, it confronts us with a sobering vision of the irrevocable consequences of a decision that must be made, an unavoidable choice that makes all the difference.

Declaring God's justice. For those believers today who find themselves in circumstances similar (if not identical) to those of the Thessalonians—that is, persecuted or afflicted for the sake of the gospel—the application of this passage is clear: *Persevere in the face of this unjust treatment* as a declaration of the fact that God is just and will vindicate his people.[23] Such faithful endurance constitutes, Paul says, a clear "evidence" (1:5) not only that God exists, but also that "[his] judgment is right" (1:5) and that he himself "is just" (1:6; cf. Rom. 3:25–26). As such, it constitutes a bold declaration that the persecutors are wrong and that they are hostile to God. Perseverance, in other words, becomes a form of proclaiming the truth about God.

---

22. J. R. W. Stott, *The Gospel and the End of Time*, 154; see John Piper, *Desiring God: Meditations of a Christian Hedonist* (Portland, Ore.: Multnomah, 1986).

23. For a discussion of the meaning of persecution and affliction, and of how and in what ways various circumstances today are or are not comparable with those of the Thessalonians, see the Bridging Contexts section for 1 Thess. 3:1–5.

What should those of us who are not experiencing persecution for the sake of the gospel do? To begin with, we have an obligation to pray for and encourage those who are being persecuted. In addition, we should *protest against unjust treatment* of our fellow believers. This will accomplish at least two things. (1) It potentially offers (in addition to prayer) a concrete means of encouraging our persecuted fellow believers. (2) Protesting against the unjust treatment of fellow believers is another way (in addition to perseverance) of declaring God's justice. Governments, nations, groups, or movements that persecute Christians are implicitly (if not explicitly) claiming the right to decide what justice means. But that is not the case; God is the one who defines what justice is. By protesting unjust actions directed toward Christians, we can remind whoever is responsible that they do not set the standard for justice and that God will hold them accountable for their injustices. In sum, if those who are persecuted declare God's justice by their perseverance, those who are not persecuted can proclaim God's justice by their protests against injustice.

How or in what way might we protest? (1) If the persecution is of believers in other countries, one way would be to adopt the model utilized by Amnesty International and groups that supported Soviet Jews prior to the fall of the Soviet Union. This involves identifying specific believers who are being persecuted and regularly writing letters on their behalf to leaders, representatives, and embassies of the responsible national government.

(2) We can lobby international organizations that distribute aid or financial resources to countries that persecute Christians to issue on a regular basis reports about the human rights conditions (with special reference to religious rights) in the countries they serve.

(3) We can lobby our own government to pay more attention to the plight of persecuted believers in other countries.

(4) We can raise the question of whether we are trading the religious rights and freedom of persecuted brothers and sisters in other countries for economic or national security considerations. At present, for example, there is in the United States a considerable debate about whether to link human rights issues to trade and economic issues in our relations with China. One side of the debate argues that the United States should not jeopardize its economic well-being by allowing human rights issues to interfere with free trade and commerce. But as

believers we should at least raise the question of whether such an approach involves the trading of the religious rights of fellow believers for our own economic advantage.

If the persecution is national or local rather than international, similar strategies (appropriately modified) can be utilized. Instead of writing or protesting to foreign governments, one might need, for example, to write the local school board to protest discriminatory policies against Christian students who wish to meet or gather for prayer or Bible study before or after school. The circumstances and situation might vary, but the principle remains the same.

2 Thessalonians 2:1–12

CONCERNING THE COMING of our Lord Jesus Christ and our being gathered to him, we ask you, brothers, ²not to become easily unsettled or alarmed by some prophecy, report or letter supposed to have come from us, saying that the day of the Lord has already come. ³Don't let anyone deceive you in any way, for that day will not come until the rebellion occurs and the man of lawlessness is revealed, the man doomed to destruction. ⁴He will oppose and will exalt himself over everything that is called God or is worshiped, so that he sets himself up in God's temple, proclaiming himself to be God.

⁵Don't you remember that when I was with you I used to tell you these things? ⁶And now you know what is holding him back, so that he may be revealed at the proper time. ⁷For the secret power of lawlessness is already at work; but the one who now holds it back will continue to do so till he is taken out of the way. ⁸And then the lawless one will be revealed, whom the Lord Jesus will overthrow with the breath of his mouth and destroy by the splendor of his coming. ⁹The coming of the lawless one will be in accordance with the work of Satan displayed in all kinds of counterfeit miracles, signs and wonders, ¹⁰and in every sort of evil that deceives those who are perishing. They perish because they refused to love the truth and so be saved. ¹¹For this reason God sends them a powerful delusion so that they will believe the lie ¹²and so that all will be condemned who have not believed the truth but have delighted in wickedness.

Original Meaning

FROM THE PERSPECTIVES of both epistolary analysis (which sees this section as the main part of the body of the letter) and rhetorical analysis (which views 2:1–2 as the *partitio*, which introduces the theme to be discussed in the following *probatio* or proof section), 2:1–12 comprise the most significant segment of 2 Thessalonians. The rest of the letter either prepares for or follows from this section.[1] With respect to its structure, verses 1–2 of this section introduce both the general topic (the *parousia* or coming of the Lord) and Paul's specific concern (that the Thessalonians not be disturbed by rumors that it has already happened). The basis on which 2:1–2 rest is given in 2:3–4; what Paul states there is spelled out in more detail in 2:5–12.

In view of the numerous interpretive difficulties associated with this passage—by common consent one of the most obscure in the Pauline corpus—it may be useful to sketch an overview of the basic aspects of the passage. Evidently some time after receiving the first letter, some members of the congregation in Thessalonica had become persuaded that the "Day of the Lord"—which Paul in 1 Thessalonians 5:2–6 had indicated would come when least expected and would surprise the unprepared—had already arrived. This apparently caused them a good deal of consternation (and may have been the root cause of their questions about the meaning and significance of the afflictions they were experiencing and about God's justice; cf. 1:3–5).

Paul and his companions somehow learned of this development, though it seems they were not sure of its cause or origin (cf. 2:2a). In response, Paul informs them that it is impossible for the Day of the Lord to have already arrived because certain events and developments (which had not yet taken place) must first occur (2:3–12). Finally, he urges them to stand firm and hold fast to the teachings they had previously received from Paul and his companions (2:13–3:5).

Has the "Day of the Lord" Already Arrived? (2:1–2)

THE MAIN TOPIC to which Paul now turns is stated in 2:1: "the coming [*parousia*] of our Lord Jesus Christ and our being gathered to him." The first element is the same one discussed in 1 Thessalonians 5:1–11; indeed, "it seems nearly impossible not to see" the discussion here "as related to some kind of misunderstanding" of that passage.[2] The second element is apparently the same event described in 1 Thessalonians 4:17 (the specific term used here echoes the Old Testament motif

---

1. Similarly G. D. Fee, *God's Empowering Presence*, 71.
2. Ibid., 71.

of the scattered exiles being gathered together again, as in Isa. 43:4–7; 56:8; Jer. 31:7–8; 2 Macc. 2:7; cf. Matt. 23:37; Mark 13:27).

Paul goes on to reveal his specific point of concern (v. 2): At least some of the Thessalonians have become "unsettled" (i.e., have lost their mental composure) or "alarmed" (perhaps "agitated"; cf. Mark 13:7) by a claim—in some way attributed to the apostle himself—"to the effect that" (NRSV; NIV "saying that") the "day of the Lord has already come."[3] The available evidence regarding the meaning of the verb used here in the perfect tense indicates that it cannot mean anything other than "has come" or "is present" (cf. Rom. 8:38; 1 Cor. 3:22; Gal. 1:4; Heb. 9:9). This observation stands strongly against attempts to find here only a sense of imminence or nearness rather than presence. In other words, at least some in the congregation had come to the conclusion that the event that Paul in 1 Thessalonians 5:1–11 spoke of as yet future had already in some way begun.[4]

This conclusion was apparently based either on misinformation or (more likely, in view of 2:15) on a misunderstanding of Paul's previous teaching on the subject. For all that Paul knows (and it clearly isn't much), this misunderstanding may have arisen or come to the Thessalonians in one of three ways. It may have come (2:2) via a "prophecy" (lit., "a spirit"; i.e., presumably a prophetic utterance, perhaps spoken by one of the congregation or a visitor; cf. 1 Thess. 5:19–20), or a "report" (lit., "word"; i.e., a nonecstatic spoken message or teaching), or a "letter" (i.e., 1 Thessalonians, though the claim is so far removed from anything he actually taught that the possibility of a forged letter crosses his mind). But Paul's primary concern is not with how the claim reached them, but with its content (i.e., the claim that "the day of the Lord has already come"), which apparently has been attributed to him.[5]

---

3. Similarly C. A. Wanamaker, *Thessalonians*, 240.

4. In the absence of any direct evidence, precisely what the Thessalonians believed on this point is cloaked in obscurity. For hypothetical reconstructions see C. A. Wanamaker, *Thessalonians*, 240; E. J. Richard, *Thessalonians*, 343–44; F. F. Bruce, *1 and 2 Thessalonians*, 165.

5. The phrase *hos di' hemon* (NIV "supposed to have come from us") is awkward. It is widely taken as an indication of source (cf. RSV, NAB, NASB, KJV). But to indicate the source of something Paul uses either the preposition *para* (cf. 1 Thess. 2:13; 4:1; 2 Thess. 3:6) or *apo*, which both mean "from," while *dia*, the preposition used here, indicates means or agent, as in Gal. 1:1 (Paul says his apostleship is neither "from [*apo*] men nor by [*dia*] man"). Moreover, *dia* also occurs before "spirit," "report," and "letter"; to translate the fourth occurrence in a row differently from the preceding three is awkward. This suggests that the phrase

Paul's Response: The Day Has Not Arrived (2:3–4)

WITH RESPECT TO this misunderstanding, Paul emphatically denies both its attribution to him (cf. 2:15, where he urges them to stand firm in what he had originally taught them, not some later misunderstanding of it) and its content: "Don't let anyone deceive you in any way" (2:3a; cf. Mark 13:5). Any claim that the Day of the Lord has arrived is false, he insists, because certain things that must happen first (before the Day comes) have not yet happened (and therefore the Day cannot have already arrived).[6]

These things that must happen first (which probably should be taken as components of a single complex event, but could be two sequential items) include (1) the occurrence of "the rebellion" (v. 3), and (2) the revealing (cf. vv. 6, 8) of "the man of lawlessness" (v. 3b). Paul takes it for granted (cf. v. 5) that his readers know what he means by "*the* rebellion [*apostasia*]" and says nothing further about it. The term could denote either political or religious rebellion; here the two ideas are likely combined, with the emphasis on the latter.[7] Paul, like other New Testament writers (cf. Matt. 24:10–12; Mark 13:5; Luke 8:13; Jude 18), probably has in view a time of increasing wrongdoing and general opposition to God (cf. 2 Tim. 3:1–9).

The leader of this rebellion is described in 2:3b–4 by means of a series of parallel phrases. He is first of all a "man of lawlessness" (cf. Ps.

---

means something like "as if said by us" and ought to be associated with what follows, rather than what precedes (so, e.g., J. E. Frame, *Thessalonians*, 246–47; R. Jewett, *Thessalonian Correspondence*, 181–86). "Paul is not saying that the letter did not come from him—it did indeed—but that *what they are now believing about the Day of the Lord did not come*" from Paul and his colleagues (G. D. Fee, *God's Empowering Presence*, 74).

6. The grammar of the sentence beginning in verse 3 is incomplete; the protasis or "if" clause of his conditional sentence (translated here as either "unless" [NRSV, NASB] or "until" [NIV]) ought to be followed by the apodosis or "then" clause. But the expected result clause never comes, perhaps because in the course of the extended description of the "man of lawlessness" (v. 4) Paul lost track of the structure of the sentence. One can either supply, as most English translations do in the middle of verse 3, the implied result clause ("that day will not come" NIV, NRSV), or put a dash at the end of verse 4 (where in Greek the missing clause would have likely come), and view the direct address of verse 5 ("Don't you remember . . .") as an interruption followed by a new sentence in verse 6 (cf. E. J. Richard, *Thessalonians*, 325).

7. It is sometimes alleged that *apostasia* should be translated as "departure" and taken as signifying the same event as the "rapture" in 1 Thess. 4:17, but there is no linguistic basis for such a view (cf. R. H. Gundry, *The Church and the Tribulation* [Grand Rapids: Zondervan, 1973], 114–18; D. E. Hiebert, *Thessalonian Epistles*, 306).

89:22 [LXX 88:23], lit., "son of lawlessness"). That is, this person is characterized by *anomia* (cf. 2:8), a word that describes willful opposition to God as well as a sinful condition (cf. 1 John 3:4).[8] (Because of this opposition he is, whether he realizes it or not, a "son of destruction," i.e., "doomed to destruction" [NIV],[9] in the sense of 1:9; the idea is developed further in verse 8 below.) Paul further characterizes this individual as one who not only "opposes" God but also "exalts himself over everything that is called God or is worshiped" (2:4a; NRSV, "every so-called god or object of worship"; cf. Acts 17:23), a description that echoes Daniel 11:36–37.

The result ("so that") and climax of this arrogant and audacious self-exaltation is the attempt by this person to usurp the very power and position of the one true God. This occurs when "he sets himself up in God's temple" (lit., the *naos*, the sanctuary itself, the holiest part of the temple complex), a symbolic action that involves nothing less than "proclaiming himself to be God" (cf. Ezek. 28:2). Moreover, like the Lord Jesus himself, this man of lawlessness will have his own "revealing" (2:3, 6, 8) or *"parousia"* (2:9), a devilish imitation of the real thing. This suggests that he is nothing less than a rival messiah or antichrist (cf. 1 John 2:18).[10]

The identity of the "temple" in which the lawless one sets himself up is a matter of some debate. In view of the way Paul's language echoes earlier attempts (some successful) to desecrate the sanctuary in Jerusalem,[11] it may be that he meant the Jerusalem temple (destroyed by the Romans in A.D. 70). Other suggestions include a rebuilt temple in Jerusalem, the church (on the analogy of 1 Cor. 3:16–17; 6:19; 2 Cor. 6:16), or a heavenly temple (cf. Ps. 11:4; Isa. 14:13–14; 66:1 [cited in Acts 7:49]; Mic. 1:2; Hab. 2:20; 1 Enoch 14:15–20; Heb. 8:1–2;

---

8. The translation "man of sin" (KJV) represents a well-attested but nonetheless secondary textual variant.

9. So most commentators; C. A. Wanamaker, however, takes it as designating "his role as an agent of destruction for Satan" (*Thessalonians*, 245).

10. Cf. F. F. Bruce, *1 and 2 Thessalonians*, 167.

11. These include the king of Tyre (Ezek. 28:2); the king of Babylon (Isa. 14:3–23, esp. vv. 12–14); Antiochus Epiphanes (Dan. 9:27; 11:31; 12:11); Pompey, the Roman general who in 63 B.C. entered the Holy of Holies (Pss. Sol. 2; 17:11–14; Josephus, *Antiq.* 14.69–76 [14.4.4]); and the Emperor Gaius Caligula, who in A.D. 40 attempted to have his statue set up in the temple in Jerusalem, a claim to divinity that the Jews refused to recognize (Philo, *Leg.* 203–346; Josephus, *Antiq.* 18.261–309 [18.8.2–9]).

9:24).[12] I. H. Marshall observes that Paul takes up a well-known motif that was derived from Ezekiel and Daniel and was given concrete illustration in previous desecrations of the Jerusalem temple (both actual and attempted), and that he uses this language metaphorically and typologically

> to portray the character of the culminating manifestation of evil as an anti-theistic power which usurps the place of God in the world. No specific temple is in mind, but the motif of sitting in the temple and claiming to be God is used to express the opposition of evil to God.[13]

Additional Information About the "Man of Lawlessness" (2:5–12)

ONE REASON FOR some of the uncertainty regarding 2:4 is that Paul takes for granted that the Thessalonians know what he is talking about. As 2:5 indicates, he had taught them about this matter previously. Clearly, then, he felt no need to repeat the details of what he is reminding them about. As a consequence, however, later readers are left in the dark regarding some aspects of what he writes. This is even more evident in what follows. Having discussed briefly in 2:3b–4 the "man of lawlessness" who must be "revealed" before the coming of the Day of the Lord, Paul alludes in 2:6–8 to what is "holding ... back" or "restraining" (NRSV) his appearing until "the proper time" (lit., "his time"). But he only alludes to this, since the Thessalonians already know what he is talking about. As a result, 2:6–8a are among the most difficult in the Pauline corpus.

The basic structure of what Paul says in these verses is clear enough: (1) "The secret power of lawlessness [lit., the mystery of lawlessness]

---

12. See further in general I. H. Marshall, *1 and 2 Thessalonians*, 190–92; for the Jerusalem temple, C. A. Wanamaker, *Thessalonians*, 247; for a rebuilt temple, R. L. Thomas, "2 Thessalonians," 322.

13. I. H. Marshall, *1 and 2 Thessalonians*, 191–92; cf. F. F. Bruce: "It may be best to conclude that the Jerusalem sanctuary is meant here by Paul and his companions, but meant in a metaphorical sense. Had they said, 'so that he takes his seat on the throne of God,' few would have thought it necessary to think of a literal throne; it would simply have been regarded as a graphic way of saying that he plans to usurp the authority of God. This is what is meant by the language actually used here, although the sacral associations of ναός [temple] imply that he demands not only the obedience but also the worship due to God alone" (*1 and 2 Thessalonians*, 169).

is already at work" (2:7a), but (2) it is operating in a manner that is somehow restrained or held back (2:6, 7b). (3) At some future time, however, "the lawless one [= 'the man of lawlessness' of 2:3] will be revealed" (2:8a; cf. 2:3, 6) or have his own "coming" (i.e., *parousia*, 2:9), at which point (4) he will be overthrown and destroyed by the far greater power and splendor of the Lord's own *parousia* (2:8b). In 2:7 Paul confirms that evil is currently at work in the world (as evidenced, e.g., by the persecutions the Thessalonians are experiencing) and is satanic in origin (2:9),[14] but it is nonetheless in some way limited or hindered. Here we come to a difficult question, that of the identity and/or character of the restraint that is currently keeping the "secret power of lawlessness" in check.

Paul first refers to this restraining influence in 2:6 as *to katechon* (a neuter participle meaning "that which restrains") and then in 2:7 as *ho katechōn* (a masculine participle meaning "the one who restrains"). What or who did Paul have in mind that he could refer to it in both impersonal and personal terms? Suggestions range widely, as is evident from the following list:[15]

(1) the Roman empire as personified in the emperor;
(2) the principle of law and order (personified in v. 7);
(3) the Jewish state;
(4a) Satan;
(4b) a force and person hostile to God (taking the verb in the sense of "possess, occupy," or "hold sway");
(5a) God and his power;
(5b) the Holy Spirit;
(6) the proclamation of the gospel (the neuter participle) by Christian missionaries, especially Paul himself (the masculine participle);

---

14. For both these conclusions see E. J. Richard, *Thessalonians*, 330–31, for a convincing discussion of the "mystery of lawlessness" phrase and an analysis of the verb "work" as a middle voice (rather than a passive, which would imply that God was the ultimate source of the power presently at work).

15. This list draws heavily upon I. H. Marshall, *1 and 2 Thessalonians*, 196–99, who also provides concise evaluations of the various proposals; see also C. A. Wanamaker, *Thessalonians*, 250–52; L. Morris, "Man of Lawlessness and Restraining Power," *DPL*, 592–94; R. L. Thomas, "2 Thessalonians," in *The Expositor's Bible Commentary*, ed. F. E. Gaebelein (Grand Rapids: Zondervan, 1978), 11:324–25.

(7)   an angelic figure restraining evil until the gospel has been
preached to all nations (cf. Mark 13:10).[16]

Despite a few proposals to the contrary, there is a general consensus that the restraining influence must be a force for good rather than evil, a conclusion that eliminates suggestions like (4a) or (4b). None of the other suggestions, however, have convinced more than a minority of scholars, and none is free from difficulties. In short, as Augustine observed,

> [Paul] was unwilling to make an explicit statement, because he said that they [the Thessalonians] knew [what he was referring to]. And thus we, who don't know what they knew, desire to understand what the apostle referred to, but even with hard work are not able, especially as his meaning is made still more obscure by what he adds [i.e., vv. 7–8a].[17]

In such circumstances, it is difficult to avoid Augustine's conclusion: "I frankly confess I do not know what he means."

Once the restraining influence (whatever or whoever it is) "is taken out of the way" (2:7), "then [Gk. *tote*, which has a clearly temporal force here] the lawless one will be revealed" (2:8a; cf. 2:3, 6). That is, he will have his *parousia* (2:9). No longer working in secret (cf. 2:7), this

---

16. See, for example, with regard to (1) F. F. Bruce, *1 and 2 Thessalonians*, 171–72, 187–88; C. A. Wanamaker, *Thessalonians*, 256–57; G. E. Ladd, *A Theology of the New Testament*, rev. ed. (Grand Rapids: Eerdmans, 1993), 606; to (2) Lightfoot, *Notes on Epistles*, 114–15; L. Morris, *The First and Second Epistles to the Thessalonians*, 227; to (3) B. B. Warfield (cited by I. H. Marshall, *1 and 2 Thessalonians*, 197); to (4a) an earlier proposal discussed favorably by J. E. Frame, *Thessalonians*, 261–62 (who ultimately, however, remains agnostic on the point); to (4b) C. H. Giblin, *The Threat to Faith: An Exegetical and Theological Re-examination of 2 Thessalonians 2* (Analecta Biblica 31; Rome: Pontifical Biblical Institute, 1967), slightly revised and reaffirmed in C. H. Giblin, "2 Thessalonians 2 Re-read as Pseudepigraphical: A Revised Reaffirmation of *The Threat to Faith*," in *The Thessalonian Correspondence*, ed. R. F. Collins (Leuven: Leuven Univ. Press, 1990), 459–69; E. Best, *Thessalonians*, 301 (hesitantly); to (5a) G. E. Ladd, *The Blessed Hope* (Grand Rapids: Eerdmans, 1956), 95; R. D. Aus, "God's Plan and God's Power: Isaiah 66 and the Restraining Factors of 2 Thess. 2.6–7," *JBL* 96 (1977): 537–53; others in I. H. Marshall, *1 and 2 Thessalonians*, 198; to (5b) R. L. Thomas, "2 Thessalonians," 324; to (6) Oscar Cullmann, J. Munck (cited by I. H. Marshall, *1 and 2 Thessalonians*, 198); and to (7) I. H. Marshall, *1 and 2 Thessalonians*, 199–200.

17. Augustine, *City of God*, 20.19. Cf. L. Morris, *The First and Second Epistles to the Thessalonians*, 228: "The plain fact is that Paul and his readers knew what he was talking about, and we do not. We have not the means at our disposal to recover this part of his meaning. It is best that we frankly acknowledge our ignorance."

one whose activity is in accord with "the work of Satan" will openly manifest himself by means of "all kinds of counterfeit miracles, signs and wonders, and in every sort of evil that deceives" (2:9–10a). The parallel with the coming of Jesus is obvious; this is nothing less than the "anti-Parousia" of the Antichrist, an evil parody of the true coming of the genuine Christ, the Lord Jesus.

The combination of miracles and signs and wonders as the work of God is common in both Testaments (e.g., Ex. 7:3; Isa. 8:18; Jer. 32:20–21; John 4:48; Acts 2:43; 6:8; 15:12; 2 Cor. 12:12; Heb. 2:4); for their association with false messiahs and prophets see Matt. 24:24//Mark 13:22 (cf. also Rev. 13:13–14; 16:14; 19:20). The real thing Paul attributes to the power of the Holy Spirit (Rom. 15:19), whereas these he just as clearly attributes to Satan. If "counterfeit" describes the character of the lawless one's actions, then the following phrase (2:10a, "evil that deceives") indicates their effect (cf. Mark 13:22; Rev. 13:13–14).

Though the *parousia* of the lawless one may be both grand (the terminology evokes the pageantry, pomp, and circumstance attending the arrival of the emperor) and cunningly deceptive, it will nonetheless be short-lived, for he is "the man doomed to destruction" (2:3b), "whom the Lord Jesus will overthrow with the breath of his mouth and destroy by the splendor of his coming" (2:8b).[18] This imagery recalls Isaiah 11:4 (cf. 30:27–28; 66:15–16a; Mal. 4:1), while the two verbs emphasize both the destruction of the evil one and especially the shattering of his power (cf. 1 Cor. 15:24, 26; also Rev. 19:11–21). The phrase "splendor of his coming" is composed of two nouns, *epiphaneia* ("appearing"; cf. 1 Tim. 6:14; 2 Tim. 4:1, 8; Titus 2:13) and *parousia* ("coming"), which have the same basic meaning. Together they suggest (esp. in view of *epiphaneia*) the suddenness or unexpectedness of Jesus' coming (cf. 1 Thess. 5:2–3) and its overwhelming greatness and glory (cf. Acts 2:20) in comparison to its counterfeit imitation. Moreover, in some contexts *epiphaneia* means "dawn" or "daybreak," a nuance particularly appropriate in view of its association here with the "day of the Lord."

---

18. Some of the differences between English translations of verse 8 (cf. NIV vs. NASB or NRSV margin) are due to minor textual variations that do not affect the main points of the verse. See further C. A. Wanamaker, *Thessalonians*, 257–58.

The counterfeit signs and wonders of the lawless one (2:9) exercise their deceptive effect on "those who are perishing" (2:10; cf. 1 Cor. 1:18; 2 Cor. 2:15; 4:3), a group (in contrast to those who are being saved) clearly not part of the community of faith. They are perishing specifically "because they refused to love the truth and so be saved" (2:10); that is, their fate is a consequence of their own choice. As I. H. Marshall observes, "Whatever one may say about divine predestination, the lost carry the responsibility for their own perdition."[19] When presented with an opportunity to "receive the love of the truth" (NASB; the unusual form of the phrase "love of the truth" probably reflects an intended contrast to the "deception of wickedness" in 2:10a) and thereby experience salvation, these people instead rejected it (cf. 1:8). As Paul puts it emphatically in 2:12b, when they could have "believed the truth," they instead "delighted in wickedness" (cf. John 3:19; Rom. 2:8).

Verses 11–12a discuss the consequence (*not* the cause) of this choice: "For this reason God sends them a powerful delusion so that they will believe the lie [i.e., the counterfeit *parousia* of the lawless one, cf. 2:9] and so that all will be condemned." (For what condemnation involves, see the discussion of 1:9.) The basic idea here is similar to that expressed in Romans 1:18–32 (especially vv. 23–28): God's actions are a response to, not the cause of, their actions.

An implication of 2:10 is that the saved will not be deceived by the false wonders.[20] This implication functions as an exhortation to remain faithful: Those who do "love the truth" should not be deceived by the counterfeit miracles and wonders.

To recapitulate: verses 1–2 introduce the general topic (the coming of the Lord) and Paul's particular concern (that the Thessalonians had become unsettled by rumors that the event has already happened). Verses 3–4 present Paul's emphatic response: the Day of the Lord cannot have yet occurred because the "man of lawlessness" (whose appearance precedes the Parousia of the Lord) has not yet been revealed. The balance of the passage (vv. 5–12) provides further information about this satanic figure, including his inevitable destruction, along with those whom he has deceived, by the Lord Jesus.

---

19. I. H. Marshall, *1 and 2 Thessalonians*, 203.
20. Ibid.; also C. A. Wanamaker, *Thessalonians*, 260.

A SUBJECT THAT Paul felt no need to write about in the first letter—when the Day of the Lord would occur (1 Thess. 5:1)—he does write about in the second letter. He does so because at least some members of the Thessalonians congregation had become persuaded that the Day had already arrived. In response, Paul basically says that is impossible because certain events that must first occur have not yet occurred, and thus the Day cannot have already arrived.

So far, so good. But at this point we begin to encounter difficulties, not so much because of what Paul said, but because of what he did *not* say. That is, in communicating with the Thessalonians, Paul took for granted information that both he and they already knew, and consequently he did not spell it out in his letter. No doubt his meaning was clear to his readers. But because he did not spell out certain critical details, his meaning is not clear to his later readers. The passage, therefore, presents a major obstacle: How does one bridge between the original meaning and contemporary significance when the original meaning at some points cannot be determined?

What we do know. Framing the question in this way (i.e., in terms of what we don't know) may not be the most effective way to approach the task of bridging contexts. Rather than worry initially about the information we lack, it may be more productive first to focus on the information we do have and what we do know about the meaning of the passage, which is considerable.

(1) To begin with, even though we do not know the cause or source of the Thessalonians' (mis)understanding of the Day of the Lord (nor, so it seems, did Paul; cf. 2:2), we do have a good idea of what the problem was: Apparently some of the Thessalonians thought that the "Day of the Lord" had already arrived. While unusual, this view is not without parallels today (e.g., Jehovah's Witnesses believe that Christ's coming occurred on October 1, 1914, but that it was invisible rather than public and involved a change of location in heaven)—though in Christian circles, one is unlikely to encounter this view. Instead of arguments among Christians today about *whether* the Day of the Lord has already come, one is much more likely to encounter arguments about *when* it will come.

(2) Paul's answer is relatively straightforward: The "day of the Lord" and "our being gathered to him" will not come until after certain other

things happen. These things (which could be two sequential items, but more likely are components of a single complex event) are "the rebellion" and the revealing of "the man of lawlessness" (2:3). What is interesting about this answer is that in speaking to the Thessalonians' uncertainty about *whether* the Day had come, Paul speaks directly to the question of *when* it will come. Thus even though the issue in Thessalonica is different from the dominant question today, Paul's answer speaks to both.

(3) Although Paul says nothing more about the first item (the rebellion), he does say a fair amount about the character and activity (though not the identity) of the "man of lawlessness." From the description given—a lawless individual doing the deceptive work of Satan, who not only opposes God but actually seeks to push God aside and exalt himself in God's place—it is clear that Paul has in mind the same figure referred to in 1 John 2:18 as the "antichrist" and in Revelation 13 as the "beast."[21]

Thus, to summarize the key elements in (2) and (3), Paul lays out a clear sequence of events. First comes the "rebellion" and the appearance of "the man of lawlessness," and then the return (*parousia*) of the genuine Christ and the gathering up of believers to be with him.

For some readers, a number of questions may well arise at this point. For example, doesn't what Paul says here contradict 1 Thessalonians 5:2, where he wrote that "the day of the Lord will come like a thief in the night"? Not at all; Paul wrote that the Day of the Lord will "come like a thief" only for *un*believers (cf. 5:3). Believers, he writes, "are not in darkness so that this day should surprise you like a thief" (5:4).

But if the Antichrist comes before the Day of the Lord (i.e., the return of Christ), couldn't someone simply add seven years (or three and a half years, depending on one's perspective) to the date of Antichrist's appearing and calculate the time when Christ will return? And would that not contradict Jesus' statement (in Matt. 24:36//Mark 13:32) that "no one knows about that day or hour"? Not at all, because Jesus also stated that "for the sake of the elect," the days of the great distress and tribulation following the appearance of Antichrist "will be shortened" (Matt. 24:21–22). By how much that time will be short-

---

21. Cf. F. F. Bruce, *1 and 2 Thessalonians*, 167; I. H. Marshall, *1 and 2 Thessalonians*, 189; Bob Gundry, *First the Antichrist* (Grand Rapids: Baker, 1997), 20.

ened no one knows; thus, no one will know the "day or hour" when Jesus will return.[22]

But what about the Rapture? Don't the Scriptures teach that believers will be "caught up" before the outbreak of the Tribulation? No, not really. Admittedly, the view that Jesus could come at any moment to take up believers carry them to heaven prior to the Tribulation, and will then come again in judgment at the end of the Tribulation, is widely publicized and wildly popular. But apart from the embarrassment this creates by having *two* "second comings" (or, if you will, both a second and a third coming), Paul in both 1 Thessalonians and 2 Thessalonians links the "catching up" (1 Thess. 4:17) and the "gathering" (2 Thess. 2:1)—terms that for Paul are synonyms—as closely as possible to the coming of the Lord on the Day of the Lord (1 Thess. 4:16; 5:2; 2 Thess. 2:1–3). And since Paul explicitly says that the Day of the Lord will not occur until *after* the revealing of the Antichrist, it follows that the "catching up" or "Rapture" will not occur until after the revealing of the Antichrist. In short, first the appearance of the Antichrist, and only then the coming of the genuine Christ and the "catching up" of believers to be with him.[23]

(4) An important implication can be drawn from what Paul says here about the sequence of events: Believers ought to be prepared to experience persecution and distress for the sake of the gospel during the time of the rebellion and Antichrist's appearing. Indeed, believers ought to be prepared to experience such things even before the appearance of the Antichrist, because, as Paul points out in 2:7, "the secret power of lawlessness is *already* at work." This explains (at least in part) why Paul took it for granted that believers "would be persecuted" (1 Thess. 3:4)—a truth that the Thessalonians certainly were ready and able to confirm in light of their own experience. To put the matter a bit differently, the "blessed hope" (Titus 2:13) for which we wait is not, as some contend, a "rapture" or escape from persecution. Rather it is, as Titus 2:13 makes clear, "the glorious appearing of our great God and Savior, Jesus Christ"—an appearing that will bring vindication and relief to God's people in the midst of persecution (2 Thess. 1:5–10; 2:8).[24]

---

22. See further Gundry, *First the Antichrist*, 26–28.

23. See further the entire book by Gundry, mentioned in the previous note.

24. See further George E. Ladd, *The Blessed Hope: A Biblical Study of the Second Advent and the Rapture* (Grand Rapids: Eerdmans, 1956), esp. 137–61.

(5) The mention of vindication brings us to an important point Paul makes in this passage, one that is even clearer than what he says about the sequence and timing of events: *in the end, Jesus wins* (2:8). In the midst of all the details about the man of lawlessness and his activities, we must not miss what Paul says about the lawless one's ultimate fate. Paul first hints at this in 2:3, where he describes him as a "man doomed to destruction," and he states his point clearly in 2:8: Jesus will "overthrow" and "destroy" him. Despite his strenuous efforts to deceive and mislead, despite "counterfeit miracles, signs and wonders" of all sorts, despite his efforts to proclaim himself God over all, the man of lawlessness will eventually fail. The outcome of the struggle between Christ and Antichrist is certain beyond any shadow of doubt: in the end, Jesus wins!

(6) Repeating a point he had made in chapter 1, Paul again makes it clear that people are responsible for their own fate. For some readers the language Paul uses in 2:11 ("God sends them a powerful delusion so that they will believe the lie") is troubling and seems to raise questions about God's fairness (e.g., if God sends the delusion, why are people held accountable for being deluded?). But even as in chapter 1 God's judgment was a *response to* people's refusal to obey the gospel (1:8), so here. Whatever action God takes is a response to people's refusal to love the truth (2:10); his judgment falls upon those "who have not believed the truth but have delighted in wickedness" (2:12).

Paul makes the same point in Romans 1. Those whom God "gives over" to their own sinful desires (Rom. 1:24, 26, 28) are those who have already "exchanged the truth of God for a lie, and worshiped and served created things rather than the Creator" (1:25; cf. 1:21, 23). In short, "whatever one may say about divine predestination, the lost carry the responsibility for their own perdition."[25]

A pitfall to avoid. In view of what is clear or what we do know about this passage, the things we do not know (esp. the identity of the restraining influence and of the man of lawlessness) constitute not so much an obstacle as a temptation—to speculate about what we do not

---

25. I. H. Marshall, *1 and 2 Thessalonians*, 203. Cf. Calvin's comments: The passage speaks of "God's righteousness punishment of those who, though called to salvation, have rejected the Gospel, and have preferred to give their mind to ungodliness and error. . . . None have perished but those who have deserved to, or who rather have died of their own choosing" (J. Calvin, *The Epistles of Paul the Apostle to the Romans and to the Thessalonians*, 407).

know. In one respect, this temptation to speculate, driven by our intense desire to know the identity of the man of lawlessness, is understandable; after all, curiosity is a powerful and well-known human characteristic. In other respects, however, there seem to be at least three problems associated with this temptation to speculate about the unknown.

(1) Such speculation distracts our attention from and obscures what we do know. It is all too easy to get so caught up in speculation about the identity of the Antichrist that one loses sight of the main points of the passage. One of the clearest points of the passage is the one discussed under (5) above: In the end, Jesus wins. In light of this, it is deeply ironic that some people get so caught up in speculation that they end up giving more attention to a doomed Antichrist than they do to the victorious Christ.

(2) Speculation on the identity of the Antichrist is, in my opinion, a waste of time, effort, and resources. The record of attempts to determine the identity of Antichrist is a long one, stretching back well over a millennium and a half. Likewise, the list of those confidently identified as Antichrist is a long one. It includes various Roman emperors, the leader of the Vandal invaders who sacked Rome, Mohammed, various popes, the papacy itself, Emperor Frederick II and Pope Gregory IX (each of whom viewed the other as the Antichrist), Martin Luther, King George II of England, Napoleon Bonaparte, Napoleon III, each side in the American Civil War, Kaiser Wilhelm of Germany, the League of Nations, Hitler, Mussolini, Stalin, King Faisal of Saudi Arabia, the United Nations, Khruschev, the Soviet Union, Mikhail Gorbachev (the birth mark on his forehead allegedly being the mark of the beast), King Juan Carlos of Spain, Pope John Paul II, Anwar Sadat, the Ayatollah Khomeini, Yasser Arafat, Saddam Hussein, the New Age Movement, theologian Matthew Fox, Henry Kissenger, and former presidents Jimmy Carter and Ronald Wilson Reagan (six letters in each name = 666 [cf. Rev. 13:18], and Reagan recovered from a serious wound [13:3]).[26]

---

26. One thing that stands out when studying the list of those who have been identified as Antichrist is how often the political, theological, or social biases or perspective of the person proposing the identification have shaped (if not determined) whom someone identified as the Satanic deceiver. In this respect, attempts to identify the Antichrist often reveal more about the one making the identification than anything else. See Robert C. Fuller, *Naming The Antichrist: The History of an American Obsession* (New York and Oxford: Oxford Univ. Press, 1995). This book is a fascinating study of efforts to discern the identity of the Antichrist from colonial days to the present that highlights the persistent influence of political, social, and

This sad history of the unsuccessful attempts to identify the Antichrist suggests that any attempts we might make will be no more successful. Surely we deceive ourselves if we think that we will be able to identify this master deceiver. Yet efforts persist, and in some quarters are even encouraged and welcomed. Most of the Christian bookstores I visit have far more shelf space devoted to the latest books and novels about the Antichrist and related topics than they do to discipleship, for example, or Christology or Bible study helps—a reflection, apparently, of reader interest and demand.

In view of the dismal record of failed attempts at identification, this persistent eagerness to read the latest speculation about the Antichrist reminds one a great deal of Paul's prediction to Timothy in 2 Timothy 4:3–4 (using NIV[ILE]):

> For the time will come when people will not put up with sound doctrine. Instead, to suit their own desires, they will gather around them a great number of teachers to say what their itching ears want to hear. They will turn their ears away from the truth and turn aside to myths.

Surely there are better ways to invest our time, energy, and money (for there can be no doubt that there is big money to be made by speculating about Antichrist) than in a fruitless attempt to predict or to read about the identity of the Antichrist. "Church history is littered with incautious, self-confident but mistaken attempts to find in Paul's text a reference to some contemporary person and event. Let this be a warning to us."[27]

(3) Jacob W. Elias suggests a third problem with speculation about what we do not know, this one involving speculation about when Christ will return. Despite the explicit statement of Jesus that no one knows the day or the hour, people have persisted in efforts to determine the time of Christ's coming (David Koresh of the Branch Davidians was only one of the more recent in a long line of date-setters).

---

theological perspectives on the way people discerned the Antichrist's presence in current events. See also the broader studies of Paul Boyer, *When Time Shall Be No More: Prophecy Belief in Modern American Culture* (Cambridge, Mass, and London: Belknap, 1992), and Bernard McGinn, *Antichrist: Two Thousand Years of the Human Fascination with Evil* (San Francisco: HarperSanFrancisco, 1994).

27. J. R. W. Stott, *The Gospel and the End of Time*, 161.

In persisting in this effort, however, Elias suggests that they run the risk of infringing on God's authority. "Date-setting essentially constitutes a usurping of God's role. God knows the future, we don't. . . . Ironically, Paul and his co-workers depict the antagonist as usurping God's authority."[28]

A broader perspective. I. H. Marshall makes an important observation with regard to 2:12.

> The effect of v. 12 is to generalise to some extent what Paul has been saying. We do not have to wait until the point when we can, as it were, identify the arrival of the final climax of evil in order to see the outworking of the divine process of judgment. It is true at all times that sin consists in delighting in what is wrong. . . . It follows that the primary significance of the passage is not that we should be trying to calculate whether or not the End is near but that we should be concerned about the moral and spiritual issues which are involved.[29]

In other words, Paul's final generalizing comment returns the focus from the future to the present: Our fate *then* will be determined by how we respond to the truth of the gospel *now*. Thus Paul reinforces a point already made in 1 Thessalonians 4:13–18 and 5:1–11: Knowledge of the future ought to shape and influence how we live in the present.

AS IN THE case of chapter 1, what one covers in applying this section of the text depends to some extent on whether 2 Thessalonians is being studied independently of or in sequence with 1 Thessalonians. For example, if 2 Thessalonians is being studied independently, it will probably be necessary to cover in some detail what Paul takes for granted in 2:1–3 regarding the return (*parousia*) of Jesus and the gathering of believers to him (for details see the discussions of 1 Thess. 4:13–18; 5:1–11).

If, however, 2 Thessalonians is being treated after 1 Thessalonians, then one might move directly to more distinctive aspects of this passage,

---

28. J. W. Elias, *1 & 2 Thessalonians*, 295. On date-setting, see further the first point under Contemporary Significance for 1 Thess. 5:1–11.

29. I. H. Marshall, *1 and 2 Thessalonians*, 205.

two of which I would like to highlight. It offers an opportunity (1) to emphasize the importance of focusing on Jesus, and (2) to reflect on the deceptive character of evil. In addition, (3) the passage provides an opportunity to revisit the question of preparation versus speculation and (4) offers an important word of encouragement in the midst of turmoil: In the end, Jesus wins. (For the importance of holding firm to the apostolic testimony and teaching, a point that arises out of 2:5, see comments on 2:15.)

Keep the focus on Jesus! In 1933, as the storm clouds of war gathered and speculation about Antichrist rose accordingly, Arno Gaebelein, the noted evangelical leader and editor of *Our Hope* magazine, wrote:

> The Editor has no use for day-and-year-setters, nor has he any use for figuring out the duration of the times of the Gentiles, nor has he any sympathy with men who prophesy that Mussolini, Hitler, Feisal or any other person is the Antichrist. It is a morbid condition which seems to suit certain minds. We wonder whom they will name next. At any rate why should a Christian have any interest at all in that coming man of sin? We have nothing to do with that lawless one. Our interest must be in Christ and not in Antichrist.[30]

Today, decades later, at a time when interest in and speculation about Antichrist is, if anything, even more intense—a time when well-known Christian leaders are writing novels whose main character is Antichrist—Gaebelein's words are no less timely, especially his final sentence: "*Our interest must be in Christ and not in Antichrist.*"

Second Thessalonians 2 is the only passage in all his letters where Paul discusses the "man of lawlessness," and he does so here only because the extraordinary circumstances in Thessalonica required him to do so. Furthermore, even as he discusses this figure, he leaves no doubt about his ultimate fate: He will be defeated by the Lord Jesus himself (2:8). Moreover, his discussion is bounded on either side by prayer or thanksgiving reports (1:11–12; 2:13–14) that focus on Jesus. The pattern Paul models here—he keeps his primary focus on Jesus and speaks of Antichrist no more than he has to—is a pattern we would do

---

30. Arno C. Gaebelein, "King Feisal Is Dead," *Our Hope* 40 (November 1933): 305, as quoted by David A. Rausch, *Fundamentalist Evangelicals and Anti-Semitism* (Valley Forge, Pa.: Trinity Press International, 1993), 134.

well to follow. When novels about Antichrist outsell books about Jesus, it seems to me that there is something seriously out of balance. Christ our Savior, not Antichrist his antagonist, deserves our attention.

The manner in which Paul emphasizes in 2:10–12 the importance of truth reinforces the importance of focusing on Jesus. Paul describes those perishing as those who refused to love or to believe "the truth." In this context, "the truth" is virtually a synonym for the gospel. And who is its focus? Jesus, of course. Moreover, Jesus himself is the truth (John 14:6; cf. Eph. 4:21). In other words, to love or believe in the truth is to love or believe in Jesus. Since our response to the truth—that is, to Jesus—determines, as Paul here makes clear, our ultimate destiny, we have all the more reason to focus on Jesus, the true Christ, and not on his antagonist, the *Antichrist*.

The familiar little song by Helen H. Lemmel, "Turn Your Eyes upon Jesus," expresses clearly what we need to do:

Turn your eyes upon Jesus,
Look full in His wonderful face,
And the things of earth will grow strangely dim
In the light of His glory and grace.

If we turn our eyes upon Jesus, "the things of earth"—including speculation about the identity of the Antichrist—"will grow strangely dim" in comparison to the light of Jesus' glory and grace, the very things Paul emphasizes in 1:12 and 2:14. As Gaebelein emphasized, our focus needs to be on Jesus.

The deceptiveness of evil. From Paul's description of the character and activities of the "man of lawlessness," it is clear that he is describing nothing less than a counterfeit christ. This counterfeit christ—"Antichrist," to use the more common terminology—seeks, by means of his own *parousia* ("coming"), counterfeit miracles, signs, and wonders (2:9), and declarations that he is divine (2:4), to deceive people into believing that he is the genuine Christ. (He is not, of course; his activities are "in accordance with the work of Satan" [2:9], not God.)

The effectiveness of a counterfeit depends, of course, on how closely it approximates that which it is imitating. A counterfeit $100 bill produced on a black and white copier will likely not fool anyone. But it is possible (or at least was, until the introduction of new safeguards in the late 1990s), using the right tools and equipment, to produce counterfeit $100 bills good enough to fool even experts on occasion. A good counterfeit so closely imitates the real thing that it is able to deceive us into thinking it is the real thing. This is how the "man of lawlessness" will work his destruction: He will so closely counterfeit the coming, power, and character of the Lord Jesus Christ that people will be duped into thinking he is the real thing. As Stott observes, "the coming of Antichrist will be such a clever parody of the coming of Christ that many will be taken in by the satanic deception."[31]

Paul's description of this satanic antagonist as a "counterfeit christ" (rather than as Antichrist) invites us to reflect on an important characteristic of evil: It is inherently and fundamentally deceptive. The effectiveness of evil has much to do with how it presents itself: not so much as the polar opposite of something good, but as a clever counterfeit of it. I suspect that most of us would like to think that if we were openly confronted by Satan and invited to become partners in evil, we would unquestionably reject the offer and inform him in no uncertain terms where he should go. But in view of the evil perpetrated by Christians in the world today, it is clear that we are not rejecting the devil's invitations to become partners in evil. Why not? Perhaps because they most often come not as clear invitations to do evil, but as camouflaged invitations to do something that appears to be good, but really isn't.[32] If "Satan himself masquerades as an angel of light" (2 Cor. 11:14), we should not be surprised if invitations to do evil are similarly masked.

How does evil mask itself? One way is by counterfeiting the good, the real, the genuine. As Cornelius Plantinga Jr. perceptively observes, when at the movies (or, frighteningly, sometimes in real life) we

> cheer for fleeing bank robbers, we do not focus on any of the damage, disturbance, or offense. We notice only those features that sin has pirated from goodness—energy, imagination, persistence, and creativity. Everything sin touches begins to die, but we do not focus on that. We see only the vitality of the parasite, glowing with stolen life.[33]

---

31. J. R. W. Stott, *The Gospel and the End of Time,* 172.

32. See C. S. Lewis, *The Screwtape Letters and Screwtape Proposes a Toast* (New York: Time, Inc., 1961).

33. Cornelius Plantinga, Jr., *Not the Way It's Supposed to Be: A Breviary of Sin* (Grand Rapids: Eerdmans, 1995), 95.

Instead of going for the real thing, we are deceived by the counterfeit, the parasite that imitates it.

The classical "seven deadly sins" offer another example of how evil masks itself. One well-known analysis views each one as an instance of "misdirected love." For example, the sins of lust, gluttony, and greed (covetousness) are seen as instances of excessive love; sloth (related to despair) is associated with defective love; and anger, envy, and pride result from perverted love (love for self rather than for others). The deceptive character of evil is clear: It can hide itself behind even one of the classical Christian virtues, love.

Other examples of evil hiding deceptively behind something that in and of itself is good, or at least morally neutral, might include the following:

- using legitimate concerns or arguments about "quality of life" issues to hide the realities of euthanasia;
- using the language of personal privacy and choice to obscure the fact that abortion involves the destruction of life;
- the way "political figures and nation states arrogate to themselves Christian symbols to legitimate their unjust and oppressive practices such as apartheid, militarism, and imperialism"— to which one could well add, in view of current events, racism and genocide.[34]
- the way business organizations use the abstract language of cost-benefit ratios and analysis to obscure the fact that what is really being discussed is a tradeoff between human lives and safety on the one hand and greater profits on the other. Confronted with specific human beings, we would almost certainly not deliberately choose to harm them. Yet repeatedly people have knowingly and consciously made decisions for the sake of economic gain that have resulted in injury or death for other people— decisions, for example, to sell cars known to have dangerous safety defects, to sell overseas pesticides banned at home because of their toxicity to humans, or to conceal evidence of a new drug's harmful or fatal side-effects in order to win product approval and get it to the market. Evil, by turning people into abstractions, generalizations, and ratios, routinely deceives us

---

34. C. A. Wanamaker, *Thessalonians*, 248–49.

into choosing courses of action that result in harm and even death for other human beings.[35]

One final consequence of the deceptive character of evil should be noted—the risk we run of overlooking what Hannah Arendt termed the "banality of evil." By this she means the way in which so much evil is the consequence of ordinary but unthinking everyday human behavior. A central example involves the Holocaust. The world was rightly shocked by Nazi extermination of six million Jews, but what is nearly as shocking is how many ordinary citizens of Germany, France, and other countries unthinkingly contributed in one way or another to the programs that led to those deaths. The most common excuse? "I was just following orders." To be sure, following orders is generally a good thing, but not when it is perverted by evil and used to bring about the deaths of other human beings.

By focusing on one of the grand masters of counterfeit and deception, the evil "man of lawlessness," who will seek to deceive people by presenting himself as nothing less than an imitation Christ, Paul reminds us of the fundamentally counterfeit and deceptive character of all sin and evil. Though it attempts to present itself as the truth, it is not; it is a cunningly deceptive parasite, whose seeming delightfulness (2:12) leads not to life but to death. Truth and life are found only in the genuine Christ, the Lord Jesus. As we reflect, therefore, on the deceptiveness of evil, let us keep our focus on Jesus.

Preparation versus speculation. This topic was discussed earlier in connection with 1 Thessalonians 5:1–11; it arises here in view of point (4) above in the Bridging Contexts section. There I suggested that the "blessed hope" (Titus 2:13) for which we wait is not escape from persecution, but rather vindication and relief in the midst of persecution. This in turn suggests that as we look forward to the return of Jesus, we should not be speculating about the identity of the lawless one but instead should be preparing ourselves for the possibility that we might be called to endure affliction and suffering for the sake of the gospel.

---

35. C. S. Lewis observed that "the greatest evil is not now done in those sordid 'dens of crime' that Dickens loved to paint. It is not done even in concentration camps and labour camps. In those we see its final result. But it is conceived and ordered (moved, seconded, carried, and minuted) in clean, carpeted, warmed, and well-lighted offices, by quiet men with white collars and cut fingernails and smooth-shaven cheeks who do not need to raise their voice" (C. S. Lewis, *The Screwtape Letters and Screwtape Proposes a Toast,* xxv).

Applying this point will require considerable pastoral sensitivity, for it touches on a much-disputed and highly controversial question about the future, specifically, the relationship of believers to the rebellion and turmoil unleashed by the "man of lawlessness." According to one widely held belief, believers will be "caught up" or "raptured" to be with Jesus prior to the outbreak of the rebellion led by the man of lawlessness, and they will thus avoid the persecution and suffering associated with this event. On this "pretribulation rapture" view, while those who remain on earth experience the horrors associated with this time of tribulation, believers will be safely ensconced in heaven with their Lord, safe above the terrible turmoil and suffering.

One reason for the popularity of this view is the vision of the future it offers: escape from suffering and affliction. Indeed, it is not unusual to encounter people who acknowledge that they hold this view precisely because it offers a vision of safety and comfort. But we should hold to our beliefs not because we like them (or their implications), but because we are convinced they are biblical. If the interpretation of Paul's teaching offered above is correct, believers will not be "gathered" to Jesus (2:1) until *after* the appearance of the man of lawlessness and the rebellion he leads. This means that believers, rather than anticipating escape from tribulation, should instead be preparing to endure it with perseverance and faith (see 1:4).

Because this point touches on a controversial question about the future, application of it requires an attitude of humility rather than dogmatism. At the same time, the circumstance that the view is controversial is no excuse to shy away from dealing with its implications. If Paul is warning believers to be prepared for persecution, as I believe he is, then we as interpreters have an obligation to point this out, regardless of the popularity (or lack thereof) of such a view.

A reason for hope in the face of oppression. In the discussion of 1 Thessalonians 2:17–3:8, I discussed how and where Christians around the world are facing persecution and affliction—and in some cases, martyrdom—for the sake of Jesus and the gospel. As C. A. Wanamaker puts it, the Thessalonians' "experience of powerlessness and alienation in the face of pervasive evil within the socio-economic and political structures" of their day "is not unknown to many Christians today."[36] To all believers who find themselves in analogous situations,

---

36. C. A. Wanamaker, *Thessalonians*, 264.

who find themselves so oppressed by systemic evil that there seems to be no way out, Paul offers in 2 Thessalonians 2:8 an important word of hope and encouragement: *In the end, Jesus wins* the battle against the forces of evil. No matter how dark the situation, in the long run Jesus will be triumphant.

This does not guarantee that we will live to see it. We may be like those Old Testament heroes described in Hebrews 11, who "were still living by faith when they died. They did not receive the things promised; they only saw them and welcomed them from a distance" (Heb. 11:13; cf. 11:39). But regardless of whether we live to see the victory or only "welcome it from a distance," Paul assures us that it will come, and that those who remain faithful will share in their Lord's triumph. Thus Paul encourages us to stand fast and faithful in the face of oppression, because in the end, Jesus wins.

2 Thessalonians 2:13–3:5

🍃

B UT WE OUGHT always to thank God for you, brothers loved by the Lord, because from the beginning God chose you to be saved through the sanctifying work of the Spirit and through belief in the truth. ¹⁴He called you to this through our gospel, that you might share in the glory of our Lord Jesus Christ. ¹⁵So then, brothers, stand firm and hold to the teachings we passed on to you, whether by word of mouth or by letter.

¹⁶May our Lord Jesus Christ himself and God our Father, who loved us and by his grace gave us eternal encouragement and good hope, ¹⁷encourage your hearts and strengthen you in every good deed and word.

³:¹Finally, brothers, pray for us that the message of the Lord may spread rapidly and be honored, just as it was with you. ²And pray that we may be delivered from wicked and evil men, for not everyone has faith. ³But the Lord is faithful, and he will strengthen and protect you from the evil one. ⁴We have confidence in the Lord that you are doing and will continue to do the things we command. ⁵May the Lord direct your hearts into God's love and Christ's perseverance.

Original Meaning

THIS IS AN important summary and transitional segment of the letter in three respects. (1) With respect to the immediate context it sharply contrasts (note the opening "but") the fate of the followers of the one true God (2:13–14) with that of the followers of the "man of lawlessness" (2:10–12). (2) With respect to the larger context it draws to a close (see 2:15–17; cf. 3:2–3, 5) the discussion of "the coming of our Lord Jesus Christ and our being gathered to him," initiated in 2:1. (3) It sets up (see 2:15; 3:4) Paul's discussion in 3:6–15 of the problem of disorderly believers.

The segment derives its coherence from its content rather than its form or structure.[1] Bounded on either side by two well-defined sections (2:1–12 and 3:6–15), it displays a wide (some would say disjointed) variety of forms: thanksgiving (2:13–14), exhortation and encouragement (2:15), prayer (2:16–17; 3:5), prayer request (3:1–2), and expressions of confidence (3:3–4). Nonetheless, two themes running through the various subunits, (re)assurance (2:13–14, 16; 3:1b, 3–4, 5) and perseverance (2:15, 16–17; 3:5), tie the segment together and reveal Paul's goals in this part of the letter. Those goals are to stabilize and to encourage the community in the face of continuing both external affliction (cf. 1:4–6) and internal problems (see 2:2–3; 3:6–15).

Thanksgiving to God (2:13–14)

THE "BUT" WITH which 2:13 opens[2] contrasts the fate of those "who are perishing" (since they "delighted in wickedness," 2:10b–12) with that of the Thessalonian believers, described as brothers and sisters[3] "loved by the Lord" (i.e., Jesus; cf. 1 Thess. 1:4) and chosen by God for salvation. Paul's major goal is to reassure the Thessalonians regarding their fate (salvation), in contrast to that of those opposing and persecuting them. Regardless of the efforts of the coming "lawless one" to deceive them, their salvation is in God's hand, who chose them "as the first fruits" (NRSV) of those to be saved in Thessalonica.[4] The word translated "chose" may echo Deuteronomy 26:18 (God's choice of Israel; for the idea, see comments on 1 Thess. 1:4).

The last two phrases of 2:13 indicate the means by which salvation has become effective. These means are the "sanctifying work of the

---

1. The segment has been resistant to both epistolary and rhetorical analysis. R. Jewett lists three epistolary and three rhetorical analyses of 2 Thessalonians, all of which differ noticeably, especially in their treatment of this section of the letter. Both Krodel (from an epistolary perspective) and Jewett (from a rhetorical perspective) agree, however, in treating 2:13–3:5 as a separate section (*Thessalonian Correspondence*, 224–25).

2. For the opening phrase of 2:13 (especially the "ought"), see comments on 1:3a; for the way 2:13 resumes the opening thanksgiving of 1:3, cf. 1 Thess. 2:13 (which resumes the introductory thanksgiving of 1 Thess. 1:2).

3. For the significance of *adelphoi*, "brothers," in 2:13 (also 2:15; 3:1), which includes the entire community and not just the male members, see comments on 1 Thess. 1:4.

4. Instead of "as the first fruits" (*aparchen*; NRSV, NAB), some significant manuscripts read "from the beginning" (*ap' arches*; NIV, RSV, NASB). The first alternative is preferable; it fits the context well, while the second phrase does not reflect Pauline usage (similarly G. D. Fee, *God's Empowering Presence*, 77).

Spirit" (the Holy Spirit, not the human spirit; cf. 1 Thess. 4:7–8) and "belief in the truth," that is, the gospel (cf. 1 Thess. 1:5; 2 Thess. 1:8), to which God has "called" them (1 Thess. 4:7; cf. 2:12, 5:24; 2 Thess. 1:11) and which the Thessalonians had received as God's own word (1 Thess. 2:13). Note again the sharp contrast with the perishing, who "refused to love the truth" (2 Thess. 2:10b, 12).

For "glory" (*doxa*, 2:14) as the future goal of God's people, see the discussion of this word at 1 Thessalonians 2:12 (cf. also Rom. 8:18, where future glory is explicitly contrasted with present suffering, a contrast implicit here in 2 Thess. 2). For the combination of "choice," "call," and "glory," see Rom. 8:29–30. Almost the same phrase as is used here (lit., "[God] ... called you ... for obtaining [*eis peripoiesin*] glory of our Lord Jesus Christ") occurs in 1 Thessalonians 5:9 ("God ... appointed us ... for obtaining [*eis peripoiesin*] salvation through our Lord Jesus Christ"), but with "salvation" in place of "glory." This close association between "glory" and "salvation" is not surprising, given that glory has in view the radiance or splendor of God's presence, and that at 1 Thessalonians 4:17 (and implicitly in 2 Thess. 1:9) Paul defines salvation as being with the Lord always.

Exhortation to "Stand Firm" (2:15)

AS USUAL, PAUL'S thanksgiving statements are multifunctional. The list of reasons why God ought to be thanked (2:13–14) quickly becomes the basis for further exhortation (2:15). "So, then" (as in 1 Thess. 5:6; cf. Rom. 12:1), he says, "stand firm" (cf. 1 Thess. 3:8), a command that stands as the positive counterpart of 2 Thessalonians 2:2 (do not "become easily unsettled or alarmed"). Moreover, he wants the Thessalonians to "hold fast to the traditions that you were taught by us" (NRSV; NIV has reversed the sentence to "the teachings we passed on to you"). Even as the first command correlated with the first part of 2:2, so this second command correlates with the second part of the same verse ("some prophecy, report or letter supposed to have come from us"). Pay attention, Paul says, to what he and his companions actually taught them, not what someone is claiming or alleging that they taught.

Even though in 2:2 Paul admits not knowing whether the problem arose via a prophetic word, an oral report or teaching, or a letter, his mention here of only the last two items ("by word of mouth or by

letter," 2:15) strongly suggests that in his view the source of the problem was a (misunderstood? misrepresented?) prophetic word, which
perhaps claimed to offer an addition to, revision of, or perhaps even
a misinterpretation of something Paul and his companions had said or
written. Regardless, the apostle's main point, toward which he has
been pointing ever since 2:2, is clear: Stick with the traditions you
learned from us and nothing else. Nothing less is at stake, he implies,
than their very salvation.[5]

The idea of authoritative tradition (*paradosis*) is thoroughly Pauline
(for the term, in addition to 2:15 and 3:6, see 1 Cor. 11:2). J. D. G.
Dunn has isolated three main types of tradition in the Pauline letters: (1) gospel tradition, concerning the central gospel message (e.g.,
1 Cor. 15:1–3); (2) church tradition, information that shapes the
practice of congregations (e.g., 1 Cor. 11:23–25); and (3) ethical tradition, dealing with proper Christian behavior (e.g., 1 Cor. 7:10;
1 Thess. 4:1–2).[6] Here in the context of chapter 2 the traditions Paul
has in mind are an example of the first type, traditions pertaining to
the basic message of the gospel. In 3:6–7 he will mention traditions
of the third type.

An Intercessory Prayer (2:16–17)

VERSES 16–17 COMPRISE an intercessory prayer much like that of
1 Thessalonians 3:11–13 in terms of its form and function. The prayer
illuminates Paul's objective in the preceding verses: to encourage and
strengthen the Thessalonians. In terms of content, verse 16 connects
with verse 13, while verse 17 echoes verse 15a.

The mention in 2:16 of Jesus before God is unusual (cf. 2 Cor.
13:14; Gal. 1:1); stylistically, it creates a chiasm with verses 13 (God)
and 14 (Jesus) and may reflect the Christological orientation of the preceding discussion. The full Christological title found here occurs frequently in 1 and 2 Thessalonians (cf. 1 Thess. 1:1, 3; 5:9, 23, 28;
2 Thess. 1:1, 2, 12; 2:1, 14; 3:6, 12, 18). Paul's use of a series of singular verbs after the mention of Jesus and God together indicates that he
probably viewed both as the source of grace and love (cf. the similar

---

5. C. A. Wanamaker, *Thessalonians*, 268.

6. J. D. G. Dunn, *Unity and Diversity in the New Testament* (Philadelphia: Westminster,
1977), 66–69; cf. C. A. Wanamaker, *Thessalonians*, 268.

close association of the two in 1 Thess. 3:11 and 2 Thess. 1:12).[7] For "grace," see comments on 1 Thessalonians 1:1 and 2 Thessalonians 1:12. For the idea of being loved, see 1 Thessalonians 1:4 and 2 Thessalonians 2:13; 3:5 (also Rom. 5:8). The second verb ("gave") expresses a consequence of the first (the giving is a result of the love).[8] The whole phrase ("who loved us and ... gave us") "reemphasizes that God's gifts are dependent on his goodness and not the worthiness of the recipient and thus gives further ground for assurance."[9]

Paul has two gifts in view in 2:16. The first is "eternal encouragement," that is, encouragement that will outlast the afflictions of this age and the judgment to come, encouragement that sustains us until we experience fully eternal life (cf. Rom. 15:15; 2 Cor. 1:3). The second is "good hope," a contemporary secular idiom (stressing "the relationship of good, responsible behavior to its optimistic effect on one's perception of the future"[10]) that Paul has Christianized by basing hope not on an individual's own behavior but on God's gracious love, thereby providing a solid basis for genuine optimism about the future.

For "encourage" and "strengthen" (2:17) see comments on these two verbs (in reverse order) at 1 Thessalonians 3:2. "Deed and word" (for this order, cf. Luke 24:19; in Rom. 15:18 and Col. 3:17 the order is reversed) is a comprehensive phrase encompassing all of human behavior, as in Colossians 3:17 ("*whatever* you do, whether in word or deed"). "Paul's desire is that inward encouragement in the face of external opposition be accompanied by godly behavior in whatever Christians say and do."[11]

Finally, it is worth noting that here (as in 1 Thess. 4:13–18; 5:1–11) talk about the future ends up serving the present. Paul's discussion of the future coming of the "man of lawlessness" ends with a prayer for encouragement in the present, based on what God has done ("loved ... gave") in the past.

---

7. Cf. Murray J. Harris, *Jesus as God: The New Testament Use of Theos in Reference to Jesus* (Grand Rapids: Baker, 1992), 168, 316; similarly I. H. Marshall, *1 and 2 Thessalonians*, 211; F. F. Bruce, *1 and 2 Thessalonians*, 196. C. A. Wanamaker, however, takes the singular verbs as referring only to God (*Thessalonians*, 270–71).

8. The phrase "by his grace" (lit., "in grace") comes at the end of verse 16 (cf. NASB); consequently, there is some uncertainty whether it modifies both "loved" and "gave" (so E. Best, *Thessalonians*, 320; C. A. Wanamaker, *Thessalonians*, 271) or only "gave" (so NIV, NRSV).

9. I. H. Marshall, *1 and 2 Thessalonians*, 211–12.

10. E. J. Richard, *Thessalonians*, 360.

11. C. A. Wanamaker, *Thessalonians*, 272.

A Request for Prayer (3:1–2)

HAVING CONCLUDED HIS prayer for the Thessalonians, Paul proceeds in 3:1–2 to ask for their prayers on his behalf (cf. 1 Thess. 5:25). The first of two closely linked requests has to do with the "message of the Lord." As in 1 Thessalonians 1:8, where the identical phrase occurs, it is essentially synonymous with the "gospel of Christ" (1 Thess. 3:2; 2 Thess. 1:8). The word translated "spread rapidly" (*trecho;* lit., "run") echoes a scriptural image (Ps. 147:15, "his word runs swiftly") that would also have been meaningful to a Hellenistic audience (cf. the athletic imagery of running a race, used by Paul in 1 Cor. 9:24). The basic idea is one of advance or progress. The gospel is "honored" (better "glorified," as NRSV, NASB; cf. Acts 13:48) when it is not merely proclaimed, but accepted or acknowledged for what "it actually is, the word of God" (1 Thess. 2:13), as the Thessalonians themselves had done (1:6).

Whereas Paul's first request is on behalf of the message (3:1), the second one is for the messengers who proclaim it (3:2): that Paul and his companions "may be delivered from wicked and evil people" (NIV[ILE]). The verb "deliver" is the same as in Matthew 6:13, the Lord's Prayer (cf. Rom. 15:31; 1 Thess. 1:10). The two adjectives (*atopos*, "wicked"; cf. Acts 25:5; 28:6; *poneros*, "evil"; cf. 1 Thess. 5:22) are roughly synonymous and convey the idea of morally perverse people who maliciously obstruct the gospel, like the people in Thessalonica who had instigated a riot in order to hinder the preaching of the gospel (Acts 17:5). Paul is speaking in general terms; it seems unlikely that he has any specific group in mind.[12]

The last phrase of 3:2—"for not everyone has faith" (i.e., "not everyone believes")—explains the hostility encountered by the missionaries, which in turn obstructs the progress of the gospel message.[13] It also sets up 3:3 by offering a point of contrast (the maliciousness of the opponents versus the protection and care of the Lord).

---

12. So F. F. Bruce, *1 and 2 Thessalonians*, 198; C. A. Wanamaker, *Thessalonians*, 275; E. J. Richard, *Thessalonians*, 374–75; differently I. H. Marshall, *1 and 2 Thessalonians*, 214 (who sees here a reference to Jewish opponents of Paul in Corinth).

13. The "for" with which the last phrase of 3:2 begins may connect the phrase to the immediately preceding request for deliverance (clearly the impression left by the NIV). But in view of the overall structure of 3:1–2 (a single sentence in which Paul makes two closely related requests: "pray for us that . . . and . . . that . . . for"), it seems more likely that the "for" links the last phrase to the request for prayer as a whole (cf. NRSV).

Expressions of Confidence (3:3–4)

IN 3:3 PAUL quickly returns to his primary concern in this section: the encouragement of the community. A double wordplay with 3:2 facilitates Paul's transition: People who are *poneros* ("evil") lack *pistis* ("faith"), but (3:3) the Lord is *pistos* ("faithful"; cf. 1 Thess. 5:24) and will continue to "strengthen" (see 2 Thess. 2:17; also 1 Thess. 3:13) and "protect" (cf. Ps. 121:7; John 17:12; Jude 24) his followers from *tou ponerou* (a phrase that can be translated as "evil" or "the evil one"). As in Matthew 6:13 (the Lord's Prayer), where the same problem is found, this phrase should probably be rendered "the evil one" (NIV, NRSV, NASB).[14] It thus not only reminds the Thessalonians of what Paul had already said in 2 Thessalonians 2:8 about the ultimate triumph of Jesus, but also reinforces the link between their opponents and opposition to God (cf. 1:4–10).

Together 3:3–4 closely parallels the pattern of 2:13–15: reassurance of God's love and concern for the community (2:13–14; 3:3) is followed by an exhortation to obedience and perseverance (2:15; 3:4). "Put somewhat differently, v. 3 assures the readers that the Lord is working in their presence while v. 4 indirectly requires obedience in response to what the Lord is doing."[15] Moreover, by praising the Thessalonians for what they have been doing (cf. 1 Thess. 4:1, 10; 5:11; 2 Thess. 1:3) and expressing his "confidence in the Lord" (cf. Gal. 5:10) that they "will *continue* to do the things we command," Paul is preparing the way for the instructions he is about to give in 3:6–15 (note esp. the triple repetition of "command" in 3:6, 10, 12).[16]

Further Prayer (3:5)

FINALLY, HAVING SLIPPED from prayer (2:16–17; cf. 3:1–2) back into further exhortation (3:3–4), Paul in 3:5 returns to prayer to close this

---

14. So E. Best, *Thessalonians*, 327–28; F. F. Bruce, *1 and 2 Thessalonians*, 200; E. J. Richard, *Thessalonians*, 370–71; the alternative view is preferred by C. A. Wanamaker, *Thessalonians*, 277.

15. C. A. Wanamaker, *Thessalonians*, 277.

16. Similarly E. J. Richard, *Thessalonians*, 371; C. A. Wanamaker, *Thessalonians*, 277–78. I. H. Marshall, however, taking 3:4 as a reference back to 3:1, understands verse 4 as an expression of confidence that they will not be hindered from praying on Paul's behalf (*1 and 2 Thessalonians*, 217). But to label as a "command" (3:4) what was essentially only a request in 3:1 is awkward; moreover, it is difficult to see how the Thessalonians could already be doing what he had only just requested them to do.

section of the letter. He prays that the Lord might "direct" (the same verb as "clear our way" in 1 Thess. 3:11, though here in the sense of Luke 1:79; cf. 1 Chron. 29:18; Prov. 21:2) the Thessalonians' attention to two important points. The first, "God's love," echoes once more a key theme running throughout 2:13–3:5, namely, assurance grounded in God. The second, "Christ's perseverance," sets before them Christ as the example of what Paul has repeatedly been encouraging them to do, that is, to persevere (cf. 2:15, 16–17; cf. 1:4 above; also 1 Thess. 1:10; 3:13).

Strictly speaking, the phrase "love of God" can indicate either "their love for God" (taking "of God" as an objective genitive) or "God's love for them" ("of God" as a subjective genitive). Both the immediate context (2:13, 16) and Pauline usage (e.g., Rom. 5:8, 5) make it virtually certain that it is the latter, as the NIV correctly indicates. Similarly, the second phrase could be translated with the KJV as "the patient waiting for Christ" (objective genitive; cf. 1 Thess. 1:3; 2 Thess. 1:4), but in view of the close parallelism between the second phrase and the first, "Christ's [own] perseverance" (subjective genitive; cf. NIV, NRSV) seems more likely.[17]

ONE OF THE first challenges of interpreting 2 Thessalonians 2–3 is deciding how to divide the chapters. While I have chosen to separate them into three segments (2:1–12; 2:13–3:5; 3:6–18), some interpreters (e.g., Stott) follow the chapter break and work with two segments (2:1–17; 3:1–18). The advantage in doing so is that it makes it easier to emphasize the way Paul's description of the saved in 2:13–15 stands in contrast to the fate of those perishing in 2:10–12,[18] and the way 3:1–5 sets up 3:6–15. On the other hand, separating 2:13–18 from 3:1–5 obscures the common

---

17. Similarly F. F. Bruce, *1 and 2 Thessalonians*, 202; C. A. Wanamaker, *Thessalonians*, 278–79; E. J. Richard, *Thessalonians*, 372, 376.

18. On the one hand, the people deceived by the "man of lawlessness" in accordance with the working of Satan (and thus who will be judged together with him) are those who have rejected the truth (2:10) and believed the lie (2:11), to the extent that they now delight in wickedness (2:12). On the other hand, the Thessalonians are loved by God and chosen for salvation (2:13), experience the sanctifying work of the Spirit in their life and believe in the truth (2:13), and are destined for glory (2:14).

themes (reassurance and perseverance) that link these two parts of the letter. More significantly, separating the two units obscures the way in which Paul emphasizes these two common themes and stresses holding fast to the apostolic teachings as the solution to both the external threat he addresses in 2:1–12 and the internal problem he deals with in 3:6–15.

As observed above, this section displays a wide variety of forms: thanksgiving (2:13–14), exhortation and encouragement (2:15), prayer (2:16–17; 3:5), prayer request (3:1–2), and expressions of confidence (3:3–4). The thanksgiving involves both praise and acknowledgment of God as the one ultimately responsible for our salvation; the theocentric prayers remind us of God's priority over everything else and provide a means of bringing our vision and desires into line with God's will. Moreover, the prayers and thanksgiving here reflect a key element observed in the other prayers and thanksgivings in the letters: They are primarily (and sometimes exclusively) other-oriented (see the comments on 1 Thess. 3:9–13). As in 1 Thessalonians 5:25, Paul's request to the Thessalonians for prayer is an implicit acknowledgment of their fundamental equality before God, irrespective of their differing levels of spiritual maturity. The confident affirmation that "the Lord is faithful" (cf. 1 Thess. 5:24; 2 Thess. 1:6) has an axiomatic quality: It expresses a truth so basic and foundational that it requires no proof, but is simply taken for granted by Paul.

In addition to the wide variety of forms, the passage also touches on a wide range of topics. There is little new here, as Paul is for the most part reaffirming or reemphasizing points he has already made, whether in person or in the first letter (for the parallels elsewhere in 1 and 2 Thessalonians, see comments in the Original Meaning, above). (1) To take one example, in many respects 2:13–14 (which touch on God's love, choice, and calling, salvation and sanctification, the work of the Spirit, and the glory of the Lord Jesus[19]) are a condensation of 1 Thessalonians 1:4–8 and 2:12–13. Here, as there, Paul grounds his advice about present problems in their past experience. He also implies that one way of dealing with apprehension about the future (e.g., the

---

19. James Denney sees in these two verses "a system of theology in miniature. The apostle's thanksgiving covers the whole work of creation from the eternal choice of God to the obtaining of the glory of our Lord Jesus Christ in the world to come" (as quoted by F. F. Bruce, *1 and 2 Thessalonians*, 192).

revelation of the "man of lawlessness") is to remember what God has done in the past.

(2) To take another example, there is the tension between divine activity and human responsibility (see 2:13, 15; 3:3–4; cf. 1:11; see also 1 Thess. 3:12; 4:10; see the Bridging Contexts section of 1 Thess. 3:9–13). If the Pauline order is always divine action (grace) followed by human response (faith), it is no less true that he consistently calls those to whom he writes to take responsibility for how they live. For Paul, these are not competing but complementary concepts.

A Trinitarian implication. With respect to 2:13, Gordon Fee points out two significant theological implications. He notes that 2:13 is a "semi-creedal" statement about salvation, which views it "as the combined activity of the triune God." The Father chooses, the Son (i.e., "the Lord") loves, and the Spirit sanctifies. "Granted, this is not Trinitarian in a later sense, but the later outworking is the direct result of such texts" as this one, which attributes to each member of the Trinity a distinct role in the work of salvation.[20] Here we have the biblical material out of which the full doctrine was later constructed.

Salvation as sanctification. Fee also highlights the significance of the fact that in 2:13 Paul describes the Thessalonians' conversion in terms of "sanctification" (i.e., "holiness"). This means that

> "sanctification" in Paul, as 1 Cor 1:30 and 6:11 also make plain, is not a second work of grace, nor does it refer primarily to something that takes place in the believer after conversion— although that, too, is surely expected. Rather, their conversion itself may be described in terms of "sanctification," both in its sense of their being now set apart for God's purposes and in its more ethical sense of their walking in God's ways, so as to reflect his character. As in 1 Thes 4:8, for Paul this is the work of the Holy Spirit in the life of the believer.... There is for him no genuine conversion that does not include the sanctifying work of the Spirit.[21]

---

20. G. D. Fee, *God's Empowering Presence*, 78. Similar passages include Rom. 5:1–5; 8:3–4; 8:15–17; 1 Cor. 6:11; 2 Cor. 1:21–22; 13:14; Gal. 4:4–7; Eph. 1:13–14; 4:4–6; Titus 3:5–7.
21. Ibid., 79.

"Set apart for God's purposes" and "walking in God's ways": not a bad description of salvation or of what it means to be God's people in the world today.

The importance of "tradition." In 2:15 Paul touches on an important point that runs throughout the second letter: the importance of holding firmly to the "traditions" (*paradoseis*; NIV "teachings"; cf. 1 Cor. 11:2) taught by the apostles (cf. 1 Cor. 4:17; Col. 2:7). Paul uses the same word in 2 Thessalonians 3:6 with respect to the disorderly, who were not living according to the "teaching" that they "received" (the same word as in 1 Thess. 4:1; cf. 1 Cor. 15:1) from the apostles. In 2 Thessalonians 3:14 the apostle emphasizes obedience to "our instruction" (*logos*), and in 2:5 he refers to "the things" he had told them. In 1 Thessalonians 4:2, he mentioned the "instructions" (*parangelias*, lit., "commandments"; the related verb *parangello* occurs in 2 Thess. 3:4, 6, 10, 12; also 1 Thess. 4:11) that the apostles "gave" to the Thessalonians.

Regardless of the terminology used, it is clear that all these passages have in view the same thing: authoritative apostolic tradition. In the Original Meaning section above, I noted three main types of tradition in the Pauline letters: gospel tradition, focused on the central gospel message; church tradition, which guides congregational conduct; and ethical tradition, focused on proper Christian living. Whatever form they took, these traditions were, as far as Paul was concerned, both authoritative and normative for the Thessalonian congregation. This is because the ultimate source of these traditions was not human but divine (cf., e.g., 1 Thess. 4:2, 15; also 1 Cor. 11:23). This means, to put it in terms of 1 Thessalonians 2:13, that these traditions are not human words but God's word. For this reason, anyone who rejects apostolic tradition rejects not a human teaching or authority but God himself (4:8).

Paul and his companions communicated these authoritative traditions to the Thessalonians either "by word of mouth or by letter" (2 Thess. 2:15). Today our only access to this apostolic tradition is through what the apostles wrote, specifically, the letters of Paul and others that have become part of the canon of Scripture. Thus, whenever Paul speaks of holding firmly, obeying, receiving, or being taught apostolic *tradition*, we need to think in terms of apostolic *Scripture*. For us today, Scripture is authoritative and normative in the same way that apostolic tradition was for the Thessalonians.

AS IS EVIDENT from the Bridging Contexts section, there are a number of topics or issues in this passage that one could focus on with respect to contemporary application. In most cases, circumstances (such as whether 2 Thessalonians is being treated after or independently of 1 Thessalonians) will determine the selection of topics for application. I would like to focus on three themes or topics, each of which occupies a significant place in this section of the letter: assurance, perseverance, and the importance of Scripture as a safeguard against deception and false or misleading information.[22]

Assurance. In light of 2:2, it appears that some of the Thessalonians were unsettled by the possibility that the "day of the Lord" might have already arrived. In view of Paul's hair-raising description of the events that would precede or accompany the coming of that Day—including the satanic deception, rebellion, and destruction—it seems likely that at least a few of these believers may have become unsettled at the prospect of what was yet to arrive. It is hardly surprising that all this talk and speculation about judgment and deception probably filled some of them with concern and anxiety.

In the face of these circumstances, Paul makes it a point to reassure the Thessalonians (he had already done so in similar terms in 1 Thess. 5:1–11; see Contemporary Significance section there). Precisely because they are loved by the Lord, because God has both chosen and called them, and because they have been saved through the work of the Spirit, they can be confident that they will share in the glory of the Lord himself (2 Thess. 2:13–14). Moreover, as Paul reminds them, "the Lord is faithful" and will therefore "strengthen and protect" them from the evil one and his associates (3:3). In other words, Paul is genuinely optimistic about the future of the Thessalonian believers because it rests securely in the care of the triune God.[23]

---

22. For topics not discussed here, see the references in the Original Meaning and Bridging Contexts sections to other parts in the commentary for guidance on applying them.

23. It is worth noting as an aside that the attitude Paul exhibits here is one of confidence, not triumphalism. Triumphalism—the belief that God is on *our* side—is foreign to Paul. But confidence—the conviction that God has called us to *his* side—runs throughout his letters.

Perseverance. Paul then makes his own application of this point: Assurance should result in *perseverance*. Calvin saw the connection clearly: In writing of 2:15–17 (cf. 3:3–4), he observes that Paul

> correctly draws this word of encouragement from his previous statement [2:13–14], because our determination and power to persevere rest on our assurance of divine grace alone. But when God calls us to salvation and stretches out His hand to us, when Christ offers Himself to us for our enjoyment by the teaching of the Gospel, and when the Spirit is given to us as a seal and pledge of eternal life, we are not to grow despondent, even though the heavens should fall.... The calling of God should defend us against all occasions for stumbling in such a way that not even the total destruction of the world should shake, much less destroy, our constancy.[24]

In short, assurance of God's faithfulness ought to prompt a response of faithfulness on our part.

It is important to observe the understanding of Christianity that underlies what Paul says here about perseverance. For Paul, Christianity is not a quick-fix treatment or a short-term solution for what ails us; it is, as someone has said, "a long walk in the same direction." The writer of Hebrews expressed much the same idea when he encouraged his readers to "run with perseverance the race marked out for us" (Heb. 12:1), for "we have come to share in Christ if we hold firmly till the end the confidence we had at first" (Heb. 3:14). Both Paul and Hebrews in turn reflect the teaching of Jesus, who on more than one occasion reminded his disciples that "the one who endures to the end will be saved" (Matt. 10:22; 24:13; Mark 13:13 NRSV).

This is not at all to say that perseverance is an easy matter. As my colleague Dan Taylor has observed,

> faith can be simultaneously incredibly strong and painfully fragile. Doctrines of eternal security notwithstanding, the choice to discontinue the whole experiment of seeking God is always present—as is the choice to begin, or to begin once more. These choices are sometimes made consciously, often by default. We

---

24. J. Calvin, *The Epistles of Paul the Apostle to the Romans and to the Thessalonians*, 411.

tire of the struggle of faith as an athlete tires in a contest or a soldier grows weary in battle.[25]

Paul's prayer in 2:16–17 is an implicit acknowledgment that we do grow weary in the struggle, that we do tire in the face of obstacles. But precisely in such circumstances, "perseverance means carrying on in the face of obstacles, continuing in what one is doing despite unfavorable circumstances" (such as the persecution the Thessalonians were experiencing). "The marathoner perseveres despite a protesting body, the sculptor perseveres despite the unyielding stone, the husband and wife persevere despite the strains of marriage."[26] God's people persist in their commitment to their Lord despite the challenges and temptations to abandon what at times must seem like an absurdity.

What keeps us going in the face of continuing struggles, trials, difficulties, doubts? Why do we persist? Because, as Paul has made clear earlier in the letter (2:8), in the end, Jesus wins. The one who has been faithful in the past will prove to be faithful in the future, and this gives us courage and hope to remain faithful in the present. Reassured by what God has done and strengthened by what the Holy Spirit is now doing (2:13; cf. 1 Thess. 1:6; 4:8), we persevere in hope, looking to the time when faith will become sight, to the time when the Lord Jesus will be revealed in all his splendor and glory.

Scripture as a safeguard. One reason the Thessalonians had become so "unsettled" (2:2) regarding the future was that they had allowed themselves to be misled by unreliable information. Instead of sticking to what Paul and his companions had actually said or written, they gave credence to information of uncertain origin and indeterminate reliability. Small wonder, then, that they became "unsettled" or "alarmed" about the future.

Paul's response was to encourage the Thessalonians to hold firmly to the teachings they have received from the apostles themselves, and nothing more. Whether in 1 Thessalonians 3:4; 4:1–2; 5:1–2; or 2 Thessalonians 2:5, 15; 3:6 (cf. also 1 Thess. 4:18; 5:11; 2 Thess. 3:14) his point was consistent: They should live in light of what they have been taught. The apostolic teaching provided the answers to

---

25. Daniel Taylor, *The Myth of Certainty: The Reflective Christian and the Risk of Commitment* (Waco, Tex.: Word, 1986), 112.

26. Ibid.

their questions and concerns, if only they would cling tightly to it and think about its implications. The best safeguard against misinformation—or, for that matter, the coming satanic deception—was the truth they had received from the apostles.

Here, I suggest, is an important word for us today: Hold tightly to the teachings we have received from the apostles. For us, this means holding tightly to Scripture. In our day and age, we find ourselves awash in false or deceptive information and teachings. Nothing, it seems, is so outrageous that it cannot find an outlet, in print, on the airwaves, or on the Internet (e.g., a recent book consisting of a long narrative interview with a man claiming to have been the apostle Paul in an earlier life, promoted via billboards and public seminars at $25.00 a pop). In such circumstances, it is more critical than ever that we hold tightly to Scripture, and Scripture alone, as our safeguard against being misled or deceived.

To be sure, in theory, we do this pretty well. Nearly all churches, "liberal" as well as "conservative," affirm the centrality, importance, and authority of Scripture. That is, we have official creeds, theological position papers, or statements of faith that say all the right things about Scripture. But if that is the situation in theory, it is something else in practice. Far too many churches and individual believers, "conservative" as well as "liberal," talk the talk but do not walk the walk with regard to Scripture. Instead of holding tightly to Scripture, we read it selectively, twist it, ignore it, supplement it, or supplant it; we find sophisticated ways to reject its relevance while appearing to follow it. In short, far too often we do everything but hold tightly to Scripture. It should come as no surprise, in such circumstances, that we find ourselves misled or deceived with respect to the truth.

What are some ways we fail to hold tightly to Scripture? Whenever, for example, we:

- take verses out of context and give them meanings the author never intended (e.g., 1 Cor. 3:16–17, a solemn warning to the Corinthians against destroying the church, is frequently applied to discussions of personal holiness or questions about suicide, two topics that have nothing to do with Paul's concern at that point in the letter).
- claim to believe in the Bible but persist in holding to unbiblical beliefs even when they clearly contradict Scripture (e.g., the

person who claims to hold to Scripture as the final authority but who continues to believe in reincarnation, even after studying Heb. 9:27, "people are destined to die once, and after that to face judgment" [NIV^{ILE}]).

- give more weight or attention to what popular teachers or novelists teach than to what Scripture does (e.g., a surprising number of my students get far more of their beliefs about evil and the demonic from popular Christian novels than from Scripture).

- uncritically accept alleged prophecies, "words of knowledge," or other charismatic "revelations" and fail to test them against Scripture (see the Contemporary Significance discussion of 1 Thess. 5:20–21).

- emphasize one part or teaching of Scripture to the exclusion of others (e.g., focusing on Jesus' teachings on love and acceptance to the neglect of what he says about sin, repentance, and holy living).

- create a new concept or term, allegedly on the basis of Scripture, and use that as a basis to set aside or overturn other portions of Scripture (e.g., one denominational task force coined a concept they called "justice-love" and used that to argue that the biblical standards of sexual morality should be set aside because they were not consistent with "justice-love").

- believe what we want to believe rather than what Scripture teaches (e.g., as one person said to me, "I believe in the Rapture of believers before the Tribulation because I don't want to have to think about going through all that hassle"). In this respect, it is certainly not difficult to find in our day numerous examples of what Paul warned Timothy about: "For the time will come when people will not put up with sound doctrine. Instead, to suit their own desires, they will gather around them a great number of teachers to say what their itching ears want to hear. They will turn their ears away from the truth and turn aside to myths" (2 Tim. 4:3–4 NIV^{ILE}).

- suggest that Scripture is not relevant to contemporary issues because circumstances were so much simpler in biblical cultures (e.g., by claiming that Scripture has so little to say about an issue that it cannot be called upon to resolve the contemporary church's debates about that issue or to address itself to the modern complexity of that issue).

This list of examples is seriously incomplete and undeveloped, but gives, I hope, some idea of the many ways we fail to hold tightly to Scripture. One consequence of our failure is that we, like the Thessalonians, are far too often "easily unsettled or alarmed" (2 Thess. 2:2); we are too easily "blown here and there by every wind of teaching and by the cunning and craftiness of people in their deceitful scheming" (Eph. 4:14 NIV[ILE]). As J. I. Packer puts it, "Western Christianity has become superficial and shallow: we do not give ourselves time to soak ourselves in Scripture, and stunted spiritual development, which includes an undervaluing of the Bible, is the unhappy result."[27]

We need to hold tightly to Scripture. As Packer observes, "other things being equal, it is the Christians who eat up the Scriptures on a regular basis who are likely to achieve most for our Lord Jesus Christ in the future, just as it was Bible-fed Christians who achieved most for him in the past." Packer explains what he means by "eat up" with a prayer from the old Anglican Prayer Book:

> Blessed Lord, who hast caused all holy scriptures to be written for our learning; Grant that we may in such wise hear them, read, mark, learn, and inwardly digest them, that by patience, and comfort of thy holy Word, we may embrace, and ever hold fast the blessed hope of everlasting life, which thou hast given us in our Saviour Jesus Christ.[28]

"Read, mark, learn, and inwardly digest" the Scriptures: Note the active engagement with Scripture conveyed by these terms! Reading the Scriptures carefully, learning and memorizing them, prayerfully meditating and reflecting on them, applying them personally and corporately—these are activities associated with holding tightly to Scripture. And as we hold tightly to Scripture, we will be able to "stand firm," as Paul commands us, in the face of the challenges and difficulties that confront us, even as others become alarmed, unsettled, or even deceived.

---

27. J. I. Packer, "Our Lifeline," *CT* 40 (October 28, 1996): 25.
28. Ibid., 23, 25.

2 Thessalonians 3:6–18

I N THE NAME of the Lord Jesus Christ, we command
you, brothers, to keep away from every brother who
is idle and does not live according to the teaching you
received from us. ⁷For you yourselves know how you
ought to follow our example. We were not idle when we
were with you, ⁸nor did we eat anyone's food without
paying for it. On the contrary, we worked night and day,
laboring and toiling so that we would not be a burden to
any of you. ⁹We did this, not because we do not have the
right to such help, but in order to make ourselves a
model for you to follow. ¹⁰For even when we were with
you, we gave you this rule: "If a man will not work, he
shall not eat."

¹¹We hear that some among you are idle. They are not
busy; they are busybodies. ¹²Such people we command
and urge in the Lord Jesus Christ to settle down and earn
the bread they eat. ¹³And as for you, brothers, never tire
of doing what is right.

¹⁴If anyone does not obey our instruction in this letter,
take special note of him. Do not associate with him, in
order that he may feel ashamed. ¹⁵Yet do not regard him
as an enemy, but warn him as a brother.

¹⁶Now may the Lord of peace himself give you peace at
all times and in every way. The Lord be with all of you.

¹⁷I, Paul, write this greeting in my own hand, which is
the distinguishing mark in all my letters. This is how I
write.

¹⁸The grace of our Lord Jesus Christ be with you all.

THE TONE OF Paul's exhortation in 3:6–15 is
the most bluntly authoritative of anything in
either letter. Both the community as a whole
and those who are the source of the problem
are explicitly commanded "in the name of the Lord Jesus" (3:6; cf.

v. 12) to obey specific Pauline instructions (cf. 3:14), and penalties for noncompliance are spelled out. Clearly this situation involves a matter that Paul approached with some seriousness.

Unlike the previous section (2:13–3:5), this segment is tightly focused. While Paul's attention travels from the congregation (3:6) to apostolic example and teaching (3:7–10) to certain members within the congregation (3:11–12) and back to the congregation (3:13–15), the entire passage focuses on a single issue: the problem of certain people who are living *ataktos* and how the community ought to deal with it. It is considerably easier, however, to identify the problem than to define it.

There is substantial disagreement as to whether 3:16 draws the preceding section (3:6–15) to a close or is part of the letter closing.[1] On the one hand, there is the parallel with the structure of the previous chapter (where 2:16–17 in some sense closes 2:1–15), a consideration that suggests linking 3:16 with what precedes it (3:6–15). On the other hand, the content of 3:16 substantially transcends the specific problem of 3:5–15. For this reason I link 3:16 with verses 17–18 and view the three verses together as the epistolary closing of the letter.[2]

Verse 16 takes the form of a benediction, which could have functioned as the close of the letter. But Paul then adds another point or two in his own hand (v. 17, sort of like adding a "P.S." after one's signature). Since this was not a suitable way in which to conclude a letter, it was necessary to add a second benediction (v. 18) as the final element.

Defining the Problem: Idle or Disorderly?

SECOND THESSALONIANS 3:6–15 is often interpreted in light of 2:1–3 as Paul's response to a situation generated by excessive interest in and excitement about the imminent return of Jesus, which led some

---

1. For the former position cf. E. J. Richard, *Thessalonians*, 385–87, 392; I. H. Marshall, *1 and 2 Thessalonians*, 230; for the latter, C. A. Wanamaker, *Thessalonians*, 291; E. Best, *Thessalonians*, 345–46; L. Morris, *The First and Second Epistles to the Thessalonians*, 262; Jeffrey A. D. Weima, *Neglected Endings: The Significance of the Pauline Letter Closings* (Sheffield: Sheffield Univ. Press, 1994), 187.

2. Attempts to find here a rhetorical *peroratio* or summary (e.g., R. Jewett, *Thessalonian Correspondence*, 87, 225) are unconvincing, primarily because this section simply does not summarize the major themes of the letter (cf. C. A. Wanamaker, *Thessalonians*, 291).

members of the church to abandon their jobs and live in idleness, dependent on the generosity and resources of others.[3] But this scenario is a hypothesis rather than a demonstrable fact. Against it stand three considerations. (1) Nowhere does Paul connect the refusal to work with the expectation of Jesus' return.[4] (2) It rests on a narrowly restricted understanding of *ataktos* as "idle" (see discussion of this word below). (3) When the same issue came up earlier in 1 Thessalonians 4:11–12, Paul stressed that he was bringing to their attention things he had already taught them (cf. 4:11: "just as we told you"). Almost certainly this happened at the time the community was established— before, in other words, any specific eschatological questions or misunderstandings arose.[5]

In sketching out these objections to the above hypothesis, I have already tipped my hand regarding what I see as the proper context within which to interpret this passage, namely 1 Thessalonians 4:11–12 and 5:14. When the community was first established, Paul apparently instructed them to devote themselves to their own concerns rather than those of others, to work for their own living and not to be dependent on others. These instructions would have affected some members more than others; in particular, clients accustomed to being supported by a patron and to looking after the patron's affairs would have had their usual lifestyle severely disrupted.

Paul reaffirmed those instructions in his first letter, stressing the need to work and to lead a quiet (i.e., nonpublic) life and thereby to avoid dependency on others (1 Thess. 4:11–12). He also encouraged the congregation to "warn the *ataktous*" (5:14). Following the sending of that letter, however, the problem seems to have continued (perhaps even intensified) rather than abated.[6] Indeed, it has been suggested that some in the community were disregarding or perhaps even

---

3. E.g., E. Best, *Thessalonians*, 331.

4. If anything, 2:13–3:5 (the somewhat awkward transitional section between 2:1–12 and 3:6–15) has the effect of separating the two issues. Even the most recent substantial attempt to connect the problem of this section with eschatological concerns acknowledges that the connection is impossible to prove (M. J. J. Menken, "Paradise Regained or Still Lost? Eschatology and Disorderly Behaviour in 2 Thessalonians," *NTS* 38 [1992]: 288).

5. Cf. R. Russell, "The Idle in 2 Thess 3:6–12: An Eschatological or a Social Problem?" *NTS* 34 (1988): 108.

6. Cf. J. E. Frame, *Thessalonians*, 297; E. Best, *Thessalonians*, 332; F. F. Bruce, *1 and 2 Thessalonians*, 205.

rebelling against Paul's instructions (cf. 2 Thess. 3:6b, 12, 14).[7] In any case, Paul now takes up the general topic again, this time in more detail, with more vigor, and with a specific focus on the behavior of those living *ataktos*.

How one defines *ataktos*, an adverb that I have so far deliberately left untranslated, is critical to the interpretation of the entire passage. The NIV translation "living in idleness" (3:6) or simply "idle" (3:11) obscures the similarity of form between Paul's phrase here and parallel statements in 1 Thessalonians 2:12 and 4:12 (cf. also 4:1). In all these verses Paul employs the verb *peripateo* (lit., "walk," metaphorically "live one's life, conduct oneself") followed by an adverb:

1 Thess. 2:12	*peripateo* + *axios*, "to live worthily" (of God)
1 Thess. 4:12	*peripateo* + *euschemonos*, "to live responsibly" (towards outsiders)
2 Thess. 3:6, 11	*peripateo* + *ataktos*, "to live *ataktos*"
2 Thess. 3:6	[*peripateo*] + *kata ten paradosin*, "[to live] according to the tradition"

This similarity does not help settle the question of the meaning of *ataktos*, but it does indicate the *character* of the behavior in question. Living *ataktos* is clearly a negative behavior in Paul's opinion, one that stands in tension with and in contrast to living "worthily of God" and "responsibly towards outsiders." It is, therefore, clearly *not* "according to the teaching" they had received from Paul and his companions (2 Thess. 3:6).

With regard to *ataktos* itself, 3:7–8 are often viewed as the key to determining its meaning. There Paul contrasts the related verb *atakteo* (3:7) with *ergazomai*, "to work" (3:8; cf. 3:10). In view of this contrast, it is often concluded that the problem is one of laziness or idleness. But in fact, the contrast only defines the term negatively, telling us what *ataktos* is not. "Idle" is one thing—but certainly not the only thing—that can stand in contrast to "work." In fact, it is 3:11 that offers the key to understanding this crucial term. There Paul repeats (from 3:6) the charge that some are "living *ataktos*," and then says, in a play on words: They are not *ergazomenous*, "working" (the same contrast he made in 3:7) but rather *periergazomenous*, "wasting their efforts," "behaving like

7. Ceslas Spicq, *Theological Lexicon of the New Testament* (3 vols.; Peabody, Mass.: Hendrickson, 1994), 1:223–26; R. Jewett, *Thessalonian Correspondence*, 104–5.

busybodies," or "meddling in the affairs of others." This immediately indicates that the people in question are in fact *active*, not "idle" or lazy.[8]

The problem, in other words, was not *in*activity, but the wrong kind of activity. Paul's mention in 3:11 of "working" (NIV "busy") hints that those whom he is criticizing may have claimed that they were engaged in legitimate "work." Whatever it was they were doing, however, was from Paul's perspective not work at all but pseudo-work, busyness that disrupted rather than benefited the community.[9] This understanding of the term here fits well with the use of the verb *atakteo* elsewhere: The primary emphasis is not on sloth or laziness "but rather on an irresponsible attitude to the obligation to work."[10] Instead of working responsibly to support themselves, the people in question were eating other people's bread (cf. 3:8, 12) and thus living (*peripateo*) "irresponsibly" or "in an undisciplined manner," which was burdensome to the rest of the congregation. Their behavior was, in other words, undisciplined, disruptive, or "disorderly" (*ataktos*) rather than merely "idle."[11]

The Apostolic Command and Example (3:6–10)

FROM PAUL'S PERSPECTIVE it should not have been necessary to "command" (*parangello*, 3:6; for this verb, cf. 1 Thess. 4:11; 2 Thess. 3:4, 10, 12) the Thessalonians[12] "to keep away from" any believer who is *ataktos*, "disorderly," because "they themselves" (3:7) already knew what they ought to be doing about this problem. But just in case the Thessalonians had any doubt about what he is talking about, Paul explicitly states for them in 3:10 the specific content of the "teaching you received[13] from us" (3:6): "If anyone refuses to work, do not permit that person to eat" (pers. trans.; cf. NASB). This translation attempts to

---

8. Similarly J. E. Frame, *Thessalonians*, 305.

9. It cannot be determined (because of a lack of information) whether the problematic behavior was taking place inside or/and outside the boundaries of the congregation.

10. G. Delling, "ἄτακτος," *TDNT* 8:48.

11. Similarly E. J. Richard, *Thessalonians*, 379, 382, 388–90; C. A. Wanamaker, *Thessalonians*, 282, 286; B. R. Gaventa, *Thessalonians*, 81–82, 128–29.

12. For the significance of *adelphoi*, which includes the entire community and not just the male members, see comment on 1 Thess. 1:4.

13. The manuscript witnesses are sharply divided at this point between "they received" (NRSV, NAB; C. A. Wanamaker, *Thessalonians*, 282; I. H. Marshall, *1 and 2 Thessalonians*, 220; F. F. Bruce, *1 and 2 Thessalonians*, 203) and "you received" (NIV, NASB). The first reading—less expected in the context and thus more likely to have been changed—is probably the original one.

convey the emphasis in Paul's sentence on the *refusal* or unwillingness to work (a point that, e.g., the CEV's "if you don't work, you don't eat" largely misses).[14] It also conveys something of its somewhat awkward structure: a conditional statement, followed by an imperative directed to the community.

What Paul and his colleagues had taught during their initial visit (3:10, "when we were with you, we gave you this rule") they had also lived themselves; that is, they deliberately practiced what they preached. Even though as apostles they had the right to be supported by others (3:9),[15] they voluntarily declined to exercise this right in order to provide an example (3:6) or model for the Thessalonians to follow (3:9; cf. Phil. 3:17). That is, they did not "act irresponsibly" or "live in an undisciplined manner" (2 Thess. 3:7b; Paul uses the verb *atakteo* here), nor did they "eat anyone's food without paying for it" (3:8a; his emphasis on these two points sets up the charges he makes in 3:11–12). "On the contrary," Paul asserts (repeating virtually word for word what he said in 1 Thess. 2:9), "we worked night and day, laboring and toiling so that we would not be a burden" (2 Thess. 3:8b).

Orders for the Disorderly (3:11–12)

THE APOSTOLIC EXAMPLE stands in sharp contrast to "some" among the Thessalonians who were "behaving irresponsibly" (3:11, repeating the charge first made in 3:6) and thereby becoming burdens to the rest of the congregation. Paul's opinion of such behavior is blunt (3:11b): rather than "working hard" (*ergazomenous*), they are "hardly working" (*periergazomenous*). It is not that these people were inactive, but that they were active in an unproductive, irresponsible, or disruptive manner. As

---

14. As L. Morris observes, "Paul is not speaking of those who cannot find work, nor of those who through injury or illness are not able to work, but of those who deliberately choose not to work" (*The First and Second Epistles to the Thessalonians*, 256).

15. On the apostolic right of support, cf. 1 Cor. 9:4–18. Paul's decision not to exercise that right in Corinth, for both pastoral and practical reasons, closely parallels the same decision he made in Thessalonica (cf. 1 Thess. 2:9). The mention here of the right to support probably does not arise in response to someone in Thessalonica claiming a similar right to support (contra R. Jewett, *Thessalonian Correspondence*, 105), but rather ties in with the authoritative tone of this entire section. Paul is asserting his authority as an apostle with considerable force and does not want anyone to think that his refusal to accept support in any way undermines that authority (as some opponents in Corinth attempted to claim; cf. 2 Cor. 12:5–12). See further J. M. Everts, "Financial Support," *DPL*, 295–300.

suggested above, those whom Paul criticizes may have claimed that they were engaged in legitimate "work." It was, however, from Paul's perspective not work at all but only pseudo-work, busyness that disrupted and burdened rather than benefited the rest of the congregation.[16]

Paul spells out his solution to the problem in 3:12–15. In 3:6 he and his colleagues had "commanded" the congregation "in the name of the Lord Jesus Christ;" here in 3:12 the "disorderly" individuals are similarly "commanded" as well as "urged [*parakaleo*, as in 1 Thess. 4:1, 10; 5:14] in the Lord Jesus Christ." The full authority of the Lord stands behind these commands; to reject them is to reject not merely Paul and his colleagues, but the Lord himself. The actual command to the disorderly is (lit.) that "quietly working (*ergazomenoi*), they should eat their own bread" (2 Thess. 3:12b).[17] That is, rather than wasting their time in pseudo-work or unproductive busyness and meddling (*periergazomenoi*, 3:11), they should engage in productive self-supporting activities, in accordance with the apostolic model.

The instruction that they do so "quietly" (*meta hesychias*) echoes 1 Thessalonians 4:11, "lead a quiet life" (i.e., avoid the strife and social pressures of the public arena and focus instead on the needs of the congregation). The point of working—and the main point of Paul's command here—is that they "eat their own bread," that is, "earn their own living" (NRSV) and (by implication) stop being an unnecessary burden on the rest of the community.

Instructions for the Congregation (3:13–15)

EVEN AS PAUL authoritatively commands the disorderly, he encourages the rest of the congregation[18] to "never tire of doing what is right" (3:13; cf. the close parallel in Gal. 6:9). Here we catch a glimpse of the negative impact the disorderly were having on the congregation. Those who were living responsibly, in accordance with the apostolic

---

16. A key reason given in 1 Thess. 4:12 for working—winning the respect of outsiders—receives no mention in the present discussion; cf. Bruce W. Winter, *Seek the Welfare of the City: Christians as Benefactors and Citizens* (Grand Rapids: Eerdmans, and Carlisle: Paternoster, 1994), 58.

17. The NIV's "settle down and earn the bread they eat" catches the gist of Paul's command, but seriously obscures both the structure of his sentence and its verbal echoes of other statements in 1 and 2 Thessalonians.

18. For the significance of *adelphoi*, which includes the entire community and not just the male members, see comment on 1 Thess. 1:4.

teaching, perhaps were being worn down by the burden of providing not only for themselves and any who legitimately deserved assistance, but also for those who refused to work.[19] In such circumstances we can see at least a twofold point to Paul's exhortation to continue to "do what is right." (1) It means continuing to care for those who genuinely need help;[20] that is, those who legitimately require assistance should not suffer a loss of aid just because a few have taken advantage of the charity of others. (2) It means being willing to carry out, should it prove to be necessary, disciplinary action against the disorderly (a point to which he turns in verse 14).

The instructions in 3:14—15 have in view everything discussed since 3:6. Paul clearly hopes that the disorderly will comply voluntarily with his instructions. If this compliance, however, is not forthcoming, the congregation itself must take steps to enforce them. What Paul said in 3:6 ("keep away from") is essentially repeated here: "Take special note" (cf. Rom. 16:17) of anyone who disobeys, in order to avoid associating with that person. The verb for "associate" that Paul uses here is the same one that he later uses in 1 Corinthians 5:9, 11. It essentially calls upon the congregation to cease having contact with any such people and thus amounts to an early instance of what later came to be termed "excommunication."

The precise extent to which contact is to be broken off is unclear. At first glance 3:14 seems rather broad: "Do not associate with" the person being disciplined. But 3:15 seems to modify 3:14 somewhat, especially the second part; the instruction to "warn him as a brother" seems to imply some limited degree of contact (unless Paul means the warning given at the time the discipline is imposed). G. D. Fee suggests that 3:15 "implies that private fellowship may not have been included in the ban" and concludes that the disciplined person was to be "shunned in terms of close fellowship in the believing community."[21]

The goal of nonassociation is clearly spelled out: "in order that he may feel ashamed." In the Mediterranean culture of the day, "shame" was

---

19. Cf. B. W. Winter, *Seek the Welfare of the City*, 58 ("There may have been those benefactors who were somewhat disillusioned with other Christians because the latter had continued to exploit them to their own advantage, in spite of Paul's specific example and teaching").

20. Cf. I. H. Marshall, *1 and 2 Thessalonians*, 226; B. W. Winter, *Seek the Welfare of the City*, 59; J. Calvin, *The Epistles of Paul the Apostle to the Romans and to the Thessalonians*, 420.

21. Gordon D. Fee, *The First Epistle to the Corinthians* (NICNT; Grand Rapids: Eerdmans, 1987), 226 (on p. 222 he refers to 2 Thess. 3).

primarily a matter of concern for one's reputation. Paul expects that the one who is "shamed" (whose reputation, in other words, is at stake) will then respond with appropriate behavior—in this case, repentance and obedience to Paul's instructions. That the unstated goal is in fact restoration is implied by what Paul says in the next sentence (3:15): In carrying out Paul's instructions, the Thessalonians are not to treat an offender as an "enemy" (i.e., an "outsider"—a course of action that "would more than likely result in their complete alienation from the community"[22]). Instead, they are to "warn [*noutheteo*, as in 1 Thess. 5:14] him as a brother," that is, treat him as an "insider," still a member of the congregation.

In short, the disciplinary action is clearly meant to be redemptive for the individual (cf. Gal. 6:1 for a statement of the general Pauline principle). At the same time, however, note that it is also protective for the community. That is, if repentance does not occur, the congregation will nonetheless have been purged of a potentially corrupting influence.

The Letter Closing (3:16–18)

VERSES 16–18 COMPRISE the letter's closing. In the benediction in 3:16, the reference to "the Lord of peace" (in which "Lord" is almost certainly Jesus) is unique in the New Testament (but cf. Col. 3:15, "the peace of Christ"). Jesus is more often linked with peace in the opening of a letter (as in 1:2 above, and every Pauline letter except Colossians) rather than in the closing (where the usual phrase is "God of peace," as in 1 Thess. 5:23; cf. Rom. 15:33; 16:20; 2 Cor. 13:11; Phil 4:9). The actual prayer is that the Lord Jesus, who is characterized by "peace," may grant to the Thessalonians "peace at all times and in every way."

The last part of the phrase indicates the breadth of Paul's concern. He has in view not simply an absence of conflict within the congregation (perhaps provoked by the problem of the *ataktoi* in 3:6–15) or (in light of the persecution and affliction they had experienced) between the congregation and the larger community (cf. 1:4). Peace, for Paul, also encompasses a state of well-being and wholeness characterized by reconciled relationships (cf. Rom. 5:1–11)—with God (cf. Rom. 5:1; 1 Thess. 1:9), with each other in the congregation (cf. 1 Thess. 3:12; 4:9), and finally with those outside the community, to the extent possible (cf. Rom. 12:18; 1 Thess. 3:12).

---

22. C. A. Wanamaker, *Thessalonians*, 290.

It was not uncommon for a person dictating a letter to take the pen from the amanuensis (the "secretary" or "scribe" who actually wrote the letter; cf. Rom. 16:22) and write the last sentence or two in his (or her) own hand.[23] Paul seems to have done this as a matter of habit (he refers to it as "the distinguishing mark in all my letters"). The exact phrase used here (lit., "the greeting in my own hand, Paul's") occurs in 1 Corinthians 16:21 and Colossians 4:18, and he comments on his writing in Galatians 6:11 and Philemon 19.

Even when Paul does not explicitly mention writing, however, there are hints that indicate he did so. For example, in 1 Thessalonians 5:27 the probable explanation of the abrupt switch from the plural to the singular pronoun is that Paul himself wrote the last two sentences. Paul's confirmation that "this is how I write" (a reference to his handwriting style rather than what he wrote) provides the recipients with an indication of authenticity (the handwriting would have matched that at the end of the first letter), without implying, however, that forgeries actually existed (see comments on 2:2). The apostolic signature also lends a note of authority, reinforcing the tone of 3:6–15 (cf. also 1 Thess. 5:27).[24]

The closing benediction in 3:18 is virtually identical to 1 Thessalonians 5:28 (cf. 1 Cor. 16:23). The only difference is that here Paul says "all of you" (as in 1 Cor. 16:24) rather than simply "you." Key terms in 2 Thessalonians 3:16 ("Lord of peace") and 3:18 ("grace") echo the content of Paul's opening greeting ("grace and peace," 1:2), thereby forming (just as in 1 Thessalonians) an inclusio that unifies the letter. For the significance of "grace" and of the phrase "Lord Jesus Christ," see the discussion of 1 Thessalonians 1:1.

Bridging Contexts

WE FACE AT least two difficulties in attempting to bridge the gap between the situation Paul faced in Thessalonica and our contemporary world. (1) The first difficulty (and,

---

23. For a photograph of a papyrus letter in which the switch from the neat, precise writing of the scribe to the irregular scrawl of the author is strikingly obvious, see Everett Ferguson, *Backgrounds of Early Christianity* (2d ed.; Grand Rapids: Eerdmans, 1993), 121 (1st ed., p. 95).

24. I. H. Marshall, *1 and 2 Thessalonians*, 232–33.

as it turns out, one more apparent than real) is that we do not know exactly what the problem was. In the preceding discussion I have outlined the range of the debate regarding the precise nature of the problem addressed in 3:6–15. Oversimplifying things a bit, it boils down to "idleness" (a refusal to work, perhaps arising out of the expectation that the Day of the Lord was coming soon) or "disorderly behavior" (activity that was burdensome or harmful to the congregation and which kept some individuals so preoccupied that they never got around to working to earn their living, subsisting instead on the generosity of other members of the congregation). I have given the reasons why I am more persuaded by the second alternative than the first.

Typically, a decision between these two alternatives would be critical to determining the contemporary application of the passage because our understanding of the situation frequently shapes our inferences and/or conclusions about the guidelines or principles with which Paul was working. But in the present case, we are relieved of the need to make inferences from the circumstances because Paul himself explicitly states his guiding principle in 3:10: "If anyone refuses to work, do not permit that person to eat" (pers. trans.). Thus the difficulty arising from our inability to determine the precise nature of the problem Paul confronts is, because of the specific circumstances of this passage, more apparent than real.

(2) The other difficulty, however, is all too real and obvious. At its heart is the immense difference between the circumstances of the Thessalonian congregation and those of most contemporary American congregations. In addressing the problem Paul takes two things for granted about the situation in Thessalonica. (a) The congregation (or members of it, acting on behalf of the congregation) was providing financial assistance to those congregational members in need of it. (b) The congregation possessed the ability to discipline its members. That many congregations today no longer (even attempt to) do the first and are unable to do the second reveal just how different the social setting of our congregations is from that of the first century.

"If anyone refuses to work, do not permit that person to eat." As we consider the contemporary significance of this principle, it is important to keep in mind exactly whom Paul has in view here: those who are able to work but refuse to do so.[25] Indeed, in this passage Paul takes it for granted that the congregation has an obligation to assist members who are in financial need as a result of circumstances beyond their control (3:13; cf. also Acts 20:35; Eph. 4:28; Titus 3:14). As Klyne Snodgrass puts it, "If a need exists, the community has a responsibility to help meet that need."[26]

As in the case of 1 Thessalonians 4:11–12, nothing is said regarding the reason(s) *why* the "disorderly" were refusing to work. "It may have been a conviction that the Day of the Lord was imminent . . . it may have been a belief in their own superior spirituality, which exempted them from such mundane concerns as earning an honest living . . . it may have been a combination of those or other factors"[27]— including attitudes toward work shaped by considerations of social class, order, and status.[28] Whatever their reason(s), the "disorderly" who were not working evidently thought that those reasons constituted a valid "need" that ought to be met by the church. Furthermore, the impression left by Paul's discussion here is that these reasons were fundamentally self-centered in their perspective. That is, the "disorderly" seem to have focused primarily on their needs or desires rather than on the needs and concerns of the congregation.

Paul, however, was not convinced of their reasons. Moreover, he apparently differed sharply from those who refused to work in how he defined "need." In his view, an unwillingness to work by someone who was able to work does not qualify as a "need." Hence his strongly worded reminder to the Thessalonians: "If anyone refuses to work, do not permit that person to eat."

At least four reasons can be discerned in support of Paul's view that individuals who are able to do so have an obligation to work. One is implicit in 3:8: so that they will not be an unnecessary burden to others in the congregation (3:8, 12). This reason is joined by two others in 1 Thessalonians 4:9–12: winning the respect of outsiders (4:12)

---

25. See the quote by L. Morris in footnote 14, above; similarly C. A. Wanamaker, *Thessalonians*, 285–86: "Paul recognized that the important question was whether or not people were prepared to work for their living. His command, therefore, was not directed to those who were unable to work or who could not find work, but to those who refused to work."

26. Klyne Snodgrass, *Ephesians* (NIVAC; Grand Rapids: Zondervan, 1996), 258.

27. F. F. Bruce, *1 and 2 Thessalonians*, 209.

28. For an excellent introduction to social class, order, and status in the Roman world, see David P. Nystrom, *James* (NIVAC; Grand Rapids: Zondervan, 1997), 123–30.

and *philadelphia*, love for others (4:9). A fourth is specified in Ephesians 4:28: to have something to share with those in need (cf. Titus 3:14; also Acts 20:35).

It is worth observing that all four reasons are other-oriented. This fits in with a significant emphasis throughout the Thessalonian letters, that Christian behavior is fundamentally other-oriented rather than self-centered. This other-oriented approach contrasts sharply with the more self-centered perspective of the "disorderly."

To summarize, Paul affirms, implicitly or explicitly, two points in this passage: Congregations have an obligation to care for members in need, and individuals who are able to work have an obligation to do so in order to avoid becoming a burden on others. This second point is for Paul no minor matter: A refusal to work is a breach of conduct serious enough to warrant the imposition of discipline.

Church discipline. Nowhere does Paul spell out fully his views about the principles and practice of church discipline. The major passages where the topic arises are here and 1 Corinthians 5.[29] On the basis of these passages, we can make the following observations. (1) Discipline is the responsibility of the congregation as a whole, not one or a few individuals within it (2 Thess. 3:6, 14; cf. 1 Cor. 5:4).

(2) Discipline should generally be reserved for matters affecting the health or well-being of the entire community. Although Paul nowhere lists or defines what qualifies for discipline, it is clear that it is not for offenses that can be dealt with privately (as per Matt. 18:15—17; Gal. 6:1). It is reserved for matters that, in Stott's words, arise "from a public, deliberate and persistent disobedience"; similarly Fee speaks of "persistent wrongdoing" that threatens to contaminate the community.[30]

(3) The disciplinary action itself involves a measure of social ostracism (3:6, 14; cf. 1 Cor. 5:11). In Fee's words, the disciplined person is to be "shunned in terms of close fellowship in the believing community"[31] (whether more is intended is unclear; see the Original

---

29. Other passages that touch on the topic include Rom. 16:17; 1 Cor. 16:22; 2 Cor. 13:1—2; Gal. 6:1—5; 1 Tim. 1:18—20; 5:19—22; Titus 3:10—11. See T. E. Schmidt, "Discipline," *DPL*, 214—18.

30. J. R. W. Stott, *The Gospel and the End of Time*, 193; Gordon D. Fee, *The First Epistle to the Corinthians*, 228, 214.

31. Gordon D. Fee, *The First Epistle to the Corinthians*, 222.

Meaning section, above). At a minimum it appears to have involved exclusion from the formal activities of the gathered community.

(4) The purpose of disciplinary action is redemptive and remedial, not judgmental or punitive, and the spirit in which it is carried out must reflect this (3:14–15; cf. 1 Cor. 5:5). Paul's command in 2 Thessalonians 3:15 ("Do not regard him as an enemy, but warn him as a brother") is especially important in this regard. As John Calvin observes,

> We ought ... to strive by whatever means we can in order that they [excommunicated persons] may turn to a more virtuous life and may return to the society and unity of the church. So the apostle also teaches: "Do not look upon them as enemies, but warn them as brothers" [II Thess. 3:15]. Unless this gentleness is maintained in both private and public censures, there is danger lest we soon slide down from discipline to butchery.[32]

Neither the above observations nor the two passages on which they are based answer all our questions about congregational discipline. They do, however, establish parameters or guidelines for its practice.

The context in which these guidelines are implemented is a critical variable with which we must reckon when we think about bringing this passage into today's world. In Paul's day, the church was essentially the only source of Christian fellowship, and churches were few and far between. Moreover, the social costs associated with belonging to the Christian community (such as loss of relationships, social ostracism, or even persecution; see comments on 1 Thess. 1:6) were generally high. This meant that people who joined the Christian movement had a high personal investment in the group and, therefore, generally had a strong motivation to maintain their association with it. In such circumstances, the threat of exclusion from the congregation of God's people is a powerful disciplinary tool.

In some situations today, especially in instances where the church and Christianity in general hold a minority position in a culture or society, the similar circumstances are present: Individuals have a high personal stake in maintaining their association with a group for which there are few or no alternatives. In other situations, however, the

---

32. Calvin, *Institutes of the Christian Religion*, ed. John T. McNeill, trans. Ford Lewis Battles (Philadelphia: Westminster, 1960), 4.12.10 (2:1238 in this ed.).

circumstances are vastly different: People have a minimal commitment to a group, to which a multitude of alternatives exist—not merely other churches, but also parachurch groups and other avenues for fellowship. Consequently they have little motivation to maintain their association with one particular group, and much less to lose (in terms of personal investment) if they do leave. In these circumstances, the challenge of application is considerably different from that faced by the Thessalonians.

In view of this wide range of circumstances in which one might face the challenge of applying Paul's guidelines regarding discipline, it becomes critically important to keep in mind the purpose and goal of discipline. (1) The purpose of disciplinary action, as noted above, is redemptive, not punitive. (2) The goal of disciplining the erring brother or sister—who throughout the process is to be regarded as a brother or sister, not as an enemy (3:15)—is restoration to full fellowship, not removal from it. In order to accomplish these goals it may be necessary to adapt or modify (but not abandon!) the means of discipline in light of the varying circumstances in which it may be needed.[33]

THERE ARE TWO primary topics that most call for attention in this section, work and church discipline. A short discussion of two other topics ("never tire of doing what is right" and the centrality of Jesus Christ) brings us to the end of the letter. (For the importance of holding firm to the apostolic testimony and teaching, a point that arises out of 3:6 and 3:14, see the discussion in the Bridging Contexts and Contemporary Significance sections of 2:15.)

Work. Even while Paul explicitly affirms that individuals who are able to work have a responsibility to do so, he takes for granted the responsibility of the congregation to meet the basic financial needs of its members. In this way Paul seeks "to make sure that no able people live unjustifiably from other people's work, and that those who are unable to work still have their basic needs met."[34] Both the affirmation

---

33. For examples of creative application of Pauline principles, see Michael E. Phillips, "Creative Church Discipline," *Leadership* 7, no. 4 (1986): 46–50.

34. Miroslav Volf, *Work in the Spirit: Toward a Theology of Work* (New York and Oxford: Oxford Univ. Press, 1991), 149.

and the assumption provide opportunities to reflect on the meaning, significance, and value of work.

Working and eating. Human beings, Jesus reminds us, do not live by bread alone (Matt. 4:4; cf. Deut. 8:3), but neither do they live without bread. Work is the means by which humans acquire "bread," that is, the necessities for life (food, clothing, shelter). In the biblical tradition, people who are able to work do so in order to provide for themselves and their families. They also work in order to provide for those who, for whatever reasons, are unable to work (Acts 20:35; Eph. 4:28). Indeed, "in the Bible and in the first centuries of Christian tradition, meeting one's needs and the needs of one's community (especially its underprivileged members) was clearly the most important purpose of work."[35]

Two observations follow from this. (1) Work is a fundamental characteristic of human life because work provides the means for sustaining life. Without work, there is no life. (2) In the biblical tradition there is an altruistic aspect to work. One works not just for self (i.e., to support oneself and one's family) but also for others (i.e., to support those unable to work).

Viewed from this perspective, the refusal of the "disorderly" to work falls short in two respects. (1) They were neglecting their responsibility to provide for themselves and their dependents. (2) They were adding to the burden of those who were working and contributing to the needs of those unable to do so. In other words, instead of working and thereby contributing to the well-being of the congregation, they were refusing to work and thereby contributing instead to its burdens. In short, their behavior was fundamentally self-centered.

In light of the preceding considerations, how might 3:10 apply today? I suggest that it establishes a linkage between a willingness to receive assistance and a willingness to work on the part of those able to do so. For those able to work, a willingness to do so is essentially a qualification for receiving financial assistance from the congregation. (I use the phrase "willingness to work" rather than "work," because not all those willing to work, indeed who want to work, are able to find employment, often for reasons well beyond their control.) By maintaining the connection between "eating" (i.e., having the necessities of

---

35. Ibid., 149.

life) and "working" (or more precisely in this context, being willing to work), Paul reinforces an important element of the biblical teaching about work.

This connection between work and sustenance is one that is under attack from a number of directions in contemporary culture. On the one hand, social policies designed to provide a necessary "safety net" for those in need—policies that have been successful to some degree in providing for the material needs of those assisted—have frequently done so in a way that has severely weakened (if not actually severed) the connection between assistance and work; this has been psychologically debilitating. The long-term negative consequences of these policies, on both the individual and the societal level, have been widely documented.

On the other hand, the rise of an "entertainment" culture, new forms of financial speculation, and the proliferation of gambling have also contributed to a weakening of the bond between "eating" and "working." Outrageous sums of money are paid routinely to people engaged in activities (e.g., sports) that have little to do with any traditional understanding of work. Moreover, the qualifications for many of these activities—e.g., height, quickness, vocal ability, or appearance—are largely a matter of genetic good luck, something one is born with.

But if one has not been fortunate in the genetic lottery, there are other, often state-sponsored, ways in which to try one's luck. I speak, of course, of the widespread presence of gambling in the United States and elsewhere today. One consequence of these developments has been the creation of a cultural environment in which the ability to "eat one's bread" becomes a matter of chance rather than work. I recall one television advertisement for a state-sponsored lottery some years ago that featured a couple sitting at a table piled high with unpaid bills and debts. The suggested solution to the problem? The purchase of a lottery ticket.

In such an environment, the connection Paul maintains between "eating" and "working" is worth emphasizing and reinforcing.

Assisting those unable to work. Miroslav Volf observes that "the stress on the pursuit of self-interest in modern societies is at odds with one of the most essential aspects of a Christian theology of work, which insists that one should not leave the well-being of other individuals and the community to the unintended consequences of self-interested activity, but should consciously and directly work for others."[36] Expressed in terms that Paul employs in the Thessalonian letters (cf. 1 Thess. 4:9–12), Volf's point is that work is not only a matter of self-interest, but also a matter of altruism, of *philadelphia* (love for sister and brother).

For Paul, "directly working for others" does not mean some form of socialism, nor does he envision holding all things in common (as did, apparently, the early Christian community in Jerusalem [see Acts 2:44] and the Qumran community), nor does it entail divesting oneself of one's property. But if "Paul does not call for the abolition of private property or for its transformation into joint ownership . . . neither does he talk of people possessing a right to it. Any idea of rights is foreign to Paul. It cuts across all that he stands for. The gospel is about not the claiming of a right but the offering of a present."[37]

What Paul envisions is that those believers who have more than they need to sustain life will voluntarily share their "present abundance" (2 Cor. 8:14, NRSV) or a sum of money they might earn from their work (1 Cor. 16:2) with those believers who are in need. The goal of this voluntary sharing with those in need is "that there might be equality, . . . as it is written: 'He who gathered much did not have too much, and he who gathered little did not have too little'" (2 Cor. 8:13, 15). This is the theological basis for his assumption that the congregation was to assist those members who were in need of financial help.

This Pauline idea of "equality" stands in sharp contrast to a contemporary culture characterized by a narcissistic sense of individualism and an atrophied sense of social responsibility.[38] In a sense, it is a question of an ethic of caring for others in contrast to an ethic of consumption. This is a point first noted and discussed in the Contemporary Significance section of 1 Thessalonians 4:9–12. What was said there applies as well to the present passage. Together the two passages present a powerful challenge to evaluate the extent to which our attitudes about work and wealth are shaped by secular

---

36. Ibid., 189.

37. Robert Banks, *Paul's Idea of Community* (rev. ed.; Peabody, Mass.: Hendrickson, 1994), 86. See further Ronald J. Sider, *Rich Christians in an Age of Hunger: A Biblical Study*, 2d ed. (Downers Grove, Ill.: InterVarsity, 1984).

38. For classic descriptions of this state of affairs see Robert N. Bellah et al., *Habits of the Heart: Individualism and Commitment in American Life* (Berkeley and Los Angeles: Univ. of California Press, 1985); Christopher Lasch, *The Culture of Narcissism: American Life in an Age of Diminishing Expectations* (New York: Warner, 1979).

cultural values rather than the Pauline value of concern for others (*philadelphia*).

Church discipline. Many (if not most) American churches today have abandoned the New Testament teaching about discipline with regard to members of the congregation. Reasons why this practice is so widely ignored include fear of lawsuits,[39] a concern about appearing judgmental or vindictive, a desire to avoid conflict or turmoil, and a desire to avoid historical or traditional stereotypes (such as those portrayed in the recent film *The Scarlet Letter*). For many congregations, it may be because the effort involved seems useless or pointless (why bother, when the person being disciplined simply leaves and joins another congregation, thereby evading the force of the action?). Other churches do not view any sin as serious enough to warrant discipline. In such instances, one is inclined to agree with Gordon Fee's observation that "maybe the most significant thing we can learn from such a text is how far many of us are removed from a view of the church in which the dynamic of the Spirit was so real that exclusion could be a genuinely redemptive action."[40]

For churches that do practice discipline, the guidelines listed in the Bridging Contexts section can inform its practice. One major problem encountered in applying the biblical texts today is defining what qualifies for discipline. As noted above, Paul does not list or define what qualifies for this last stage of discipline. We can observe, however, that it seems to be reserved for matters affecting the spiritual health or well-being of the congregation as a whole. In the absence of definitive guidance from Scripture, application requires careful prayer and consideration by a congregation and its leadership.[41]

In any case it is important to remember that what Paul discusses in this passage represents a final step, not the first one, in the process of holding one another accountable for our conduct as members of the congregation. How, and especially the attitude with which, the church

---

39. A concern that is legitimate, but need not be paralyzing. See the guidelines offered by Karl F. Pansler, "Church Discipline and the Right of Privacy," in *Christian Ministries and the Law*, ed. H. Wayne House (Grand Rapids: Baker, 1992), 65–78.

40. Gordon D. Fee, *The First Epistle to the Corinthians*, 214.

41. See further the following helpful books on this topic: Thomas C. Oden, *Corrective Love: The Power of Communion Discipline* (St. Louis: Concordia, 1995); John White and Ken Blue, *Church Discipline That Heals: Putting Costly Love Into Action* (Downers Grove, Ill.: Inter-Varsity, 1985); J. Carl Laney, *A Guide to Church Discipline* (Minneapolis: Bethany, 1985).

handles those earlier stages may well determine the success or failure of this final stage.

It is always possible, of course, no matter how prayerfully or carefully the process is carried out, that the person being disciplined will simply walk away from the situation and thereby short-circuit the process. Should this happen, the effort will nevertheless not have been entirely in vain. While restoration of the erring member may be the primary goal of a disciplinary process, it is not the only reason for exercising discipline. As Calvin points out, one important purpose for discipline "is that the good be not corrupted by the constant company of the wicked, as commonly happens. For (such is our tendency to wander from the way) there is nothing easier than for us to be led away by bad examples from right living."[42] Thomas C. Oden makes a similar point ("like an astringent amid an epidemic, corrective love seeks to *resist the infectious process by which the pollution of one infects another* in the community") and contributes an additional consideration: "Corrective love seeks to *bear testimony against deceptive egocentricity and bring truth to light*. It refuses to collude with deception."[43]

Love for and concern about the spiritual health of an erring brother or sister, concern for the health of the congregation, a refusal to collude with deception (cf. the discussion of the deceptiveness of evil under 2:1–12 above)—these are reasons enough to consider seriously what Paul has to say about the topic of congregational discipline.

"Never tire of doing what is right" (3:13). Donor fatigue. Volunteer burnout. No one involved with fundraising or volunteer organizations is unacquainted with these terms or their symptoms. After a while, no one seems to notice; no one seems to care. No matter how hard one works, it doesn't seem to make any difference or have any effect on the situation. On top of that, perhaps those whom one is trying to assist are not appreciative of one's efforts. In circumstances such as these, it is not surprising that we sometimes grow weary of "doing good" (cf. Gal. 6:9).

John Calvin's comment on this verse indicates that he too was familiar with this problem. He also suggests what our response ought to be:

It often happens that those who are otherwise particularly ready and eager to do good grow cool on seeing that they have spent

---

42. Calvin, *Institutes of the Christian Religion*, 4.12.5 (2:1233 in McNeil/Battles edition).
43. Thomas C. Oden, *Corrective Love*, 84, 85 (italics in original).

their favours to no purpose by misdirecting them. Paul therefore admonishes us that although there are many who are undeserving, and others who abuse our generosity, we are not on this account to give up helping those who need our aid. His statement is worth noting—however the ingratitude, annoyance, pride, impertinence, and other unworthy behavior . . . may trouble us, or discourage and disgust us, we must still strive never to abandon our desire to do good.[44]

Though Paul in this passage does not state why we ought not to "tire of doing good," we can infer it from what he says elsewhere in his letters: "Serve wholeheartedly, as if you were serving the Lord, not men, because you know that the Lord will reward everyone for whatever good he does" (Eph. 6:7–8).[45]

Paul's final word: The centrality of the Lord Jesus Christ. In the closing verses of the letter (3:16, 18) Paul echoes the key ideas and concepts of his opening verses (1:1–2). By so doing he ends the letter as it began—with the spotlight, focus, and emphasis squarely on Jesus Christ the Lord. In the course of the letter he has talked a fair amount about the Thessalonians and their problems, and some about the evil "man of lawlessness." But in the end, the last word is about Jesus. He is the one who loved us (3:13) and from whom we receive grace and peace (1:2, 1:12; 3:16, 18); he is the one who is faithful and will strengthen and protect us from the evil one (3:3) and whose representative, the lawless one, he will overthrow and destroy (2:8) when he comes to deliver his people (1:7), who then will share in his glory and splendor (1:10; 2:14), having been counted worthy of God's kingdom (1:5).

In short, our future rests entirely on the power and faithfulness of God as revealed through the Lord Jesus his Messiah. That was a good place for the letter to begin; it is an even better place for it to end, as we persevere in faith (1:4) and await with eternal encouragement and good hope (2:16) the revelation from heaven of the Lord Jesus himself (1:7).

---

44. J. Calvin, *The Epistles of Paul the Apostle to the Romans and to the Thessalonians*, 420.

45. See further on this passage Klyne Snodgrass, *Ephesians* (NIVAC; Grand Rapids: Zondervan, 1996), 328–29, 333.

Scripture Index

Subject Index

We want to hear from you. Please send your comments about this book to
us in care of the address below. Thank you.

ZondervanPublishingHouse
Grand Rapids, Michigan 49530
http://www.zondervan.com